CASTLEREAGH AND ADAMS

JOHN QUINCY ADAMS

Portrait by C. R. Leslie

CASTLEREAGH

AND ADAMS

ENGLAND
AND THE UNITED STATES

1812-1823

BY BRADFORD PERKINS

UNIVERSITY OF CALIFORNIA PRESS
BERKELEY AND LOS ANGELES · 1964

UNIVERSITY OF CALIFORNIA PRESS
BERKELEY AND LOS ANGELES, CALIFORNIA
CAMBRIDGE UNIVERSITY PRESS
LONDON, ENGLAND
© 1964 BY THE REGENTS OF THE UNIVERSITY OF CALIFORNIA
LIBRARY OF CONGRESS CATALOG CARD NO. 64-19696
DESIGNED BY WARD RITCHIE
PRINTED IN THE UNITED STATES OF AMERICA

FOR DEXTER PERKINS

PREFACE

In this volume, the last of a trilogy devoted to Anglo-American relations for three decades after 1795, I have continued the approach of *The First Rapprochement* and *Prologue to War*. This third volume tells the story of America's search for true independence and recognition as a sovereign power, with the political, economic, and psychological implications that accompany independence and sovereignty.

As the earlier volumes attempt to show, the United States proceeded from the Federalists' realistic decision to make haste slowly to the nearly ruinous Republican assertion of unattainable rights and thus to war in June, 1812. For two and a half years thereafter, through warfare and negotiation, the United States invested her limited power in a struggle to preserve the position gained prior to 1812 or even 1803, and this theme dominates the first half of the present volume.

After the treaty of Ghent America moved forward in negotiations with Great Britain and other powers, notably Spain. By 1823 she had carved out a position dialectically combining the realism of the Federalists with Republican aspirations. This clearly appears in the dialogue preceding promulgation of the Monroe Doctrine, when the administration decided to proclaim American isolation from Europe and at the same time to act independently of Great Britain in facing the challenge to Latin America.

I have not attempted either an entirely American, purely diplomatic, or all-encompassing history. As previous scholars have tended to slight the development of British policy, so fundamental a part of the American quest for diplomatic respectability, I have emphasized this subject. Because emotional as well as political and economic factors contribute to a nation's international posture, I have examined postwar nationalism in some detail. On the other hand I have felt free to ignore minor aspects of Anglo-American relations. John Quincy Adams' negotiations with Spain and the controversy over recognition of Latin America appear only

vii

when they bear upon America's relations with England, her most formidable antagonist and traditional enemy.

Once again I express my deep gratitude to the many persons in England who opened family archives. Her Majesty, Queen Elizabeth II, graciously permitted me to use material from the Royal Archives at Windsor. For freedom to use the manuscripts of Viscount Castlereagh, the Earl of Harrowby, George Canning, Charles Bagot, and Admiral Warren I owe great thanks to the Marchioness Dowager of Londonderry, the Earl of Harrowby, the Earl of Harewood, Oliver R. Bagot, and Lord Vernon.

For the illustrations in this volume I am indebted to Robert Homans, San Francisco, California, owner of the portrait of John Quincy Adams, and to the National Portrait Gallery, London, owner of the portraits of Castlereagh and Canning by Lawrence.

Research for this volume and its predecessor could not have been done without generous assistance from the University of California, Los Angeles, and particularly the Social Science Research Council, which granted me a faculty research fellowship for the period 1957–1960. Assistance in the preparation of this volume has been provided by the Horace H. Rackham School of Graduate Studies of the University of Michigan. The patient toil of J. Fraser Cocks III has saved me from numerous errors of fact and reference, while Mrs. Grace H. Stimson of the University of California Press has performed the editorial chores with her usual aplomb, care, and skill. Finally, I am most grateful to the John Simon Guggenheim Memorial Foundation and its officers, Henry Allen Moe and James Mathias, for enabling me to devote a year, free from distraction, to the composition of this book.

As always my wife and my parents gave freely of their time and energy, performing that most unrewarding of tasks, criticism of the manuscript. As I end my task and come to a period and subject with which he has dealt so brilliantly, I dedicate this volume to Dexter Perkins. His success and his kindness remain both stimulus and challenge.

BRADFORD PERKINS

June, 1963
Ann Arbor, Michigan

CONTENTS

We must learn to know ourselves, to esteem ourselves, to respect ourselves, to confide in ourselves under heaven alone. We must hold Europe at arm's length, do them justice, treat them with civility, and set their envy, jealousy, malice, retaliation, and revenge at defiance.

JOHN ADAMS, 1814

We must support our rights or lose our character, and with it, perhaps, our liberties. A people who fail to do it can scarcely be said to hold a place among independent nations. National honor is national property of the highest value.

JAMES MONROE, 1817

The line of policy which that speech [Monroe's message of December 2, 1823] disclosed became a great, a free, and an independent nation; and he hoped that his majesty's ministers would be prevented by no mean pride, no paltry jealousy, from following so noble and so illustrious an example.

HENRY BROUGHAM, 1824

CHAPTER

I

PROLOGUE

For nearly fifty years after the rattle of musketry at Lexington the Americans sought to become an independent people capable of following their own destiny without European assistance. In the early years, weak, cautious and lacking confidence, they leaned first upon France and then upon England to preserve a precarious existence. No European power considered the United States more than an upstart, perhaps transitory, nation, and as late as 1814 a friendly British newspaper referred quite naturally to America as "the Colonies." [1] This dependent position, always considered degrading by many citizens, particularly irked the Republicans. Attaining power in 1801, they sought a different road. Baffled by their own incompetence and by foreign intransigence toward neutrals during a world war, they felt forced to commit the United States to war in 1812.

This decision, because it was quixotic or misguided in the view of many citizens, threatened the union and woefully undermined

[1] *Morning Chronicle* (London), Oct. 20, 1814.

military efforts. It also destroyed phil-Americanism in England, and in 1813 John Quincy Adams pronounced Opposition leaders "as wrong headed and stiff-necked . . . as the Ministry themselves." [2] Only by great good fortune, and after a trying period of negotiations at Ghent, did the Americans emerge without loss from the war. Because the conflict lasted some months beyond the first abdication of Napoleon, an effective if disliked magnet for British attention, Americans interpreted their negative success as proof they could survive without European aid. "Their first war with England made them independent—their second made them formidable," the London *Times* admitted in 1817.[3]

Adjusting British policy to American confidence and power, Viscount Castlereagh broke free from old attitudes after 1814. He treated the Americans with consideration, avoided controversy whenever possible, and settled outstanding issues on a basis of parity. Thus he became the first British foreign secretary to accept the reality of American independence. After Castlereagh took his life in 1822, the new policy continued under George Canning. The next year the Americans, educated by the two foreign secretaries to act as equals, turned down a British offer of coöperation because they did not wish to play the role of a satellite. They struck out on their own. Monroe's message of December 2, 1823, completed the work of the Declaration of Independence.

[2] Adams to Abigail Adams, Feb. 10, 1813, Adams Family Papers, Massachusetts Historical Society, Vol. CXXXIX.

[3] *Times* (London), April 5, 1817.

CHAPTER

II

RELUCTANT DRAGONS

Shortly after lunch on June 18, 1812, Chief Clerk John Graham strode briskly from the Department of State to the nearby British legation. Ushered into the presence of His Britannic Majesty's envoy, Graham solemnly invited that young man to wait upon Secretary of State Monroe at three o'clock. Monroe's purpose was plain, for Congress had already passed a war bill. The minister, Augustus John Foster, knew the proper forms; four years earlier he had been at Stockholm when the Swedes broke relations with England. Cold formality and disdain were the attitudes to adopt toward upstart powers casting their lot with the tyrant of the Tuileries against Britain, defender of world liberties.

Promptly at three—tardiness might suggest faintness of heart—Foster entered the Secretary's office. The Englishman later wrote in his journal that Monroe nervously jiggled his watch chain, mumbled words, and accompanied the expected notice of war with an invitation to make peace. At another interview two days later, "We endeavoured to frighten one another for a whole Hour by descanting on the Consequences of the War." Monroe

3

alluded to the inevitable American conquest of Canada; Foster riposted by speaking of slave rebellion and Yankee sedition. These topics at last exhausted, the two men amiably shared Monroe's pot of tea.

On June 23 Foster accepted an invitation from the White House. President Madison asked as the price of peace only that Britain repeal the Orders in Council (news that she had just done so was then racing across the Atlantic) and consent to negotiate on impressment. At the close of the interview Madison warmly clasped the young man's hand and wished him well. Earlier that day, far out in the Atlantic, Commodore John Rodgers' squadron sighted a lone frigate flying the white ensign. Abandoning his search for a West Indian convoy, Rodgers turned in pursuit. His flagship, U.S.S. *President,* exchanged the first shots of the war with H.M.S. *Belvidera* before the Englishman finally drew away.

Neither this action nor the progress of General William Hull, already marching with his men toward the advance base at Detroit and the invasion of Upper Canada, was known at Washington for some time. Foster coolly attended the theater, received visits from congressmen both curious and sympathetic, and finally left the capital only at noon on June 25. After an uneventful overland trip and a leisurely stay at New York he sailed for home via Halifax on the twelfth of July.[1] That day, nearly four weeks after the declaration of war, General Hull crossed over into Canada.

By their indecisive actions, the Secretary, the President, Commodore Rodgers, and General Hull unconsciously reflected the nation's lack of enthusiasm. None of the grievances against Great Britain—ship seizures, impressment, intrigue among the Indians, a pervasive attitude of arrogance—was new. The War Hawk Congress fumbled and hesitated for six months, and most members hoped desperately for some miracle that would avert a clash of arms. When finally, almost impulsively, Congress voted for war, nearly two-fifths of the representatives and just under half the Senate opposed it, while others assented simply to preserve the

[1] June 17–July 12, 1812, Augustus J. Foster journal, Library of Congress.

4

last shreds of their own or their party's reputation. Opponents of war, particularly in New England, were far more united and determined. "The seditious opposition in Mass. & Con^t. with the intrigues elsewhere," the President wrote only two months later, ". . . have so clogged the wheels of the war, that I fear the campaign [against Canada] will not accomplish the object of it."[2]

America's woeful weakness frightened even loyal citizens. The War Hawk Congress stopped just short of imposing war taxes, passed ineffective recruiting legislation, and refused to expand the navy. Although the Peninsula could be expected to absorb British land forces for months to come (the campaign of Salamanca had not yet reached its successful climax, and the triumph at Vittoria still lay a year away), at sea the threat was obvious. The American navy had 170 gunboats, a dubious and often rotten legacy from Jefferson, but only ten frigates, two in such bad repair that they never put to sea. Frigates and swarming privateers might despoil British commerce. They could not hope to protect American trade from seven British ships of the line, twenty-three frigates, and scores of small craft in the Western Hemisphere, to say nothing of whatever reinforcements the Admiralty sent to American waters.

Not too inaccurately, albeit stridently, a leading Federalist journal summed up the arguments against war when it wrote, two days after the declaration: "For the government of a country, without armies, navies, fortifications, money or credit, and in direct contradiction to the voice of the people, to declare war against a power which is able in a few months time to sweep from the ocean millions of property belonging to the people of that country, is an act of imprudence, not to say wickedness, such as, perhaps, was never before known since civil government was established."[3] Moreover, a quarrel with France, nearly as long-

---

[2] Madison to Jefferson, Aug. 17, 1812, James Madison Papers, Library of Congress.
[3] Adam Seybert, *Statistical Annals . . . of the United States of America* (Philadelphia, 1818), pp. 646, 657–658; *New-York Evening Post*, June 20, 1812. In July the Halifax station alone, counting three frigates en route, had more seagoing ships than the entire American navy. Endorsement on Edward Cooke to John W. Croker, secret, July 25, 1812, Admiralty Archives, Public Record Office, Adm 1/4222.

standing and almost as bitter as that with England, undermined the war. Napoleon's armies and the blockade of the Continent drew off British resources; otherwise the United States got no aid from England's great enemy. On the contrary, he seized American ships which eluded the Royal Navy to trade with his empire. Pointing to the past, Federalists charged that Madison had chosen the wrong enemy. Pointing to the present, they argued that the United States should fight both powers or neither.

The President was by no means exempt from anti-French feeling, for he had suffered at Napoleon's hands. In the early months of the war with England, through his minister at Paris and the columns of the *National Intelligencer*, Madison warned the Emperor that the United States might join the ranks of his enemies, possibly even take on a double war without waiting for peace with Britain. Deafened by the still exhilarating tramp and jingle of the Grand Armée marching toward Moscow, Napoleon ignored the President.[4]

Madison recognized the inconsistencies that preceded and the perils that would accompany war. In 1813 he reminded a friend that the "circumstances under which the war commenced . . . require that it should be reviewed with a liberality above the ordinary rules and dispositions indulged in such cases." War could no longer be avoided, he said, and yet neither Congress nor the nation would consent to effective preparation before hostilities began. More bluntly, his statement meant that British arrogance and the ineffectiveness of American protests made war the only honorable recourse. It meant, too, that the vindictive seditiousness of Federalist opposition to American policy had helped close the door to success without war. In the words of Boston's *Independent Chronicle*, a citadel in the enemy's kingdom, the Federalists "forced the United States to the alternative, either to *surrender their independence*, or *maintain it by war*."[5]

[4] Irving Brant, *James Madison: Commander in Chief* (Indianapolis, 1961), chap. 5 *passim*.

[5] Madison to Nicholas, April 2, 1813, Gaillard Hunt, ed., *The Writings of James Madison* (9 vols.; New York, 1900–1910), VIII, 242; *Independent Chronicle* (Boston), July 16, 1812.

Such logic, which had much to commend it, failed to convince the electorate. The elections of 1812 showed no surge of support for the war president and his party. For the presidency some Federalists supported Rufus King. Most endorsed Lieutenant-Governor De Witt Clinton of New York, sure that only by alliance with a dissident Republican, no matter how disreputable, could their party unseat Madison. Madison won a narrow victory. Pennsylvania, at one time considered doubtful but actually carried by a majority of 20,000, provided the margin.

Although Republicans gained control of the House of Representatives for the seventh consecutive time, successes in the North increased the Federalists' share from one-fourth to almost two-fifths of that body. Thanks to an increase in total membership, the Federalists actually held more seats than at any other time in their history. Not one New Hampshire Republican survived the election, and eighteen new administration enemies won in New York. In Massachusetts, where the Embargo once resuscitated a challenged party, war granted Federalism a third life; a fairly evenly divided delegation became one containing fifteen Federalists and only five Republicans. As no less than 52 of 114 Republicans were new and untried, the party phalanx from the South, the West, and Pennsylvania faced serious difficulty. "Barbers who shave Democrats at Washington," a Federalist winner gleefully commented, "ought to have an increase of fees on account of the unusual lengthening of faces." [6]

The War Hawk Congress, slow to abdicate, remained at Washington for more than a month after the declaration of war, then met again in November for a lameduck session. At no time did the members contribute much to their war. They put off discussion of many war taxes and even hesitated before prohibiting the export of military supplies to Canada. Most important, the quondam war hawks and their colleagues took so weak a position on trade

[6] *Niles' Weekly Register* (Baltimore), June 26, 1813; Taggart to Rev. John Taylor, Nov. 12, 1812, George H. Haynes, ed., "Letters of Samuel Taggart, Representative in Congress, 1803–1814," American Antiquarian Society, *Proceedings*, n.s., XXXIII (1923), 409.

with the enemy that a war editor could protest, in October, that "the receipt of *British* goods and the supply of *British* armies with flour and grain, [make] it hard to believe that we are really at war." [7]

Sophistical reasoning alone could justify this failure to press the war. Jefferson asked, since Britain "is to be fed at all events, why may we not have the benefit of it as well as others?" He went on to argue, as if a world war could be compartmentalized, that French defeats in Spain and Napoleonic successes in northern Europe alike benefited America. Thus grain and beef sold to Wellington's commissary served a useful purpose. Moreover, the ex-President added, "If we could by starving the British armies, oblige [t]hem to withdraw from the peninsular, it would be to send them here; and I think we had better feed them there for pay, than feed and fight them here for nothing."

Taking a different tack, John C. Calhoun urged Congress to concentrate on the military crusade and forget lesser matters which, operating unequally upon different parts of the country, might undermine unity. "Tie down a hero," this war hawk said, "and he feels the puncture of a pin; but throw him into battle, and he is scarcely sensible of vital gashes." [8] Calhoun both won and lost. In June, 1812, the House of Representatives refused to loosen restrictions on imports from Britain. The vote, sixty-three to fifty-eight on a motion to postpone the subject, was close and confused. Both parties split. Some war hawks joined Calhoun while others clung to nonimportation either as an adjunct to or a substitute for effective military action. [9] Only a small amount of British goods slipped into the United States in 1812.

Far more important, after the prewar embargo expired, was the tremendous flow of exports to England and Spain. In the autumn session of Congress spokesmen for consuming states pressed for

[7] *Annals of Congress,* 12th Cong., 2d sess., pp. 1558–1559, 1560, 1570, 1572, 1574; *Niles' Register,* Oct. 17, 1812.

[8] Jefferson to James Ronaldson, Jan. 12, 1813, Andrew A. Lipscomb and Albert E. Bergh, eds., *The Writings of Thomas Jefferson* (Memorial ed.; 20 vols.; Washington, 1903–1904), XIII, 205–206; *Annals,* 12th Cong., 2d sess., p. 1540.

[9] *Annals,* 12th Cong., 2d sess., pp. 1535–1544.

an embargo on exports. They were borne down by Calhoun and others. One of Calhoun's allies, Richard Wright, "is a Marylander, where they raise a vast deal of wheat," a Federalist noted, "and altho' a violent democrat, furious for the war, and formerly in favor of restrictive measures, had now rather feed the enemy and supply her armies in Spain and Portugal, than not get a good price for his wheat, and this appeared to be the sentiment of all the Marylanders, Virginians & Pennsylvanians formerly so fond of Embargoes." A second effort, to embargo provision exports alone, failed by a narrow margin in December.[10]

So the export trade flourished. Before Foster left Washington he issued scores of licenses to protect shipments to the Peninsula from seizure by the Royal Navy. Commanders at Halifax continued this practice and also encouraged the use of false flags by American ships. By autumn the clandestine trade had become fairly well formalized, and the commander of naval forces in American waters asked the Admiralty to decide between Saint Bartholomew and Bermuda as "the Emporium for American Vessels navigated under the Swedish, or Portuguese Flags." At last, in February, 1813, Madison asked Congress to end what he called an uncivilized and un-Christian system, "equally distinguished by the deformity of its features and the depravity of its character," by prohibiting the acceptance of British licenses. After controversy between the two houses of Congress, this limited attack upon trade with the enemy became law in July, 1813.[11] A few months later Wellington entered the rich farming areas of southern France.

---

[10] Bigelow to Hannah G. Bigelow, Nov. 8, 1812, Clarence S. Brigham, ed., "Letters of Abijah Bigelow, Member of Congress, to His Wife, 1810–1815," American Antiquarian Society, *Proceedings*, n.s., XL (1930), 342; *Annals*, 12th Cong., 2d sess., pp. 212–214.

[11] Admiral Sawyer to Croker, July 18, Aug. 6, 1812, Adm 1/502; Admiral Warren to Viscount Melville, Nov. 11, 1812, Adm 1/503; James D. Richardson, ed., *A Compilation of the Messages and Papers of the Presidents* (10 vols.; Washington, 1907), I, 522–523; *Annals*, 12th Cong., 2d sess., pp. 1150–1151; 13th Cong., 1st and 2d sess., pp. 55, 485. At the same time the Senate refused to approve a bill urged by Madison and passed by the House to prohibit most exports carried in foreign ships.

In one month in 1812 the British issued 722 licenses for American grain shipments to Lisbon and Cadiz. Memorandum encl. in Clancarty to Melville, Jan. 13, 1813, Adm 1/5216.

Madison, burdened with a recalcitrant Congress, perhaps envied the Earl of Liverpool. After June, 1812, when repeal of the Orders in Council deprived his opponents of almost their only effective weapon, Liverpool faced few parliamentary challenges. Leaders of the campaign against the orders, notably Henry Brougham, promised to support the ministry if Madison made a *casus belli* of any other issue. For the first time since 1807 the British government enjoyed nearly universal support in Parliament.

The expectation that in the end America would not dare go to war muted or delayed criticism of past policy. Even news that the House of Representatives had voted for war was not considered final. After all, observed the *Times,* American actions, while "unpleasant enough, . . . spring from a state of things which no longer exists, and are, therefore, as reversible as those acts of ours have been found, which have occasioned them." Only William Cobbett firmly predicted war unless Britain ended all seizures of American ships and seamen, and only Cobbett warned, "Nothing . . . will ever make an American war popular in England." [12]

A fortnight later, on the evening of July 30, news of the declaration of war reached London. The *Courier,* always America's most strident critic, castigated her unmercifully, and most newspapers joined the chorus in a lower key. Even the *Morning Chronicle,* mouthpiece of the Opposition, regretted the Yankees' precipitancy and criticized the petty spirit of Madison's message. On the other hand, the *Chronicle* placed chief blame upon the British government: ". . . our mode of proceeding towards America has been most irritating to her, as well as most injurious to ourselves. . . . The charge against us of obstinate perseverance in error, from pride rather than conviction, is just." The outbreak of war cast a shadow over a Liverpool dinner to celebrate repeal of the orders, but, the principal speaker told his audience, "it is not the Americans who wish for war. It is the war faction in England, that

[12] *Times* (London), July 10, 1812; *Cobbett's Political Register* (London), XXII (1812), 101–107.

. . . have heaped upon America, injuries upon injuries, insults upon insults, until human nature can no longer endure them; until America is forced to draw the sword." [13]

Such criticisms, formerly just, were now out of date. In May, 1812, the Admiralty directed commanders in American waters to "take especial care" to avoid clashes with the United States Navy and to exercise "all possible forbearance towards the Citizens of the United States." In the last months of peace the flag officer at Halifax, successor to the quite different Sir George Berkeley of *Chesapeake* fame, withdrew his ships fifteen leagues from the American coast, and as late as July 8 the cabinet told the navy to turn the other cheek even if the United States sent letters of marque to sea before learning of the repeal of the Orders in Council.[14]

The *President-Belvidera* clash discouraged but did not dismay Liverpool and his colleagues. Spokesmen pointed out that two earlier affrays, the *Chesapeake* and *Little Belt* incidents, sputtered out without war. This false hope lasted only a few days, until news of the declaration of war. After two meetings on July 31 the cabinet embargoed American vessels and cargoes bound for the United States. At the same time it ignored a plea from insurers at Lloyds and permitted large shipments to go to Halifax despite the risk of capture.[15] Expecting the war to end when Madison learned that the orders had been repealed, the cabinet wanted British manufactures near the American market when peace came.

For several months the English government worked to abort a conflict begun, in their view, by mistake. At first they counted on

[13] *Courier* (London), July 31, 1812; *Morning Chronicle* (London), July 31, 1812; *Liverpool Mercury*, Aug. 14, 1812.

[14] Lords Commissioners of the Admiralty to Admirals Duckworth, Stirling, Sawyer, and LaForey, most secret, May 9, 1812, Adm 2/1374; Sawyer to Croker, June 25, 1812, Adm 1/502; Castlereagh to Lords of the Admiralty, July 8, 1812, Adm 1/4222.

[15] *Courier*, July 28, 30, 31, 1812; *Chronicle*, Aug. 1, 1812. The *Chronicle* reported that some members of the government even wanted to permit American ships to depart freely, and an Opposition peer conjectured that "Government is seriously frightened, & disposed from pure fear to act moderately." *Chronicle*, Aug. 4, 1812; Earl of Rosslyn to Brougham, July 27, 1812, Papers of Henry, Lord Brougham, University College, London.

negotiations at Washington. On June 17 and again on the twenty-fifth, Castlereagh sent instructions to Foster. The first, after announcing repeal of the orders,[16] threatened to restore them unless America lifted restrictions on British trade within a fortnight of receiving the news. Moreover, Britain reserved the right to resume her system in May, 1813, if French or American action made resumption necessary. A week of reflection produced instructions somewhat more liberal and far less peremptory in tone. Castlereagh abandoned the two-week deadline, permitting Foster to arrange American repeal with Monroe, and eliminated the threat to restore the orders in 1813. If French policy forced England to consider new trade controls, the instructions stated, "the Absense of all irritating and restrictive [English and American] Regulations" might permit negotiations to render the new controls "more acceptable to the American Government than those hitherto pursued." [17] For the first time a British ministry proposed to take American wishes into consideration before setting maritime policy.

Unfortunately Anthony Baker, who succeeded to Foster's functions, rushed to the State Department as soon as the first instructions arrived. Ignoring Castlereagh's injunction to avoid specifics until he received more detailed instructions, Baker stated both the time limit and the threat. Although the second instructions would almost certainly not have satisfied the American government, the young chargé's brusquerie choked off all hope. Madison, the only administration leader then in Washington, declined to receive Baker. Castlereagh's more supple proposals did not come before the Americans, and when Secretary of State Monroe returned from vacation he formally declared that "no measures could be taken founded on the Order in Council of June 23, in consequence of the total change in the relations of the two Countries which had

---

[16] Technically the Orders in Council were not to be repealed until August 1, when it was expected that Madison would have heard of the British decision and have had the opportunity to reciprocate by removing American restrictions on trade with England. Castlereagh stressed, however, that if the Americans reopened trade the act of British repeal would have "a retrospective effect" to May 18, 1812.

[17] Castlereagh #20, most secret, #21 to Foster, June 17, 25, 1812, Bernard Mayo, ed., *Instructions to the British Ministers to the United States, 1791–1812*, American Historical Association, *Annual Report, 1936*, III (Washington, 1941), 381–387.

occurred since it was issued." [18] Britain's belated change of course failed to alter the administration's equally tardy decision to risk the chance of arms.

London did not know that Foster had left Baker behind to manage British affairs. Consequently the cabinet, still hoping to stifle the conflict, opened a new channel of communication with the Americans. Admiral Sir John Borlase Warren, the newly appointed commander of all naval forces in the Western Hemisphere, had not yet left for his post. As flag officer at Halifax from 1808 to 1810, Warren's chief task, only partially successful, had been to curb aggressive naval officers unleashed by Admiral Berkeley. Too old, lazy, and pacifically inclined to direct an energetic naval offensive, in fact almost a duplicate of Admiral Howe of Revolutionary days, the sea dog with Opposition connections seemed well suited to the task of making peace. Your "first duty," Castlereagh instructed him, "will be to endeavour to re-establish . . . Peace & Amity." As the Orders in Council, still in British eyes the sole cause of war, had been revoked, Madison might agree to suspend hostilities. This settled, Warren was to follow the instructions of June 25—that is to say, to arrange for withdrawal of restrictions on British commerce with America—but he had no authority to engage in detailed negotiations.[19]

On September 30, shortly after his arrival in American waters, Warren sent his offer to Washington. A month later Monroe replied, insisting that impressment follow the orders into discard. This chilling demand caused Warren to return to his military

[18] Memorandum enclosed in Graham to Russell, Aug. 10, 1812, Department of State Archives, National Archives, Diplomatic Instructions, All Countries, Vol. VII; Baker #19 to Castlereagh, most secret, Aug. 10, 1812, Foreign Office Archives, Public Record Office, FO 5/87; Madison to Gallatin, Aug. 8, 1812, Albert Gallatin Papers, New-York Historical Society; Baker #23 to Castlereagh, Aug. 24, 1812, FO 5/87. On August 25 the National Intelligencer (Washington), speaking for the administration, explained that the form taken by the repeal of the Orders in Council was inacceptable because Britain still claimed a right to legislate over neutrals, showed that repeal was conditional by hinting at restoration of the orders, and failed to make the effect of repeal retroactive to 1810, when repeal of the French decrees allegedly took place.

[19] Castlereagh to Lords of the Admiralty, secret and confidential, Aug. 12, 6, 1812, Adm 1/4222. For a summary of Warren's negotiations see Alfred T. Mahan, Sea Power in Its Relation to the War of 1812 (2 vols.; Boston, 1905), I, 390–392.

role, though without any greater success. Late in the year he talked about a raid on Southern ports, including New Orleans (the same honeypot of prize money attracted another admiral two years later), but for the most part he confined his energies to the composition of letters pleading for reinforcements.[20]

The American government brushed off Baker and Warren because it preferred to negotiate through Jonathan Russell, the chargé at London. After all, only the cabinet could end impressment, and having secured victory over the Orders in Council the Americans decided to press this second grievance. No doubt Madison felt that, while impressment had been tolerated to preserve peace, once at war America must present her full demands. Probably he believed England's eagerness for peace would bring concessions withheld when she doubted the United States would really fight. Conceivably Madison at last truly realized that national honor was something more than the subject of diplomatic correspondence and messages to Congress; perhaps he now agreed with Thomas Ritchie of the Richmond *Enquirer,* who felt that "We are slaves to a pretension which stamps our character with disgrace and our sovereignty with the marks of subjection." [21]

The first wartime instructions to Russell proclaimed a desire for peace. If Castlereagh promised to end impressment and lift the Orders in Council Russell might "stipulate an armistice." In return the United States promised to prohibit by law the enlistment of foreign seamen in her merchant marine. (Resuscitation of this old scheme, rejected in 1807 by Jefferson because it threatened to cripple the American marine, showed the administration's avidity for peace.) A month later, to make the demand more palatable, Monroe agreed to consider informal assurances on impressment an adequate preliminary to an armistice.[22]

The cabinet, as devoted to impressment as most Britons, de-

---

[20] Warren to Melville, Nov. 18, 1812, Sir John Borlase Warren Letters, Greenwich Naval Museum MSS 9629. Sir George Prevost, the land commander in Canada, who negotiated with General Dearborn a temporary armistice quickly repudiated by Madison, showed a similar lack of vigor.

[21] *Enquirer* (Richmond), Nov. 10, 1812.

[22] Monroe to Russell, June 26, July 27, 1812, Instructions, Vol. VII.

clined to accept either American proposal. In rejecting the first, Lord Castlereagh told Russell that Britain could not give up impressment in return for a promise to pass a possibly ineffective law. The American thereupon called for his passports. The arrival of Monroe's second, slightly more moderate proposal interrupted his struggle to close his portmanteaus and secure safe passage. In a formal note and during an evening interview at Castlereagh's home Russell pressed for an early reply. The cabinet found it easy to oblige. "Our answer," one minister informed an absent colleague, "will of course be little more than a reference to the former Answer: there being in substance no difference" between the two proposals. In a formal note dated September 18 the Foreign Secretary even professed to find the second offer more dishonorable than the first, since it attempted "the same purpose in a more covert and therefore in a more objectionable manner." Two days later Jonathan Russell left London, cherishing an Anglophobia he never lost. The ministry, reversing an earlier stand, unleashed privateers to prey upon American commerce.[23]

England at last abandoned hope for peace. The Prince Regent's speech at the opening of Parliament laid the blame for war at the door of the Americans. Two months later, in January, 1813, ministerial presses spawned a lengthy paper bearing the jawbreaking title, "Declaration of his Royal Highness the Prince Regent relative to the Causes and Origin of the War with America."

---

[23] Russell to Castlereagh, Aug. 24, 1812, FO 5/91; Castlereagh to Russell, Aug. 29, 1812, *ibid.*; Russell to Castlereagh, Sept. 1, 1812, *ibid.*; Russell to Castlereagh, Sept. 12, 1812 (2 letters, 1 "private"), *ibid.*; Earl Bathurst to Harrowby, Sept. 16, 1812, Papers of Dudley Ryder, First Earl of Harrowby, Sandon Hall, Staffordshire; Russell to Monroe, Sept. 17, 1812, Department of State Archives, National Archives, Despatches, Great Britain, Vol. XVIII; Castlereagh to Russell, Sept. 18, 1812, FO 5/91; Castlereagh to Harrowby, private, Oct. 9, 1812, Harrowby MSS. Russell's negotiations are traced in detail, on the basis of conversations with the American, in a memorandum by Thomas Mullett, n.d. [1812], Samuel Whitbread Papers, Southill Park, Biggleswade, Bedfordshire, fol. 3923.

It should be noted that the Americans offered only a military armistice, not an end to prohibitions of British imports into the United States. While no doubt necessary to maintain the economic pressure designed to force England to agree to a favorable treaty of peace, continued nonimportation meant that Great Britain would, at least for the life of the negotiations, be deprived of the chief advantage she expected to gain from repeal of the Orders in Council.

On all issues, it appeared, Britain had shown noble moderation. The declaration reaffirmed the right of impressment, "a cause of war, now brought forward as such for the first time," and hostilely dissected America's position. Clearly, the ministry maintained, a malign influence lay behind the decision for war: its "real origin . . . will be found in that spirit, which has long unhappily actuated the councils of the United States: their marked partiality in palliating and assisting the aggressive tyranny of France . . . and their unworthy desertion of the cause of neutral nations. . . . America has been associated in policy with France, and committed in war against Great Britain." [24] Whether intended as serious analysis or, far more credibly, as anti-Republican propaganda, this state paper marked a return to the tone of *War in Disguise,* the famous pamphlet by James Stephen which marked the opening of controversy in 1805.

A few English voices challenged the declaration. An American-born propagandist, George Joy, hastily published a pamphlet answering it point by point. The *Liverpool Mercury,* ally of Henry Brougham, asked, "Is the trade of America to be totally sacrificed to the interests of those who make a trade of war?" The *Edinburgh Review,* which often printed Brougham's articles, blamed the ministry for the war and argued that impressment had been "exercised . . . without either moderation or justice," though at the same time insisting that the practice, properly regulated, must continue. Samuel Whitbread, probably America's staunchest parliamentary supporter, took Madison's part on the orders and even on impressment, but ended by criticizing the precipitancy—the quarrel had lasted nearly a decade—of the declaration of war. Alexander Baring, husband of a Philadelphia girl, banker for the United States, and a veteran opponent of ministerial policy, most unreservedly supported the Americans. In a short, hard-hitting speech in the House of Commons, Baring argued that the Orders in Council brought on the war, that earlier repeal would have frustrated the war hawks. After declaring war, Baring

[24] *Hansard,* XXIV, 14, 363–377. The declaration was presented to Parliament on February 3, 1813, and appears in *Hansard* at that point.

continued, the United States naturally resuscitated other griev-ances. Her offer on impressment was not unfair and would even benefit Great Britain by preventing desertions to American service.[25]

Few members of Parliament agreed, nor did the enfranchised, if one may judge from an election that strengthened the ministry and cost Brougham his seat. The *Times,* one of the wolves that helped harry the Orders in Council into the grave, now spoke of the "paltry cavils" against them. The *Morning Chronicle,* mouth-piece of the Opposition, ignored the orders as though they had never existed, and postively defended the principle of impress-ment. The *Chronicle* praised Castlereagh, an almost unprece-dented use of its columns, for rejecting Russell's propositions. Lord Grenville, the Opposition's aging field marshal, believed Madison in league with France; the *Times* considered this ques-tion open, but added, "whether engaged by BUONAPARTE or not, he is alike doing that Monster's dirty work." [26] Such com-ments rendered supererogatory the stale bias and shrill distortion of the *Courier,* the *Sun,* and other ministerial satraps.

With marvelous restraint the Prince Regent's declaration kept silent upon American designs against Canada. George Canning, untrammeled by the restraints of office, bluntly accused the United States of seeking conquest, "a plan long cherished, and not wholly, I fear, repugnant to . . . that party . . . whom it is usual to designate as our friends." The *Times* accused the Americans of seeking not only Canada but also the West Indies, the domination of world commerce, and even the complete destruction of British power.[27]

Once again the language of others made the ministry seem almost moderate. Those who had enlisted under Spencer Perceval

---

[25] George Joy, *Anticipation of Marginal Notes on the Declaration of Government of the 9th of January, 1813. In the American National Intelligencer* (London, 1813); *Liverpool Mercury,* Oct. 16, 1813; *Edinburgh Review,* XX (1812), 451–456; *Hansard,* XXIV, 629–632, 619–622.

[26] *Times,* Nov. 28, 1812; *Chronicle,* Jan. 13, 1813; *Hansard,* XXIV, 47–48; *Times,* Dec. 15, 1812.

[27] *Hansard,* XXIV, 639–640; *Times,* Dec. 25, 1812.

and now followed the grim banners of Liverpool believed England was fighting against "the most desolating tyranny that ever afflicted the race of man," [28] and, like many in a later contest, they considered neutralism tinged with hostility. Toward America they acted in a fashion often harsh and arrogant, often shortsighted and selfish. Still, they neither sought nor welcomed the war; indeed, in 1812 they sought to avert it, and except briefly at the climax of the fight over the Orders in Council they were never effectively attacked for harshness toward the United States. Generally a sterner policy would have commanded popular and parliamentary support. Not surprisingly, therefore, the House of Commons nearly unanimously voted approval of the Prince Regent's declaration. Baring and Whitbread recruited few allies. The House and the people responded far more positively to Canning's complaint that ministers, clinging too long to delusive hopes of peace, failed to press the war with vigor.[29]

Certainly the opening months seemed to justify Canning's criticism. In Upper Canada, it is true, tiny British forces under Isaac Brock captured General Hull and his army at Detroit, and then repulsed a foray across the Niagara River. A third American attack, directed at Canada's jugular, the St. Lawrence, bogged down even before it reached the international boundary. Against these successes could be laid Brock's death while leading a charge at Queenston and the apparent certainty—despite her arrogance, England still underestimated American ineptitude—that 1813 would see renewed, reinforced, and coördinated invasion attempts all along the Canadian border. Privateers ranged the Atlantic and positively infested waters around Halifax. So many dispatches were lost that the Admiralty replaced unarmed packets with sloops of war.

Most humiliating of all for the nation of Nelson, three frigates —*Guerrière*, *Macedonian*, and *Java*—struck their flags to the Americans. "It is a cruel mortification to be beat by these second-hand Englishmen upon our own element," a cabinet minister ad-

[28] *Hansard*, XXIV, 641 (Canning).
[29] *Ibid.*, pp. 593–649.

mitted. His countrymen clamored for revenge. They scorned erudite proof that the Americans had, most unfairly, built frigates so large that they upset the odds of battle. The Admiralty prudently kept secret new orders forbidding single-ship duels with these vessels;[30] if made public this directive would have caused a furor. The Royal Navy had not gained preëminence by fleeing its enemies.

In the autumn of 1812, at last resigned to war, London tried to prod Admiral Warren into action. Gentle hints failing, peremptory orders followed in December and again in March, by which time the Admiralty had diverted one-seventh of its available strength to Warren's command. Expressing pained surprise at the Admiral's failure to move earlier, the First Lord ordered a blockade of Chesapeake and Delaware bays and, in the second instructions, the entire coast south of Rhode Island. Moreover, Lord Melville told Warren to abandon his gentle treatment of Yankee ships unless New England seemed ready to secede. In sum, wrote Melville, making it clear the cabinet had changed its tune, "we cannot consent to the War being conducted on any other principles than . . . the annoying the Enemy to the utmost of your power." Still the naval campaign dragged.[31]

While Warren lay quiet during the war's second year, bloody conflicts took place along the Canadian-American frontier. On Lake Erie Oliver Hazard Perry patched together a flotilla, manned it with a motley collection of sailors and buckskin-clad riflemen, and triumphed over an equally jerry-built British squadron in a contest of endurance at Put-in-Bay on September 10. This success cleared the way for a rebuilt army of regulars and volunteers under William Henry Harrison to recapture Detroit and cross into Canada. In October Harrison defeated the combined

[30] Harrowby to Countess of Harrowby, Dec. 25, 1812, Harrowby MSS; Melville to Warren, private, March 23, 1813, Greenwich MSS 9629. The Americans, too, found alibis when their ships were defeated. After the *Chesapeake*'s loss, the *Independent Chronicle* (June 3, 1813) complained that the British had used hand grenades, boarded the ship instead of engaging in an artillery duel, and in general acted in a manner "base and cowardly in the extreme."

[31] Melville to Warren, private, Dec. 3, 1812, private, March 26, 1813, Sir John Borlase Warren Papers, Sudbury Hall, Derbyshire.

forces of Tecumseh and General Henry Proctor at the battle of the Thames. Tecumseh died, and Proctor abandoned his baggage and fled at top speed.

Harrison's victory rekindled fires doused by Isaac Brock. "In a few days we anticipate a new harvest of glory," Thomas Ritchie's *Enquirer* declared in language reminiscent of 1812. *"Kingston will be ours. We shall again meet our enemy, and he will again be ours.* From Kingston to Montreal we can pass down the St. Lawrence in 2 or 3 days in boats, and *Montreal is ours."* [32] This ebullience soon subsided. Harrison withdrew, and invasion attempts at both ends of Lake Ontario were foiled. In 1814 the enemies would fight from old bases.

Neither side paid much attention to the possibility of peace. As early as August, 1812, upon learning of the war, the Russian chancellor thought of mediation. Cautiously encouraged by John Quincy Adams, the American minister, Count Rumiantzov pressed ahead. When the British ambassador reacted frostily Rumiantzov bypassed him and sent the offer to London. Similar orders soon went to André de Dashkov, Russia's young chargé at Washington. On his own responsibility, Dashkov had already suggested Russian mediation. The President appeared cool in January, 1813, but by the time Rumiantzov's instructions arrived in February, Madison knew of Napoleon's disaster in Russia and the consequently improved position of Britain. The *National Intelligencer* immediately announced acceptance of the Russian offer. Without any reason to suppose Britain would agree, James Madison and James Monroe eagerly adopted Rumiantzov's scheme three days after Dashkov presented it. Unseemly haste apparently counted for little when success in war seemed so elusive. [33]

[32] *Enquirer,* Oct. 19, 1813.
[33] Aug. 21, 1812, Charles F. Adams, ed., *Memoirs of John Quincy Adams* (12 vols.; Philadelphia, 1874–1877), II, 101–104; Rumiantzov to Baron de Nicolay, Sept. 6/18, 1812, Russian Ministry of Foreign Affairs, Correspondence dealing with the Russian offer of mediation in the War of 1812, transcripts, Library of Congress. On this entire episode, see Frank A. Golder, "The Russian Offer of Mediation in the War of 1812," *Political Science Quarterly,* XXXI (1916), 380–391; memorandum of conversation with Dashkov, June 25–27, 1813, Rufus King Papers, New-York Historical Society, Vol. XIII; Dashkov to Monroe, Feb. 24/March 8, 1813, Gallatin MSS; *National Intelligencer,* March 9, 1813; Monroe to Dashkov, March 11, 1813, Gallatin MSS.

Envisioning a glittering success, young Dashkov pressed ahead. He adopted as his own an American suggestion to suspend hostilities without awaiting word from London. Unfortunately Admiral Warren declined to risk another rebuke from his superiors. Writing from his flagship at anchor in nearby Lynnhaven Bay, Warren categorically rejected the new proposal. He went on to give his "private" opinion that, to secure peace, the United States must end restrictions on British commerce, tolerate impressment, and—this is the first hint of an important theme—agree to "a proper Arrangement relative to the Frontiers and Country belonging to the Indian Nations . . . being Allies of the British Nation." [34] Ignoring this chilling tone, the Americans named commissioners to represent them at St. Petersburg and in general acted as though English acceptance of Rumiantzov's proposition was foreordained.

As usual on those infrequent occasions when the President allowed himself to be sanguine, optimism was unjustified. Britain rejected, not once but repeatedly, suggestions that a third power mediate her quarrel with the Americans. According to a plausible account later communicated to John Quincy Adams, the cabinet made the decision unanimously and with no hesitation at all. Rumiantzov refused to consider the first rejection as final. For almost a year he tried to reactivate the project. Lord Cathcart, British representative at the Czar's headquarters, twice stated his government's disapproval of the scheme and believed he had convinced Alexander to drop it. Rumiantzov, both physically and politically separated from his sovereign, sent still another offer through his ambassador in London in the autumn of 1813. For the fourth time the cabinet refused to accept it.[35]

Ministerial obduracy is easy to understand. Although recently

[34] Warren to Croker, secret, March 28, 1813, and enclosures, Adm 1/4359; Warren to Croker, secret and confidential, April 20, 1813, and enclosures, especially Warren to Dashkov, confidential, April 12, 1813, *ibid.*

[35] Nov. 3, 1813, Adams, *op. cit.,* II, 542–543; Castlereagh to Nicolay, Nov. 18, 1812, Correspondence dealing with Russian mediation; Adams #132 to Monroe, April 15, 1814, Worthington C. Ford, ed., *The Writings of John Quincy Adams* (7 vols.; New York, 1913–1917), V, 34–39; Castlereagh to Cathcart, July 14, 1813, Charles K. Webster, ed., *British Diplomacy, 1813–1815* (London, 1921), pp. 14–15; Cathcart #79 to Castlereagh, Aug. 5, 1813, *ibid.*, p. 16; Rumiantzov to Lieven, n.d. [Aug. 16/28, 1813], Correspondence dealing with Russian mediation.

become an ally, Russia and particularly Rumiantzov had quarreled with England in the past. The Chancellor's failure to sound out Great Britain before approaching America raised the suspicion that he did not mind putting the onus of refusal on England. Most important of all, mediation would, as Lord Castlereagh wrote, allow the United States "to Mix directly or Indirectly her Maritime Interests with those of Another State." The British government could not allow the United States and Russia to combine against her maritime code. In any event Parliament would never approve; ". . . no Government dare surrender," Castlereagh wrote, "the right of search for enemy's property, or British subjects." [36] Rumiantzov's failure to understand these evident truths deeply annoyed Whitehall.

Direct negotiations did not invite the same objections. As early as May, 1813, London papers suggested them, although the *Sun* insisted upon peace terms based on "British vengeance and retributive justice." In July Castlereagh sent an offer to negotiate directly to St. Petersburg.[37] Rumiantzov, still determined to force mediation, concealed this initiative from the Americans for months. His trickiness baffled and angered the commissioners, but then, both anger and bafflement were common at St. Petersburg.

Informal correspondence with London opened the Americans' eyes. En route to Russia one commissioner, Albert Gallatin, wrote to Alexander Baring, the London banker who handled the American government's accounts. Baring, sure that Gallatin expected something more in reply than "a gossiping letter about American politics," offered himself to the Foreign Secretary as an informal channel of communication, and Castlereagh promptly took advantage of this opportunity. There followed several exchanges of letters, nominally private but actually the product of careful consideration by the American commissioners on one hand and Castlereagh and Liverpool on the other. The English invited direct

[36] Castlereagh to Baring, Oct. 8, 1813, FO 5/98; Castlereagh to Cathcart, July 14, 1813, Webster, *op. cit.*, p. 14.

[37] *Times*, May 13, 1813; *Sun* (London), May 12, 1813; Nov. 3, 1813, Adams, *op. cit.*, II, 542; Castlereagh to Cathcart, July 14, 1813, Webster, *op. cit.*, pp. 14–15.

negotiations but warned the Americans—and Baring, sometimes overeager in his striving for peace—that they must not expect Britain to abandon impressment. The Americans hinted that they would settle for regulations preventing abuses of the practice. While their letters pointed out that they had authority to act only under Russian mediation, clearly they did not object to direct negotiations. Although they never told Castlereagh so, they even considered violating their instructions by going to London for peace talks.[38]

The commissioners at St. Petersburg in effect invited Great Britain to secure presidential approval of direct negotiations. Writing to Monroe in November, 1813, Castlereagh accepted the suggestion. Britain offered to negotiate, he said, "upon principles of perfect reciprocity," a statement somewhat contradicted by a later passage announcing devotion to "the maritime Rights of the British Empire." Madison and Monroe ignored this ominous reservation, perhaps because Castlereagh's communication arrived on the heels of reports of Napoleon's defeat at Leipzig and American setbacks on the Niagara frontier. The administration accepted the British offer early in January, and the goddess of peace forwarded the news to London in unusually rapid time.[39]

Down to the end of 1813, when H.M.S. *Bramble* arrived in America with Castlereagh's letter, everything about the war had been strangely inconclusive. Blood had been shed, lives had been lost and even wantonly thrown away. More often the campaigns of 1812 and 1813 had been a matter of marching and countermarching, a contest in braggadocio and insult, or a conflict of wills

[38] Gallatin to Baring Bros., June 22, 1813, enclosed in Baring to Castlereagh, July 6, 1813, FO 5/98; Baring to Gallatin, July 22, 1813, Gallatin MSS; Baring to Castlereagh, July 25, 1813, Henry Goulburn Papers on the Ghent Negotiations, William L. Clements Library, Ann Arbor, Vol. I; Gallatin to Baring, Aug. 15/27, 1813, Gallatin MSS; Baring to Castlereagh, Sept. 26, 1813, Goulburn MSS, Vol. I; Castlereagh to Baring, Oct. 2, 1813, *ibid.*; Baring to Castlereagh, Oct. 5, 1813, *ibid.*; Baring to Gallatin, Oct. 12, 1813, Gallatin MSS; Nov. 19, 1813, Adams, *op. cit.*, II, 548–551.

[39] Castlereagh to Monroe, Nov. 4, 1813, Department of State Archives, National Archives, Records of Negotiations Connected with the Treaty of Ghent, Vol. I; Monroe to Adams and Bayard, Jan. 8, 1814, Instructions, Vol. VII; *Chronicle*, Feb. 4, 1814.

between field commanders and their superiors. Neither the battle of the Thames nor tardy British blockades seriously altered the situation. The campaigns of the new year promised to be more serious. Similarly, on the diplomatic front, eighteen inconclusive months were to be followed by the direct confrontation of negotiators. The fate of these negotiations, the fate of military campaigns upon which the very existence of the United States might rest, would become known in 1814.

CHAPTER

III

JONATHAN FACES A DRUBBING

Unlike Madison, Castlereagh was in no hurry to get negotiations going. He offered direct negotiations as much to end Russian importunities as from any desire for peace, and he and his colleagues allowed the rapidly changing European scene to monopolize their attention in the early months of 1814. Only in August did plenipotentiaries come together at Ghent. By that time the scene, very discouraging to Madison in January, had become even more so. Above all, Napoleon had fallen, leaving England free to concentrate her ships and troops against the Americans. While the Duke of Wellington made a thrust northward into France, his allies dealt with Napoleon's main force. The Emperor refused peace after Leipzig, so at Christmastime the armies of Russia, Prussia, and Austria crossed the Rhine. Political and military coördination was poor, but the sheer weight of numbers defeated Napoleon. On the last day of March, after storming Montmartre, allied troops entered Paris. The Emperor soon abdicated.

Federalists thanked God for his aid to the allies. When Napoleon fled Russia, William Ellery Channing composed a thanksgiving prayer which, a friendly newspaper claimed, "united the elegance, and what the French call the 'Onction' of FENELON, with the simplicity of the Apostolic age." In New York, with "hearts glowing with gratitude to the Supreme Ruler of the Universe," editors of the *Post* celebrated "the deliverance of the world from one of the most cruel and detestable tyrants that ever disgraced humanity. . . . This is the Lords doing, and it is marvelous in our eyes." [1] Probably the *Post* would have found it as marvelous, and as clearly the work of the Lord, if Wellington disembarked at the Battery to force another abdication and perhaps restore another *ancien régime*.

For as long as possible Republican editors refused to believe Napoleon was doomed. One leading journal declared, Channing to the contrary, that the "fate of France appears peculiarly under the protection of Heaven. . . . Their hero . . . seems the peculiar charge of an overruling Providence." (Of course Republicans notoriously profaned religion.) *Niles' Register* foretold "the most signal disasters that have marked the pages of history" when the allies marched on Paris. Another paper cautiously predicted that, chastened by misfortune, Napoleon would negotiate a compromise peace uniting the Continent against "the tyranny of England." Less than a week before news of the abdication, the semiofficial *Intelligencer* printed the "GREAT NEWS" that the Austrian and Russian emperors and the King of Prussia had entered Paris as prisoners.[2]

When the Corsican's fall could no longer be denied, ingenious Republicans found usually implausible grains of consolation. The *Independent Chronicle* professed to consider the Bourbon restoration a triumph for the original principles of 1789. The *Intelligencer* hoped American privateers would find it easier to use the ports of Bourbon France than the blockaded harbors of Napoleon's

---

[1] *Columbian Centinel* (Boston), March 27, 1813; *New-York Evening Post*, June 6, 1814.
[2] *Independent Chronicle* (Boston), Oct. 28, 1813; *Enquirer* (Richmond), April 6, 1814; *Niles' Weekly Register* (Baltimore), April 2, 1814; *National Intelligencer* (Washington), June 2, 1814.

empire.[3] Republicans also hoped the victors would quickly fall out, forcing Britain to liquidate her American quarrel for another nearer home. Encouraged by Anglo-Russian friction culminating in unpleasantness during the Czar's visit to London, William H. Crawford, a leading war hawk who was now minister to France, stressed this possibility.[4] Finally, peace in Europe encouraged Republicans by promising to convert impressment and blockades into purely theoretical issues. Perhaps England would become less stubborn.

The British government bluntly warned against this hope. When, at a Paris dinner attended by Crawford and the visiting Castlereagh, a Frenchman raised his glass to toast "universal peace," the Foreign Secretary appended the warning phrase, "upon just principles." Crawford understood his meaning. At about the same time, in an order of the day explaining why sailors must serve until the American war ended, the Admiralty declared that "the question now at issue in this war is the maintenance of those maritime rights which are the sure foundation of our naval glory." The men below decks, like the regiments marching over dusty roads to take ship for America, had been freed for service there by the French collapse. Only a blind optimist could find much hope in European events. The Nestor of Monticello summed up the actual fact: ". . . the downfall of Bonaparte [is] a great blessing for Europe, which never could have had peace while he was in power. . . . To us alone this brings misfortune."[5]

Jefferson's successor faced financial difficulties more challenging and political opposition more virulent than any other wartime president. The two plagues ran together because many wealthy

---

[3] *Independent Chronicle*, June 6, 1814; *National Intelligencer*, June 10, 1814.

[4] Crawford to Monroe, private, March 26, 1814, Department of State Archives, National Archives, Despatches, France, Vol. XIV.

[5] Crawford to Monroe, private, April 20, 1814, *ibid.;* Croker to fleet, April 30, 1814, Christopher Lloyd, ed., *The Keith Papers*, III, Navy Records Society, *Publications*, XCVI (n.p., 1955), 253–254; Jefferson to William Short, Aug. 20, 1814, Andrew A. Lipscomb and Albert E. Bergh, eds., *The Writings of Thomas Jefferson* (Memorial ed.; 20 vols.; Washington, 1903–1904), XVIII, 283.

Federalists sought to end the war by withholding financial support. In the past Federalist bankers and the house of Baring in London had aided Gallatin. With the ministry's tacit approval, the Barings handled routine accounts all through the war. London papers charged the Barings with participating in American war loans.[6] Since this politically inspired charge was false and the United States found foreign loans impossible to obtain elsewhere, the Treasury had to depend upon its own resources and the coöperation of loyal Americans.

Cherished Jeffersonian principles of low taxation, surpluses, and debt reduction followed other tenets into the discard. The national debt, so laboriously reduced, rose by more than $80 million during the war until it was 50 per cent higher than the inheritance from John Adams. Even more important, on several occasions the government almost exhausted cash reserves. "We have hardly money enough to last till the end of the month," Secretary Gallatin reported in March, 1813. Rumor had it that the Department of State could not meet a stationery bill, and Andrew Jackson once had to pay his command out of his own pocket.[7]

As early as June, 1812, Congress authorized interest-bearing

[6] Ralph W. Hidy, *The House of Baring in American Trade and Finance* (Cambridge, Mass., 1949), pp. 51–52; *Sun* (London), Aug. 12–16, 1813. In the issue of August 13 the *Sun* stated that considerations of finance "loosen the tongues and give a spring to the influence of many men who have heretofore pretended to act from the impulse of patriotism, and the fashionable feelings of modern philanthropy." On this theme, see also Warren to Liverpool, private, Nov. 16, 1813, Papers of the First and Second Earls of Liverpool, British Museum (Add. MSS 38190–38489, 38564–38581), Add. MSS 38255.

In 1814, toward the end of the peace negotiations, Baring briefly considered refusing to pay dividends on American bonds. As almost all United States government bills had been protested, he had no balance upon which to draw and would, by the dividend payments, in effect grant credit to a nation at war with his own. On Gallatin's appeal the banker changed his mind and made the payments. Otherwise Baring extended only small credits to cover costs of the peace mission, expenses of prisoners of war, etc. Baring to Gallatin, Nov. 15, 29, 1814, Albert Gallatin Papers, New-York Historical Society; Gallatin to Baring, Nov. 24, Dec. 9, 1814, *ibid.*

[7] *Historical Statistics of the United States, Colonial Times to 1957*, Bureau of the Census (Washington, 1960), p. 711; Gallatin to Madison, March 5, 1813, James Madison Papers, Library of Congress; Bray Hammond, *Banks and Politics in America* (Princeton, 1957), p. 230; Marquis James, *The Life of Andrew Jackson* (Indianapolis, 1938), pp. 149–150.

treasury notes, much like the Continentals of Revolutionary days. During the war the Treasury issued $37 million, although never more than half of this amount was in circulation at any one time. In July and August, 1813, a year after war began, Congress reluctantly restored and even increased internal taxes repealed in Jefferson's time. Even as late as 1814, however, internal taxes covered only one-twentieth of the government's expenditures. From start to finish they provided only a fraction of the revenue produced by import duties despite British blockades, and less even than the amount realized from the sale of public lands.[8]

The government depended primarily upon loans. Congress authorized $60 million in bonds from 1812 to 1814. Despite sale at a discount and in return for depreciated currency, Gallatin and his agents found it difficult, often impossible, to dispose of the bonds. Only $8 million worth were sold at par, and the total specie return was about $28 million. Wealthy but Federalist New England purchased less than $3 million of bonds while at the same time accepting British paper. "The Specie is constantly going in Cart Loads to Canada, between which country & the Eastern States, especially this, there is an uninterrupted trade in Bills of the British Gov't," a Bostonian reported late in July, 1814; "from two Banks in Boston there have departed 1,800,000 Dollars since the first of June." [9]

A handful of wealthy patriots saved the Treasury from total humiliation. When Gallatin offered a $16 million issue in the spring of 1813, New England virtually boycotted it while Republican states proved short of cash. At Gallatin's urging three foreign-born bankers, David Parish, John Jacob Astor, and Stephen Girard, agreed to take more than $9 million worth, more than half the total issue. The bankers extorted a discount of 12 per cent and a promise that the government would seek honorable peace

[8] Paul Studenski and Herman E. Krooss, *Financial History of the United States* (New York, 1952), pp. 76–77; *Historical Statistics*, p. 712.
[9] Studenski and Krooss, *op. cit.*, p. 78; Hammond, *op. cit.*, p. 229; Christopher Gore to King, July 28, 1814, Charles R. King, *The Life and Correspondence of Rufus King* (6 vols.; New York, 1894–1900), V, 403.

or, that failing, would urge vigorous financial legislation. In 1814 Jacob Barker, a Quaker from New York, secured similarly favorable financial terms after the administration rejected political terms Federalist bankers attempted to impose.[10]

Federalists opposed the administration with their voices, votes, and hearts as well as with their dollars. They had always considered the war evilly inspired, and they saw political advantages in pressing their opposition. Federalist governors in New England challenged the government's right to send militia beyond the borders of their home states. Because they had no desire to see the Republicans conquer Canada, Federalists on the New York City Council defeated a resolution of thanks to General Harrison for his success there. Federalists in the Massachusetts Senate killed a proposed commendation of Captain James Lawrence for his defeat of a British ship. When, after a less successful engagement, the nation rang with praise of Lawrence's dying words, "Don't give up the ship," Federalists refused to march in his funeral procession.[11]

In Congress the opposition consistently harried Madison. In June, 1813, an energetic young recruit named Daniel Webster presented a string of particularly embarrassing resolutions. They called for information from the President upon issues, like Napoleon's alleged repeal of the Berlin and Milan decrees, which the administration wished to consider dead and buried. The debate gave Federalists fertile opportunities for slander, hyperbole, and innuendo, yet the resolves were so skillfully drawn that Republicans had to accept them or invite charges of not daring to face the truth. When the Secretary of State provided the documents, Federalist congressmen renewed their attacks upon the policy that had led to war.[12]

[10] Gallatin to Secretaries of War and Navy, April 17, 1813, Madison MSS; Philip G. Walters and Raymond Walters, Jr., "The American Career of David Parish," *Journal of Economic History*, IV (1944), 160–161; Samuel E. Morison, *The Life and Letters of Harrison Gray Otis* (2 vols.; Boston, 1913), II, 72–73.

[11] Freeman Cleaves, *Old Tippecanoe: William Henry Harrison and His Time* (New York, 1939), pp. 211–212; Hervey P. Prentiss, *Timothy Pickering as the Leader of New England Federalism, 1800–1815* (n.p., 1932), pp. 98–99.

[12] *Annals of Congress*, 13th Cong., 1st and 2d sess., pp. 169–485 *passim*.

Belated Republican attention to trade with the enemy provided opponents with another attractive target. Federalist opposition helped to defeat an embargo proposed by Madison in the summer of 1813. When the President returned to the charge in December, asking both an embargo on exports and the prohibition of imports that came primarily from Britain, his enemies took up the challenge. They scoffed at the hope of moving England to peace "by depriving her woollen drapers and cotton weavers of the sale of a few bales of goods." Refurbishing another theme used against earlier commercial restrictions, they charged the administration with abusing power. "If, sir," said a congressman from a district trading extensively with the enemy, "a parallel can be found in all the annals of ancient or modern despotism, (always excepting that of France,) of equal commercial oppression, let her abettors show it." Republicans declined the challenge. Almost silently they forced the new legislation through Congress.[13]

The embargo caused so much hardship and presented the Federalists with such good ammunition that the Republicans abandoned it after only five months. They found an excuse in the collapse of Napoleon, arguing that peace in Europe created commercial opportunities which Britain should not be allowed to monopolize, and that Europe's eagerness for trade with America would cause trouble for England. Everyone knew the real reason was the swell of protest, particularly in New England.[14]

Federalists were not so united as they appeared. A few, most notably Rufus King, who neither liked nor respected Madison, gave national considerations priority over partisan interest. King urged wealthy Federalists to take up the bond issues and warned Yankee extremists against "measures, which neither the actual State of public affairs, temporary as it must be, nor their permanent welfare will justify." A larger group opposed the war but shrank from sedition or rebellion. "Since our nation is so wicked and unjust as to enter upon this war, its sufferings will be salutary," George Cabot moralized. He and others expected the war to purge

---

[13] *Ibid.*, pp. 549–550, 554–561, 602–611, 2032–2058.
[14] *Ibid.*, pp. 731–734, 738–740, 1961–2002, 2014.

the nation of guilt—and of Republican domination.[15] Extremists saw no way to deprive the Republicans of power under the existing political system. They therefore embraced the chance of dissolution. Some, including Timothy Pickering, hoped after an interval to reconstitute the union on sounder principles. Most of these men expected the union, only twenty-five years old, to collapse peaceably and easily. A few talked of armed rebellion. A Dartmouth classmate wrote Webster, for example, that he was prepared to "march at 6 days notice for Washington . . . and I would swear . . . never to return till Madison was buried under the ruins of the capitol."[16]

Until 1814 Federalist groups lived in fairly good harmony. King's faction was relatively unimportant, although aided by Republican votes he won election to the Senate in 1813. Extremists knew that even in New England the people were not ready to break up the union. The entire party tacitly agreed to the purely negative course of criticizing the administration. This tactic, however, had little appeal outside New England. Even discontented citizens wished to know the intentions of those who sought political power and refused to cheer national victories. In New York, where Federalists won three-quarters of the congressional seats in 1812, the next year Madisonians captured the governorship and one house of the legislature. The next spring Republicans won the other house and reversed the ratio of parties in the congressional delegation. Other states shifted less spectacularly, sometimes because not even 1812 shook Republican control and sometimes because Madison's willingness to negotiate mollified antiwar Republicans. Nevertheless, if elections in 1812 and 1814 are a valid barometer, Federalism lost ground outside New England despite the war's unpopularity.

A tightened grip on New England compensated for these losses.

---

[15] King to Gore, Aug. 29, Sept. 30, 1813, King, *op. cit.*, V, 342, 346; Cabot to Pickering, June 11, 1813, Henry Cabot Lodge, *Life and Letters of George Cabot* (Boston, 1877), pp. 408–409.

[16] Pickering to Gouverneur Morris, Oct. 29, 1814, Lodge, *op. cit.*, pp. 535–536; George Herbert to Webster, April 20, 1813, Claude H. Van Tyne, ed., *The Letters of Daniel Webster* (New York, 1902), p. 27.

In 1813 the party gained control of all states north of the Hudson, and in Massachusetts the incumbent governor received a majority ten times as large as in 1812. The next year saw further gains as internal taxes, the embargo, a blockade of Yankee shores, and invasion of the Maine district brought war home to the Northeast. Governor Strong's majority dropped only slightly despite the attractiveness of his opponent, and in the section as a whole Federalists captured forty-one of the forty-three congressional seats.[17]

Party extremists decided the time had come. For a year they had talked about a convention of disaffected states. In February, 1814, the Massachusetts General Court recommended this step by overwhelming margins in both chambers. A justificatory report emphasized the evil effect of the embargo, "an act more unfeeling and odious than the Boston port bill, which aroused the colonies into independence. . . . We think it the duty of the present generation, to stand between the next and despotism." A convention of the "Wise and Good," the report continued, should propose "and even insist" upon proper safeguards. To gain hesitant members the ultras agreed to postpone a formal call to a convention until the next general court. Their faith in the electorate was justified in April, when the party swept to victory in a virtual referendum on the convention issue.[18] At this time no one could foresee that extremism had reached its peak, that firebrands would be checked when a convention met.

Ever a pessimistic man, Madison was sorely tried as bad news flowed to his office in the spring and summer of 1814. Secretary Monroe brought reports of the changes in Europe, Secretary Gallatin warned that the Treasury was drying up, and Madison's correspondents sent news of agitation in New England. Military prospects, although not universally dark, certainly seemed gloomy. The British government appeared, in an English officer's words,

[17] The preceding paragraphs rest upon a number of works including Morison, *op. cit.*; Prentiss, *op. cit.*; Irving Brant, *James Madison: Commander in Chief* (Indianapolis, 1961); Henry Adams, *History of the United States during the Administrations of Jefferson and Madison* (9 vols.; New York, 1889–1891), VII-VIII.

[18] Herman V. Ames, ed., *State Documents on Federal Relations*, II (Philadelphia, 1900), 69–75; Adams, *op. cit.*, VIII, 10–11.

to "have determined to give Jonathan a good drubbing." In August, in the same week that negotiations began at Ghent, a sardonic British admiral smiled to an American visitor, "M^r. Maddison will have to put on his armour & fight it out." [19] As Cockburn's grin implied, the odds did not lie with the Americans.

Until 1814 Liverpool's ministry tolerated extensive trade with the enemy. All the Empire needed American foodstuffs, and the commander in Canada later reported that two-thirds of his army's beef came from the United States. Midland mills lived upon American cotton. Nor could Britain lightheartedly abandon her largest foreign market. "Notwithstanding the Prohibitions of the Americans," Liverpool wrote, "there are some Articles of this Country which must have become really matters of necessity to them, & which they must be desirous . . . of procuring at some Risk." The Earl's government encouraged Americans to violate Madisonian law for economic reasons and to foment discord in the United States.

Yet the ministry also wanted Americans to feel the economic pinch. A colleague reminded the premier that "the exclusion of the American Produce, not only injures the Enemy, but upholds our Independence of them." In this spirit the government banned American rice and tobacco. But what of cotton? "Cotton Wool is the Produce of the most Anti Anglican part of the United States," Lord Bathurst noted; "a rigorous blockade of their Rivers, & Ports would make them feel the pressure of that War, of which they are the authors: while a free importation of their Cotton Wool would be a relief to them." The government compromised. It blockaded the South but permitted imports to continue via ports in New England. [20]

Carriage presented another problem. The British marine, largely occupied with wartime tasks, was in any event banned from

[19] Col. Henry Torrens to Maj.-Gen. Sir George Murray, April 14, 1814, Arthur R. Wellesley, Duke of Wellington, ed., *Supplementary Despatches, Correspondence, and Memoranda of Field Marshal Arthur Duke of Wellington, K.G.*, IX (London, 1862), 58; J. S. Skinner to Madison, Aug. 13, 1814, Madison MSS.
[20] Liverpool to Wellington, private, Nov. 21, 1812 [1811], Liverpool MSS, Add. MSS 38236; Bathurst to Liverpool, Oct. 3, 1812, *ibid.*, Add. MSS 38250; *Times* (London), Feb. 4, 1814.

American ports. Neutral shipping, permitted to come from enemy ports even with American-owned goods on board, could carry but a small part of the burden. Consequently the ministry tolerated a licensed trade, often in American ships, and regularized it by various orders in council. In 1813, after parliamentary attacks, the government curbed trade with the West Indies and required American ships to unload most European-bound goods at Halifax, which developed a thriving trade with the United States.[21] These changes foreshadowed greater rigor in 1814.

Vice-Admiral Sir Alexander Cochrane, who replaced Warren early in that year, shared the ministry's belief that coddling New England paid few dividends. Even before assuming command he wrote that "it will be absolutely necessary to place all the Northern ports, in the same state of strict blockade, as those to the Southward have hitherto been." Ships were not lacking, for even in Warren's time squadrons permanently blocked harbors where American frigates took refuge. In April, 1814, almost as his first act, Cochrane announced a general blockade.[22]

Despite licenses and evasion by wagons and ships which slipped along the Maine coast to British North America, Cochrane's blockade struck America a thundering blow. The prices of coffee, sugar, and textiles, already far higher than in peacetime, rocketed upward. Staple growers suffered a further decline in the prices of cotton and foodstuffs. The blockade and the American embargo which preceded it crippled shipping interests in New England. Whereas in 1813 a Yankee Republican could write complacently, "The violents cannot carry with them the main body,"[23] in 1814, thanks largely to the blockade, "violents" like Pickering, Gouverneur Morris, and John Lowell dreamed of success.

The British government showed its determination to give Jon-

---

[21] *Times*, Feb. 4, 1814; James Buller to Croker, Feb. 2, 1814, and encl., Admiralty Archives, Public Record Office, Adm 1/5219; Walter R. Copp, "Nova Scotian Trade during the War of 1812," *Canadian Historical Review*, XVIII (1937), 141–155. Buller's letter explains and encloses Orders in Council issued to that date. Further information may be found in many sources, particularly minutes of the Board of Trade, Public Record Office, BT 5/22.

[22] Cochrane to Croker, March 7, April 28, 1814, Adm 1/505, 1/506.

[23] William Eustis to Monroe, confidential, Feb. 9, 1813, James Monroe Papers, Library of Congress.

athan a drubbing in other ways. Reports slipping past the block-aders repeatedly told of the dispatch of redcoats to America. The movement began on a limited scale early in the year, when, despite the outcry of the young Sir Robert Peel, who was on the spot, some troops were sent from Ireland. With Napoleon's abdication the transfers swelled. Less than a week later the Duke of Wellington received orders to ready 13,000 troops for redeployment. The Admiralty soon received a blizzard of requests, all marked "Immediate," for frigates to escort the transports. As early as May everyone knew that, as the *Morning Chronicle* put it, "the *elité* of the army" was bound for America.[24]

Four regiments, three of them combat veterans from France, were detailed to raid the American coastline. The idea was not new; even Admiral Warren had talked about attacks upon New Orleans, Baltimore, and Washington to destroy military stores and "probably shake the Union to it's Centre." Now, with new commanders, things could go beyond the talking stage. Some eager officers wished to stir up Negro rebellion or support the Creeks, but the ministry preferred to avoid permanent commitments. London did order the occupation of eastern Maine, but for the rest limited its commanders to hit-and-run raids. These, the cabinet hoped, would hasten Madison's downfall and, most important of all, "give a diversion . . . in favour of the Army employed in the defence of Upper and lower Canada."[25] By June, 1814, it was obvious to all, not least the Americans, that these raids would soon come.

Preparations for the major thrust along Lake Champlain took

[24] Peel to Goulburn, Feb. 9, 1814, Henry Goulburn Papers, County Hall, Kingston-on-Thames; Duke of York to Wellington, April 14, 1814, Wellington, *op. cit.*, IX, 82–84; Goulburn to Croker (2) and H. E. Bunbury to Croker, immediate, April 19, 1814, Adm 1/4229; *Morning Chronicle* (London), May 19, 1814; *Edinburgh Evening Courant*, Sept. 22, 1814.

[25] Warren to Croker, Feb. 21, 1813, Adm 1/4359; Cochrane to Croker, June 20, 1814, Adm 1/506; Sir Edward Codrington to Melville, private, May 22, 1814, Papers of Viscount Melville, William L. Clements Library, Ann Arbor; Goulburn to Croker, secret, April 28, 1814, and encl., Adm 1/4229; Bathurst to Maj.-Gen. Barnes, May 20, 1814, encl. in Goulburn to Croker, secret, May 20, 1814, *ibid.* Cochrane did give small amounts of aid to the Indians and carried off some Negro slaves, but the British made no major efforts to stir racial conflict in the United States.

somewhat longer. Remembering that broken communications had doomed Burgoyne in 1777, the British tried to secure control of the lake. To strengthen their flotilla took time, as did the movement of troops from their landing places to the frontier. Ten thousand reinforcements placed a heavy burden on Canada's primitive logistic system. In recognition of these facts, authorities at London first urged but did not positively order an invasion. When Governor-General Sir George Prevost persisted in delays and excuses, his government stepped up the pressure.[26] In August the reluctant general crossed the border. Neither his superiors nor the cocky European veterans under him had serious doubts of success.

Other theaters became almost sideshows in 1814. Commodore Perry's victory exasperated Britons—"Despicable in the Cabinet, ridiculous in the field, upon the waves they retain the blood and spirit almost of Englishmen," the *Times* exclaimed in pique and wonder[27]—and sparked demands for stronger efforts beyond Niagara. The ministry chose, however, to write off this portion of the Great Lakes. The Americans, for their part, did not exploit Harrison's victory at the Thames, concentrating their energies against Indians south of the lakes. On the Niagara frontier the tide flowed to and fro. Although the Americans did well at Chippewa and Lundy's Lane and held snippets of Canadian territory until autumn, Sir George Drummond seized the offensive in midsummer.

Privateers strengthened Madison's hand as his armies and navy could not. Overwhelming British forces swept the frigates from the seas. Privateers and a few small naval vessels continued to disrupt British commerce, although about one-third of the captures were retaken before reaching American ports. Estimates of the number of captures varied tremendously, even after the war. Lloyds admitted the loss of 1,200 merchantmen; *Niles' Register* claimed about 2,350.[28] Whatever the true figures, Britain suffered severely. Communications were interrupted, valuable ships and

[26] Bathurst to Prevost, secret, June 3, 1814, Colonial Office Archives, Public Record Office, CO 43/23; Bathurst #71, #75 to Prevost, July 11, Aug. 22, 1814, *ibid.*
[27] *Times*, Oct. 7, 1813.
[28] *Hansard*, XXIX, 649–650; *Niles' Register*, Jan. 6, 1816.

cargoes were lost. Insurance rates doubled or even tripled. Corsairs did best early in the war, and convoys reduced their effectiveness in 1813. In the spring of 1814 the number of captures rose again, to nearly two a day.[29] French ports offered haven to privateers despite energetic British protests to the new Bourbon government. Some New Englanders, deprived of trading opportunities, put idle ships to work in more bellicose business. American ships infested waters around the British Isles, Parliament became restive, and at least one American observer believed the privateers made Liverpool seek peace.[30]

Yet by and large the gods appeared to smile upon Great Britain in 1814. Looking back afterward, an American diplomat summed up British advantages as negotiations began:

The events which took place last spring in Europe left us to contend single handed against Great Britain. She was inflated by success . . . of a force which under no other circumstances could have been at her disposal. She was in a singular degree united against us & she had . . . all the means to subjugate and punish us in a single campaign. We were on our part unprepared & divided & faction had literally tied one of our hands behind us.[31]

Except that it omitted financial problems, this catalogue fairly stated American difficulties. Only time would show whether the British ministry intended to press its advantages, whether the cabinet intended to fight for what one London paper described as a "Peace such as America *deserves,* and British *generosity* may bestow . . . upon . . . a faithless, unprincipled, and corrupt Government." [32] Only time would show whether five Americans who came together at Ghent in July, 1814, could secure peace without humiliation.

[29] *Hansard,* XXIX, 649–650.
[30] Erving to Gallatin, Aug. 15, 1814, Gallatin MSS.
[31] Russell to John M. Forbes, Jan. 31, 1815, Jonathan Russell Papers, Brown University Library.
[32] *Sun,* May 17, 1814.

CHAPTER

IV

AMERICANS AT GHENT

A month in advance of the British commissioners, five well-traveled Americans arrived in a Flemish town to negotiate peace. John Quincy Adams and Jonathan Russell, already quarreling as they would for years, reached Ghent in uneasy company on June 24, 1814. Three afternoons later James A. Bayard joined them at the Hotel des Pays-Bas, and the next evening, striding past puddles left by heavy rain, Henry Clay entered the hotel. On July 6 the quartet greeted Albert Gallatin, who brought discouraging information from London and Paris. In a few days the commissioners left the inconvenient, expensive Hotel des Pays-Bas for the Hotel d'Alcantara on the Rue des Champs, leased from Baron Lavendeghem. At Adams' insistence they took a month's lease renewable at their option; if negotiations collapsed they would thus save expense.[1]

[1] Adams #125 to Monroe, July 3, 1814, Worthington C. Ford, ed., *The Writings of John Quincy Adams* (7 vols.; New York, 1913–1917), V, 56–57; diary entries of June 27, 28, July 6, 1814, Elizabeth Donnan, ed., *Papers of James A. Bayard, 1796–1815*, American Historical Association, *Annual Report, 1913*, II (Washington, 1915), 513–514; July 9, 1814, Charles F. Adams, ed., *Memoirs of John Quincy Adams* (12

Not one of the envoys came from the Republican heartland south of the Potomac. All other sections were represented, as was Federalism by ex-Senator Bayard. "With us," Monroe wrote, "every part of the nation ought to be represented to ensure confidence." [2] The Secretary did not add that Madison originally nominated only Gallatin, Adams, and Bayard, adding Clay and Russell as substitutes for the Czar, so to speak, after Castlereagh suggested direct negotiations. "Take out Bayard—and what are they?" a staunch Federalist asked; ". . . from such discordant materials I anticipate no good." The mission was indeed a bundle of contradictions. Extreme submissionists and extreme war men alike distrusted it. "The only serious difficulty in the American commission was its excess of strength," Henry Adams comments, [3] meaning that this strength led to frequent squabbles. Yet on balance their very great strength, different talents, and similar argumentativeness—only Gallatin apart—well served the men of Ghent. They did not reveal their cross-purposes to outsiders. Mark the contrast with Franklin and Jay in 1782, with Wilson and House and Lansing in 1919. [4]

Accident made John Quincy Adams chairman of the commission; membership he deserved. In 1813 Madison and Monroe intended Gallatin to hold the first position, only to have the Senate reject his appointment. Adams succeeded to the leadership and was permitted to hold it even after Gallatin's successful reappointment in 1814. His experience, omnivorous reading, and marvelous memory made Adams indispensable. He alone of the commissioners, for example, knew where in Martens' massive *Receuil des*

---

vols.; Philadelphia, 1874–1877), II, 656–657. The fullest description of the Ghent negotiations, freely used here, is Fred L. Engelman, *The Peace of Christmas Eve* (New York, 1962).

[2] Monroe memorandum, n.d. [Jan., 1814], James Monroe Papers, Library of Congress, fol. 3847.

[3] Charles Goldsborough to Bleecker, Feb. 4, 1814, Harriet L. P. Rice, *Harmanus Bleecker* (Albany, 1924), p. 37; Henry Adams, *History of the United States during the Administrations of Jefferson and Madison* (9 vols.; New York, 1889–1891), IX, 14.

[4] Historians, though overemphasizing the practical importance of quarrels within the American commission, have given the envoys too much credit for the final settlement. See below, pp. 49–50, 131.

traités to find the prescription for opening negotiations with the enemy.[5] On his forty-fifth birthday two years earlier, Adams had written in his journal, "Two thirds of a long life are passed, and I have done nothing to distinguish it by usefulness to my country or to mankind." [6] The most important offices, secretary of state and president, did lie ahead of him, as well as service in the House of Representatives. But even in 1812 John Quincy Adams had reached the top of the diplomatic corps, had served in the Senate, had been appointed to the Supreme Court, and (greatest glory of all?) had occupied a professorial chair at Harvard.

Few Adamses have been masters of *suaviter in modo, fortiter in re*, a fact that alternately provokes self-congratulation and self-criticism in the family. Of his son's service at Ghent, ex-President John Adams wrote, "I hope his Phylosophy held out the siege. Oh! how glad I am, that I was not in his place. I am very much afraid that I should have been very impudent." James A. Bayard, who later came to appreciate Adams, found him "singularly cold and repulsive" at St. Petersburg. At Ghent both Adams' colleagues and the British suffered the lash of his tongue. Adams himself frequently admitted and regretted, in his diary, that "I cannot always restrain the irritability of my temper." [7]

Optimism too is not a notable characteristic of this greatest American family. Certainly John Quincy Adams had less of this quality and particularly of its handmaiden, humor, than his father. The Americans, save possibly Clay and to a lesser extent Russell, arrived at Ghent in pessimistic mood. In Adams despond reached an acme. He knew that his colleagues often considered him, in Russell's later words, "a kind of laborious pedant without judgment enough to be useful or taste sufficient to be admired." [8] Since Adams, egotistical as well as self-critical, knew his wisdom ex-

---

[5] Aug. 7, 1814, Charles F. Adams, *op. cit.*, III, 3–4.
[6] July 9, 1812, *ibid.*, II, 387.
[7] John Adams to Richard Rush, Oct. —, 1814, Adams Family Papers, Massachusetts Historical Society, Vol. CXXII; diary entry of Aug. 3, 1813, Donnan, *op. cit.*, p. 427; Sept. 20, 1814, Charles F. Adams, *op. cit.*, III, 37.
[8] Russell to Clay, Oct. 15, 1815, James F. Hopkins, ed., *The Papers of Henry Clay* (Lexington, 1959———), II, 75.

ceeded his colleagues', his failure to dominate them deepened the negative mood imposed by the shadow of Britain.

Both before and after 1814 Adams' nationalism most often took the form of Anglophobia. He left the party of his father to enlist under Jefferson largely because he considered the Federalists too tolerant of British insult, and he seldom concealed his feelings. Even Alexander Baring distrusted him, and the London *Times* declared: "Mr. Adams may be considered as pledged by principle, and want of principle, to the most bitter and durable hatred of Great Britain." [9] Above all Adams looked forward to the day when America would cease to be a cockboat in the wake of H.M.S. *Britannia*. Progress in this direction seemed impossible in the summer of 1814. All Adams hoped to do at Ghent was to place the onus for continued war upon England. Although he had little faith in Madison's administration, Adams preferred the uncertain arbitrament of arms to the surrender of American honor at Ghent.

As chairman, Adams claimed the head of the table, the right to present formal statements to the British, and the privilege (soon dubious, then abandoned) of preparing the first draft of all papers. Through influence, and by accommodating quarrels and arranging compromises, Albert Gallatin really gained the place President Madison originally planned for him. Gallatin was not an assertive man, and only the hypercritical Russell considered him arrogant. Still his request for a private cipher and his extensive separate reports to the Secretary of State show that Gallatin considered himself *primus inter pares*.[10]

In 1813 Gallatin had volunteered to go to St. Petersburg. Mon-

[9] Baring to Castlereagh, July 6, 1813, Foreign Office Archives, Public Record Office, FO 5/98; *Times* (London), Aug. 11, 1814.

[10] Adams to Louisa Adams, Jan. 10–17, 1815, Ford, *op. cit.*, V, 267; Russell to Clay, Oct. 15, 1815, Hopkins, *op. cit.*, II, 76; memorandum encl. in Gallatin to Monroe, April 22, 1813, Department of State Archives, National Archives, Records of Negotiations Connected with the Treaty of Ghent, Vol. I. Adams' appreciation of Gallatin sprang in part from a recognition that his colleague accomplished by tact what he himself often failed to obtain by direct argument. In the words of Adams' grandson, "In no instance did Mr. Gallatin allow himself to be drawn into the conflicts of his colleagues, and yet he succeeded in sustaining Mr. Adams in every essential point without appearing to do so." Henry Adams, *The Life of Albert Gallatin* (Philadelphia, 1879), p. 522.

roe and the new secretary of war, John Armstrong, objected,[11] and Gallatin's plan to hold on to his treasury office and resume its chores upon his return raised complaints against pluralism. Yet Gallatin lobbied for appointment and even left the United States before the Senate acted on his nomination. After twelve arduous years, after putting wartime finance in as good shape as he thought politically possible,[12] Gallatin wanted to escape Washington. Moreover the Secretary believed that "the great incapacity for conducting the war" and the "want of union" made peace imperative. Essentially he sought a mere truce. "Taught by experience," he wrote, "we will apply a part of our resources to such naval preparations & organisations of the public force as will, within less than five years, place us in a commanding situation." [13] So Gallatin, with his fellow commissioner, James A. Bayard, and twenty secretaries and servants, sailed for Europe in May, 1813.

Haste proved unwise. Federalists, Republican factionalists, and some of Monroe's friends, seeking to cripple a rival for the presidential succession, combined against the appointment. The chief stated reason, and for many the real one, was Gallatin's plan to hold office as peace commissioner and secretary of the treasury simultaneously. The President satisfied no one by explaining that the Secretary of the Navy, notoriously a bungler, would hold the fort until Gallatin returned. Just as Gallatin's ship entered the Gulf of Finland the Senate rejected the appointment that sent him on his long journey.[14] Before learning of defeat Gallatin acted

[11] Monroe to Jefferson, June 7, 1813, Stanislaus M. Hamilton, ed., *The Writings of James Monroe* (7 vols.; New York, 1898–1903), V, 267–268; memorandum of June 25–27, 1813, Rufus King Papers, New-York Historical Society, Vol. XIII.

[12] Gallatin believed all possible had been done to prepare for 1813. Gallatin to Jean Badollet, May 5, 1813, Albert Gallatin Papers, New-York Historical Society. On the other hand, he considered the long-term fiscal prospects threatening. At St. Petersburg, replying to a comment that it would be almost impossible to finance another year's campaign, Gallatin said: "You are right and if I had not thought so also myself, you would not see me here upon this sofa." Diary entry of Aug. 26, 1813, Donnan, *op. cit.*, p. 442.

[13] Gallatin to James W. Nicholson, May 5, 1813, Gallatin MSS.

[14] *Annals of Congress*, 13th Cong., 1st and 2d sess., pp. 83–87, 89; King to Oliver Wolcott, Jr., June 10, 1813, Wolcott Family Papers, Connecticut Historical Society, Vol. XXIII; Thomas Worthington to Hannah Gallatin, July 19, 1813, Gallatin MSS; Madison to Gallatin, Aug. 2, 1813, Gaillard Hunt, ed., *The Writings of James Madi-*

officially at St. Petersburg, and afterward he traveled to London to assay the chances of peace. In February, 1814, discovering that Gallatin had not left Europe, President Madison capitulated to the Senate. He appointed a replacement to the Treasury and added Gallatin to the commission to negotiate directly with the British. This nomination won quick approval from the Senate but displeased many Englishmen who believed the old canard that "in affections, politics, & morals, he is a confirmed Frenchman." [15]

The concept *reculer pour mieux sauter* no longer played a major part in Gallatin's thinking. "In present circumstances," he wrote Monroe from London, "the most favorable terms of Peace that can be expected are the status ante Bellum." Gallatin expected even this to be strongly resisted by a nation exhilarated by European victory, full of "vindictive passions" toward America, and possessed of large fleets and armies without employ. To unite the American people and to encourage peace sentiment in Britain he believed, like Adams, that the commissioners must above all seek to fix the blame for continued war upon Great Britain. [16]

Gallatin's traveling companion, James A. Bayard of Delaware, had been a Federalist politician almost as long as the Pennsylvanian, six years his senior, had served Republicanism. The President's opponents considered Bayard's appointment a shoddy trick to weaken the Federalists; Adams doubted his two colleagues could work in harness; and one Englishman said he would not be more surprised if the Prince Regent appointed a member of the cabinet and its most violent opponent, Samuel Whitbread, joint commissioners to negotiate at Paris. [17] Actually Gallatin and Bayard were moderates. In backing Jefferson over Burr in 1801 and supporting the war after strenuously opposing its declaration, Bay-

son (9 vols.; New York, 1900–1910), VIII, 252–256; John W. Eppes to Madison, June 29, 1813, William C. Rives Collection, Library of Congress; William H. Crawford to Gallatin, April 20, 1814, Gallatin MSS.

[15] Irving Brant, *James Madison: Commander in Chief* (Indianapolis, 1961), p. 241; *Times*, Aug. 11, 1814.

[16] Gallatin to Monroe, June 13, 1814, Ghent Negotiations, Vol. I.

[17] Killian K. Van Rensselaer to Bayard, April 17, 1813, Donnan, *op. cit.*, p. 206; June 15, 1813, Charles F. Adams, *op. cit.*, II, 474; John Mansfield to Whitbread, April 20, 1814, Samuel Whitbread Papers, Southill Park, Biggleswade, Bedfordshire.

ard showed patriotism. The Senator, who knew his political friends considered it treachery to serve Madison, felt "a Solemn duty not to refuse . . . any means in my power which could aid in extricating the Country from its embarrassments." He believed the administration, chastened by military failures, "desire[d] peace if it can be obtained upon decent terms." [18] Bayard sacrificed his health on the altar of peace. Dysentery assailed him in Russia, travel exhausted him. Neither a stay in London nor the generous use of wine improved him. He too faced negotiations at Ghent with "very slender" hopes, yet had no intention of begging for peace. There was, Clay testified, "not a more genuine American in the mission." [19]

Clay and Bayard nearly became colleagues in 1813 when Monroe recommended the appointment of Clay instead of Gallatin. In 1814, when Madison enlarged the commission, he selected Clay after toying with the name of another war hawk, William H. Crawford, the minister at Paris. Doubtless the President believed the appointment would show he did not intend to capitulate to England, and at the same time, by making Clay partly responsible, might disarm criticism of any future compromises. Federalists charged Madison with sabotage of the negotiations, an accusation echoed in England. After all, a Federalist pamphleteer pointed out, Clay stood "pledged not to make peace till Britain yields what she never will yield—her maritime rights." [20] This charge maligned Madison and Clay. In July the Kentuckian said he would accept a treaty silent on impressment. At the same time he was somewhat more sanguine than his colleagues, although not the pure optimist they considered him. He did not expect peace to come easily, if at all. He depended upon events in America and Europe which he knew were hopes rather than certainties. Above all he believed, as he wrote in remonstrance to the dispirited Gallatin and Bayard, "we shall best promote the objects of our Mis-

[18] Bayard to Samuel Bayard, April 23, 1813, Donnan, *op. cit.*, p. 211.
[19] Bayard to Andrew Bayard, Aug. 6, 1814, *ibid.*, pp. 312–313; Clay to Monroe, private, Oct. 26, 1814, Monroe MSS.
[20] Brant, *op. cit.*, pp. 239–240; John Lowell (*pseud.* A Massachusetts Lawyer), *Review of a Treatise on Expatriation* (Boston, 1814), p. 3.

sion . . . by presenting a firm and undismayed countenance." [21]

Clay, most observers have noted, was a gambler. At Ghent he whiled away idle hours at cards; the censorious Adams complained, although on one occasion he joined his colleague in a social game which bored Clay because the stakes were too low. The Kentuckian considered diplomacy much like gambling: "He was for playing *brag* with the British Plenipotentiaries. . . . He said the art of it was to beat your adversary by holding your hand, with a solemn and confident phiz, and outbragging him." [22] Like all but the best gamblers Clay found it difficult to maintain a "confident phiz" in the face of adversity. At the dreariest point in the negotiations John Quincy Adams noted with grim satisfaction that "Mr. Clay, who was determined to foresee no public misfortune in our affairs, bears them with less temper, now they have come, than any other of us." [23] Whatever his outward mien, Clay did not differ overmuch from his colleagues.

Just as Bayard and Gallatin, two moderates, traveled together on the *Neptune,* so Jonathan Russell, a former war hawk, accompanied Clay on the *John Adams.* The Rhode Islander got on board just before the *Adams* sailed from New York on February 23, 1814. For six weeks the two commissioners passed hours in conversation. Although four years the younger, Clay quickly gained the ascendancy. By the time they arrived in Sweden, then the expected scene of negotiations, he had captured Russell's soul. At Ghent and forever after Russell served as Clay's sometimes overzealous adjutant.

To explain Russell's subordination to Clay it is necessary to look beyond their political views and the former speaker's force and charm. Russell was by nature extremely touchy; he sullenly removed from common lodgings at Ghent and later complained he had been underpaid for his services. Even before leaving for

---

[21] Clay to Crawford, July 2, 1814, William H. Crawford Papers, Library of Congress; Clay to Bayard and Gallatin, May 2, 1814, Hopkins, *op. cit.,* I, 891.

[22] Bayard gruffly replied: "Ay, . . . but you may lose the game by bragging until the adversary sees the weakness of your hand." Dec. 11, 1814, Charles F. Adams, *op. cit.,* III, 101–102.

[23] Oct. 14, 1814, *ibid.,* III, 53.

Europe he harbored grievances against Gallatin and Adams; the latter hatred is particularly baffling, for Adams said he knew Russell only through "a frequent and very agreeable correspondence" when both headed legations in Europe.[24] Largely as a reaction, Russell enlisted under Clay, and Adams' cold and condescending manner at Ghent confirmed his attitude.

The London *Times* unfairly considered Russell "a mere cypher." He had served at Paris and London just before the declaration of war and presented the peace proposals of the summer of 1812, thus gaining a firsthand knowledge even Adams lacked. The appointment of Russell and Clay to the mission reassured Republicans troubled by the selection of a Federalist and a renegade, Bayard and Adams. Russell also strengthened the balance so treasured by Monroe. He represented mercantile interests, and even a Rhode Island Federalist admitted that Russell's *"practical commercial knowledge* is undoubtedly *sound* and extensive."[25] Finally, Russell's nomination gave Madison a chance for a small political victory. The Senate, which had disapproved Russell's appointment as minister to Sweden on nominal grounds of economy, had to swallow it when coupled with the larger job.

Among them the five American commissioners traveled some 20,000 miles before reaching the Hotel des Pays-Bas. Gallatin and Bayard joined Adams in St. Petersburg at the end of July, 1813, leaving the next January after collapse of the mediation project. After a brutal trip by sleigh and coach—snow fell on twenty-two of the first twenty-eight days, and the travelers often slept in their conveyances—they reached Amsterdam, then crossed the Channel to England in April. The two visitors, arriving dur-

[24] Russell to Monroe, private and personal, Feb. 6, 1814, Monroe MSS; Adams to Abigail Adams, March 30, 1814, Ford, *op. cit.*, V, 25.

[25] *Times*, August 11, 1814; William Hunter to Bayard, Jan. 29, 1814, Donnan, *op. cit.*, p. 266. Hunter, a moderate Federalist like Bayard, took an essentially negative view of Russell: "He has been a Lawyer, a Merchant, a Traveller, his vicissitudes of Fortune have been frequent and extreme, his *practical commercial knowledge* is undoubtedly *sound* and extensive. If he is not secretly instructed to obstruct the Negotiation he certainly may be eminently useful, but in his Sincerity and Honesty I have not an implicit Confidence. You will find him cold, reserved, *artful* tho inelegant in manners and unamiable in Temper. He knows how to conceal his resentments, he can even supplicate those he hates."

ing wild celebrations of Napoleon's downfall, found most Englishmen eager for revenge upon the United States and virtually wrote off chances of an honorable peace.

When Lord Castlereagh offered direct negotiations he suggested London or Gothenburg, Sweden, as the meeting place. Madison chose Gothenburg, and to this port—or, more accurately, to the mouth of the ice-blocked harbor twelve miles away—the *John Adams* sailed. There Clay and Russell received suggestions from their brethren in London to move the negotiations. With misgivings the newcomers agreed to go to Ghent, a town then garrisoned by British troops. They firmly resisted hints by Gallatin that the best hope lay in negotiating at London under the eye of the ministry, presumably more peace-minded than any agents it might select. When, upon his arrival in Sweden at the end of May, John Quincy Adams learned of these developments, he too reluctantly accepted the transfer to Ghent. As Clay had already left for a visit to Paris en route to Holland, Adams and Russell sailed alone in the *John Adams* from Gothenburg to the Texel. As previously recounted they anticipated the other Americans at Ghent.[26]

No American wife brightened life at Ghent. Russell was a widower, Gallatin and Clay and Bayard left their wives in the United States, and Louisa Adams remained at St. Petersburg. The men, thrown upon one another, conversed to the point of exhaustion and irritation about their mission and American politics. Entertainments by city dignitaries, sight-seeing excursions during lulls in the negotiations, and even Clay's efforts to find amusement outside the common lodgings granted only temporary relief. Unfortunately Christopher Hughes, the mission's official secretary, remained in the hotel on the Place d'Armes. Hughes, one of those rare people who make friends with almost everyone, drew Adams' praise as "lively and good-humored, smart at a repartee, and a thorough punster, [in] theory and practice." [27] This young man

[26] For the travels of the American commissioners, see Engelman, *op. cit.*, Part II.
[27] Adams to Louisa Adams, Aug. 1, 1814, Ford, *op. cit.*, V, 69.

might have eased tensions at the rented quarters on the Rue des Champs.

The temporary bachelors grated upon one another, the more so because of British pressure. They disagreed about housing, had differing views about diplomatic protocol, and even quarreled when Ghent's Society of Fine Arts and Letters offered membership to only three of them. Always pugnacious, John Quincy Adams found himself at the center of disagreement. He had argued with Gallatin and Bayard in Russia, and although he came to respect both, particularly Gallatin, as a pessimist himself he sometimes found their even greater lack of hope intolerable. At Ghent he exchanged many a shot with Henry Clay, afterward regretting that he allowed the younger man to provoke him.

The disagreements are often exaggerated. Aside from one sharp conflict at the very end, the Americans agreed upon basic strategy. They argued over tactics and, most frequently, over the phraseology of notes to the British or of reports to Washington. With little else to do, each commissioner insisted upon the precise language, the exact nuance he preferred. Gallatin most often exercised his talents as peacemaker in reconciling drafts that littered the conference table. The give-and-take, the constant examination of alternatives, helped the Americans compose more powerful notes than their opponents, and the commissioners successfully concealed their differences. Only once did controversy within their ranks reach the ears of the British emissaries, and on no issue did it weaken the American position.

The commissioners did not consider themselves disunited. Just after arriving at Ghent they celebrated Adams' forty-seventh birthday. Bayard, his antagonist at St. Petersburg, offered the toast. "We appear all to be animated with the same desire of *harmonizing* together," Adams informed his wife. At Clay's urging he agreed to dine regularly with his colleagues, even at the risk of wasting time. Britain's high tone solidified the Americans. "No former diversity of opinion here shews itself in the smallest degree," Clay reported in August, and at the end of their labors

Adams described the disagreements as trivial.[28] His memoirs, always most complete in describing quarrels, and Russell's later denigration of Adams and Gallatin have left an unjustified impression.

The true relationship, bittersweet if you will, is symbolized by an exchange in December. Adams, the former professor of rhetoric, chided Clay for misusing English. The Kentuckian described a British negotiator, Henry Goulburn, as full of "irritation" when he should have used the word "irritability." Looking slyly at Clay, Adams added that Goulburn resembled someone else he knew. Laughing, Clay replied that this other irritable person was known by "none better than yourself." Gallatin chimed in with a similar remark. Then "we passed on in perfect good humor to another topic. There was, however, truth in the joking on all sides." [29]

The five unhopeful, sometimes quarrelsome Americans brought fifty manuscript pages of instructions with them to Ghent, the earliest written in April, 1813, and the most recent a year later. The instructions neither offered concessions to secure peace nor, with one important exception, demanded extensive British concessions. Washington weakly sought a favorable maritime code and the cession of Canada, but the one *sine qua non* was an agreement to end impressment.

President Madison's war message had emphasized impressment; peace talks in the first summer of war had collapsed on this issue, and the instructions of 1813 repeated the same theme. "If the encroachment of Great Britain is not provided against," Secretary Monroe wrote, "the United States have appealed to arms in vain.

[28] Adams to Louisa Adams, July 12, 1814, *ibid.*, V, 61; Clay to Monroe, private, Aug. 18, 1814, Monroe MSS; Adams to John Adams, Dec. 26, 1814, Adams Family MSS, Vol. CXXXIX. Adams' memoirs, although the most valuable source for the internal history of the Ghent commission, abound in excessive criticism of himself and his colleagues. As always Adams was even harsher when scribbling in his diary than he was in speaking to living flesh. Jonathan Russell, a silent intriguer at Ghent, developed exaggerated views for political purposes later on. So united in basic purpose were the Americans at Ghent that it is hard to accept Henry Adams' assertion (*History*, IX, 16–17) that Lord Castlereagh missed an easy opportunity to divide the commissioners.
[29] Adams to Louisa Adams, Dec. 16, 1814, Ford, *op. cit.*, V, 237–238.

If your efforts to accomplish it should fail, all further negotiations will cease, and you will return home without delay." [30]

The administration showed weakness from the very beginning. No doubt the President, like all nationalists, considered impressment humiliating; he certainly saw the political risk of admitting British pretensions. He also knew he could not possibly expect outright British capitulation. As always he offered to arrange other ways by which the Royal Navy might recover deserters, and in the summer of 1812, seeking to end the war just begun, the President offered an armistice on a mere promise by Britain to negotiate seriously. The instructions of 1813 somewhat sugared the pill of Monroe's *sine qua non*, demanding a ban on impressment only during the existing European war. [31]

Wheedling legislation sponsored by the administration accompanied these instructions. As early as the preceding December congressmen had talked of a ban on the enlistment of foreigners by American merchantmen. Gallatin and Monroe drafted a bill, then had it copied into a hand less distinctive than Gallatin's to conceal their responsibility. After the present war the secretaries proposed to forbid employment of seamen from any nation—all knew they meant England—which reciprocated by closing its own marine to Americans. (Those already naturalized and others who began naturalization before the war ended were exempted from the ban.) [32]

Felix Grundy introduced this bill late in January along with a report from the Foreign Relations Committee, actually also a product of the executive. After endorsing the bill the report denounced the impressment of Americans: "It is incompatible with their sovereignty—it is subversive of the main pillars of their independence." Silence in a treaty of peace, the report maintained, would tacitly admit English claims. [33] The bill came under heavy

---

[30] Monroe to Gallatin, Adams, and Bayard, April 15, 1813, Department of State Archives, National Archives, Diplomatic Instructions, All Countries, Vol. VII.

[31] *Ibid.*

[32] Baker to Castlereagh, separate and secret, Dec. 16, 1812, FO 5/88; Gallatin to Monroe, n.d., Monroe MSS, fol. 3547; *Annals*, 12th Cong., 2d sess., pp. 937–939.

[33] *Annals*, 12th Cong., 2d sess., pp. 932–937, esp. p. 936.

fire. "I am for going on . . . to a ten or twenty years' war . . . rather than succumb to tyranny," an aged war hawk declaimed. Some Federalists opposed a bill that, by showing moderation, might rally the people behind the war. Loyal Madisonians defended the bill as a possible contribution to honorable peace and a certain one to unity, a compromise that withdrew American protection from "wandering foreigners" to forge a shield over "the natives, the possessors, and the cultivators of the soil of this country." Aided by Federalists who either did not wish to or dared not oppose a peace move, the bill became law in February, 1813.[34]

Jefferson had once rejected the same plan, fearing it would ruin the American marine, which desperately needed foreign seamen. To secure relief from impressment, his heir agreed to forbid the employment of Englishmen; to show London that Congress would not block the bargain, Madison gained its approval in advance. The administration hoped to take "from G. Britain all motive for the war [and thus] terminate it by an honorable peace, or unite the country in a vigorous prosecution of the war," the Secretary of State said.[35] The act failed in both respects. It scarcely affected the conflict between Federalists and Republicans. In England a few praised it, but only as a prelude to further concessions. A law officer spied out many loopholes, so the ministry made no move to take up Madison's offer. On the contrary, Liverpool and his colleagues justly considered it a sign of weakness. Within a few months even Secretary Monroe felt that the administration had miscalculated.[36]

In April, 1813, when the departing Gallatin received his instructions, the administration had not learned its lesson. The instructions embodied the new law and positively insisted on the termination of impressment. Even silence, Monroe wrote, "would be the abandonment . . . of all claim to neutral rights, and of

[34] *Ibid.*, pp. 111, 960–1010, 1015, 1017–1019, 1022–1055. The quotations from Desha and Goldsborough are on pp. 1000 and 1054.
[35] Monroe to John Adams, [Feb. 15, 1813], Hamilton, *op. cit.*, V, 243.
[36] *Times*, March 22, 1813; *Liverpool Mercury*, Feb. 11, 1814; Christopher Robinson to Castlereagh, May 31, 1813, FO 83/2205; Monroe to Madison, Aug. 16, 1813, Rives Collection.

all other rights on the Ocean." The Americans, he went on threateningly, were learning military arts in a practical school and would strike heavy blows if war continued.[37] When, meeting Gallatin at Philadelphia, Bayard first saw these instructions, they filled him with despair. He had no faith in the new law, against which he voted in the Senate, and he had hoped for more flexible instructions. Reporting the conversation, Gallatin left the impression that he shared Bayard's misgivings. Monroe and Madison remained obdurate. They would accept almost any conditions to induce the British to abandon impressment, but abandonment there must be. "This practice being essentially a cause of war & the primary object of your negotiation," Monroe replied, "a treaty of peace leaving it in silence, and trusting to a mere understanding liable to doubts and different explanations, would not be that security which the United States have a right to expect." Bayard and Gallatin glumly promised to obey orders.[38]

Neither they nor John Quincy Adams, when he received the instructions, considered this the end of the issue. In correspondence with Alexander Baring, Gallatin went to the limit of his instructions in suggesting only a temporary curb on impressment. Adams positively preferred, instead of compromise or mutual concession, to "leave the question just where it was, saying nothing about it." In the climate of 1814 Britain would not concede, and the United States might better wait for a more favorable opportunity. Clay agreed. When negotiations opened every member of the commission was willing to abandon the sole positive stipulation in their instructions.[39]

A shift at Washington enabled them to avoid defiance. In January, 1814, Monroe urged the negotiators to hold firm, and the next month he informed them that the United States would no

[37] Monroe to Gallatin, Adams, and Bayard, April 15, 1813, Instructions, Vol. VII. Discussion of the impressment problem occupied twenty-one of the thirty-two pages of these instructions.
[38] Gallatin to Monroe, private, May 2, 1813, Monroe MSS; Monroe to Gallatin, private, May 5, 1813, ibid.; Gallatin to Monroe, May 8, 1813, ibid.; Bayard to Monroe, May 5, 1813, ibid.
[39] Gallatin to Baring, Aug. 15/27, 1813, Gallatin MSS; Adams to John Adams, Feb. 17, 1814, Ford, op. cit., V, 22; Clay to Crawford, July 2, 1814, Crawford MSS.

longer settle for abandonment of impressment only during the existing war in Europe. Then, on news of Napoleon's abdication, the administration collapsed. First the President and the cabinet agreed to postpone the subject if Britain formally promised negotiation on the heels of peace. "The United States having resisted by war, the practice of impressment, and continued the war until that practice had ceased by a peace in Europe," the resulting instructions stated, "their object has been essentially obtained for the present." [40]

Secretary Monroe asked Minister Sérurier to delay a French packet while the Department of State put the instructions in proper form. In the interim further news arrived, this time doleful reports sent by Gallatin and Bayard from London early in May. Convinced that British opinion would tolerate no retreat or concession, Madison and his subordinates abandoned the last shred of pretense. New instructions dated June 27 dropped the insistence on postwar negotiations. "You may omit any stipulation on . . . impressment," Monroe wrote, "if found indispensably necessary to terminate" the war. For the record, the Secretary exhorted his agents to accept silence only as a last resort.[41] He and the President knew they would virtually disregard this passage.

The new instructions completed a sorry story. Without ever forging weapons strong enough to bring Britain to defeat, Jefferson and then Madison engaged in humiliating controversy, let impressment help bring on the war, made it the sole reason for continuing a contest weakly prosecuted, insisted in public and private that the nation's honor required positive treaty stipulations, and then finally collapsed, authorizing a treaty that made no mention of this criminal invasion of American sovereignty. By their course the Republicans revealed the too-frequent emptiness of their bombast, the need to harmonize resources and aims, and the actual importance of emotion as opposed to rationality.

After the Orders in Council fell, other maritime issues seemed

[40] Memorandum of June 23–24, 1814, Hunt, *op. cit.*, VIII, 280–281; Monroe to commissioners, June 25, 1814, Instructions, Vol. VII.

[41] Brant, *op. cit.*, pp. 267–268; memorandum of June 27, 1814, Hunt, *op. cit.*, VIII, 281; Monroe to commissioners, June 27, 1814, Instructions, Vol. VII.

less important than impressment. In the instructions of April, 1813, Monroe discussed the problems of blockade, the Rule of the War of 1756, and so on, in clearly routine fashion. Nine months later the Secretary added: "Further reflection . . . has added great force to the expediency and importance of a precise definition of the public [i.e., international] law on this subject." [42] This dictum fell far short of an imperative, leaving the negotiators free to make any agreement or none.

Territorial ambition, many Englishmen believed, explained the declaration of war. They quoted war hawks, generals, editors, but could not cite the President or the Secretary of State. In 1812 Madison and Monroe looked upon Canada as no more than a vulnerable target. Neither to Foster nor through Russell did the American government ask title to Canada, and General Hull's disgraceful surrender soon made it ridiculous to talk even of temporary occupation.

Monroe's successive instructions clearly demonstrate the phases of administration thought. In April, 1813, pointing out the nearly full employment of British resources in Europe, he warned that if war continued "her [North American] provinces must soon become an easy prey." This circumstance, Washington felt, strengthened the administration's hand. England might well make concessions to secure a "reciprocal stipulation . . . for the restoration of any Territory, which either party may have acquired by the War." [43]

Ten weeks later, mildly intoxicated by successes on the Niagara frontier and anticipating General Harrison's advance into Canada, the administration cautiously raised the ante. American forces, Monroe wrote, might well occupy all Upper Canada. If England, which then held no lodgments in American territory, demanded restitution of conquests, "it is not intended to carry on the War, rather than yield to that unequal condition." On the other hand the envoys might find it "worth while" to suggest a transfer of

---

[42] Monroe to Gallatin, Adams, and Bayard, April 15, 1813, Instructions, Vol. VII; Monroe to Adams, Bayard, Clay, and Russell, Jan. 28, 1814, *ibid.*
[43] Monroe to Gallatin, Adams, and Bayard, April 15, 1813, *ibid.*

"the upper part and even the whole of Canada to the United States." [44] In this cautious fashion the administration exposed new ambitions, ambitions that attracted modest support throughout the nation after the battle of the Thames.

Dreams of Canada lasted on into the next year. Arguments for cession, stated new instructions penned in January, had "gained much additional force from further reflection." Clashes appeared inevitable as long as Britain held Canada and had forces on the Great Lakes. Postwar settlement "spreading rapidly over all our vacant Territory" would bring Americans to the international border, where "collisions may be daily expected." Either conquest or internal rebellion must soon deprive Britain of Canada anyway. So ran the administration's arguments. They led to the obvious conclusion that "these evils had . . . better be anticipated . . . by timely arrangement between the two Governments." [45] Again the President did not demand cession, for these instructions represented dreams, not determined purpose. When they reached Europe the changing scene had made them preposterous hallucinations, as the recipients recognized.

Impressment and, to a lesser extent, neutral rights and Canada dominated instructions sent from the Department of State down to the opening of direct negotiations at Ghent.[46] Thanks to the last-minute retreat from the impressment *sine qua non*, the five residents of the Hotel d'Alcantara had no peremptory orders on any one major issue. Had there been such that displeased them the ministers, all but Russell self-confident men, would have ignored them. They knew what their presumed masters at Washington at last began to learn, that negotiations would center on English and not on American demands. They knew, and had warned Madison and Monroe, that Britain ached to punish American presumption.

[44] Monroe to Gallatin, Adams, and Bayard, June 23, 1813, *ibid.*

[45] Monroe to Adams, Bayard, Clay, and Russell, Jan. 28, 1814, *ibid.* See also Monroe to Adams and Bayard, Jan. 1, 1814, *ibid.*

[46] Other items discussed at one time or another included the prewar privileges enjoyed by Canadians trading with Indians in the United States, limitations on American armaments on the Great Lakes, possible appeals to Russia and Sweden for aid, protection for Canadians who aided the American invaders, indemnities for prewar captures and wartime damages, and the return of Astoria to American hands.

The negotiations into which the emissaries plunged have come to occupy a special and in many ways a deserved place in American legend, not, however, because they lasted longer than any other negotiations for peace. Franklin and Jay, with assistance from John Adams toward the close, endured a longer period in 1782, and the Paris negotiations of 1919 as well as the seemingly interminable talks at Panmunjom lasted longer than those at Ghent. Nor do the negotiations at the close of the War of 1812 stand out because of the superhuman talents of the American diplomats involved. Admittedly no one would place Nicholas Trist in 1847–48 or the five-man commission of 1898 or the Korean puppeteers on a par with the quintet at Ghent. Probably Wilson's entourage at Paris comprehended less raw ability than the group of 1814. Yet it is clear that Franklin, Jay, and John Adams present a level of diplomatic talent unequaled in any other American negotiation, including that in which John Adams' son played a major role.

The negotiations of 1814 are unique, and the negotiators therefore gain special applause, because of all the American negotiations for peace, Korea perhaps excepted, in these alone did the nation not face a defeated foe or one who thought himself defeated. The Americans came to Ghent in the spring of 1814 not to demand terms but to defend their country against British demands. The presence of a leading member of the opposition, James A. Bayard, symbolized the national character of the negotiations, whereas the appointment of antiadministration representatives in 1898 and 1918 was little more than window dressing to ease a resulting treaty through the Senate. In 1814, as at no other time in the history of the United States, the peace negotiators were on the defensive.

CHAPTER

V

THE BRITISH DILEMMA

The pessimists in the Hotel d'Alcantara at least knew that unhappy news simplified their task. They could not press for concessions; they had the tactically easier if morally more demanding duty of defense. How much more subtle a task faced Lord Liverpool and his colleagues! They must first of all prepare defenses against demands they still mistakenly expected to receive. They had also to decide whether to press for total victory, perhaps rupturing the American union or driving Madison to an American Elba, or to accept a standoff leaving the United States with *points d'appui* for renewed assaults. Naturally they dreamed of the former, and British opinion clamorously demanded it. Liverpool, Chancellor of the Exchequer Vansittart, Castlereagh, and Bathurst, cautious men all, knew that triumph would be expensive and might be unattainable, so they also kept the door open to compromise. Their inconsistencies baffled and irritated both British and American commissioners and produced, toward the end of August, 1814, the first great crisis at Ghent.

Liverpool thought a single negotiator should meet the five Americans. "What is wanted," he wrote, "is a Man of legal mind

& of a very accurate Understanding," later adding that the envoy must also have standing with the public.[1] These desiderata were obvious, particularly when the government balanced between two contradictory courses. A keen man's reports would help in the decision, a well-known signature might muffle criticism of a compromise treaty if it came to that, and a single envoy could maneuver more deftly than a commission. As past events showed, the Americans excelled at legalistic arguments which the ordinary diplomat found it hard to meet. Liverpool failed to find a man combining all the desired qualities. Indeed it is hard to imagine even the most towering Englishman standing alone before the attack of the strong American commission.

To meet the enemy on legal battlefields the ministers selected Dr. William Adams, an admiralty lawyer. To reassure the nation on maritime issues they appointed Vice-Admiral Lord Gambier, a veteran of more than forty-five years of service, beginning with the American Revolution, who had led the successful assault upon Copenhagen in 1807. Like John Quincy Adams, Gambier became the nominal rather than the effective chairman of his commission. To complete the delegation and to do most of the work, the government approached George Hammond, the first envoy to independent America twenty years before. Despite urging by his friend George Canning, Hammond declined, wisely pointing out that the Americans still cherished bitter feelings toward him.[2] The cabinet substituted Henry Goulburn of the Colonial Office, an energetic undersecretary already marked for advancement. Goulburn was expected to provide expertise on territorial questions and to serve as liaison with London. To him the government looked, often in vain, for that "accurate Understanding" so desired by Liverpool.

[1] Liverpool to Castlereagh, private, Feb. 4, 1814, Papers of Robert Stewart, Viscount Castlereagh, Second Marquis of Londonderry, Mount Stewart, Newtownards, County Down; Liverpool to Castlereagh, private and confidential, April 29, 1814, *ibid.*

[2] Hammond to William Hamilton, April 30, 1814, George Hammond Papers, Foxholm, Cobham, Surrey; Canning to Liverpool, May 5, 1814, Papers of the First and Second Earls of Liverpool, British Museum (Add. MSS 38190–38489, 38564–38581), Add. MSS 38193.

All three envoys were sturdy British nationalists of rather simple views. They failed to grasp the quandary of their masters, having no doubts about the proper course to follow. Neither did they possess the talents to meet the Americans in argument. Perhaps understandably they sometimes became irritable, and William Adams positively disgraced himself in one dinner-table spat with Bayard. Still it is wrong to suggest, as have Henry Adams and others, that the British commissioners spent much of their time quarreling with the Americans or that they alone were responsible when tempers rose. Most meetings were models of sometimes overelaborate decorum and cordiality, the two sets of negotiators occasionally dined one another throughout their stay, and Clay at least corresponded with Gambier and Goulburn in later years. Of course there were quarrels, particularly in December, but only John Quincy Adams considered them part of a bitter personal vendetta.

Only he, an indefatigable critic, rated Dr. William Adams a malevolent opponent. The undeniably blunt lawyer possessed a certain relieving wit and humor. So unprepossessing that Liverpool forgot his name, Dr. Adams troubled no one but his namesake. Even John Quincy Adams sometimes granted Gambier grudging praise. This aging sea dog, also vice-president of the English Bible Society, appealed to Bayard as "a wellbred, affable and amiable man." Liverpool described the Admiral's views as "very clear & temperate & at the same time very firm." [3] Had the Americans raised maritime questions they might have drawn Adams and Gambier into bitter arguments. As it was, these Englishmen rarely did more than parrot their instructions. Gambier in particular played a minor role, although his uniform served as a reminder of British power.

Henry Goulburn, thirty-one, declined to go to Ghent unless permitted to take his wife and small child. They hardly brightened his stay, for Mrs. Goulburn suffered from and complained

---

[3] Liverpool to Castlereagh, private and confidential, April 29, 1814, Castlereagh MSS; Bayard to Richard H. Bayard, Oct. 27, 1814, Elizabeth Donnan, ed., *Papers of James A. Bayard, 1796–1815*, American Historical Association, *Annual Report, 1913*, II (Washington, 1915), 350.

about a long autumn cold she could not shake, raised problems about the care of the baby, and sometimes embarrassed her husband by failing, because of poor eyesight, to recognize dignitaries even when they came into close range. In the autumn a family problem further complicated Goulburn's life. His ne'er-do-well brother became engaged to a girl whose father refused to supply a dowry. To aid the lovers, Goulburn's widowed mother proposed to settle a substantial sum upon them. Henry spent several long evenings over letters designed to convince his mother that her generosity, although it did credit to her heart, violated traditional practice, discouraged self-reliance in the groom, and—*sotto voce*—was unfair to the elder brother.[4]

Despite his distractions Goulburn was the most active English delegate at Ghent. He corresponded privately with Bathurst, his regular chief, and less frequently with the traveling foreign secretary. Largely because, like the Americans for their part, he sometimes believed his opponents did not really want peace, he often favored a more rigid line than his superiors.

Goulburn occasionally fell into unpleasant public arguments with the Americans, and a private visit from John Quincy Adams turned, with Adams' coöperation, into a veritable donnybrook.[5] On most occasions he managed, sometimes with obvious effort, to hold his tongue and his temper. Since failure to understand the Americans was almost endemic in England, Goulburn's attitude is not surprising. Like most of his countrymen he simply refused to recognize that he was dealing with representatives of a proud, independent nation.

The Earl of Liverpool completed his commission early in May. To the annoyance of the Americans, who soon learned the fact of the appointments if not the correct names, three months elapsed

[4] Goulburn to Mrs. Goulburn, Oct. 18, 25, 1814, Henry Goulburn Papers, County Hall, Kingston-on-Thames.

[5] Wilbur D. Jones, ed., "A British View of the War of 1812 and the Peace Negotiations," *Mississippi Valley Historical Review*, XLV (1958–1959), 485–486; Goulburn to Bathurst, private, Sept. 16, 1814, Henry Goulburn Papers on the Ghent Negotiations, William L. Clements Library, Ann Arbor, Vol. I; Goulburn to Castlereagh, private, Sept. 5, 1814, Foreign Office Archives, Public Record Office, FO 5/102; Adams #139 to Monroe, Sept. 5, 1814, Worthington C. Ford, ed., *The Writings of John Quincy Adams* (7 vols.; New York, 1913–1917), V, 110–120.

before Gambier, Goulburn, and Adams arrived at Ghent. Discussing the delay with Bayard later, Dr. Adams excused the commissioners: "Why it is some time since we have been riding at single anchor ready to cut & make sail upon receiving orders." [6] Distracted by the European furor and still undecided on its American policy, Downing Street prevented an earlier meeting.

During these months almost no English voices called for compromise with the Americans. William Cobbett, often the advocate of unpopular causes, warned against the cost in blood and treasure of any effort to crush the United States. Although Cobbett himself criticized the *Morning Chronicle* as the "chameleon of this war," this Opposition bellwether gave him more support than any other organ. The *Chronicle* at least balanced harsh nationalistic sentiments with praise of Madison's moderation and criticism of the "disgraceful reasoning" of Englishmen who wanted to demolish the United States.[7] All other important journals shared in what Gallatin called "the general hostile Spirit" of the English people. After the triumph over Napoleon, Britons wanted to move on to crush a less sturdy enemy. As late as October Cobbett reported that "the only opposition, as to the war, will arise out of our *failures*. The Opposition will only *blame* the Ministers for not having burnt *more* ships, plundered *more* towns, and done *more* mischief." [8]

The vengeful spirit virtually prohibited compromise. Englishmen could understand the hostility of European states bludgeoned by Napoleon, the Home Secretary told John Trumbull, a visiting American artist-politician, "but America was out of Reach of the common Enemy—and the declaration of war, at the very moment when G.B. had done all in her power to conciliate . . . is con-

---

[6] Bayard to Crawford, Aug. 16, 1814, William H. Crawford Papers, Library of Congress.

[7] *Cobbett's Political Register* (London), XXV (1814), 804–807 and *passim;* XXVI (1814), 550; *Morning Chronicle* (London), May 18, 19, 1814.

[8] Gallatin to Monroe, June 13, 1814, Department of State Archives, National Archives, Records of Negotiations Connected with the Treaty of Ghent, Vol. I; *Cobbett's Register*, XXVI, 547.

sidered here as a wanton act of rancorous & unappeasable ill will.
—and as such we must meet it:—this cannot be a *Sentimental
War.*" The Americans, British papers argued, must suffer for their
temerity in declaring war. Madison's "faithless, unprincipled, and
corrupt Government" must pay an indemnity in territorial or other
concessions. Finally, the *Sun* in particular argued, the Americans
should not be "left in a condition to repeat their insults, injuries,
and wrongs, whenever the situation of Europe should encourage
them to resume their arms." British security required harsh terms.[9]

Two or three London newspapers spurned negotiations with
James Madison. The *Times* considered him as tyrannical as Napoleon, "and as we firmly urged the principle of *No Peace with*
BUONAPARTE: so . . . we must in like manner maintain the
doctrine of *No Peace with* JAMES MADISON." At relatively
little cost the United States might be broken up, New England
perhaps drawn back into the Empire, and Madison put to flight.
"Nothing can save him but an ill-judged forbearance on the part
of Great Britain," the *Times* declared. John Walter's paper maintained this attitude, once shared by the *Star*, all the way through
to the end of negotiations. The *Morning Post*, praising its own
moderation, censured such extremism, arguing that Britain might
well settle for Madison's submission rather than for his removal.[10]

All Englishmen wanted to cripple the United States. Their
demands varied in detail but might, the *Times* said, "be couched
in a single word, submission." Sir John Sinclair, once George
Washington's friendly correspondent, considered the opportunity
heaven-sent. "The Americans if they are not now humbled," he
wrote Liverpool, "will not only rival us in Agriculture, in Commerce in naval force, but also in Manufactures." In a widely circulated pamphlet a spokesman for British North American interests
demanded boundary changes, American exclusion from the Great

[9] Trumbull memorandum, n.d. [fall, 1814], Col. John Trumbull Papers, Yale
University, transcript; *Sun* (London), May 17, Feb. 3, 1814.
[10] *Times* (London), April 15, May 17, Dec. 20, 1814; *Star* (London), Feb. 3,
1814; *Morning Post* (London), May 19, 1814. Interestingly enough the *Times* (Feb.
3, 1814) was the only paper to suggest regulations to make impressment less oppressive
to the United States.

Lakes, a permanent Indian state carved out of American territory, the cession of New Orleans, and the exclusion of American ships from colonial ports, to say nothing of lesser requirements. The war abrogated "all former treaties, all impolitic concessions," so that England could insist upon terms suited to her interest.[11]

The best summary of British aspirations appeared in the *Courier* when Gambier, Goulburn, and Adams were appointed:

Vigorous war! till America accedes to the following demands:

A new boundary line for Canada.

A new boundary line for the Indians.

The independence of the Indians, and the integrity of their boundaries, to be guaranteed by Great Britain.

The Americans to be excluded from the fisheries . . . [and] from all intercourse with the British West India Islands . . . [and] our East India possessions, and their *pretended* right to the north-east coast of America to be extinguished forever.

The Americans not to be allowed to incorporate the Floridas with their Republic; and the cession of New Orleans to be required, in order to ensure to us the due enjoyment of our privilege to navigate the Mississippi: and here it may also be a question, in how far the arrangements made between Spain, France, and America, respecting Louisiana, can come into discussion.

Finally, the distinct abandonment of the new-fangled American public law; the admission of the international law as it is at present received in Europe; the recognition of our right of search.[12]

Everyone knew the *Courier* often printed ministerial propaganda. On this occasion editor Daniel Stuart spoke for himself. Uninformed by ministers who had not made up their minds, Stuart joined the general call for vengeance.

Like almost all ministries in the first century of American independence, Liverpool and his colleagues were less hostile to the United States than most Britons. "We wish for peace. . . . We

---

[11] *Times*, June 2, 1814; memorandum encl. in Sinclair to Liverpool, May 2, 1814, Liverpool MSS, Add. MSS 38257; Nathaniel Atcheson, *A Compressed View of the Points To Be Discussed in Treating with the United States of America; A.D. 1814* (London, 1814), *passim*.

[12] *Courier* (London), May 21, 1814.

ask only reciprocal security of our mutual essential interests," [13] the Home Secretary told a visiting American. Lord Sidmouth's statement gilded the lily or at least concealed vast differences of opinion over the meaning of "reciprocal security." Still, unlike the public, the ministry recognized that the climax of the war did not make all American rights fair game or justify a refusal to negotiate with James Madison.

Again unlike the public, ministers weighed practical as well as emotional considerations. Even a relatively small war with America would increase the national debt, already raised from £240 million to £861 million by the French war. No level of expenditure, no quantity of reinforcements, certainly no plotting in New England could positively guarantee military success. Nearer home, rivalries among the victors threatened Europe's equilibrium. Moreover, although the Czar for the moment declined to support the Americans on maritime issues, he might yet revive his opposition to the British code. "I fear the Emperor of Russia is half an American," Liverpool complained. Louis XVIII seemed to have similar prejudices. Only repeated bludgeoning induced France to give an often unobserved pledge to close her ports to American privateers, and in a mild fashion Paris apparently used its influence on behalf of the United States.[14]

All three ministers who shared control of the Ghent negotiations understood these things. The Earl of Liverpool prided himself on taking a long view. Although, as an American envoy later delicately put it, "splendour of genius was not his characteristic," the premier was industrious, thoughtful, and distrustful of extremism. In a time of European conflict, he believed, war with America at least provided a good excuse for breaking up all European-American trade. When Europe returned to peace, "it was our decided Interest to bring the War with America to a termination as speed-

---

[13] Gallatin to Clay, April 22, 1814, Henry Clay Papers, Library of Congress; Trumbull memorandum, n.d. [fall, 1814], Trumbull MSS.
[14] Liverpool to Castlereagh, Sept. 27, 1814, Arthur R. Wellesley, Duke of Wellington, ed., *Supplementary Despatches, Correspondence, and Memoranda of Field Marshal Arthur Duke of Wellington, K.G.*, IX (London, 1862), 291; Guillaume-Jean Hyde de Neuville, *Mémoires et Souvenirs*, II (Paris, 1890), 22–23.

ily as possible." Above all Liverpool did not want the war to become a heavier charge upon British resources. To Sidmouth he wrote that "it is not a Contest in which we are likely to obtain any Glory or Renown, at all commensurate to the Inconvenience it will occasion." [15]

Most Americans distrusted Viscount Castlereagh. Albert Gallatin, it is true, considered the Foreign Secretary the most favorably inclined member of the cabinet, but William H. Crawford's charge that he lacked "talents and discretion" and that "his greatness is wholly adventitious" presented the more typical American view. Castlereagh left England for Paris and Vienna shortly after preparing the first two, most demanding instructions for the British commissioners. Thereafter he played a minor role in Anglo-American discussions. He regarded with distaste if not with positive horror the prospect of a break, partly because of the probable effect at Vienna. From the very beginning he showed that he was quite aware of the possible cost of attaining American submission.[16]

Earl Bathurst, immediate supervisor of the negotiations after Castlereagh's departure, also managed the military campaigns in America. Until the middle of September he clearly hoped military victories would panic Gallatin and his colleagues. On the other hand Bathurst had long considered the United States "an opulent independent Kingdom" which could not be pushed around like a feather. According to one report, when vindictives presented a map on which they had sketched a new Canadian border, "his Lordship asked them if they thought such an acquisition worth the Loss of 10 to 20,000 men, & as many millions of money." He

---

[15] Richard Rush, *A Residence at the Court of London* (3d ed.; London, 1872), p. 46; Liverpool to James Stephen, private and confidential, March 24, 1814, Liverpool MSS, Add. MSS 38257; Liverpool to Sidmouth, Sept. 15, 1814, Papers of Henry Addington, Viscount Sidmouth, The Castle, Exeter, Devon.

[16] Gallatin to Clay, April 22, 1814, Clay MSS; Crawford to Monroe, Dec. 28, 1814, Department of State Archives, National Archives, Despatches, France, Vol. XV; Castlereagh to Goulburn, private, Aug. 24, 1814, Goulburn MSS, Vol. I; Castlereagh to Liverpool, Aug. 28, 1814, Charles W. Vane, Marquess of Londonderry, ed., *Correspondence, Despatches, and Other Papers, of Viscount Castlereagh, Second Marquess of Londonderry*, X (London, 1853), 100–102.

sought moderate advantages, not American capitulation. He believed European powers would soon protest British blockades that
prevented trade with America, and expected opposition to the war
to arise in England.[17]

At first the Earl of Liverpool and his lieutenants concealed their
misgivings. Although at the end of 1813, with Europe still in tor-
ment, they were willing to settle for an American peace based on
the *status quo ante bellum*,[18] six months later they hoped for a
good deal more. After all, for the first time in twenty years the
Americans faced a victorious power, not a beleaguered one. Perhaps this fact, perhaps British victories in the impending summer
campaigns, would produce important concessions. It was worth a
trial. Sometimes the cabinet spoke peremptorily for tactical reasons; sometimes their emissaries exceeded instructions. Never did
British leaders stick to a position the Americans refused to discuss.
Thus an American could gloat, after the peace, over "John Bull's
translation of a *sine qua non*—'*If you think I do ask too much, I
shall be very willing to take less.*'"[19]

In this spirit Castlereagh turned briefly from European problems to draft first instructions to Gambier, Goulburn, and Adams
in July, 1814. The war annulled previous treaties, he informed

[17] Bathurst to Castlereagh, Oct. 21, Sept. 22, 1814, Castlereagh MSS; Bathurst to
Perceval, Aug. 24, 1808, Spencer Perceval Papers, 33/107, examined while temporarily on deposit with the Register of National Archives; Reuben G. Beasley to Monroe,
May 13, 1814, James Monroe Papers, Library of Congress; Bathurst to Goulburn,
Sept. 12, 1814, Goulburn MSS, Vol. I.
[18] Cabinet memorandum, Dec. 26, 1813, Charles K. Webster, ed., *British Diplomacy,
1813–1815* (London, 1921), p. 126. This memorandum, prepared for Castlereagh's
guidance in European negotiations, states the British position, which he is permitted to
reveal if interrogated by the European powers. As the full text, merely paraphrased
by Webster, shows (FO 139/1), the British government did not wish to reveal its hand
unless forced to do so: "G[t]. Britain to declare her readiness, should a general Peace be
signed [by the European powers], to sign a Separate Peace with the United States of
America on the *Status Quo ante Bellum*, without Involving in such Treaty any decision upon the Points in dispute at the Commencement of Hostilities.
"a direct Proposition to treat in London having been lately made to the American
Gov[t]. this Offer not to be stated, unless the Subject be brought forward.
"Should such an offer be made to America, a Time to be limited [?] within which
her acceptance or refusal must be declared."
[19] *Aurora* (Philadelphia), Feb. 22, 1815.

them, thus opening to renegotiation such matters as the rights of American fishermen in Newfoundland waters. Beyond announcing this fact the Admiral and his colleagues, Castlereagh advised, should avoid committing England on any issue while probing the powers and the spirit of the American commissioners. As George Dangerfield has observed, "it was not a set of proposals, but a state of mind, that the British presented to their American colleagues." Castlereagh discarded extremely harsh, brutally specific instructions prepared in the Foreign Office in favor of his own much vaguer ones.[20]

For guidance, not for communication to the Americans, Castlereagh sketched out the cabinet's views on four issues. The cabinet expected the Americans to raise the first—maritime rights and impressment. They did not share the feeling of British ultras that "to suffer these even to be discussed would be a dereliction of duty." A few months before, on Liverpool's initiative, ministers considered impressment at length. Unwilling to abandon it, all agreed the practice was "liable to considerable abuse" and endorsed various rather far-reaching controls.[21] If pressed they would have brought them forward at Ghent. They preferred silence, "considering the question to be practically at rest by the Return of Peace" in Europe.

In the instructions Castlereagh turned next to Britain's Indian allies south of the Great Lakes. Here the Foreign Secretary's pen scratched vigorously, writing that "an adequate Arrangement . . . is considered by your Gov^t. as a *sine qua non* of Peace." This meant, he wrote, peace between the United States and the Indians as well as "a full and express Recognition of their Limits." Disingenuously or stupidly Castlereagh went on to argue that Indian lands should be guaranteed, the westward advance of settlement

---

[20] George Dangerfield, *The Era of Good Feelings* (New York, 1952), p. 68; Castlereagh to commissioners [not sent], n.d., FO 5/101; Castlereagh to commissioners, July 28, 1814, *ibid*. Except where otherwise noted, the following paragraphs rest upon the latter document.

[21] Atcheson, *op. cit.*, p. 1; Liverpool to law officers, private and confidential, March 14, 1814, Liverpool MSS, Add. MSS 38256; Liverpool memorandum, n.d., with cabinet endorsements, *ibid*.

halted in its tracks, to prevent Canadian-American friction. "The best prospect of future Peace appears to be that the two Governments should regard the Indian Territory as a useful Barrier between both States."

Castlereagh did not direct his agents to convey the *sine qua non* to the Americans in specific terms; this Goulburn later did on his own responsibility. Moreover, he clearly considered the inclusion of the Indians in the peace more important than the establishment of a barrier state. While he made "Recognition of their Limits" part of the *sine qua non,* he did not equally explicitly insist upon the barrier idea. The Foreign Secretary thus demanded, in these instructions, that boundaries be fixed, but strongly suggested rather than absolutely required that they be permanently guaranteed. Nobody at Ghent, save briefly Henry Clay, suspected the truth, that the barrier-state proposal was part of a probing operation.

The Canadian-American boundary, Castlereagh said in turning to another item of discussion, had been "very hastily and improvidently framed" at the end of the Revolution. Britain desired—Castlereagh did not say she required—unstated revisions to improve Canadian security, threatened like the rest of the continent by American expansionism. In discussing his last point, the fishery, Castlereagh maintained that the United States must offer an equivalent for the return of privileges abrogated by the war. Again he did not indicate his exact wishes.

The ministry dared not make a compromise peace while English sentiment remained at fever pitch. On the other hand, expected British victories might crack the Americans' resistance. Unless the British government drifted until another year of campaigning became inevitable, delay could only assist it. Thus the government dawdled in selecting its agents, reneged on a promise to send them off by the beginning of July, and only finally ordered a ship to carry them across the Channel on July 30.[22] The instructions, vague on some issues and silent on others, notably armaments on the Great Lakes, clearly showed that the government desired an

[22] Gallatin to Monroe, June 20, 1814, Ghent Negotiations, Vol. I; John Barrow to Hamilton, Aug. 2, 1814, FO 5/103.

extensive feeling-out period. When the Americans revealed their position, Castlereagh wrote, more precise instructions would follow.

Perhaps to ensure that their agents gave the policy of conquest a full trial, the ministry failed to explain what the commissioners could not divine. Earl Bathurst's tardy explanation, in September, astounded Henry Goulburn. "I confess," he replied in embarrassed surprise, "that I was impressed with the idea that the government did not wish the negotiation to be protracted." Goulburn had, he said, considered the last preceding note to the Americans "as not so much calculated to delay the conclusion of the negotiation as to throw upon them the responsibility of its rupture." [23]

As, before this time, Goulburn and his colleagues supplied deficiencies in argument and precision they thought they found in their instructions, it is not surprising that their American opposites also failed to penetrate the cabinet's policy. Gallatin in June and Clay in August briefly suspected delay to be calculated.[24] On balance the Americans failed to see this until at least October, when they began to rail against temporizing.

Early in August, the day after a great fireworks show celebrated victory in Europe, Britain's representatives set out in all innocence to impose terms on the Americans. On the evening of Saturday the sixth, accompanied by secretaries and the Goulburn family, they drove into Ghent. On Sunday morning their secretary, Anthony Baker, called at the Hotel d'Alcantara, found Bayard at home, and presented an invitation to open talks at the British residence on Monday. The Americans, declining a summons to the presence of the Englishmen, sent Christopher Hughes to suggest neutral ground. He arranged a meeting at the Hotel des Pays-Bas at one o'clock the next day.[25]

[23] Bathurst to Goulburn, private, Sept. 12, 1814, Goulburn MSS, Vol. I; Goulburn to Bathurst, Sept. 16, 1814, Wellington, *op. cit.*, IX, 265–266.

[24] Gallatin to Monroe, June 20, 1814, Albert Gallatin Papers, New-York Historical Society, unsent portion of draft; Clay to Monroe, private, Aug. 18, 1814, Monroe MSS.

[25] At the first meeting the negotiators agreed to meet alternately thereafter at their respective residences. Clay memorandum, n.d., Monroe MSS, fol. 3661. They did not strictly observe this procedure.

Since ennui had driven Jonathan Russell on a trip to Dunkirk, surely a desperate measure, only four American envoys and secretary Hughes appeared at the hotel. They found the Englishmen waiting. As senior British delegate, Admiral Gambier opened proceedings, elaborately assuring the Americans that his country regretted the war and hoped for peace. Goulburn and Dr. Adams mumbled similar sentiments; John Quincy Adams replied in kind. With the exchange of credentials formal negotiations began.[26] Nobody in the room foresaw that they would last four and a half months.

To the British as initiators of the talks fell the first statement. The Admiral stepped aside to leave this chore to Goulburn, who, in paraphrasing the instructions he held in his hand, somewhat exceeded the Foreign Secretary's intentions. On impressment, the young delegate found himself saying that, although Great Britain had no desire to negotiate, so prominent a cause of war must probably be discussed. This virtual invitation to the Americans to raise the subject did not accord with cabinet views. Similarly, Goulburn explicitly stated that Britain would close the fishery unless the Americans offered an equivalent for its renewal.

On the other two points, where Britain asked something from America, Goulburn necessarily spoke extensively. Britain's Indian allies, he said, must be included in the general peace and their territory must be "definitively marked out, as a permanent barrier between the dominions of Great Britain and the United States." His government considered this, Goulburn solemnly avowed, a *sine qua non*. By this statement he coupled the barrier state to other aspects of the Indian question far more firmly than his in-

[26] Accounts of the meetings of Aug. 8, 9, 10, 1814, include Gambier, Goulburn, and Adams #1 to Castlereagh, Aug. 9, 1814, FO 5/102; Adams, Bayard, Clay, and Russell #2 to Monroe, Aug. 12, 1814, Ghent Negotiations, Vol. I (not signed by Gallatin but written by him); journal, Aug. 7–10, 1814, James F. Hopkins, *The Papers of Henry Clay* (Lexington, 1959———), I, 952–959; Clay to Monroe, private, Aug. 18, 1814, *ibid.*, pp. 962–968; Aug. 8–10, 1814, Charles F. Adams, ed., *Memoirs of John Quincy Adams* (12 vols.; Philadelphia, 1874–1877), III, 4–13. Except where otherwise noted the following description rests on these materials. In describing these and later conferences, I have ignored unimportant issues and extensive argument to permit concentration on the essential points.

structions warranted. Goulburn did not describe the Indian boundary he had in mind—indeed his instructions were silent on the subject—and spoke in generalities when he turned to the other British demand, revision of the Canadian boundary.

At the close of his long presentation Goulburn asked if the Americans had instructions on the topics he had raised. John Quincy Adams evaded an immediate reply. To be sure that he and his colleagues fully grasped the British position he recapitulated the four points. In particular he probed a bit on impressment, receiving assurances that Great Britain did not intend to take the initiative, certainly would not insist that specific approval be written into the treaty. This accomplished, the Americans requested an adjournment to prepare a reply to Goulburn's question, arranged a meeting at their residence the next morning, and marched back to their quarters at the Hotel d'Alcantara.

In a lengthy conference not even interrupted by the evening meal, the American commissioners agreed that the situation was ominous. Goulburn sounded more like London newspapers than like the pacific Castlereagh presumably descried by Gallatin and Bayard on their visit to England. "We did not however wish to prejudge the result," they reported to Washington, "or by any hasty proceeding, abruptly to break off the negotiation." They decided to answer the British on each point. They would say that they had had no instructions concerning the fishery or the Indians, but had received orders on the boundary and impressment.[27] Of course they did not plan to reveal that their instructions, far from authorizing boundary revisions at American expense, requested the cession of Canada. Nor did they propose to inform the British that, so far as they then knew, their government demanded the prohibition of impressment.

Fortunately for the American commissioners' peace of mind, the new instructions of June 25 and 27 arrived this same evening. When finally completely decoded after midnight, they proved to authorize the silence foreshadowed by Adams' queries earlier in

[27] Journal, Aug. 8, 1814, Hopkins, *op. cit.*, I, 954; Adams, Bayard, Clay, and Russell #2 to Monroe, Aug. 12, 1814, Ghent Negotiations, Vol. I.

the day. Thus the British escaped payment for Goulburn's over-expansiveness. At the next meeting both sides touched only perfunctorily upon impressment. Months later, at Henry Clay's insistence, the Americans included an article prohibiting it in a draft treaty. When the English struck out this provision the Americans did not complain.

British nationalists, so often infuriated by events at Ghent, enjoyed a rare opportunity to exult. "Whilst BUONAPARTE was upon the throne, impressment is the prime cause of the war, and the justification of its continuance. But no sooner has BUONAPARTE been driven from the throne, than Mr. MADISON finds out it is not worth contending for, and is willing to slink it out of the Negotiation." [28] So wrote Daniel Stuart of the *Courier*, and few would deny the justice of his comment. Ill-considered Republican policy had come to its inevitable end, leaving a taste of humiliation and failure.

Not impressment but Indians dominated the strategy session in Adams' room. The character of the demand, even more than Goulburn's explicit avowal of a *sine qua non*, made such discussion inevitable. The real challenge lay in the British attempt to leap over the border, so to speak, to limit the right of the American government to deal in its own way with Indians resident in its own dominions. No self-respecting nation could tolerate such effrontery. The envoys might have refused even to consider the question. They decided instead to state that, although without powers, they would discuss it. They hoped to talk the English out of their *sine qua non* or, alternatively, to bring it into sharper focus before breaking off negotiations.[29]

The three Englishmen walked to the Hotel d'Alcantara on the morning of August 9, their only forward movement of the day. In a meeting marked by outward calm and rather labored courtesy the Americans led Goulburn and Adams into embarrassing disclosures without giving away their own position. At the outset

[28] Journal, Aug. 8, 1814, Hopkins, *op. cit.*, I, 955; Nov. 4, 1814, Adams, *op. cit.*, III, 63; *Courier*, Nov. 21, 1814.
[29] Adams, Bayard, Clay, and Russell #2 to Monroe, Aug. 12, 1814, Ghent Negotiations, Vol. I.

John Quincy Adams stated that his commission had power to negotiate on impressment and boundaries but not on the Indians or the fishery. The latter two subjects, not being among the causes of war, he maintained, naturally formed no part of Monroe's instructions. The British might have asked if Adams' statement meant that territorial questions, say a desire for Canada, had played a part in the coming of war. They might also have asked if the Americans were not tacitly admitting that prewar charges of British intrigues among the Indians had no substance, but they could not get the floor and later forgot these questions.

Firmly resisting interruption, Adams proceeded. Despite Monroe's silence, he said, the American commissioners agreed to discuss—he carefully omitted to say they agreed to negotiate—the Indian and fishery questions. Through all this and in mentioning items his side wished to raise, notably the definition of neutral rights and an indemnity for seizures by the Royal Navy, Adams spoke quietly. He touched with such unwonted mildness upon the fishery that the Englishmen, particularly Goulburn, who should have known the Adams family's devotion to the cod, concluded that the Americans would not press the issue.[30] This delusion lasted for some months.

When at last the British got the floor they concentrated upon the Indian question. Instructed or not, they argued, the Americans must see that Great Britain could not abandon her Indian allies. Would they accept a provisional article, Dr. Adams asked, leaving to their government a decision between accepting it and throwing the whole treaty to the ground? The Americans' response, that negotiations with the tribes had already begun and would inevitably succeed after an Anglo-American treaty, that (in Clay's words) "the branch would fall with the trunk," failed to satisfy their opponents. Insisting that Britain must judge the terms extended to her allies, the Englishmen again suggested a provisional article. The Americans refused to promise one, and Clay clearly "stated his opinion that none could be framed" which would satisfy Washington.

[30] Goulburn to Bathurst, Aug. 9, 1814, Wellington, *op. cit.*, IX, 177.

In any event, the Americans argued, they still did not know what sort of provisional article the British had in mind. Did England propose to alter boundaries in favor of the Indians and to limit American sovereignty over tribal territory? Here they struck precisely at Goulburn's initial indiscretion. Their opponents at first rather vaguely denied either intention. Finally Goulburn admitted that his government wished to establish permanent tribal reserves. Within those territories, Dr. Adams added, neither the United States nor (a note of ostensible reciprocity) Great Britain would be free to acquire lands by purchase or otherwise. This demand, the Americans later reported, was so obviously unacceptable, whatever the extent of territory involved, that they did not even press for a description of the proposed boundary.

At last the conversation dragged to a halt. Having unwisely allowed themselves to be dragooned into an exposition of their plans, the British commissioners declared that since the Americans would not promise to negotiate *sub spe rati* there was no point in further conversation. Politely the Americans expressed regret "at the danger of the negotiation breaking off thus at the threshold," and, hoping for further useful revelations from the blundering Britons, urged a continued exchange of views. Gambier, Goulburn, and Adams agreed to meet the next day only to arrange a protocol of the first two conferences. Struggling to keep the protocol brief, the English showed more temper than in the regular sessions.

On the protocol they got their way, but they could not prevent the Americans from communicating the full British demands to their government. After much argument over drafts prepared by Adams and Bayard, on August 17 the Americans consigned to U.S.S. *John Adams* a monster of a dispatch composed by Gallatin.[31] As a response from America would require months, all eyes turned to London.

Lord Castlereagh, in the throes of last-minute consultations before departing for the Congress of Vienna, quite possibly left

---

[31] The dispatch, dated Aug. 12, 1814, but actually only begun by Gallatin on that date, seems to have gone forward five days later. Aug. 17, 1814, Adams, *op. cit.*, III, 16.

the drafting of new instructions to someone else. At most, as his subsequent actions show, he considered them a trial balloon. The directive passed rapidly over the fishery, maritime rights, and spoliation claims, rejecting concession on all three, and barely mentioned boundary changes. It raised an issue, control of the Great Lakes, mentioned neither in the first instructions nor in the talks at Ghent. For "strictly defensive" reasons and to construct "a military Barrier" against attack, the instructions said, Great Britain required the United States not to build ships upon the lakes or maintain forts upon their shores.

The instructions, though admitting it was perhaps not surprising that the Americans had no instructions on boundaries for the Indians, insisted that the United States could not expect England to abandon her allies. The instructions repeated that "their being included in the Peace is considered to be a sine quâ non," and, as the commissioners had already committed Britain on this point, directed them to reëmphasize it. Describing a precise boundary for the first time, the government suggested roughly the nineteen-year-old Greenville line, long since rendered obsolete by later treaties and by the advance of settlement. Since Goulburn, by English standards an expert, later expressed astonishment that many Americans lived beyond the old line, ignorance rather than malice probably explains this particular suggestion. As in the earlier orders, the discussion of Indian reserves was less peremptory than the insistence that they be included in the peace. The British government, it was said, "was prepared" to negotiate on the Greenville basis and to stipulate "against any acquisition, by purchase, on the part of either State." [32] Insertion of the phrase "by purchase" weakened the request, for it left the way open to other means of acquisition.

Packing the instructions into one of his red dispatch boxes, Lord Castlereagh set out for Ghent en route to Paris and Vienna. Late on August 18 he reached the Flemish city and convened his subordinates. They advised a high line, particularly Goulburn, who especially welcomed the insistence upon British control of the

[32] Castlereagh #3 to commissioners, Aug. 14, 1814, FO 5/101.

Great Lakes.[33] All present shared the view that the first task was to find out if the Americans would negotiate a provisional article on the Indians. On a favorable answer, the instructions and the commissioners agreed, depended the continuation of negotiations. That night the Americans received an invitation to meet the next day at three o'clock. This time the meeting was held in the British residence, the Hotel du Lion d'Or. Castlereagh may even have been in the building—certainly he was not far away—but he did not join the plenipotentiaries.

Goulburn again led off. Sometimes reading and sometimes paraphrasing Castlereagh's instructions, he ran over all the points with brutal precision. Once again, particularly on control of the lakes and on the Canadian boundary, which the Foreign Secretary had flicked off in one sentence, he exceeded the instructions in detail and emphasis. Afterward a barrage of American questions cleared up the few points remaining in doubt; later on, in their report, the British commissioners half apologized to their superiors for excessive candor. When Gallatin asked about the fate of the hundred thousand settlers living beyond the Greenville line, Dr. William Adams responded: "They must shift for themselves." Bayard asked if the Indian and lakes proposals were *sine qua non*'s; Dr. Adams replied that the former was, but, as for the second, "One *sine qua non* at a time is enough. It will be time enough to answer your question when you have disposed of what we have given you."

Finally John Quincy Adams requested the British to put their views in writing. Despite some misgivings on the part of his namesake, that day the most obdurate of the British trio, the Englishmen agreed. The meeting adjourned.[34] Once again the Americans had evaded a clear statement of their willingness or unwillingness to negotiate a provisional article; once again they had drawn much information, albeit not much encouraging information, from their opponents.

[33] Goulburn to Bathurst, Aug. 21, 1814, Wellington, *op. cit.*, IX, 188.
[34] Accounts of the meeting of Aug. 19, 1814, include Gambier, Goulburn, and Adams #3 to Castlereagh, Aug. 26, 1814, FO 5/102; Adams, Bayard, Clay, Russell, and Gallatin #4 to Monroe, Aug. 19, 1814, Ghent Negotiations, Vol. I; Aug. 19, 1814, Adams, *op. cit.*, III, 17–20.

After the visitors disappeared Lord Castlereagh and his subordinates convened to discuss the next move. That the Americans had largely limited themselves to questions, that they had refrained from direct challenges, apparently misled Goulburn and his colleagues. After the first two meetings they had reported that the Americans probably would not accept a provisional article. Now all three Englishmen assured the Foreign Secretary that, in their opinion, the "American Commissioners were disposed both to treat and sign on the Frontier and Indian arrangements. No surprize or repugnance was at the moment disclosed, to any of the Suggestions." They advised firmness. Castlereagh, who would have preferred a milder line, generally deferred to his subordinates' wildly erroneous tactical judgment. Working at breakneck speed, Goulburn completed that evening a written statement of the British position, which was delivered to the Americans the next day.[35]

Concealed in Goulburn's vigorous prose lay one major loophole upon which Castlereagh insisted. He agreed that the Indians must share in a treaty of peace and that "any acquisition [of their lands], by purchase," should be prohibited. He refused to go further, vetoing the commissioners' deceptively minor proposal that the phrase be expanded to read, "any acquisition, by purchase or otherwise." Specifically he warned them not to insist upon outlawing American acquisitions by "Conquest in a War justifiably declared, however open such a plan might be to Evasion." As Goulburn protested to Bathurst, Castlereagh's caveat made a mockery of the whole project. America always claimed that her Indian wars were defensive, that conquest was punishment of the aggressor. Goulburn's appeal failed because Castlereagh had discussed this very issue with Liverpool and Bathurst before leaving London.[36]

The Americans either took no notice of or placed no particular value on the omission of a ban upon conquest. After all, peremp-

[35] Castlereagh to Liverpool, private, Aug. 28, 1814, Liverpool MSS, Add. MSS 38259; Gambier, Goulburn, and Adams to American commissioners, Aug. 19, 1814, Ghent Negotiations, Vol. I.
[36] Castlereagh to Liverpool, private, Aug. 28, 1814, Liverpool MSS, Add. MSS 38259; Goulburn to Bathurst, Aug. 21, 1814, Wellington, *op. cit.*, IX, 188–189.

tory demands to transfer border territory to Canada, to disarm on the lakes, and above all to establish an Indian state on lands more extensive than the British Isles were serious enough. The conversation of August 19 and the subsequent note threw the commissioners into despair. Even Henry Clay, who had prepared a private report to the Secretary of State forecasting British retreat, tore open his letter and hastily scratched a postscript apologizing for mistaken optimism.

Convinced their reply to the British would wind up negotiations, the Americans quarreled even more than usual over a first draft prepared by Adams, a demon for punishment. Refusing even to transmit the English proposals to Washington, they ringingly and rightly declared that a "Treaty concluded upon such terms would be but an armistice. It cannot be supposed that America would long submit to conditions so injurious and degrading." [37] That same day, three thousand miles away, British troops cheered the flames that devoured the American capital.

The first confrontation had come. In John Quincy Adams' words, Britain "opened to us the alternative of a long, expensive and sangwinary War, or of submission to disgraceful conditions, and sacrifices little short of Independence itself." [38] The choice between these alternatives presented no problem to an American patriot.

Would the alternatives remain so stark? The answer lay with Liverpool, Bathurst, and Castlereagh. They delayed negotiations as long as possible and shilly-shallied between the vengefulness of London newspapers and their own inclinations toward compromise. Now they must decide. For reasons of honor they might insist yet a while upon including the Indians in a peace settlement, just as for reasons of prudence they had already privately opened a gaping rent in the barrier-state project. Thanks to their own carelessness and the excessive explicitness and blundering analyses of the British commissioners, they were on record as demanding an

---

[37] Clay to Monroe, private, Aug. 18, 1814, and postscript, Hopkins, *op. cit.*, I, 965–968; Aug. 21, 1814, Adams, *op. cit.*, III, 21; Adams, Bayard, Clay, Russell, and Gallatin to British commissioners, Aug. 24, 1814, FO 5/102.

[38] Adams to Crawford, Aug. 29, 1814, Crawford MSS.

end to land purchases from the Indians, even a rollback of the frontier. Would they hold to this demand? The Americans thought so and canceled the lease upon their residence at Ghent. Goulburn thought so. To Castlereagh, who had gone on to Paris, he wrote that a "rupture in effect has taken place by the answer of the American commissioners." [39] The first two weeks of negotiations, although they had seen the end of the impressment issue, seemed to have killed the chances of peace.

[39] Goulburn to Castlereagh, private, Aug. 26, 1814, Goulburn MSS, Vol. I.

CHAPTER

VI

ABANDONING THE
"SABLE HEROES"

Downing Street viewed the Indian question as two distinct problems, only one involving the honor of the Prince Regent. In the weeks following the first confrontations at Ghent, London surprised both sets of commissioners by abandoning the barrier-state project, which ministers considered a desideratum, not an imperative. They clung more stubbornly to the real *sine qua non,* some protection for Indian allies; indeed British opinion virtually forbade naked betrayal of the tribes. Finally the logic of events and harassment by American diplomats forced the ministry into a settlement which preserved only the barest shadow of British honor.

Most tribes took up arms after Hull's surrender demolished American power around the western Great Lakes. In all battles west of Niagara red men fought beside redcoats, and the contrast between Tecumseh's death and General Proctor's flight at the Thames suggests the Indians' importance. Far to the south, particularly in the second year of war, British contacts with the always restless Creeks helped open a new theater of conflict.

Field commanders considered their country honor-bound to aid those who fought shoulder to shoulder with British troops. As early as October, 1812, the Governor-General of Canada first urged his government to remember the Indians when the time came to impose terms upon the Americans. Sir George Prevost found a ready hearing in the office of his superior, Earl Bathurst. Late in 1813 and again the next spring Admiral Cochrane, whose marauding on the Mobile coast had involved him with the Creeks, urged that in a treaty of peace "stipulations . . . be made for repossessing the Indians of the Territory they have been deprived of" by losses in a war encouraged by Great Britain.[1]

Beginning in October, 1813, as a result of the disaster at the Thames, some northern tribes made peace with the Americans. By July a number had even agreed to fight against England. In the south, in a campaign capped by his victory at Horseshoe Bend in March, 1814, Andrew Jackson destroyed Creek military power, and on the day of the second Anglo-American conference at Ghent the border captain forced the Creeks to sign a treaty ceding huge territories. Thus most Indian tribes had already made peace when their cause became a major issue at Ghent.

Inklings of these developments had already arrived, but not until the end of September did Britain learn, from the Americans, of the treaty by which northern tribes changed sides. Until that time the government felt obliged to defend the Indians. The premier and his colleagues knew that much British opinion, dangerous to challenge, insisted that "these sable Heroes . . . be for ever secured against Yankee encroachment and barbarity."[2]

The barrier-state project, to which Liverpool did not attach so much importance, had a long history. Shelburne's surrender of the

---

[1] Prevost to Bathurst, Oct. 5, 1812, encl. in Goulburn to Hamilton, Nov. 27, 1812, Foreign Office Archives, Public Record Office, FO 5/94; Julius W. Pratt, "Fur Trade Strategy and the American Left Flank in the War of 1812," *American Historical Review*, XL (1934–1935), 255 and 246–273 *passim;* Cochrane to Croker, Dec. 7, 1813, June 22, 1814, Admiralty Archives, Public Record Office, Adm 1/505, 1/506.

[2] *Sun* (London), June 1, 1814.

American Northwest in 1782 irritated many Englishmen, particularly because cession threatened the fur trade in the Great Lakes basin. To save this trade the Pitt ministry found excuses to hold Detroit and other Western posts for more than a decade after the end of the American Revolution. Since not even the most aggressive colonialist proposed a war to recover the lost territory, the British fell back on the barrier-state plan. Professedly designed to create a buffer that would minimize Canadian-American friction, the barrier-state project really contemplated an English satrapy, rich in furs, south of the Canadian border. In March, 1792, the Foreign Office sent long instructions to its American representative, George Hammond. Hammond, who had sense enough to know that the project could not be consummated, did not press it.[3] Although far more impractical than in 1792, when America was a babe among nations, the barrier-state project arose anew in 1814. John Quincy Adams later guessed that Britain put forward this proposal, outwardly less selfish than a direct request for boundary improvements, because she could not justify a demand for territory until the occupation of Maine later in the summer.[4] An independent Indian nation, presumably easier to obtain than boundary revision reaching to the Ohio River, would serve the purposes of the fur trade almost as well. Guaranteed by British power, it would equally well stifle the westward development of the United States.

Barrier-state propaganda had begun as early as 1808, when Nathaniel Atcheson produced a pamphlet calling for revision of the post-Revolutionary settlement. This man, secretary and mainspring of a committee of British North American merchants organized in London in 1809, proved indefatigable. In 1812 his *Compressed View of the Points To Be Discussed in Treating with the United States* belabored Shelburne's unjust treatment of the Indians and the fur traders. Atcheson called for the Greenville line—perhaps the government got the idea from this presumed

---

[3] Samuel F. Bemis, *Jay's Treaty: A Study in Commerce and Diplomacy* (rev. ed.; New Haven, 1962), pp. 160, 181, and chap. vi *passim*.

[4] Adams #137 to Monroe, Aug. 17, 1814, Department of State Archives, National Archives, Records of Negotiations Connected with the Treaty of Ghent, Vol. I.

expert—and a guarantee of Indian holdings. A barrage of demands, mostly inspired by Atcheson, descended upon Liverpool, Castlereagh, and Bathurst in the spring of 1814. The Colonial Secretary, at least, seems to have found the vision tempting.[5] Probably at his instigation the proposal went forward in August, 1814.

Goulburn took the demand seriously. Two days after receiving the defiant American note of August 24, at dinner with his opponents (for social contacts continued), he complained to James A. Bayard that the United States acted as if war could be declared on speculation, bets withdrawn if the gamble failed. This notion seemed to Goulburn so unjust that he prepared a note chastising "the spirit of Aggression & Aggrandizement" of the United States, and interpreting the last note as a decision "not to suspend the negotiation, but finally to determine it." He sent his draft to Castlereagh at Paris, explaining as he had to Bayard that reference to London was unnecessary. To London Goulburn forwarded a brief statement of his intention to wind up negotiations and return home.[6]

This insouciance shocked both Castlereagh and Bathurst, Hastily the Foreign Secretary replied that London must see and approve the Goulburn draft. Scarcely pausing to consult Liverpool, Bathurst rushed off orders to withhold the note if still undelivered,

[5] Nathaniel Atcheson, *American Encroachments on British Rights* (London, 1808), *passim;* Donald G. Creighton, *The Commercial Empire of the St. Lawrence* (Toronto, 1937), p. 170; Nathaniel Atcheson, *A Compressed View of the Points To Be Discussed in Treating with the United States of America; A.D. 1814* (London, 1814), pp. 4–7, 12–15; minute encl. in Atcheson to Castlereagh, Feb. 8, 1814, FO 5/103; memorandum encl. in ———— to Liverpool, May 17, 1814, Papers of the First and Second Earls of Liverpool, British Museum (Add. MSS 38190–38489, 38564–38581), Add. MSS 38257; David Anderson, *Canada: or, a View of the Importance of the British American Colonies* (London, 1814) ; *Times* (London), May 24, 1814; Bathurst to Prevost, secret, June 3, 1814, Colonial Office Archives, Public Record Office, CO 43/23. Charles M. Gates takes a contrary view of Bathurst's position in his article, "The West in American Diplomacy, 1812–1815," *Mississippi Valley Historical Review,* XXVI (1939–1940), 502.

[6] Memorandum of Aug. 27, 1814, Elizabeth Donnan, ed., *Papers of James A. Bayard, 1796–1815,* American Historical Association, *Annual Report, 1913,* II (Washington, 1915), 338; Castlereagh to Liverpool, private, Aug. 28, 1814, and encl., including Goulburn draft, Liverpool MSS, Add. MSS 38259; Bathurst to Goulburn, Aug. 30, 1814, Henry Goulburn Papers on the Ghent Negotiations, William L. Clements Library, Ann Arbor, Vol. I.

whatever Castlereagh might say. The ministry refused to take the responsibility for a rupture. It considered the American note, in the premier's words, "capable of an irresistible answer," and it had not quite forgotten, although it no longer placed much faith in, the commissioners' earlier assurance that in the end the Americans would negotiate on the Indian question. Upon receiving rebukes from London and Paris the British commissioners sent Anthony Baker to tell the Americans their reply would be delayed. Both Baker and Goulburn, who a day later had a long interview with John Quincy Adams which raised neither in the opinion of the other, assured the Americans the delay was purely technical, designed to give proper solemnity to a final break.[7]

While the Americans pressed for a reply expected to release them from cramped bachelor quarters at Ghent, Liverpool and Bathurst struggled to compose one that would keep negotiations simmering. Considering Goulburn's draft, forwarded by Castlereagh, "too conclusive" for use even after editorial changes, the two cabinet members set to work on an alternative.[8] Liverpool, particularly incensed at the bland American declaration that the United States had never sought Canada and thus that Canadian security needed no new protection, prepared an answer to this argument. "It is notorious to the whole world," he maintained in a summary sentence, "that the avowed object of the American Government was the conquest of Canada, and the expulsion of British power from North America." This point demonstrated to his satisfaction, Liverpool left most of the note to his lieutenant. Bathurst repeated the old arguments on lakes disarmament and boundary changes. Then, modifying the tone of earlier instructions, he requested the Americans to suggest alterations as long as they were "not incompatible with the object[s]" in view.

---

[7] Castlereagh to Goulburn, Aug. 28, 1814, encl. in Castlereagh to Liverpool, private, Aug. 28, 1814, Liverpool MSS, Add. MSS 38259; Bathurst to Goulburn, Aug. 30, 1814, Goulburn MSS, Vol. I; Liverpool to Wellington, Sept. 2, 1814, Arthur R. Wellesley, Duke of Wellington, ed., *Supplementary Despatches, Correspondence, and Memoranda of Field Marshal Arthur Duke of Wellington, K.G.,* IX (London, 1862), 213; Adams #139 to Monroe, Sept. 5, 1814, Ghent Negotiations, Vol. I.

[8] Bathurst to Goulburn, private, Sept. 1, 1814, Goulburn MSS, Vol. I.

Turning to the major issue, Bathurst insisted that his country could not in honor abandon her allies. He visibly retreated on Indian boundaries. The Colonial Secretary did not state that agreement on a barrier state was a *sine qua non*. The Greenville suggestion, he maintained, had been put forward merely for purposes of discussion. With Liverpool's approval Bathurst now belatedly injected a specious touch of reciprocity, declaring Britain ready to guarantee Indian lands north as well as south of the international boundary. The draft note closed with another paragraph by Liverpool inviting discussion on all points. "The last Paragraph is the most material," Bathurst privately advised Goulburn, "as it will I think make the Americans unwilling to break off the Negotiation without reference home." [9]

Despite Liverpool's argumentative prologue and Bathurst's usual awkward circumlocutions, the second British note marked a major withdrawal. Preparation by two ministers personally not only downgraded the residents of the Hotel du Lion d'Or but revealed that London had learned negotiations would be neither simple nor one-sided. Although Goulburn and his colleagues received and used, advantageously in the view of the original authors, permission to modify their superiors' language, they otherwise had no discretion (and indeed never regained much). Above all, Earl Bathurst cautioned his overbellicose agents, they must not alter "the disposition manifested throughout not to consider our first project as an ultimatum, from whence we should not depart." [10] In plain language, the Prince Regent's ministers did not consider the barrier state, perhaps even treaty protection for the Indians, a *sine qua non*, whatever instructions might say or the men at Ghent might desire.

The Americans looked upon the sixteen-page note delivered by Baker on September 5 simply as an effort to avoid responsibility for breaking negotiations. They found it annoying that they must

[9] Gambier, Goulburn, and Adams to Americans, Sept. 4, 1814, FO 5/102; Bathurst to Goulburn, private, Sept. 1, 1814, Goulburn MSS, Vol. I.

[10] Liverpool to Bathurst, Sept. 12, 1814, Francis Bickley, ed., *Report on the Manuscripts of Earl Bathurst* (London, 1923), p. 286; Bathurst to Goulburn, private, Sept. 1, 1814, Goulburn MSS, Vol. I.

halt their packing to compose a reply to a note "still hammering upon the old anvil." Their second note, dated September 9, answered Liverpool at length, although Clay thought half a page could do the job, refused to treat on the Indians and the Great Lakes, and in effect asked Great Britain to choose between those demands and a break in negotiations. The British commissioners, once burned by excessive zeal, referred the new communication to London without comment.[11]

Again the reply prepared in London, mainly by Bathurst as his chief was visiting Walmer Castle, combined obfuscation, complaint, and concealed surrender. As preludes, either to excuse retreat or to soften the blow to underlings in the diplomatic salient, both earls wrote privately to Goulburn explaining that "there are many political reasons to make us anxious to conclude a Peace if we can do it on proper Terms." This meant, among other things, the abandonment of Henry Goulburn's favorite project, "exclusive military possession of the Lakes." Liverpool and Bathurst agreed to bury this demand, put forward only in the instructions of August 14 and apparently never taken seriously despite the complaints of Americans at the time and of historians since.[12]

The Indian problem still predominated. In the mildest possible

[11] Adams to Louisa Adams, Sept. 9, 1814, Worthington C. Ford, ed., *The Writings of John Quincy Adams* (7 vols.; New York, 1913–1917), V, 120; Russell to Crawford, Sept. 12, 1814, William H. Crawford Papers, Library of Congress; Adams, Bayard, Clay, Russell, and Gallatin to British, Sept. 9, 1814, FO 5/102; Gambier, Goulburn, and Adams #5 to Castlereagh, Sept. 9, 1814, *ibid.*

[12] Bathurst to Goulburn, Sept. 16, 1814, Goulburn MSS, Vol. I; Liverpool to Goulburn, private, Sept. 17, 1814, *ibid.*; Bathurst to Wellington, Sept. 16, 1814, Wellington, *op. cit.*, IX, 263. Although the Americans made a great deal of the British proposal to disarm them on and around the Great Lakes it is difficult to believe that Downing Street ever considered this demand a serious one. The opening instructions to the British commissioners ignored it, and Goulburn admitted that at the time of his departure from London he understood the ministers to be relatively uninterested in a project he valued highly. Goulburn to Bathurst, Aug. 21, 1814, *ibid.*, p. 188. Although debated at length in notes between the two sides, the lakes proposal, like many other collateral issues, never assumed a tithe of the importance of the Indian question or, later, the Canadian boundary. Liverpool and Bathurst abandoned it without any visible embarrassment. Even Goulburn hinted, in a private talk with Adams, that it might have been pressed too hard. Adams #139 to Monroe, Sept. 5, 1814, Ghent Negotiations, Vol. I.

language, the note prepared for signature by Gambier, Goulburn, and Adams merely stated that the British commissioners were "instructed to offer for discussion an Article" prohibiting both Canadian and American land purchases from the Indians within agreed geographical limits for a stipulated length of time, after which the subject might be reopened and the border adjusted, by implication in favor of the whites.[13] Even this proposal, essentially a febrile and temporary guarantee of probably circumscribed Indian dominions, was not made a *sine qua non*. Clearly the Americans would refuse to discuss it. For a month the British government tried to prod their enemies into accepting the barrier state; now they abandoned the project.

Still, Albion must avoid open perfidy. The Earl of Liverpool believed, and apparently convinced his colleagues, that the Americans would agree to include the tribes in a peace treaty and give them their prewar boundaries. After all, England had abandoned two major demands, for a barrier state and for control of the lakes. Surely a sense of relief and an understanding of diplomatic proprieties would lead the Americans to offer a concession in return. In any event Britain could go no further. The note drafted in London had Gambier and his colleagues say that "the Undersigned are authorized distinctly to declare, that they are instructed not to sign a treaty of peace . . . unless the Indian nations are included in it, and restored to all the rights, privileges, and territories, which they enjoyed in the year 1811. . . . From this point the British Plenipotentiaries cannot depart." [14]

Finely worded, admirably firm, fit for later transmission to Parliament—so the third British note seemed. In reality it was a pose, a genuflection to the goddess Fidelity. Any sensible man knew that with this meager protection the Indians would soon lose their 1811 rights, that at best the proposal delayed American vengeance. As a Foreign Office official wrote two years later, when Indians sought British assistance because the treaty had been violated, "If . . . the American Government admitted the Indians

[13] Gambier, Goulburn, and Adams to Americans, Sept. 19, 1814, FO 5/102.
[14] Liverpool to Bathurst, private, Sept. 14, 1814, Bickley, *op. cit.*, p. 287; Gambier, Goulburn, and Adams to Americans, Sept. 19, 1814, FO 5/102.

. . . to return to their former Situation for a week or a month they complied with the Treaty literally." [15] All that remained of the original British position was insistence that the tribes be included in the treaty.

This insistence troubled the Americans, for it placed the Indians upon the footing of sovereign nations rather than of wards. Gallatin and Bayard at first thought the bitter medicine must be swallowed. The majority brought them around, partly on Adams' prediction that the cabinet would abandon this stand as it had earlier *sine qua non*'s. After several meetings, including four hours devoted to the now-habitual task of gutting an Adams draft, they returned a defiant reply on September 26. They boldly avowed their nation's intention "progressively and in proportion as their growing population may require to reclaim from a state of nature, and to bring into cultivation every portion of the territory contained within their acknowledged boundaries." Citing British precedent at wearisome length, this third American note pronounced the recognition of Indian sovereignty absolutely inadmissible.[16] Then the commissioners sat back to await the test of Adams' prediction of another British retreat.

The next day London learned that a force under General Robert Ross had sacked Washington. The good news encouraged Bathurst to write to Ghent once more; in his enthusiasm he nearly destroyed the negotiation. He authorized the commissioners to suspend negotiations if the Americans stuck to their refusal to negotiate *sub spe rati* on the Indians. Only the fact that they had already forwarded their opponents' note to London prevented the commissioners from acting on this advice. Liverpool too found the news exhilarating, but he counseled delay before sending any new demands to the Americans at Ghent. "Let them feast in the mean time upon Washington," he advised.[17]

[15] Edward Cooke to Goulburn, May 20, 1816, FO 5/118.
[16] Clay to Crawford, Sept. 20, 1814, Crawford MSS; Sept. 20, 25, 1814, Charles F. Adams, ed., *Memoirs of John Quincy Adams* (12 vols.; Philadelphia, 1874–1877), III, 36–38, 41–42; Adams, Bayard, Clay, Russell, and Gallatin to British, Sept. 26, 1814, FO 5/102.
[17] Bathurst #5 to commissioners, Sept. 27, 1814, FO 5/101; Liverpool to Bathurst, private, Sept. 30, 1814, Bickley, *op. cit.*, p. 295.

Yet within a week the British government backed down once more, making Adams a prophet. Apparently the initiative came from the Earl of Liverpool, for Bathurst's note to Ghent showed no inclination to compromise. The premier's generally exultant letter, on the contrary, suggested a way around the impasse. Might not the Anglo-American treaty simply stipulate that both nations make peace with the Indians, restoring the rights they held in 1811? Stifling whatever disquiet he felt, Bathurst put Liverpool's suggestion into diplomatic form, accepted a few softening changes desired by the premier (the commissioners later made others), and alerted Goulburn, who must have been weary of assurances that a final British position had been established, to expect an absolutely unwithdrawable ultimatum.[18]

The fourth British note, sent across the Channel on October 5, began with a rehearsal of stale arguments. Then followed a renewed demand for boundary revision, evidently a prelude to the next act in negotiations. Finally the note turned to the main subject. Outwardly it breathed fire, speaking of a "last effort," an "Ultimatum," and warning that "however reluctant . . . the Prince Regent may be to continue the War, that evil must be preferred if Peace can only be obtained" by keeping silent on the Indians.[19] Without admitting so the note abandoned the demand, to which British honor allegedly stood pledged, that the Indians become parties to the peace. Liverpool's proposal was a mere gesture. Neither side considered it substantively important.

Instinctively the Americans looked askance upon Britain's "last offer," delivered while they sat at dinner on October 8. Even Gallatin was reluctant to give England a shadow of justification for interference in American-Indian affairs. None believed the English retreat presaged an early peace, but all felt the issue had become too small to justify a break in negotiations. On October 13 an American note, drafted by Clay, accepted, subject to Washington's approval, the article forwarded from London. Clay could

[18] Liverpool to Bathurst, Oct. 1, 1814, Wellington, *op. cit.*, IX, 298; Bathurst to Goulburn, Oct. 4, 14, 1814, Goulburn MSS, Vol. II.
[19] Gambier, Goulburn, and Adams to Americans, Oct. 8, 1814, FO 5/102.

not resist gloating that the article proposed "only what the Undersigned have so often assured the British Plenipotentiaries would
necessarily follow" an Anglo-American settlement, namely the
end of Indian hostilities.[20] With this sally the Indian controversy
disappeared.

Why did the British government retreat? Why did not news of
the capture of Washington cause them to increase rather than
whittle down their *sine qua non?* Clearly the answers involve many
factors. Although Castlereagh's opening instructions made Indian
participation in the treaty a *sine qua non,* the commissioners and not
their superiors elected to emphasize a broader aspect of the Indian
question, the barrier state, rather than, say, the Canadian boundary. Committed by their subordinates and assured that the Americans would give way, the ministers naturally were reluctant to
draw back. What had been put forward as part of the probe-and-
delay strategy became a major issue. When London abandoned the
barrier-state plan it gave up something that, like a monopoly of
military power on the Great Lakes, it never really expected to
obtain.

Hastily drawn, perhaps after reference only to Atcheson's work,
and ineptly presented, the barrier state never received unequivocal
cabinet support. Castlereagh did not want to prohibit American
conquests in an Indian war justly begun, although, as Goulburn
pointed out, this stance opened an enormous loophole. Liverpool
never believed, he said in September, "the proposition that the
Americans should not be at liberty to make purchases from the
Indians within their own *recognized sovereignty* (however desirable) was tenable as a sine qua non." [21] Yet these exceptions made
quite ridiculous a demand for the Greenville line, prewar boundaries, or any other limits.

In fighting for the Indians the English stood upon treacherous

---

[20] Gallatin to Monroe, Oct. 26, 1814, James Monroe Papers, Library of Congress;
Oct. 12–13, 1814, Adams, *op. cit.,* III, 51–52; Adams, Bayard, Clay, Russell, and
Gallatin to British, Oct. 13, 1814, FO 5/102.

[21] Liverpool to Bathurst, private, Sept. 14, 1814, Bickley, *op. cit.,* p. 287. Liverpool
also recognized that the Americans had the best of the early exchanges. Liverpool to
Bathurst, Sept. 15, 1814, *ibid.,* p. 288.

ground. Reality challenged them, for much of the proposed Indian state had long since been ceded away and, in a rough sense, "reclaim[ed] from nature" by frontiersmen. Precedent challenged them, for previous ministries had insisted the Indians were not sovereign nations but dependencies of the white power within whose boundaries their territory lay. Time after time the Americans, who had little else to do but prepare diplomatic notes, repeated these arguments. At last they wore down Liverpool and Bathurst, who would not trust their subordinates even in disputation. In the end the Americans nearly convinced Bathurst that they would accept no article whatsoever regarding the Indians.[22]

Because the British commissioners, at the opening conferences and in their note of August 9, so closely united the separate issues of Indian peace and Indian boundaries, surrender on one point necessarily weakened defense of the other. Moreover, only a few days after learning of General Ross's success London received less favorable news, kindly forwarded by the Americans at Ghent, that many tribes had made peace with the United States and had even agreed to fight Britain. Should war continue for these traitors and the few tribes not yet at peace? It seemed unwise.

The lengthy Indian disputes convinced Liverpool that the question was not so simple as England had believed in the spring. The diplomatic scouting expedition, clumsily converted into an expensive reconnaissance in force, revealed the stubbornness of the quintet at Ghent, even of the Federalist Bayard. As early as the middle of September Liverpool considered the Indian question "one of growing embarrassment, and one not so easily solved by military success as the question of more or less extent of frontier." [23] Britain, having already lost her toehold in the barrier-state area, might

---

[22] Bathurst to Goulburn, Oct. 4, 1814, Goulburn MSS, Vol. II.

[23] Liverpool to Bathurst, private, Sept. 14, 1814, Bickley, *op. cit.*, p. 287. When John Quincy Adams called upon him on September 1, Goulburn stated that Britain considered the Canadian boundary and not Indian limits the key issue; ". . . when the boundary is once defined, it is immaterial whether the Indians are upon it or not. Let it be a desert." Adams #139 to Monroe, Sept. 5, 1814, Ghent Negotiations, Vol. I. Adams considered this shift of emphasis a mere tactical ploy.

have better luck fighting for changes in the Canadian border. She must move on before a decision for another year of campaigning was forced upon her and before, too, political skies closed in upon the ministry.

Until the very end of the battle over the Indians the backdrop, drawn in Britain's spring of victory, remained unchanged. Until late September only shadowy, contradictory reports of battles and marches across the sea reached Europe. The parliamentary recess freed ministers from open challenge; political London became nearly deserted, and even editors dozed. The Foreign Secretary did not reach Vienna (the "Great Congress" which, in Jonathan Russell's appropriately capitalized phrase, threw "in the background the little congress at Ghent" [24]) until September 13, and at first Lady Castlereagh, who sometimes wore her husband's Order of the Garter atop her coiffure, attracted more interest than her spouse.

In the late autumn bold strokes appeared upon the old canvas, painted by an uncoördinated group of stagehands: dashing British generals and inept ones, editors and opposition politicians in both countries, the half mystic, half realpolitiker who was Czar of All the Russias, and the small man who until driven to flight by redcoats occupied the White House. These changes invigorated the diplomatic cast and, for British actors at least, sharply altered the approach to the second act at Ghent.

The Liverpool-Castlereagh-Bathurst policy of delay rested largely upon the not unjustified expectation that the summer of 1814 would see important successes for British arms. London counted upon amphibious operations against the seaboard and a descent along the historic Lake Champlain invasion corridor, as well as upon lesser accomplishments on the Niagara frontier. On September 22 Earl Bathurst wrote Castlereagh, "Our prospects in America are I think good," and he went on to list at some length the victories he expected. His superior, less bellicose and

---

[24] Russell to John L. Lawrence, Oct. 7, 1814, Jonathan Russell Papers, Brown University Library.

less optimistic, counted no specific chickens, but even Liverpool expected events to strengthen Britain's hand.[25]

Less than a week after Bathurst consigned his letter to the Vienna messenger one prediction came true, as we have seen. Borne like so much good news on the wings of Mercury, accounts reached London that late in August a small force under General Robert Ross had landed from Admiral Cochrane's transports, brushed aside feeble resistance, and captured Washington. Madison fled. The invaders put to the torch the Capitol, the White House, and other public buildings as well as Gallatin's house, a sniper's nest, before withdrawing to their ships. Although Secretary of State Monroe, writing to Ghent, and President Madison, in a message to Congress, claimed that Ross had fled the field, the raid humiliated the United States. A "capitulatory propensity," as Monroe so delicately phrased it, took hold of Americans who saw their own neighborhoods equally exposed to British wrath.[26]

George Canning seized his pen to congratulate a friend at the Admiralty on "the splendid events at Washington, & . . . the exemplary justice inflicted on the most malignant of our Enemies." Newspaper editors repeated these themes and sometimes added new ones. The *Sun* considered the rape of Washington a painful duty, admitting that "were it not that the course of punishment they are undergoing, is necessary to the ends of moral and political justice . . . we should feel ashamed of victory over such ignoble foes." Nevertheless the *Sun* compared the victory with Wellington's greatest successes, and even pronounced it "full and perfect in all its parts." The *Manchester Mercury* pointed out with the satisfaction reserved today for unscored-upon football teams that "Save *London* alone, . . . there is not now the capital of a great power in the civilized world (if we may reckon America under that

[25] Bathurst to Castlereagh, Sept. 22, 1814, Papers of Robert Stewart, Viscount Castlereagh, Second Marquis of Londonderry, Mount Stewart, Newtownards, County Down; Liverpool to Castlereagh, Sept. 23, 1814, Wellington, *op. cit.*, IX, 279; Liverpool to Wellington, Sept. 27, 1814, *ibid.*, p. 290.

[26] Monroe to Nicholson, Sept. 21, 1814, Joseph H. Nicholson Papers, Library of Congress. Alexandria capitulated to the British and paid ransom. Baltimore seemed likely to do so at one time. Nicholson to Hannah N. Gallatin, Sept. 4, 1814, Albert Gallatin Papers, New-York Historical Society.

description) which has not been visited by a hostile and victorious enemy." [27]

Ministers welcomed the sack of Washington not merely because success in the field reflected glory on Downing Street. Chastisement inflicted by British arms made it somewhat less necessary, in the view of many Englishmen, to impose humbling terms at the peace table. "The taking of Washington," Chancellor Nicholas Vansittart observed, ". . . was felt as a reparation for the supposed insults our Flag had suffered." To make sure the news would not be differently interpreted at Ghent, Bathurst carefully informed his agents that the ministers did not intend to raise their demands as a consequence of Ross's victory.[28]

At the same time that success made compromise more palatable to British opinion, the cabinet expected it to undermine American resistance at Ghent. Bathurst sent the news to Henry Goulburn, urging his agent "to put on a face of compress'd joy . . . in communicating the News to the American Ministers." Goulburn forwarded London newspapers to Clay with a covering note archly suggesting that they might help pass the time during Clay's forthcoming visit, with Russell and Hughes, to Brussels. Only a few days later the British plenipotentiaries handed to the Americans their last proposal on the Indians. The peremptory manner in which they demanded its acceptance, although not the terms of the proposal itself, reflected the news from Chesapeake Bay. Goulburn, at least, thought this success alone prevented the Americans from rejecting the ultimatum.[29]

In the longer run Ross's marauding had less uniformly helpful

[27] Canning to Croker, private, Sept. 29, 1814, John W. Croker Papers, William L. Clements Library, Ann Arbor, Canning Letters; *Sun*, Sept. 27, 28, 1814; *Manchester Mercury*, Oct. 4, 1814. The *Morning Post* (London) commented (Sept. 27, 1814): "It remained for the Americans to display a pusillanimity hitherto unknown in the long course of the ages."

[28] Vansittart to Castlereagh, confidential, Nov. 26, 1814, Papers of Nicholas Vansittart, Lord Bexley, British Museum (Add. MSS 31229–31237), Add. MSS 31231; Bathurst #5 to commissioners, Sept. 27, 1814, FO 5/101.

[29] Bathurst to Goulburn, Sept. 27, 1814, Goulburn MSS, Vol. I; Goulburn to Clay, private [Oct. 3, 1814?], James F. Hopkins, ed., *The Papers of Henry Clay* (Lexington, 1959——), I, 982; Goulburn to Bathurst, Oct. 21, 1814, Wellington, *op. cit.*, IX, 366.

effects. Europeans already inclined to cheer an underdog contesting with Albion considered the incendiarism barbarous. Some Englishmen came to agree. Even more important, as a few thoughtful men foresaw, the raid, which "exasperated without weakening" the United States, stimulated American patriotism. Most Federalists in Congress supported a statement prepared by Rufus King which read, "Althô the Declaration of war was unnecessary, and highly inexpedient, the Manner in which it has been prosecuted by the Enemy, and the avowed Purpose of waste & Distruction that he proclaims, have so changed the Character of the War, that it has become the Duty of all to unite in the Adoption of vigorous measures to repel the Invaders of the Country, and to protect its essential Rights & Honor." [30] King and his friends could not speak for Pickering, Cabot, and Gouverneur Morris. Still, national unity benefited from the capture of Washington.

Lesser events in the summer tended to strengthen Britain's hand. Despite successes on the Niagara frontier which reflected the increasing skill of their commanders, American forces ultimately withdrew to the New York side of the river. In August the citizens of Nantucket formally declared their neutrality in return for relaxation of the British blockade, and sanguine Englishmen expected other parts of New England to follow this pattern. The next month British troops secured key positions on the Maine coast with the greatest of ease, providing a territorial pawn for play on the chessboard at Ghent. These "base capitulations," Jonathan Russell complained, increased the commissioners' difficulties. [31]

Three weeks after the Washington news and only a few days after the Americans accepted the feeble British proposal anent the Indians, two crushing reports reached London. While success had not led Britain to raise her terms, these calendars of defeat in-

---

[30] Crawford to Monroe, private, Oct. 21, 1814, Department of State Archives, National Archives, Despatches, France, Vol. XV; Sir J. Willoughby Gordon to Abbot, private, Oct. 1, 1814, Charles Abbot, Lord Colchester, ed., *The Diary and Correspondence of Charles Abbot, Lord Colchester*, II (London, 1861), 520; *Edinburgh Review*, XXIV (1814), 254; memorandum of Oct. —, 1814, Rufus King Papers, New-York Historical Society.

[31] *Sun*, Sept. 29, 1814; Russell to Alexander J. Dallas, Oct. 26, 1814, Russell MSS.

spired her to relax them. News from Baltimore and Plattsburg helped ease the way to peace.

After reëmbarking on the fleet of Admirals Cochrane and Cockburn the British army moved up the Chesapeake to Baltimore. Fort McHenry, named after a singularly inept Federalist secretary of war, and troops led by Samuel Smith, otherwise one of the least respectable personages in contemporary public life, balked the attempt to reënact the Washington raid. A sniper killed General Ross, the only effective British commander since Brock. The fleet fell sullenly down the bay, releasing an involuntary guest, Francis Scott Key, who composed a proud but worried ode to the defenders during his confinement.

The black news reached London on October 17. Some papers claimed a victory, partial perhaps but clear-cut. American troops had been driven back, shipping destroyed, the harbor blocked. Thus the *Sun* carried a headline, "AMERICAN ARMY DEFEATED NEAR BALTIMORE—GENERAL ROSS KILLED—REEMBARKATION OF THE EXPEDITION." This pretense soon collapsed. The public and certainly the ministry knew that failure at Baltimore had "materially counteracted" the impact of Washington.[32] The success of British raids, including a planned descent upon New Orleans,[33] could no longer simply be assumed.

Even more serious news came from the Champlain front. Prodded by London and the cocky Wellingtonians sent to join him, Sir George Prevost inched southward from Canada with the largest army—more than 10,000 men—employed during the war. Prevost encountered only weak opposition until he reached Plattsburg, where General Alexander Macomb, with a force one-quarter the size of his, blocked his route. On Sunday morning, September 11, in a bloody melee watched by the armies on shore, an American flotilla under Thomas Macdonough defeated the British squadron guarding Sir George's communications on Lake Champlain. Pre-

[32] *Sun*, Oct. 17, 1814; *Morning Chronicle* (London), Oct. 18, 1814.
[33] The British intention to attack New Orleans was widely suspected; even the temporarily retired militarist on Elba anticipated it. Col. Neil Campbell to Castlereagh, Sept. 17, 1814, Wellington, *op. cit.*, IX, 270. Bathurst had great hopes for the expedition. Bathurst to Castlereagh, Oct. 21, 1814, Castlereagh MSS.

vost broke off a land attack then in progress and withdrew to Canada, preferring retreat to emulation of Gentleman Johnny Burgoyne. A disgusted veteran, commander of the recalled assault column, wrote home that the game was up. "This country," said General Sir Frederick Robinson, "can never again afford such an opportunity, nothing but a defensive war can or ought to be attempted here, and you will find that the expectations of his Majesty's ministers and the people of England will be utterly destroyed in this quarter." [34]

Prevost's earlier reports, although mixed in tone, had not prepared his country for the shock of defeat. "He has a noble army, and ought certainly to be in Possession at this time of Sacketts Harbour, and of Plattsburg," Liverpool wrote a week before quite contrary news arrived. The newspapers were equally surprised. Ministerial journals minimized the defeat, sometimes suggesting that American transmitters had inflated the news and often insisting that temporary reverses occurred even in victorious campaigns. After all, even Wellington had had his ups and downs. In one such effort Stuart of the *Courier* inadvertently used the word "disaster," and such Plattsburg really was. The *Times* considered it "a defeat still more disastrous" than the battle of Lake Erie the preceding year, Opposition journals combined to attack ministers who tolerated Prevost's ineptness, and calls for a parliamentary inquiry echoed through the capital.[35] Only death from natural causes saved Sir George from a court-martial.

All principals in the Ghent negotiations recognized the importance of Plattsburg. Liverpool belatedly regretted sending troops to Prevost instead of Ross, who had used his smaller share much better. Henry Goulburn considered the setback nearly decisive: ". . . if we had either burnt Baltimore or held Plattsburg, I be-

[34] Robinson to ———— Merry, Sept. 22, 1814, Bickley, *op. cit.*, p. 293.
[35] Liverpool to Harrowby, private, Oct. 10, 1814, Papers of Dudley Ryder, First Earl of Harrowby, Sandon Hall, Staffordshire; *Post*, Oct. 20, 1814; *Sun*, Oct. 19, 1814 ("The affair at Plattsburgh is but a feather in the general scale"); *Star* (London), Oct. 19, 21, 22, 1814; *Courier* (London), Oct. 18, 19, 1814; *Times*, Oct. 19, 1814; Cobbett's *Political Register* (London), XXVI (1814), 545–560.

lieve we should have had peace on the terms which you have sent to us in a month at latest. As things appear to be going on in America, the result of our negotiation may be very different." Bathurst drew much the same conclusion from "this unfortunate Adventure on Lake Champlain." [36] All knew that, unless Britain accepted the demands of another year of war, she could not hope to impose terms at Ghent.

At home too the autumn skies clouded. Ever more loudly British taxpayers demanded relief from a burden borne for more than two decades. "Economy & relief from taxation are not merely the War Cry of Opposition," Nicholas Vansittart observed, "but they are the real objects to which public attention is turned." Public resentment over the tax burden bothered all the cabinet, particularly the premier, who chafed under the "prodigious expense" of a war in which he had lost hope for sweeping victory. "We must expect . . . to hear it said," he complained, "that the property-tax is continued for the purpose of securing a better frontier for Canada." In debate at the opening of Parliament on November 8 Liverpool proved wrong only in that the chief assault fell upon the income tax rather than the property tax.[37]

Because events at Ghent soon took a turn for the better, largely as a result of the ministry's decision to drop its Canadian demands, the government escaped serious challenges in the House of Commons. Still the nation had clearly lost enthusiasm for the war. By the end of November the people had become, the Chancellor of the Exchequer guessed, "very indifferent . . . to the final issue of the War, provided it be not dishonorable." [38]

The Earl of Liverpool, whose letters in the autumn of 1814

[36] Liverpool to Castlereagh, Oct. 21, 1814, Wellington, *op. cit.*, IX, 367; Goulburn to Bathurst, Oct. 21, 1814, *ibid.*, p. 366; Bathurst to Castlereagh, Oct. 21, 1814, Castlereagh MSS.

[37] Vansittart to Castlereagh, confidential, Nov. 26, 1814, Vansittart MSS, Add. MSS 31231; Vansittart to Castlereagh, confidential, Oct. 17, 1814, *ibid.*; Liverpool to Castlereagh, Nov. 2, Oct. 28, 1814, Wellington, *op. cit.*, IX, 402, 383; *Hansard*, XXIX, 1–18, 41–75.

[38] Vansittart to Castlereagh, confidential, Nov. 26, 1814, Vansittart MSS, Add. MSS 31231.

betrayed fatigue and depression, received no encouragement from events in Europe. The French continued to permit American privateers to use their harbors, and in October the Admiralty's ranking civil servant had to be dispatched to Paris to handle this problem. France and indeed all Europe clearly sympathized with the Americans. To complete Liverpool's discomfiture, Paris seethed with discontent against the Bourbons. A successful revolution, either Bonapartist or republican, would certainly mean serious friction, if not war, with Great Britain.[39]

Meanwhile events at Vienna built to a crisis. Throughout October, while Metternich dawdled over the ladies and Talleyrand bided his time, Castlereagh fought against Russian claims in Poland and sought unsuccessfully to forge a united front against Alexander. Like Stalin after him, Alexander refused to disgorge the booty of battle. A first confrontation took place early in October, just at the time the Indian question was settled at Ghent. A more serious one—to anticipate our story—occurred early in November, when the Czar and Castlereagh's brother and aide even exchanged talk of war. At the peak of this tension the cabinet dropped territorial claims against the United States. After Britain retreated from Polish and Canadian battlegrounds, Vienna took up the question of Saxony, claimed by Austria and Prussia. The threat of a European war which would entangle England hung over Castlereagh and Liverpool during the closing negotiations at Ghent.[40]

When at last the Americans saw through the British policy of delay they ascribed it largely to uncertainty about Vienna. Jonathan Russell believed that "if the pacification of Europe should be confirmed [Britain intended] to direct the undivided strength of Great Britain to the recolonization of America." John Quincy Adams did not expect much immediate advantage from discord at Vienna. In the long run he considered it highly important, for

---

[39] *Chronicle*, Oct. 17, 1814; *Star*, Oct. 21, 1814; Bathurst to Goulburn, Nov. 21, 1814, Goulburn MSS, Vol. II.

[40] Charles K. Webster, *The Foreign Policy of Castlereagh, 1812–1815* (London, 1931), *passim*.

post-Napoleonic rivalries prevented the European tranquillity that would, in English eyes, make it advisable to continue the American war.[41]

The impact of Viennese developments on Ghent and London is hard to establish. The Earl of Liverpool even found a good reason for abandoning Poland in the danger of Russian aid to the Americans; if not a mere excuse, his argument suggests that Ghent influenced Vienna, not the reverse. Three weeks later both Liverpool and Bathurst gave friction at Vienna as one among several reasons for dropping attempts to improve the Canadian boundary.[42] Probably in both instances the explanations combined truth with an alibi for decisions taken on broader grounds. It is of course clear that Castlereagh's troubles did not strengthen his country's hand at Ghent.

Events at Vienna, Washington, and Plattsburg, as well as in the houses of Parliament, changed the stage setting as a new act began at Ghent. By the middle of October two issues had been settled. The first, impressment, disappeared when both sides agreed to silence on a major cause of war. The second, involving the Indians, occupied the negotiators for nine weeks. Finally, on October 13, this issue also disappeared. Although the British eventually gained an article nominally assuring lenient treatment of their Indian allies, in effect they abandoned the field almost as completely as the Americans had abandonded their efforts to outlaw impressment. Remembering the breadth of British pretensions during the quarrel, Adams and his fellow commissioners did not allow themselves to become optimistic. Recalling the stubbornness of their opponents, the British too by no means looked for clear sailing ahead. Both were right, for a new set of British demands soon set the diplomats at loggerheads again.

[41] Russell to James Fenner, Oct. 26, 1814, Russell MSS; Adams #143 to Monroe, Nov. 20, 1814, Ford, *op. cit.*, V, 201.
[42] Liverpool to Castlereagh, Oct. 28, Nov. 18, 1814, Wellington, *op. cit.*, IX, 382–383, 438; Bathurst to Goulburn, Nov. 21, 1814, Goulburn MSS, Vol. II.

CHAPTER

VII

CONQUEST OR COMPROMISE?

The Dover-Ostend packet, bearer of four increasingly weak statements on the Indians in one direction and a quartet of sturdy American rejoinders in the other, soon found substitute freight. For six weeks Downing Street and the Hotel d'Alcantara turned to boundary questions foreshadowed by interpolations, sometimes lengthy and always argumentative, in earlier exchanges. Again notes flowed back and forth across the Channel, accompanied in the westerly direction by comments from Goulburn's gloomy Greek chorus. Only at the end of November did these exchanges cease, leaving the packet to carry a less ominous cargo in December.

Secretary Monroe's instructions spoke less forcefully on Canada than on impressment. His agents, willing to drop the *sine qua non* without permission, naturally abandoned less peremptory instructions. Indeed, Monroe and Madison no longer hoped to see their dream fulfilled. A few Americans wanted to fight until Britain gave up Canada. Most shared Clay's soberer judgment that, since the invasion of Canada had been "not the end but the means" in 1812, the spirit of conquest should not lengthen the war.[1]

All the Americans at Ghent knew that Britain would never cede Canada. Thus they never demanded Canada, and even denied Washington had ever entertained designs upon it. To give this argument a shred of respectability they repudiated as unauthorized the bombastic proclamations of a series of unfortunate invasion commanders.[2] The assertion infuriated Lord Liverpool particularly because it undermined his claim that Canada needed protection against invasion, but neither he nor subordinates poring over published American state papers could quite disprove it. Naturally the Americans never offered to aid the researchers by showing their instructions, but they were nagged by fear the British might have intercepted these.

Many Englishmen wanted to revise "the mischievous and ignorant Line drawn at the close of the American war" of independence. Nathaniel Atcheson demanded the entire St. Lawrence–Great Lakes watershed, and a Tory exile from the United States urged the Earl of Liverpool to pen up the Americans east of the Alleghenies.[3] Lacking accurate knowledge of the geography, London newspapers seldom made their demands precise, merely arguing in general terms for boundary changes to punish the Americans and protect Canada.

The ministry agreed to seek, in the interest of security, revisions in the boundary so "very hastily and improvidently framed in this respect." A draft prepared in the Foreign Office spelled out British requirements in detail: the Maine salient blocking the route from Quebec to Halifax; a strip of territory west of the Niagara River,

[1] Plumer to Elbridge Gerry, March 5, 1814, William Plumer, Jr., *Life of William Plumer* (Boston, 1857), p. 418; Clay to Thomas Bodley, Dec. 18, 1813, James F. Hopkins, ed., *The Papers of Henry Clay* (Lexington, 1959———), I, 841–842.

[2] Adams, Bayard, Clay, Russell, and Gallatin to British, Sept. 9, 26, Oct. 14, 1814, Foreign Office Archives, Public Record Office, FO 5/102.

[3] Maj.-Gen. Charles Stevenson to Sidmouth, Feb. 16, 1814, Papers of Henry Addington, Viscount Sidmouth, The Castle, Exeter, Devon; Nathaniel Atcheson, *A Compressed View of the Points To Be Discussed in Treating with the United States of America; A.D. 1814* (London, 1814), p. 9; Daniel Coxe to Liverpool, June 27, 1814, Papers of the First and Second Earls of Liverpool, British Museum (Add. MSS 38190–38489, 38564–38581), Add. MSS 38257.

including Fort Niagara and Buffalo; and Michilimackinac, which controlled the upper Great Lakes and was occupied by British troops in 1812.[4] In keeping with his probe-and-delay strategy, the Foreign Secretary included no such list in his opening instructions. He simply directed Gambier, Goulburn, and Adams to find out if the Americans would negotiate on territorial questions and, purely for the guidance of the British commissioners, explained that their government planned to improve Canadian security.[5]

During August and September the Indian question obscured other things. The instructions carried to Ghent by Castlereagh in person devoted only a single phrase to boundary changes. They also justified American disarmament on the lakes, a project here fleetingly brought forward, as a substitute for territorial cession. Either would improve Canadian security. Later communications kept the Lake of the Woods and Maine issues alive, although receding from a demand for changes to a proposal to settle disputed portions of the line. Demands for cessions near the lakes, these notes stated, awaited settlement of the Indian question.[6]

Behind this screen the two earls, Liverpool and Bathurst, laid plans to "treat on the Uti possidetis," a principle confirming to belligerents the territory they actually controlled. Perhaps the Americans, who refused to concede to abstract assertions of Canada's helplessness, would give greater respect to military force. To

---

[4] In addition, although not to serve Canadian security, the Foreign Office staff wanted Britain's title to islands in Passamaquoddy Bay confirmed, a boundary drawn from Lake of the Woods, and the Americans driven back from the Columbia Basin on the Pacific Coast. The cabinet adopted the first two suggestions but ignored the third. Unused draft instructions, n.d., FO 5/101. The carelessness of British preparation is indicated by Goulburn's request, in October, for a map showing "a river called the Passamaquoddy." The commissioners had none. Goulburn to Bathurst, Oct. 24, 1814 [misdated Aug. 24], Arthur R. Wellesley, Duke of Wellington, ed., *Supplementary Despatches, Correspondence, and Memoranda of Field Marshal Arthur Duke of Wellington, K.G.*, IX (London, 1862), 191.

[5] Castlereagh #1 to commissioners, July 28, 1814, FO 5/101.

[6] Castlereagh #3 to commissioners, Aug. 14, 1814, *ibid.*; Gambier, Goulburn, and Adams to Americans, Aug. 19, Sept. 4, 19, Oct. 8, 1814, FO 5/102. Bathurst professed to believe that the Americans had accepted British arguments with respect to the boundary from Lake of the Woods to the Mississippi. Bathurst #8 to commissioners, Oct. 18, 1814, FO 5/101.

make *uti possidetis* more attractive the two ministers proposed to modify it, giving up the positions in Maine taken by Sir John Sherbrooke. They kept their eyes on Fort Michilimackinac, already in British hands, and the Niagara enclave they hoped General George Drummond would secure. Bathurst considered acquisition of these two posts "indispensable," and Liverpool longed for them.

As a delaying tactic the premier proposed to ask more, particularly Sackets Harbor on Lake Ontario near the St. Lawrence, should the Indian controversy end before news arrived from America. Both peers planned to exploit any successes Sir George Prevost might gain.[7] Since, shortly after the Indian question sank from sight, not good but bad tidings had come from Sir George, Liverpool and Bathurst never had a chance to show how far their ambitions ran.

On October 18 the Colonial Secretary officially put forward the doctrine of *uti possidetis*. "Considering the relative situations of the two Countries," he wrote, "the Moderation evinced by His Majesty's Gov^t. in admitting this principle, in the present state of the Contest, must be manifest." This sentence, penned the day after news from Plattsburg, is somewhat baffling. Aside from lightly held Maine, English commanders occupied no American territory except Mackinac Island. The British actually asked to negotiate on the basis not of what they held but of what, despite Prevost's catastrophe, they expected soon to hold or thought they could take. In a private letter to Goulburn, Liverpool maintained that the Americans could never mount a land offensive, would be strangled by the blockade, and could not hope for assistance from Europe.[8] Surely, Liverpool implied, these evident truths must lead

---

[7] Bathurst to Goulburn, private, Sept. 12, 1814, Henry Goulburn Papers on the Ghent Negotiations, William L. Clements Library, Ann Arbor, Vol. I; Liverpool to Bathurst, Sept. 14, 1814, Francis Bickley, ed., *Report on the Manuscripts of Earl Bathurst* (London, 1923), p. 287; Bathurst to Goulburn, Sept. 20, 1814, Goulburn MSS, Vol. I.

[8] Bathurst #8 to commissioners, Oct. 18, 1814, FO 5/101; Liverpool to Goulburn, private, Oct. 21, 1814, Goulburn MSS, Vol. II.

the American commissioners to accept what was, in effect, a doctrine of *uti possidebitis*.

Canadian security continued to dominate the thoughts of Bathurst and his chief, as is shown by instructions of October 18 and a note to the Americans of the twenty-first, the fifth formal communication since August. Britain proposed *uti possidetis* "subject to such modifications as mutual convenience may be found to require." This meant American cessions in three areas, all of them important to Canadian defense. To gain a convenient, ice-free route from Halifax to Quebec, Bathurst urged Goulburn to "fight hard" for extensive gains in northern Maine, to recede to minor ones if the Americans resisted, and ultimately to "yield the whole rather than break off. But you must be *inflexible*," Bathurst went on, "in insisting on the retention of Fort Niagara & Fort Michilimackinac. From these points I think the News must be bad, before we can be brought to relax." [9] These demands, although ignoring military realities of the moment, were essentially defensive in outlook and moderate by comparison with earlier dreams.

Such one-sided moderation failed to appeal to the Americans. After less argument than usual they sent a brief, blunt note to the Hotel du Lion d'Or on the morning of October 24. Pointing out that the British piously claimed to abhor conquest, the reply challenged their sincerity. The Americans agreed to treat "only upon the principle of a mutual restoration of whatever territory may have been taken by either party." Pretending to assume acceptance of this principle, the note repeated an earlier proposal to exchange *projets*.[10]

Pessimism still gripped the Americans. Clay predicted a British retreat from the new demand and noted that the *Courier*, "the most ministerial print, has constantly and with apparent anxiety maintained" that negotiations were continuing. Nevertheless Clay considered the odds to be against peace. Russell thought the pros-

[9] Bathurst #8 to commissioners, Oct. 18, 1814, FO 5/101; Gambier, Goulburn, and Adams to Americans, Oct. 21, 1814, FO 5/102; Bathurst to Goulburn, private, Oct. 18, 1814, Goulburn MSS, Vol. II.
[10] Adams, Bayard, Clay, Russell, and Gallatin to British, Oct. 24, 1814, FO 5/102.

pects hopeless. Adams attached no significance to a dinner-table conversation with Lord Gambier, who castigated "the incendiaries who were constantly employed in the English newspapers, blowing the flames of war." Bayard admitted only a tiny ray of optimism, and Gallatin kept silent.[11]

Both Liverpool and Bathurst considered the negotiation effectively ended by the American reply, but shrank from a final break. When Goulburn obliquely suggested a rupture Bathurst told him to keep the moribund talks alive a little longer. A temporizing statement prepared by Bathurst and delivered to the Americans on October 31 pictured the preceding British note as a *projet* and asked an American one in return. The two ministers wished to delay a breach beyond the opening of Parliament on November 8, and to find better justification than a demand for conquest.[12] At the most critical time in the negotiation Liverpool and Bathurst resisted the momentum of their own prior course. They refused to admit that the probing strategy had clearly shown the impossibility of moving the intransigents at the Hotel d'Alcantara. The choice now lay between a standoff peace, however humiliating, and another campaign, an alternative extremely unpalatable to Liverpool and possibly ruinous to his ministry.

On November 3 the carriages of the cabinet, or as much of it as was within range of London, clattered into the cul-de-sac that is Downing Street. For the first time the entire ministry met to go over the American question.[13] They did so against a cheerless European background. At Vienna the Polish crisis had reached its peak, and on the morrow the Czar and Lord Stewart would talk of

[11] Clay to Monroe, private, Oct. 26, 1814, James Monroe Papers, Library of Congress; Russell to Monroe, private, Oct. 26, 1814, *ibid.;* Oct. 26, 1814, Charles F. Adams, ed., *Memoirs of John Quincy Adams* (12 vols.; Philadelphia, 1874–1877), III, 58–59; Bayard to Andrew Bayard, Oct. 26, 1814, Elizabeth Donnan, ed., *Papers of James A. Bayard, 1796–1815,* American Historical Association, *Annual Report, 1913,* II (Washington, 1915), 348–349.
[12] Liverpool to Wellington, Oct. 28, 1814, Wellington, *op. cit.,* IX, 384; Goulburn to Bathurst, Oct. 24, 1814 [misdated Aug. 24], *ibid.,* pp. 190–191; Bathurst to Goulburn, private, Oct. 28, 1814, Goulburn MSS, Vol. II; Liverpool to Bathurst, Oct. 24, 1814, Bickley, *op. cit.,* p. 302; Bathurst #11 to commissioners, Oct. 28, 1814, FO 5/101; Gambier, Goulburn, and Adams to Americans, Oct. 31, 1814, FO 5/102.
[13] Liverpool to Castlereagh, Nov. 2, 1814, Wellington, *op. cit.,* IX, 402.

war. In Paris, the Earl of Harrowby, who had just returned, informed his colleagues, plots threatened Louis XVIII and, in British eyes far more important, the life of the Duke of Wellington, His Majesty's ambassador.

In subsequent letters to the Duke both Liverpool and Bathurst stressed that he must at all events find a pretext for leaving Paris. The cabinet offered him the choice of going to Vienna or America. No one dared order Wellington to take the American command. Liverpool tried blandishment, writing, "The . . . idea which has presented itself to our minds is, that you should be appointed to the chief command in America, and that you should go out with full powers to make peace, or to continue the war, if peace should be impracticable, with renewed vigour." [14] The premier explained himself more fully to Castlereagh. He hoped the Duke would go to America, revitalize Prevost's army, and thus "give us the best chance of peace." Wellington wanted peace "if it can be made upon terms at all honourable. It is a material consideration," Liverpool wrote in a very significant passage, ". . . that if we shall be disposed for the sake of peace to give up something of our just pretensions, we can do this more creditably through him than through any other person." [15] This letter, written after the cabinet meeting, clearly reveals that the ministers thought of peace in less than triumphant terms. British patriots could scarcely criticize a settlement acceptable to Wellington, yet negotiating through him instead of at Ghent would avoid the embarrassment of surrender to the disputatious envoys there.

At first the Iron Duke expressed a preference for America over Vienna, solely because it provided a better excuse for leaving Paris.[16] On second thought he had misgivings, communicated at

[14] Bathurst to Wellington, Nov. 4, 1814, *ibid.*, p. 416; Liverpool to Wellington, Nov. 4, 1814, *ibid.*, p. 406; Bathurst to Wellington (2), Nov. 3, 1814, FO 27/99. Bathurst broached the American scheme to Wellington a few days before the cabinet met. At that time the Duke reacted cautiously but not unfavorably. Wellington to Bathurst, Nov. 4, 1814, Bickley, *op. cit.*, p. 303.

[15] Liverpool to Castlereagh, Nov. 4, 1814, Wellington, *op. cit.*, IX, 404–405.

[16] Wellington to Liverpool, Nov. 7, 1814, *ibid.*, pp. 422–423. The Duke wrote, "I feel no disinclination to undertake the American concern," provided departure could be delayed, perhaps until March. He felt that his presence in Paris powerfully aided the French government.

length to Liverpool on November 9. His letter provided a curtain behind which the cabinet maneuvered into a new position, accepting the principle of the American demand for return to the *status quo ante bellum*. The Duke began by asking to remain in Paris but agreed to leave if the cabinet insisted, as indeed it did.[17] He proposed that the government recall him to serve on courts-martial, leaving a decision on the American mission to a later date. Should Paris or Vienna break into flame, Wellington wrote with characteristic self-assurance, "there is nobody but myself in whom either yourselves or the country, or your Allies, would feel any confidence." Departure for America was out of the question for some months. Although Wellington did not say so, the delay would mean that he probably could not arrive in the New World soon enough to negotiate peace before spring campaigns began.

Wellington repeated his willingness to go to America, "though I don't promise myself much success there." Britain, he wrote with only the faintest suggestion that he might be oversimplifying, could not prevent American incursions into Canada or press an offensive southward until she gained naval superiority on the lakes. Without this "I shall do you but little good in America; and I shall go there only to prove the truth of Prevost's defence [of his retreat after losing naval support], and to sign a peace which might as well be signed now." Again coolly appraising his own eminence, Wellington admitted that his signature on a treaty of peace would reconcile "England to terms of which they would not now approve."

In conclusion Wellington scornfully dissected *uti possidetis*. He pointed out that American forces still held Canadian territory and minimized the lightly garrisoned conquests of Sir John Sherbrooke. "An officer," he scoffed, "might as well claim . . . the ground on which his piquets stand, or over which his patrols pass." At the moment "you have no right . . . to claim a concession of territory. . . . Why stipulate for the uti possidetis? You can get no territory . . . and you only afford the Americans a popular and creditable ground . . . to avoid to make peace." Having

---

[17] Liverpool to Wellington, Nov. 18, 1814, Liverpool MSS, Add. MSS 38260; Liverpool to Wellington, Nov. 21, 1814, Wellington, *op. cit.*, IX, 449.

used language no real subordinate dared risk, the Duke explained that he wanted the government to understand his position before sending him to America.[18]

On Sunday, November 13, the carriages returned to Number 10. The cabinet decided to insist upon the Duke's departure from Paris. They left the cover story to him, although they preferred an appointment to the American command. Bathurst, the responsible minister, later grumbled that Wellington's desire for peace distorted his military analysis, but the cabinet accepted it. Liverpool promised to work hard for control of the lakes or at least some of them. Even more important, he assured the Duke the cabinet awaited the American *projet* "anxiously" and with an open mind. "We shall be disposed," the premier went on, "to meet your views." When the *projet,* accompanied by the usual negative Goulburnisms, arrived the next day, Bathurst quickly warned his subordinate "to prepare . . . for our giving up the Basis of the Uti possidetis." [19]

A week passed before the cabinet met again. Then, by agreeing to negotiate on the basis of the American draft, the ministers confirmed the death of *uti possidetis* and gave up the last hope of imposing a real war penalty on the United States.[20] The Americans, having swept the stage in the first two acts, could look forward with confidence to the third. Even John Quincy Adams, a congenital gloom, relaxed. "For the first time," he wrote Louisa, winter-bound at St. Petersburg, "I now entertain hope that the British government is inclined to conclude the peace. . . . We are now in sight of port. Oh! that we may reach it in safety!" [21]

Why did Downing Street breathe hope into the pessimistic

[18] Wellington to Liverpool, Nov. 9, 1814, Wellington, *op. cit.,* IX, 424–426.

[19] *Morning Chronicle* (London), Nov. 15, 1814; Bathurst to Goulburn, private, Nov. 21, 1814, Goulburn MSS, Vol. II; Liverpool to Wellington, Nov. 13, 1814, Wellington, *op. cit.,* IX, 430–431; Goulburn to Bathurst, Nov. 10, 1814, *ibid.,* p. 427; Bathurst to Goulburn, Nov. 15, 1814, Goulburn MSS, Vol. II. See also Goulburn's detailed analysis, Goulburn to Bathurst, Nov. 14, 1814, Wellington, *op. cit.,* IX, 432–433.

[20] *Courier* (London), Nov. 23, 1814; Bathurst #12 to commissioners, Nov. 21, 1814, and enclosure, FO 5/101.

[21] Adams to Louisa Adams, Nov. 29, 1814, Worthington C. Ford, ed., *The Writings of John Quincy Adams* (7 vols.; New York, 1913–1917), V, 220.

Yankee? Bathurst explained the decision in international terms. The ministry feared that a revolution in Paris would kindle a new Anglo-French war. After the bitter quarrel over Poland, Russia might seize the chance to humiliate Britain. Wellington's bleak analysis made it seem wise to write off the American war and turn to face the new European challenge. Finally, Bathurst expected the Americans at Ghent to present demands offering better grounds to break negotiations, if Britain chose, than rejection of *uti possidetis*. Liverpool's even longer catalogue of alibis added financial and parliamentary considerations.[22] All explanations rationalized a decision unconsciously taken long before. Ever since August the British ministers had been sliding downhill. The plan to vest Wellington with diplomatic powers clearly doomed *uti possidetis* before the cabinet formally abandoned it. While the ministers dreamt of conquest and certainly expected an American forfeit for beginning the war, from the very beginning their efforts were halfhearted, their secret reservations apparent in every exchange. Now they admitted to themselves that they must accept a treaty without plums, without prizes.

When the two major architects of the decision spoke of a possible increase in American demands, they had in mind instructions known to have arrived recently at Le Havre in the ship *Fingal*. "A few days will . . . inform us," Liverpool wrote with concern, "whether we are likely to have Peace or whether the American Govt. will have advanced new Pretensions in consequence of the Clamour wch they have excited throughout the Country on account of the Demands brought forward by us in the Month of August."[23] On October 10, two days after reports from Ghent reached Washington, President Madison submitted the dispatches as well as the instructions of June, 1814, granting permission to drop impressment, to Congress and the country. Clearly he intended to rally the nation behind a war against aggression.

---

[22] Bathurst to Goulburn, Nov. 21, 1814, Goulburn MSS, Vol. II; Liverpool to Castlereagh, Nov. 18, 1814, Wellington, *op. cit.*, IX, 438; Liverpool to Canning, Dec. 28, 1814, Charles D. Yonge, *The Life and Administration of Robert Banks, Second Earl of Liverpool* (3 vols.; London, 1868), II, 74–76.

[23] Liverpool to Wellington, Nov. 26, 1814, Liverpool MSS, Add. MSS 38260.

Madison was not, indeed never expected to be, completely successful, for Federalist extremists considered any British demand legitimate. Timothy Pickering regarded the barrier-state proposal as "an act of benevolence" as well as "interested policy," and Gouverneur Morris opposed war to settle "the Right or the Wrong of shooting Indians in the Western Wilderness." John Lowell, the leading Federalist propagandist, enthusiastically praised the barrier-state and disarmament proposals,[24] and aggressive British demands did not prevent New Englanders from pressing plans for a convention at Hartford.

A swell of protest concealed these ripples from Liverpool. "No nation, not already fitted for the chains of a conqueror," one editor wrote, could consider the demands. "We have been free too long to be slaves," echoed another. More important, dissident Republicans rallied behind the war. Senator Thomas Worthington of Ohio, a sturdy opponent of war in 1812, trusted the nation to unite against a proposal to turn most of his state into an Indian refuge. Former Governor Thomas McKean of Pennsylvania, who considered the declaration of war "improvident and very wrong," wrote to another retired politician in Quincy, "War . . . is the order of the day: We will never be British colonies again." [25]

While Liverpool doubtless discounted predictable Madisonian outcries and was too ignorant of American politics to note the rallying of Republican factionalists, he could not ignore Federalist pledges, many reported in newspapers borne by the *Fingal*, to support the war. The documents produced in Congress "sentiments . . . purely national, and almost unanimous." Alexander C. Hanson, formerly a secret correspondent of British ministers in America and manager of a newspaper sacked by a mob because of its vehement opposition to war, now declared that the conflict

[24] Pickering to Strong, Oct. 12, 1814, Henry Adams, ed., *Documents Relating to New-England Federalism* (Boston, 1877), pp. 394–398; Morris to Pickering, Oct. 17, 1814, Timothy Pickering Papers, Massachusetts Historical Society; Lowell to Pickering, Oct. 19, 1814, *ibid*.
[25] *Pennsylvania Republican* (Harrisburg), Oct. 18, 1814; *Enquirer* (Richmond), Oct. 22, 1814; diary entry, Oct. 10, 1814, Thomas Worthington Papers, Library of Congress; McKean to John Adams, Oct. 15, 1814, Thomas McKean Papers, Historical Society of Pennsylvania.

"ceased to be a party war, and of necessity became national." Federalists supported a motion to scatter ten thousand copies of the documents across the land. John Jay, whose own British treaty many considered weak, protested that Downing Street employed "a Language rarely used, unless by the victorious to the vanquished." The *Alexandria Gazette*, breakfast-table reading for Federalist congressmen, called upon all citizens, whatever their opinions of past policy, to unite in defense of American sovereignty.[26]

The shock wave reached London after Liverpool assured Wellington of the government's desire for peace and after Bathurst told Goulburn to prepare to abandon *uti possidetis*. On November 21, when the cabinet met to ratify a decision already effectively taken, Bathurst added the new development to his alibis. The Ghent reports, he said, united America, so much so that Madison's fall from power would no longer help, "His Opponents being abler Men, and as hostile to us."[27] Thus Madison's maneuver, so successful at home, did not influence the basic British decision, although it did embarrass Downing Street and discourage a reversal of policy.

By publishing during negotiations, the Earl of Liverpool complained, "M^r. Madison has acted most scandalously," and in the House of Lords he sniffily declined to answer the uncouth American publication with an English one. The dispatches revealed just what Liverpool wished to conceal, that in August, at least, the war was one of conquest. Rumors of territorial demands had already called down criticism from Lord Grenville,[28] the semiretired Opposition leader who journeyed from Cornwall for the opening of Parliament, and clear proof would strengthen the attack. On the

[26] *Niles' Weekly Register* (Baltimore), Oct. 15, 1814; *Annals of Congress*, 13th Cong., 3d sess., pp. 381–383; Taggart to Taylor, Nov. 2, 1814, George H. Haynes, ed., "Letters of Samuel Taggart, Representative in Congress, 1803–1814," American Antiquarian Society, *Proceedings*, n.s., XXXIII (1923), 430–431; *New-York Evening Post*, Oct. 12, 1814; Jay to Pickering, Nov. 1, 1814, Pickering MSS; *Alexandria Gazette*, Oct. 13, 1814. The *Evening Post*, Oct. 13, 1814, mildly qualified its first reaction.

[27] Liverpool to Castlereagh, Nov. 18, 1814, Wellington, *op. cit.*, IX, 438; Bathurst to Goulburn, Nov. 21, 1814, Goulburn MSS, Vol. II.

[28] Liverpool to Wellington, Nov. 26, 1814, Liverpool MSS, Add. MSS 38260; Hansard, XXIX, 368–376, 15–16.

other hand the government faced ridicule if, after taking a high tone, it accepted a peace on prewar terms. No wonder Liverpool, normally an even-tempered man, sputtered furiously!

Quite possibly at his request, the *Courier* carefully differentiated Indian pacification from other issues not made ultimatums. Except for the *Morning Post,* which described the demands as "formal overtures" rather than unalterable propositions, no other newspaper grasped the subtle difference. Many justified the attempt to disrupt the United States. "These terms are just and indispensable to our national safety," the *Sun* commented. "Let us, therefore, hope, that their justice will also *unite all parties in this Country* in their support." This sentiment echoed in London and provincial papers.[29] With a wringing of hands the *Times* maintained that the event proved what it had always asserted, that no good could come of the negotiations. Not that the *Times* reprobated the claims made, for in fact it considered them modest. The mistake lay in negotiating with Madison at all, in bringing forward unenforceable demands, and in thus uniting the American people. "Such," said the *Times,* which desired negotiations to take place at advanced British headquarters in Washington or Philadelphia, "is the consequence of *talking,* instead of acting." [30]

The Opposition took quite a different view. After a confused start owing to editor James Perry's absence from town, the *Morning Chronicle* swung into action. Perry very effectively stated the Opposition case, writing that "when the American Commissioners had actually given up the original pretext of the war, the impressment of Seamen, we set up a new cause, that of cutting up their territorial possessions, and demanded the lion's skin before we had killed the lion." Thus, the editorial continued, "the war is made altogether to change its character, and to become a war of aggression and conquest, instead of a contest for the maintenance of our maritime rights." In Parliament, Grenville attacked the ministry, although privately admitting that "if we had the power of dictating terms" he would change the Canadian-American boundary.

---

[29] *Courier,* Nov. 21, Dec. 7, 1814; *Morning Post* (London), Nov. 21, 22, 1814; *Star* (London), Nov. 21, 22, 1814; *Sun* (London), Nov. 21, 1814.

[30] *Times* (London), Nov. 21, 23, 1814.

Lord Lansdowne, son of the negotiator of that boundary, solemnly warned Liverpool that he would not support a war of conquest, and other peers nodded their agreement.[31]

The premier's oarsmen thus found themselves between Scylla and Charybdis with no option but to push straight ahead. They could not escape criticism from British nationalists for jeopardizing Canadian security, but if they pulled rapidly through to peace they might escape the worst currents, particularly since most nationalists far preferred the ministry to the Opposition. Opposition criticism also counseled speed. Encouraged by war weariness and a dislike of taxes, they now in effect served notice that if peace did not speedily come they would assault the government with heavier weapons. "You must understand," Bathurst counseled Goulburn, "that we are . . . anxious . . . to bring the Treaty to a conclusion. Meetings are beginning to petition against the Income Tax— & we have difficulty in keeping the Manufacturers particularly at Birmingham quiet." [32] Clock and calendar now served the Hotel d'Alcantara, not Number 10.

The clock ran on for almost exactly a month, the pendulum swinging between Ghent and London in narrowing arcs until the ticking stopped on Christmas Eve. After virtually ignoring the negotiations from August until the end of November, the British capital seethed with rumors, usually optimistic ones, though as late as December 23 the *Post* and the *Times* reported an impasse. Speculators, some uncomfortably close to the American delegation, gambled on the prices of raw materials, particularly cotton, and the consols rose and fell with peaceful and warlike news. Couriers battled winter storms in the Channel, and a messenger who chartered a ship for speed perhaps saved his life, for the regular packet capsized in a tempest.[33]

As the flow of couriers indicated, the cabinet continued to man-

---

[31] *Chronicle*, Nov. 21, 22, 1814; *Edinburgh Review*, XXIV (1814), 251–256; *Liverpool Mercury*, Dec. 2, 1814; Grenville to Grey, Oct. 21, Nov. 23, Dec. 12, 1814, Papers of Charles Grey, Second Earl Grey, The Prior's Kitchen, Durham University; *Hansard*, XXIX, 377–383.

[32] Bathurst to Goulburn, private, Dec. 6, 1814, Goulburn MSS, Vol. II.

[33] *Post*, Dec. 23, 1814; *Times*, Dec. 23, 20, 1814; Dec. 2, 1814, Charles F. Adams, *op. cit.*, III, 90–91.

age negotiations despite Henry Goulburn's complaint that "the Americans . . . have rather hoaxed us for the number of our references home." Leaving Goulburn and his associates to bear American scorn, the cabinet met several times on American affairs and consulted informally in addition. Liverpool, who wanted to go to Bath, and Harrowby, eager to join his countess for Christmas, chafed at confinement in the capital.[34]

At Ghent the commissioners supplemented notes with face-to-face meetings. At the first, held on December 1 in the British residence, now shifted to a former Carthusian monastery on the outskirts of Ghent, Admiral Gambier "said he was happy that we had now met again, and that it was with much fairer prospects of success than when we had met last," a sufficiently delicate reference to the harsh confrontation of August 19. The promise was not completely fulfilled. Goulburn pronounced this meeting long and tiresome. After another on December 10, during which, Goulburn grudgingly admitted, the Americans acted "with better grace than usual," the delegations clashed on the twelfth in a session John Quincy Adams considered the most unpleasant yet held. After an exchange of correspondence which breached the last logjam, the negotiators devoted three hours on December 23 to an exercise in textual criticism and gathered the next day to stamp finis upon their work.[35]

The five Americans met even more often to consider their position, and for almost the first time tempers flared high. One marathon session, marked by a direct clash between Adams and Clay, lasted more than five hours before Gallatin herded his fractious colleagues into tenuous agreement. A little later Adams virtually dared his colleagues to sign a treaty without him, and at the very last moment, for reasons that both baffled and irritated his colleagues, even the tolerant Gallatin, Henry Clay made the same

[34] Goulburn to Bathurst, private, Dec. 13, 1814, Bickley, *op. cit.*, p. 316; Harrowby to Countess of Harrowby, Dec. 13, 1814, Papers of Dudley Ryder, First Earl of Harrowby, Sandon Hall, Staffordshire.
[35] Dec. 1, 10, 12, 23, 24, 1814, Charles F. Adams, *op. cit.*, III, 79–90, 93–98, 104–112, 122–125, 126; Goulburn to Hamilton, private, Dec. 2, 1814, FO 5/102; Goulburn to Bathurst, Dec. 10, 1814, Wellington, *op. cit.*, IX, 471; Adams to Louisa Adams, Dec. 16, 1814, Ford, *op. cit.*, V, 237.

threat. These spats, lovingly recorded in Adams' diary, left a permanent mark only upon the rancorous Russell, who destroyed his modest reputation some years later by raking them up and misstating his role. "Upon almost all the important questions," Adams informed the family patriarch at Quincy, "we have been unanimous." [36]

As early as October 29, as much to while away time as anything else, since the British declined to exchange *projets*, the Americans began work on one. Two days later their opponents reversed themselves, argued speciously that their own note outlining *uti possidetis* was a *projet* and asked the Americans to reciprocate. After almost daily discussions—they did observe the Sabbath—the Americans patched together a draft treaty forwarded to Downing Street through Gambier, Goulburn, and Adams.[37]

In the draft and its covering letter [38] the Americans presented an unimpressive mixed bag of proposals. They never expected success on prewar controversies: impressment, definition of blockade, and compensation for ship seizures. Nor could they have had much hope for a proposal to prohibit the use of Indians in future wars, as England stood to gain little from such prohibition. Their useful plan to settle the Canadian-American boundary by commissions was neither earthshaking nor unprecedented. The American proposal to draw the boundary west of Lake of the Woods along the forty-ninth parallel, thus disposing of an ancient controversy extended westward by the purchase of Louisiana, was more important, but even here the commissioners did not intend to press very hard for their views.

Gallatin wanted to confirm both America's liberty to fish in British waters and dry and cure on Newfoundland shores and the right of Canadians to use the Mississippi as a highway from the interior. As he admitted, he inclined to accept the British claim

[36] Nov. 28, Dec. 14, 22, 1814, Charles F. Adams, *op. cit.*, III, 71–75, 117–122; Adams to John Adams, Dec. 26, 1814, Adams Family Papers, Massachusetts Historical Society, Vol. CXXXIX.

[37] Oct. 29–Nov. 10, 1814, Charles F. Adams, *op. cit.*, III, 60–68; Gambier, Goulburn, and Adams to Americans, Oct. 31, 1814, FO 5/102.

[38] Adams, Bayard, Clay, Russell, and Gallatin to British, Nov. 10, 1814, and encl., FO 5/102.

that these rights had expired with the war. Clay violently opposed renewal of the Mississippi privilege, swearing he would not sign a note along the Gallatin lines. Then, picking up Adams' earlier suggestion, he proposed to reassert American rights to the fishery and remain silent on the Mississippi question. The Kentuckian's comments made it clear he was willing to adopt this position for bargaining purposes only; if necessary he would accept silence on the fishery. As he had gone some distance to meet the majority, Adams, Bayard, and Gallatin accepted his suggestion.[39]

Still unaware of London's crumbling will, the Americans considered the evacuation of all conquests their most important demand. Clay and Russell wanted to settle this matter before taking up any other subject. Adams on the other hand desired to apply the *status quo ante bellum* to all controversies, not merely territorial questions. After Madison and Monroe backed down on impressment, "the very object of the war," they could not very well object to silence on lesser issues, he pointed out, and instructions sent via the *Fingal* soon confirmed his argument. Some of his colleagues, willing to abandon items in the *projet* one by one, drew back from a blanket withdrawal in advance. Adams' draft suffered the usual fate, but after strenuous arguments he wore down his opponents, most notably Clay. Thus the note accompanying the *projet* declared, in a deceptively casual aside, that the Americans were "ready to sign a Treaty placing the two Countries in respect to all the subjects of difference between them, in the same state that they were at the commencement of the present War, reserving to each party all its rights, and leaving whatever may remain of controversy between them for future negotiation." This sentence offered a second treaty quite different from the *projet*, or at least invited substantial British deletions.[40]

The Americans, considering the request for a *projet* a mere

[39] Oct. 30–Nov. 7, 1814, Charles F. Adams, *op. cit.*, III, 60–65; Clay to Russell, July 9, 1822, Henry Clay Papers, Library of Congress.

[40] Nov. 1, 10, 1814, Charles F. Adams, *op. cit.*, III, 62, 66–68; Adams, Bayard, Clay, Russell, and Gallatin to British, Nov. 10, 1814, FO 5/102. Monroe's instructions of October 4, 1814 (Department of State Archives, National Archives, Diplomatic Instructions, All Countries, Vol. VII) arrived in Ghent on November 24, 1814. Charles F. Adams, *op. cit.*, III, 69–70.

tactic, expected refusal of both offers. Clay warned that he might refuse to sign a treaty should Britain unexpectedly accept. Adams, author of the broad *status quo ante bellum* proposal, merely intended to "put the continuance of the war entirely at the door of England." In this spirit of gloomy gamesmanship the Americans dispatched Secretary Hughes with their proposals after supper on November 10. Had they learned Henry Goulburn's reaction—absolute disapproval plus annoyance at having to stay up late to examine the proposals—their gloom might have deepened.[41]

More than a fortnight passed before the Americans received a reply. Goulburn, warned by Bathurst to expect instructions he would dislike, naturally did not relieve the Americans' anxiety. When London's response, dispatched on November 21 and delivered on the twenty-sixth, reached the Hotel d'Alcantara, John Quincy Adams threw away a pessimistic letter to a French friend (who finally got a quite different letter five months later) and joined his colleagues in welcoming the "first dawn of Peace that had arisen to our hopes."[42] Although the cabinet devoted most of its long dispatch to proposed deletions and changes in the American *projet*, the pivotal parts were two short sentences. At the end, as if they wished it smuggled in unnoticed, the British announced the abandonment of *uti possidetis*, though a ritualistic sentence added that "should this negotiation terminate in a way contrary to their hopes & just expectations" they might again press for territory. In the opening passage they agreed to negotiate on the basis of the American draft. As they suggested no important additional articles, it was obvious that in general they were reconciled to a return to the conditions of 1812.[43]

During the subsequent month of haggling almost everyone consistently assumed that the "dawn of Peace" foreshadowed an irenic day. Arguments flared as high as ever, as if both commissions

[41] Nov. 10, 1814, Charles F. Adams, *op. cit.*, III, 66–68; Goulburn to Bathurst, Nov. 10, 1814, Wellington, *op. cit.*, IX, 427.

[42] Adams to P. P. F. DeGrand, April 28, 1815, Adams Family MSS, Vol. CXXXIX; Nov. 27, 1814, Charles F. Adams, *op. cit.*, III, 70.

[43] Gambier, Goulburn, and Adams to Americans, Nov. 26, 1814, and encl., Department of State Archives, National Archives, Records of Negotiations Connected with the Treaty of Ghent, Vol. I.

sought to employ passion to replace the more impressive weapon of earlier months, a threat to continue the war. Adams, who found several British demands unpalatable, sometimes feared they concealed a desire to break negotiations at a propitious moment. More often he admitted that negotiations now turned upon "atoms." The commissioners directed William H. Crawford to delay negotiations with Paris bankers for a war loan and to discourage French officers seeking employment in the American army.[44]

In the new spirit the Americans abandoned most of their disputed proposals with a minimum of recrimination. Impressment, blockade, indemnity for seizures, the use of Indian allies—all disappeared from view. The Americans also accepted a suggested change in the boundary commissions. Remembering the Jay treaty commissions—in one of them the Americans consistently outvoted the British member, and in another the American seceded to prevent decisions he opposed—Goulburn argued that "the Americans always cheat us" and urged negotiation rather than arbitration. Instead, his superiors proposed that the commissions consist of one member from each nation, with the final decision by a third power if the commissioners deadlocked. The Americans did not object.[45]

Two points, trivial in themselves, had symbolic importance. Before 1812 Canadians enjoyed the privilege of trading with Indians south of the border. Clay swore he would never sign a treaty that granted or implied, as did a full return to the *status quo ante bellum*, the continuation of this privilege. Actually the British never mentioned it. They sacrificed not only the "sable heroes" but the merchants of Montreal on the altar of peace, peace in 1814 and harmony in the future. Speaking for the West, Thomas Hart Benton later declaimed, "Vast as had been her losses, her sacrifices of brave citizens . . . , she felt herself compensated by the single

[44] Dec. 11, 1814, Charles F. Adams, *op. cit.*, III, 99–100; Adams to Louisa Adams, Dec. 2, Nov. 29, 1814, Ford, *op. cit.*, V, 223, 219; Gallatin and Adams to Crawford, Dec. 2, 1814, William H. Crawford Papers, Library of Congress; commissioners to Crawford, Dec. 2, 1814, Hopkins, *op. cit.*, I, 1002.

[45] Gambier, Goulburn, and Adams #15 to Castlereagh, Dec. 1, 1814, and encl. (Adams, Bayard, Clay, Russell, and Gallatin to British, Nov. 30, 1814), FO 5/102; Dec. 1, 1814, Charles F. Adams, *op. cit.*, III, 79–90; Goulburn to Bathurst, Nov. 14, 1814, Wellington, *op. cit.*, IX, 432.

advantage of excluding British traders from all intercourse with her Indians." [46]

The other point showed how deeply Britain distrusted the United States. The Americans had struck one article from Jay's Treaty, eviscerated a boundary convention of 1803 so badly that Britain let it die, and failed to ratify the Monroe-Pinkney treaty of 1806.[47] The British feared similar chicane on this occasion. From the very beginning they planned to insist upon prompt, unconditional ratification, and in the first instructions Castlereagh wrote: "The difficulties which have arisen with that Government on former Occasions will sufficiently explain the Necessity of this Precaution." They certainly did not wish to relax military pressure, particularly the blockade, until the Americans accepted the treaty. Thus they proposed, when returning the *projet,* to end hostilities with the exchange of ratifications, not, as was customary, after formal signing of the treaty. Moreover, at the last minute the British agents at Ghent inserted a phrase requiring ratification without change. "But even if peace is signed," wrote Liverpool the day before that event, "I shall not be surprised if Madison endeavours to play us some trick in the ratification of it." [48]

Some Americans believed, and others still believe, that had Sir Edward Pakenham taken New Orleans a month later the British government would have repudiated the treaty and demanded large sections of the American heartland. Secretary of State Mon-

---

[46] Dec. 11, 1814, Charles F. Adams, *op. cit.,* III, 103; *Annals,* 18th Cong., 1st sess., p. 434.

[47] Not only the British experienced Washington's penchant for altering the work of American representatives abroad. The convention of Mortefontaine, signed in France in 1800, was virtually rewritten in the United States.

[48] Castlereagh #1 to commissioners, July 28, 1814, FO 5/101; Bathurst to Goulburn, private, Dec. 9, 1814, Goulburn MSS, Vol. II; Gambier, Goulburn, and Adams #22 to Castlereagh, Dec. 24, 1814, FO 5/102; Liverpool to Castlereagh, Dec. 23, 1814, Wellington, *op. cit.,* IX, 495. See also Croker to Rear-Admiral Manley Dixon, Dec. 27, 1814, Gerald S. Graham and R. A. Humphreys, eds., *The Navy and South America, 1807–1823,* Navy Records Society, *Publications,* CIV (London, 1962), 150. In this letter the admiral in command of the South American station is told that, "in the event of the President of the United States of America's ratifying the treaty of peace," he will receive from the British agent sent to Washington with the treaty orders to cease hostilities. Until then, he is ordered to continue operations against the Americans.

roe, for one, shared this view.[49] Monroe could not read the cabinet's private correspondence, but he ought to have realized that his suspicions were (like the premier's) habitual rather than logical. Without waiting for news from Pakenham, England ratified the treaty so quickly that her ratification reached America with the document itself. From the very first the fate of the agreement lay in Madison's hands, not Liverpool's. The American commissioners at Ghent were neither simpletons nor Anglophiles, yet they accepted the unusual British proposal with equanimity and dispatch.[50] The episode is simply an indication of the distrust each party held for the other.

The Americans more strongly resisted one other British alteration in their draft. At issue were islands in Passamaquoddy Bay between Maine [51] and Nova Scotia. The British, who claimed the islands but did not occupy them until 1814, refused to include them in the general restoration of territory, arguing that occupation should continue until arbitration settled the title. The Americans, who wanted to regain control of the islands without waiting for arbitration, had a very weak hand to play; even Adams, the most determined, admitted that it was unthinkable to risk peace on this slender issue. Ultimately the Americans agreed to exempt the disputed islands from the general restoration, although they insisted upon language that impaired their country's claim as little as possible.[52]

The last issue settled involved use of the Mississippi River and the curing and drying of fish on Newfoundland shores. Should both privileges, affirmed in the treaty of 1783, be reconfirmed?

[49] Monroe to Madison, May 3, 1815, Monroe MSS.

[50] Gambier, Goulburn, and Adams #22 to Castlereagh, Dec. 24, 1814, FO 5/102; Bathurst #1 to Baker, Dec. 31, 1814, FO 5/105; Adams, Bayard, Clay, Russell, and Gallatin to British, Nov. 30, 1814, FO 5/102; Dec. 1, 1814, Charles F. Adams, *op. cit.*, III, 82–83. The British readily accepted an American proposal to activate the treaty with its formal ratification by both parties, not with the exchange of instruments of ratification. This suggestion, put forward in recollection of the loss at sea of official ratifications of Jay's Treaty, clearly lessened the chance of delay which Monroe thought Britain desired.

[51] Then part of the state of Massachusetts.

[52] Bathurst #12, #15 to commissioners, Nov. 21, Dec. 6, 1814, and encl., FO 5/101; Gambier, Goulburn, and Adams #15 to Castlereagh, Dec. 1, 1814, FO 5/102; Adams to John Adams, Dec. 26, 1814, Adams Family MSS, Vol. CXXXIX; Adams, Bayard, Clay, Russell, and Gallatin to British, Dec. 14, 1814, Ghent Negotiations, Vol. I.

Should one be dropped, the other preserved? Should both be passed over in silence? Although they dominated the conversations of December and delayed a settlement, neither the Mississippi nor the fishery compared in importance with the barrier state or *uti possidetis*. Morever, although each side tried to euchre the other into concessions, long before the final agreement the likely line of settlement was clear. The issues were, in short, minor and in a sense artificial.

This was particularly true of the Mississippi question. Although the Americans, notably Clay, took seriously the English demand for use of the river, London did not. The British asked access to the river, the source of which had been found since 1783 to lie in American territory, and confirmation of the right of navigation. When the Americans spurned these suggestions London did not press for reconsideration. The British sought only to get the Americans to agree that the right expired with the war, thus destroying the claim to the fishery, or to offer compensation for closing the river if, to justify their demand for fishing rights, the Americans claimed that these two provisions of the treaty of 1783 continued in force.[53]

London considered the fishery question the more important. In the last year of peace the American fishing trade employed 43,000 tons of shipping and brought in catches worth $1,400,000, much of it from waters around Newfoundland. Nathaniel Atcheson alleged that 1,200 American ships used British waters in a peak year. Petitions imploring the government to drive off the Americans descended upon Whitehall; the use of Newfoundland shores led to friction and encouraged smuggling; and as early as April, 1814, the British ministry determined to abrogate the concession of 1783. To justify their position they maintained, and law officers supported them, that the War of 1812 canceled earlier treaties.[54]

[53] Bathurst #15 to commissioners, Dec. 6, 1814, FO 5/101; Bathurst to Goulburn, private, Dec. 6, 1814, Goulburn MSS, Vol. II; Gambier, Goulburn, and Adams #15 to Castlereagh, Dec. 1, 1814, FO 5/102.

[54] Adam Seybert, *Statistical Annals . . . of the United States of America* (Philadelphia, 1818), p. 341; Atcheson, *op. cit.*, p. 16; Bathurst to Castlereagh, April 21, 1814, Papers of Robert Stewart, Viscount Castlereagh, Second Marquis of Londonderry, Mount Stewart, Newtownards, County Down; Bathurst to Goulburn, private, Nov. 21, 1814, Goulburn MSS, Vol. II.

By the time the fishery, previously mentioned *sotto voce*, became a key item at Ghent, the British position had narrowed. Privately ministers were ready to tolerate fishing in British waters. They merely sought to end drying and curing on Newfoundland soil, a likely source of future controversy. This privilege—the Americans called it a right—benefited some fishermen, but in the normal course of events most fish were dried and cured in home ports of the fishing ships. Although Goulburn assured Bathurst he had made clear to the Americans the distinction between what Britain desired and what she would tolerate,[55] no American records indicate that he or Gambier or Dr. Adams actually did so. If not, these men, who pressed harder than London on several issues raised in December, were largely responsible for the tribulations of that month. The Americans thought they were fighting to preserve the right to fish in onshore waters as well as the right to cure.

Such a contest did not appeal to most of the American delegation. Privately the majority accepted England's argument that war erased the grant of 1783; Clay opposed any payment in western coin for Yankee interests; and Russell hated John Quincy Adams, chief patron of the fishermen. Russell accused Adams of narrow parochialism, of a willingness to "barter the patriotic blood of the West for blubber, and exchange ultra-Alleghany scalps for codfish." Adams, though recognizing his vulnerability to such a charge, refused to abandon American rights and honestly believed what he had written a few years earlier: "In the association of ideas, there is no very unnatural transition from cod fishing on the Grand Banks to the History of the United States." [56]

With sporadic assistance from Bayard, Adams dragooned his colleagues into defense of the fishery, but their hearts were never in the cause. Consequently the Americans changed their position several times within a few weeks. In their *projet,* largely because

[55] Samuel E. Morison, *The Maritime History of Massachusetts* (Boston, 1921), p. 135; Bathurst to Goulburn, private, Dec. 16, 1814, Goulburn MSS, Vol. III; Goulburn to Bathurst, private, Dec. 20, 1814, *ibid.*

[56] Russell to Clay, Oct. 15, 1815, "Letters of Jonathan Russell, 1815," Massachusetts Historical Society, *Proceedings,* XLIV (Boston, 1911), 311; Adams to Plumer, Aug. 16, 1809, Plumer, *op. cit.,* pp. 376–377.

silence might imply acceptance of British declarations that war terminated the privilege, they maintained the contrary. In conference on December 1 they defended this argument, but undermined it by offering to reopen the Mississippi in return for confirmation of the fishery. This proffered exchange suggested, the British commissioners reported, that the Americans really considered the arrangement "purely of a conventional nature." London, which welcomed the partial admission but did not consider the Mississippi a fair trade for the fishery, tried to exploit the opening. The British emissaries proposed to refer both matters to future negotiations to arrange separate compensation for the renewal of two distinct privileges. The Americans quickly rejected this plan. Instead they proposed either a simple declaratory article reserving both parties' claims or, preferably, silence on the two questions.[57]

Although none of the Americans thought Great Britain would agree to silence, even the offer represented a defeat for Adams. As Gallatin warned his Yankee colleague, he stood almost alone. Indeed Gallatin told Goulburn privately that his commission wished to leave the questions to the future. When Clay, seated next to Goulburn and Gambier at a dinner proffered by the town, repeated the same sentiment, the Admiral replied that such deferral might mean war when British ships forcibly closed the fishery; the United States would never fight for the fishery, Clay replied. Had London insisted upon explicit acceptance of its position, there is every probability that four of the Americans would have surrendered despite Adams' avowal that he would refuse to sign a treaty that did so.[58]

The game of "brag," as Clay called it, required two players, and in the end the British proved as eager as their opponents to save some of their bets. At the outset Bathurst, whose private correspondence hints that he disapproved the decision, informed Goulburn that the cabinet would not press things to a climax,

---

[57] Gambier, Goulburn, and Adams #15, #17 to Castlereagh, Dec. 1, 10, 1814, FO 5/102; Adams, Bayard, Clay, Russell, and Gallatin to British, Dec. 14, 1814, *ibid.*

[58] Dec. 14, 1814, Charles F. Adams, *op. cit.*, III, 117–119; Goulburn to Bathurst, private, Dec. 13, 1814, Bickley, *op. cit.*, p. 316.

would even settle for silence. "Our silence, after the declaration made of our Interpretation . . . does not necessarily abandon our right to prevent the Americans renewing this Privilege," he wrote. "Practically, however it does, and we are all I think pretty well aware of it." London permitted the underlings at Ghent to try for something better during the first half of December. Then, just as the Americans began to show signs of weakness, Goulburn unaccountably became convinced of their irresistible firmness and recommended compromise.[59]

Ministers willingly agreed to divide the pot. The American offer of silence reached London on the night of December 18, and Liverpool summoned the cabinet to Downing Street the next day. They discussed the American treaty in detail, perhaps using as an agenda draft instructions Earl Bathurst had prepared. At four that afternoon a courier set off for Ghent with instructions announcing Britain's willingness to settle for silence.[60]

Only three afternoons later the British delegation sent a note of acceptance to the American residence in Ghent. Although the note contained some irritating language, the authors fairly described it as "removing . . . the only objection to the immediate conclusion of the Treaty." James A. Bayard hastened into the streets to find Adams, who had gone off for a solitary, dreary walk. Bayard's news so warmed that argumentative man that when the commission met to consider the British note Adams waved aside a suggestion that the Americans reaffirm their own position for the record before concluding the treaty. At a three-hour conference the next day, marked to be sure by haggling over language and minor spats on other issues, the two sides easily agreed to delete from the draft treaty Article VIII, dealing with the Mississippi and the fishery.[61]

And so, after nearly twenty weeks of travail, they reached the

---

[59] Bathurst to Goulburn, private, Nov. 21, 1814, Goulburn MSS, Vol. II; Goulburn to Bathurst, private, Dec. 13, 1814, Bickley, *op. cit.*, p. 316.

[60] Bathurst #17 to commissioners, Dec. 19, 1814, FO 5/101; *Courier*, Dec. 20, 1814; *Chronicle*, Dec. 20, 1814.

[61] Gambier, Goulburn, and Adams to Americans, Dec. 22, 1814, Ghent Negotiations, Vol. I; Dec. 22, 23, 1814, Charles F. Adams, *op. cit.*, III, 119–120, 122–125.

end. There remained the preparation of fair copies, the collation of texts, the addition of signatures, and the affixing of the wax seals and the red ribbons that enliven the somber parchment of all treaties. Perhaps, as the commissioners laboriously scratched out copies of the treaty in their own hands or, on the British side, supervised copying by others, their minds ran back to August, when they had first met. How the formal British position had changed! Agreement to accept silence on the fishery was the last and certainly not the most important instance in which Downing Street took counsel of its secret misgivings rather than its hopes of conquest and victory.

VIII

THE SHOCK OF PEACE

Opening the London *Post* of December 23 at Ghent a few days after its publication, one of the Americans, perhaps Henry Clay, may have allowed himself to smile. "The ridiculous mockery at Ghent," the *Post* reported on the very day when the final terms were settled, was approaching an unsuccessful end. On the twenty-fourth, an hour late because Clay dawdled over his copying chores, the Americans descended into the Rue des Champs shortly before four and set out by carriage for the signing ceremony. In their laps they held copies of a treaty not one of them had expected until recently to see.

Outside the Chartreux they found a carriage, horses already harnessed, waiting to carry Anthony Baker toward London with the official news. Inside the old monastery Admiral Gambier, re-capturing the lead from Goulburn for this purely formal occasion, presided as the two delegations laboriously collated the various texts of the treaty. A word was changed here, a comma there, but all agreed to overlook slight discrepancies in the writing out of dates. These painstaking tasks occupied the diplomats for about two hours, the actual signing half an hour. Lord Gambier and John Quincy Adams exchanged hopes that the peace would be permanent.[1] Gambier, the religious sea dog, may have been sincere; Adams, who counted Great Britain an inveterate enemy, doubtless considered the sentiment diplomatic persiflage.

The commissioners remained at Ghent for periods of from ten days to a month. On December 28 the Americans entertained their companions in labor for the last time. A week later—Goulburn complained that the delay prevented him and his wife from celebrating New Year's in London—city fathers feted the peacemakers at a dinner for ninety people. The band, Adams noted, alternately played "Hail Columbia" and "God Save the King" "until Mr. Goulburn thought they became tiresome. I was of the same opinion." Labored toasts and the recitation of a local baron's undistinguished couplets added no more to the occasion, but even Adams found the dancing lively.[2] At Vienna that season, amidst the pleasant company of wives and mistresses, they danced fully as well, heard more varied music as well as sprightlier toasts, and failed to finish their task.

Tidying up, the Americans terminated their lease on Baron Lavendeghem's town house and moved back to the Hotel des Pays Bas. Auctioneers sold their furniture. Since Ghent considered the treaty a signal American success, the desks and chairs and beds brought high prices as mementos of that rare event, a British diplomatic defeat. Wily dealers smuggled additional furniture, some from the Chartreux, and bad wine—the Americans had not left a drop—into the sale.[3]

Secretary Baker's carriage cast a wheel shortly after leaving Ghent. Even so, traveling all Christmas Day, he reached London

---

[1] *Morning Post* (London), Dec. 23, 1814; Dec. 24, 1814, Charles F. Adams, ed., *Memoirs of John Quincy Adams* (12 vols.; Philadelphia, 1874–1877), III, 126; Adams to Louisa Adams, Dec. 27, 1814, Worthington C. Ford, ed., *The Writings of John Quincy Adams* (7 vols.; New York, 1913–1917), V, 253–254.

[2] *Times* (London), Jan. 12, 1815; Goulburn to Bathurst, Dec. 30, 1814, Arthur R. Wellesley, Duke of Wellington, ed., *Supplementary Despatches, Correspondence, and Memoranda of Field Marshal Arthur Duke of Wellington, K.G.*, IX (London, 1862), 516; Jan. 5, 1815, Adams, *op. cit.*, III, 138–139.

[3] Adams to Louisa Adams, Jan. 10–17, 1815, Ford, *op. cit.*, V, 267–268.

in forty-three hours. Within a few hours the treaty was approved by the government and officially ratified by the Prince Regent. A week later, accompanied by Clay's secretary, who arrived with an official American copy, Anthony Baker sailed for America in H.M.S. *Favourite*. Lord Bathurst warned him not to accept conditional ratification by the United States or even any formal statement of Washington's views on the many questions omitted from the treaty.[4]

Granted at last the time to stand back and examine their handiwork, the Americans at Ghent and the cabinet at London found it acceptable, but worried about the reaction elsewhere. The Americans expected bitter criticism from their countrymen, who approved only spectacular success and either rejected or heaped obloquy upon compromise. Henry Clay melodramatically predicted that the treaty would "break him down entirely, and we should all be subject to much reproach." Gallatin and Adams anticipated much the same fate, and only Bayard, who as it turned out did not live long enough to enjoy the praise, predicted popular applause. On Christmas Day both Gallatin and Clay wrote apologias to Monroe. The most the former could say was that the treaty was the best possible under existing circumstances. Clay, admitting that no war aims had been won, nevertheless maintained that the treaty "cannot be pronounced very unfavourable. We lose no territory, I think no honor."[5]

John Quincy Adams considered the treaty "an unlimited armistice [rather] than a peace, . . . hardly less difficult to preserve than . . . to obtain." Like Clay and Gallatin, he expected criticism but believed the treaty the best possible under the circumstances. "We have abandoned no essential right," he wrote to his mother, "and if we have left everything open for future controversy, we have at least secured our Country the power at her own

---

[4] Bathurst #18 to commissioners, Dec. 26, 1814, Foreign Office Archives, Public Record Office, FO 5/101; Bathurst #1 to Baker, Dec. 31, 1814, FO 5/105.

[5] Dec. 11, 1814, Adams, *op. cit.*, III, 104; Gallatin to Monroe, Dec. 25, 1814, Albert Gallatin Papers, New-York Historical Society; Clay to Monroe, Dec. 25, 1814, James F. Hopkins, ed., *The Papers of Henry Clay* (Lexington, 1959——), I, 1007.

option to extinguish the war." [6] This hint that his countrymen might prefer continued war to ratification of the treaty shows how far John Quincy Adams was from a spirit of exultation.

In later years Henry Clay boasted about his part in the negotiations, while Gallatin expressed quiet satisfaction. Adams' attitude also changed. He came to view Ghent as an honorable draw, neither a victory nor a defeat nor a mere escape from war. On the fourth anniversary of the treaty his thoughts turned back to "that great blessing to my country and myself—a blessing great in itself, greater in its consequences, and which affords me a continual source of pleasure in the remembrance." [7]

Great blessing though it was, the Treaty of Ghent does not necessarily demonstrate the superhuman talents of the Americans who negotiated it. Indeed the envoys themselves made no such claims, leaving patriotic historians to make the assertion for them. Actually Adams and his colleagues deserve substantial but less extreme praise. They failed to divine the weakness of London's will, accepting as an authentic replica the pose of Goulburn, Gambier, and Dr. Adams. They acted purely defensively, and they neither obtained a single major concession nor extorted from England renunciation of any item the British cabinet chose to press to a final issue. On the other hand the Americans never panicked. They offered no substantial concessions to obtain peace. Despite their pessimism and to avoid putting America in the wrong, they declined to break off the negotiations in the face of provocation by Goulburn and his colleagues. This refusal was their most important decision and their greatest triumph. Unlike the British trio, they made no major mistakes and held the fort until London made the key decisions which led to peace. This is credit enough for the five Americans at Ghent.

In 1814 the British cabinet, like the American delegates, ac-

[6] Adams to Louisa Adams, Jan. 3, 1815, Dec. 23, 1814, Ford, *op. cit.*, V, 261, 245–246; Adams to Abigail Adams, Dec. 24, 1814, Adams Family Papers, Massachusetts Historical Society, Vol. CXXXIX.

[7] Dec. 24, 1815, Adams, *op. cit.*, IV, 197.

cepted the treaty without enthusiasm. In Lord Sidmouth's words, the ministers considered it "a great relief, though not in all respects a subject of exultation." [8] They could but admit that their probing had revealed no American weak points, that they and particularly their agents had been outargued at Ghent. Like the American commissioners they were well aware that the treaty postponed rather than decided many issues. They took consolation in the defeat of American assertions, most of them (for example, on impressment) never actually pressed by Adams and his colleagues but nonetheless threatening in British eyes.

The ministry believed the treaty—any treaty—would strengthen Lord Castlereagh's hand at Vienna. News of peace reached that city on the morning of New Year's Day, surprising everyone and particularly pleasing the British delegation, which passed the day receiving congratulations from persons even as exalted as the Czar. "We have become more European," Castlereagh commented with satisfaction, ". . . and by the Spring we can have a very nice army on the Continent." Boldly he proposed an Austro-Franco-British alliance to press Prussia and her supporter, Russia, on the Saxon question. *Post hoc, ergo propter hoc* is dangerous reasoning. Yet it seems likely that, as Downing Street expected, the Treaty of Ghent influenced events at Vienna. A year later John Quincy Adams reported, apparently on the basis of conversations with English leaders including Castlereagh, that during the congress Russia exploited Britain's difficulties with America and therefore regretted the conclusion of the war.[9]

In Paris, too, British diplomats welcomed the treaty. The Duke of Wellington, pictured by Liverpool as a sort of *deus ex machina* of the peace, was particularly enthusiastic. He hastened off a congratulatory note to the American minister and, in violation of

[8] Sidmouth to J. Hiley Addington, Dec. 27, 1814, George Pellew, *The Life and Correspondence of the Right Honble Henry Addington, First Viscount Sidmouth* (3 vols.; London, 1847), III, 122.

[9] Charles K. Webster, *The Foreign Policy of Castlereagh, 1812–1815* (London, 1931), pp. 370–372; Adams #12 to Monroe, Sept. 5, 1815, Department of State Archives, National Archives, Despatches, Great Britain, Vol. XIX.

protocol which called for a first visit by the American, followed this up with a call at the residence of William H. Crawford.[10]

The British cabinet most valued the treaty for its impact upon domestic politics. Writing to George Canning, a very uncertain political ally, the Earl of Liverpool excused rather than defended the peace. Canning's reply, that "upon the whole you have done what was wise and necessary," can hardly have warmed the premier. (Privately Canning went further, describing the treaty as unsatisfactory.) Canning, however, hit upon the crux of the matter when he observed that peace ripped a promising weapon from the hands of Liverpool's parliamentary opponents. Lord Grenville, abandoning his plan to challenge the ministry for extravagant demands and military incompetence, complained that ministers, "having now trod back their own steps, & replaced us at last, no matter with what . . . humiliation, in that state of Peace for which the Country sighed, . . . will find a very ready & very obedient majority to quash all questions of retrospect." [11]

This does not mean that the treaty was popular, only that it was preferred to war. While audiences at Covent Garden and Drury Lane, traditional barometers of public opinion, applauded the peace, an undercurrent of groans and hisses could also be heard. A few days later, after acrimonious debate, the London Common Council only narrowly defeated a resolution that, although welcoming the end of the war, criticized the peace terms. British North American interests complained bitterly, as did many Canadians when they heard the news. If the antitreaty *Times* may be believed, less understandable protest arose even in Liverpool, which as the chief port for trade with the United States stood to

[10] Crawford to Madison, Dec. 28, 1814, William C. Rives Collection, Library of Congress.
[11] Liverpool to Canning, Dec. 28, 1814, Wellington, *op. cit.*, IX, 513–515; Canning to Liverpool, Jan. 14, 1815, Papers of the First and Second Earls of Liverpool, British Museum (Add. MSS 38190–38489, 38564–38581), Add. MSS 38193; Canning to Lord Boringdon, Jan. 7, 1815, postscript, Papers of the Family of the Lords Morley, British Museum (Add. MSS 48218–48301), Add. MSS 48219; Grenville to Thomas Grenville, Jan. 3, 1815, Thomas Grenville Papers, British Museum (Add. MSS 41851–41859), Add. MSS 41852.

benefit particularly from the reopening of commerce. Midland manufacturers and Scottish traders, on the other hand, naturally welcomed the peace.[12]

Of all the newspapers only the *Courier* tried to picture the treaty as a triumph, and the exceptionally labored quality of editor Stuart's prose suggests he found this task, probably assigned by the ministry, most uncongenial. The *Courier* pointed out that the Americans failed to secure a single item for which they went to war and maintained that, while a more easily defended boundary for Canada was theoretically desirable, the Americans had absorbed so much punishment that they would not again attack it. Apparently the management of Covent Garden swallowed these arguments. Several years later the American minister to London discovered to his annoyance that his country's standard, like those of defeated countries, lay at the feet of the heroic picture of Britannia painted upon the fire curtain of the theater.[13]

Most commentators viewed the treaty as a devastating defeat. The *Public Advertiser* wailed that only a rebirth of the spirit of Elizabeth, Cromwell, and William I could save England. The *Times*, consistent to the end, inveighed against the "deadly instrument, . . . degrading manner of terminating the war, . . . premature and inglorious peace." The *Times* hoped the Americans would reject the treaty, thus prolonging the war until Madison fell, New England perhaps seceded, and the Royal Navy erased the stains of disgrace. Rumor held that the Prince Regent, sharing these sentiments, excoriated his ministers for their weakness.[14]

William Cobbett, who also considered the treaty an American victory, gloried in the ministry's defeat. The government, he argued, had continued the war since August simply because it hoped to deal a blow to the idea of liberty. Thanks in part to Opposition

[12] *Star* (London), Dec. 27, 1814; *Times,* Jan. 13, 1815, Dec. 31, 1814; Baker to Hamilton, March 23, 1815, FO 5/106; *Caledonian Mercury* (Edinburgh), Dec. 29, 1814.

[13] *Courier* (London), Dec. 27, 28, 29, 1814; Richard Rush, *A Residence at the Court of London* (3d ed.; London, 1872), p. 180.

[14] *Niles' Weekly Register* (Baltimore), Feb. 18, 1815, quoting *London Public Advertiser; Times,* Dec. 27, 28, 29, 1814; *Edinburgh Evening Courant,* Dec. 26, 1814.

grumbling, Cobbett went on, Liverpool and his minions had been forced to give up their scheme and, in an event more important than any since Johann Gutenberg's invention four centuries before, to accept a treaty that "blasted the malignant hopes of the enemies of freedom."

The Opposition press, not so republican as Cobbett, went not quite so far in criticism of the ministers. "That they have humbled themselves in the dust, and have thereby brought discredit on the country, is certain," the *Chronicle* commented; "but they have seen their folly, and it is better to cover themselves with sackcloth, than to devote the kingdom to the calamities inseparable from the vain attempt of maintaining their . . . demands." [15]

Most Englishmen rejected the simple analyses of the *Courier* and *Cobbett's Register*. Writing to Admiral Lord Gambier, a colleague in the Bible Society, William Wilberforce expressed the mixed view. "American compositions and threatenings and false accusations," he wrote, ". . . tempted [me] . . . to long to inflict [sharp punishment] on the detestable American Government. . . . But here," Wilberforce continued, "the religion of the blessed Jesus steps in, and forces on me with irresistible authority the duties of peace and love." America even seemed to contain some "true Christians" (by which Wilberforce appears to have meant Anglophiles), and they deserved gentle treatment.[16] Although Wilberforce's sanctimonious reasons for setting aside dreams of vengeance were uniquely his own, many of his countrymen were, like him, torn between a desire for peace and hatred of the American government. The *Sun* sympathetically reported general regret that the American government had escaped payment for the war, yet welcomed the end of "this wasting and useless" contest. The *Post* regretted that General Ross and other commanders had not burned more private property, simply to punish the Americans for declaring war. "The crouching submission of our

---

[15] *Cobbett's Political Register* (London), Jan. 7, 14, 1815; *Morning Chronicle* (London), Dec. 27, 1814.
[16] Georgiana, Lady Chatterton, *Memorials, Personal and Historical of Admiral Lord Gambier, G.C.B.* (2d ed.; London, 1861), II, 347–348.

foe," the *Post*'s phrase for the *status quo ante bellum,* unfortunately forestalled a campaign of arson. Both the *Post* and the *Star,* in a bizarre distortion of the treaty's meaning, expected the boundary commissions to arrange cessions to Britain. This prospect alone, they suggested, reconciled them to the settlement.[17]

As Liverpool, Canning, and Grenville predicted, peace destroyed the American war as a political issue in Great Britain. After only a few days editorials turned to other subjects. Parliament did not debate the treaty until April, 1815. In the upper chamber Marquis Wellesley assailed the "monstrous, egregious, and unreasonable demands" so unsuccessfully put forward at Ghent. He complained that "the American commissioners had shown the most astonishing superiority over the British" and called for papers. By this time in his career the once impressive Wellesley had become a rather faulty Roman candle, and his attack fizzled out. By nearly a three-to-one margin the peers declined to call for correspondence.[18]

The House of Commons likewise scorned "questions of retrospect." Only a thin house attended the debate, quite a contrast with the packed benches during earlier battles over the Orders in Council and the conduct of the naval war. As had Bathurst in the Lords, Henry Goulburn disingenuously blamed the delay from August to December on the presumed necessity of awaiting new instructions from Washington. The Opposition mobilized only thirty-seven members in support of an amendment converting an address in praise of the treaty into a criticism of ministerial diplomacy.

Surprisingly, during the debate not a single speaker turned his guns upon the United States. On the contrary, George Ponsonby, who led off for the Opposition, drew cheers when he declared that "to consider America as the child of England, growing up and flourishing under her fostering hand—this, Sir, is a situation of more true glory and of more real happiness, than any other nation . . . can boast of." Sir James Mackintosh, the respected liberal

---

[17] *Sun* (London), Dec. 27, 28, 1814; *Post,* Dec. 27, 28, 29, 30, 1814; *Star,* Dec. 27, 1814.
[18] *Hansard,* XXX, 587–607.

lawyer, maintained that peace with America, like the preservation of Dutch independence, should be a basic tenet of English diplomacy.[19] By these statements the Opposition in effect announced its return, at least temporarily, to the philopacifism it had shown before the war. The ultranationalists' silence, on the other hand, probably reflected concern aroused by Napoleon's return from Elba, with all its international implications, rather than a basic shift in attitude toward the United States.

A few months later Admiral Gambier complained that exposure to "the unpleasant animadversions of the public as well as both Houses of Parliament" entitled him to special reward for his services at Ghent. Ministers apparently agreed, for they soothed him with £2,250 and Dr. William Adams with £2,000. (Goulburn, who had done more work than the other two combined, declined payment beyond his regular salary.) [20] In a way the Admiral had a point. Ministerial retreats exposed the commissioners to charges of weakness and incompetence, whereas the treaty they signed, but for which they were not responsible, dissatisfied Britons who wished more stripes had been laid on James Madison's back.

During the Commons' debate a government spokesman, Hart Davis, forecast a new ministerial tack when he emphasized the importance of Anglo-American trade. "Will it be maintained, in the present day," the *Caledonian Mercury* asked, "that the prosperity of America is a loss to this country? The jealousy of the prosperity of other countries is among the antiquated prejudices of the last century." [21] Old prejudices died hard. Most Englishmen continued to be jealous of the United States and fearful of her rising power.

In fact the treaty was a British surrender only when contrasted with the perfervid sentiments of the spring of 1814 and their weaker expression in proposals put forward at Ghent. Britain maintained her maritime pretensions. Canadian interests lost nothing save wildly optimistic hopes for boundary rectification and

[19] *Ibid.*, pp. 500–533.
[20] Gambier to Liverpool, Aug. 23, 1815, and endorsement, FO 5/111.
[21] *Caledonian Mercury*, Dec. 31, 1814.

commercial control of the American interior. If the Indians were abandoned, only contempt for American sovereignty excused Britain's earlier connection with them. Psychologically England came close to recognizing American equality at Ghent, thus troubling British nationalists and indeed forecasting a new sort of relationship. Materially, Great Britain surrendered very little by the Treaty of Ghent.

The evident advance toward equality, discomfiting to Englishmen, assured the treaty a far warmer reception in the United States. External factors, too, made the peace a subject of congratulation. Americans welcomed the news partly because it was so unexpected, partly because it made ridiculous an otherwise threatening movement in New England, and partly because peace followed military victories decisive enough to bring honor to the country without reigniting dreams of conquest.

A second set of dispatches from Ghent, covering the period to the end of October and published in Washington a month later, seemed, like the first, to show that Britain, confident she could have peace on prewar terms at any time, drew out the negotiations in an effort to secure more. *Uti possidetis* seemed nearly as fearsome as the now-abandoned Indian demands. As the President put it, Britain still "speculate[d] on the fortune of events" and showed no eagerness for peace. Indeed, if James Madison had any complaint against his representatives, it was that they tolerated "the gambling procrastinations of the other party" instead of forcing a decision one way or the other. Only *Niles' Register* predicted, none too confidently, the conclusion of peace.[22]

If peace did not come it seemed certain that New England sedition would deepen and perhaps turn to secessionism. In October Massachusetts called a convention of states to plan New England defense and consider constitutional reform. On December 15 delegates from the Bay State, Connecticut, and Rhode Island, plus a few informally selected representatives from New Hampshire and

---

[22] Madison to John Adams, Dec. 17, 1814, Gaillard Hunt, ed., *The Writings of James Madison* (9 vols.; New York, 1900–1910), VIII, 322–323; *Niles' Register*, Dec. 10, 1814.

Vermont, where the state legislatures declined to go along with the Massachusetts plan, gathered in secret conclave at Hartford. Years later apologists maintained, apparently with a straight face, that "a small and peaceful deputation of grave citizens . . . assembled at Hartford. There, calm and collected,—like the Pilgrims from whom they descended . . . ,—they deliberated on the most effectual means of preserving . . . the civil and political liberty which had been won and bequeathed to them." [23] At the time few observers shared this view.

President Madison believed the New Englanders would stop short of secession, if only because the Yankees depended for their prosperity upon trade with other sections and because the Federalists, despite recent electoral successes, held power by relatively narrow margins. As a matter of prudence the President took precautions. He dispatched Colonel Thomas Jesup, a wounded veteran, to Connecticut, nominally to raise troops but actually to keep an eye on proceedings, and alerted Governor Tompkins of New York to the possibility of civil war. At the very end the President approved a plan to raise antisecessionist volunteers in New England if it became necessary, and ordered General Robert Swartwout northward with contingent authority to spend $350,000 on preparations.[24]

Fortunately for the union, Federalists disagreed among themselves. A few, including the always bitter John Lowell, opposed the meeting, sure it would not have the courage to go beyond talk. A larger number, including Massachusetts delegates Harrison Gray Otis and George Cabot, who became chairman, opposed secession but wanted to use the national crisis to extort concessions from the central government. Others, notably Timothy Pickering, preferred temporary dissolution of the union to continued Repub-

[23] Appeal of the Massachusetts Federalists, Jan. 28, 1829, Henry Adams, ed., *Documents Relating to New-England Federalism* (Boston, 1877), pp. 80–81. The best account of the convention is Samuel E. Morison, *The Life and Letters of Harrison Gray Otis* (2 vols.; Boston, 1913), II, 125–159, used here and below.

[24] Irving Brant, *James Madison: Commander in Chief* (Indianapolis, 1961), pp. 343–344, 359–361; Monroe to Madison, Jan. 10, 1815, Rives Collection; Tench Ringgold memorandum, Jan. 10, 1815, James Monroe Papers, New York Public Library.

lican rule. Before adjourning on January 5, the convention agreed to demand constitutional amendments that, among other things, reduced Southern representation in Congress and required a two-thirds majority for a declaration of war. Pickering and others never expected ratification of these amendments, perhaps did not even wish it. The convention recommended a second meeting in June if the war continued and if relief was not granted.[25]

After the event, everyone from ultra-Federalist Gouverneur Morris on one hand to loyal Republican legislatures on the other scoffed at the mountain that produced such feeble mice.[26] Before the treaty arrived jocularity was not possible. Colonel Jesup reported secessionist sentiment throughout New England; tight secrecy at Hartford encouraged speculation about unpublished agreements; and the call for a second meeting hung like a lowering cloud over the nation.

After a short visit to Boston, Harrison Gray Otis and two other emissaries set out for Washington to present the convention's demands to President Madison. Otis never dreamed that he and his companions were engaged in a three-way race. H.M.S. *Favourite,* the herald of surprise, was nearing American shores. A post-rider was approaching Washington from the south with equally unexpected good tidings, the news that American troops had repulsed a British attack on New Orleans. Otis' trio reached the capital just ahead of the news of peace, having previously collided at Baltimore with accounts from New Orleans. The victory alone was enough to "put the Administration on stilts," as Otis put it, and destroy the already feeble hope of extorting concessions from the President and his party.[27]

The New Orleans attack was probably the worst-kept military secret of a war in which both sides freely advertised their intentions. Crawford and Gallatin sent warnings from Europe in August; British officers unsuccessfully sought the assistance of the

---

[25] Resolutions of the Hartford convention, Herman V. Ames, ed., *State Documents on Federal Relations,* II (Philadelphia, 1900), 83–86.

[26] Morris to Moss Kent, Jan. 10, 1815, Henry Adams, *op. cit.,* p. 421; Ames, *op. cit.,* pp. 86–88.

[27] Otis to Sally F. Otis, Feb. 12, 1815, Morison, *op. cit.,* II, 164.

Baratarian pirate, Jean Laffite (who informed the Americans), early in September; and both British and American newspapers weighed the prospects of victory and defeat. Although many Americans thought Britain intended to occupy Louisiana, the planned descent actually was simply an extension of the raid-and-pillage strategy to an area fit for winter campaigning. Lord Bathurst, mastermind of the expedition, had little hope that British troops could even temporarily occupy more than the city of New Orleans, and he believed the cost of holding Louisiana far beyond British means.[28]

Thus it was with ambitions of booty and burning, not empire building, that Admiral Sir Alexander Cochrane anchored off Louisiana early in December. Some 8,000 troops, most of them the Wellingtonians whose departure alerted Crawford and Gallatin, inched through the bayous toward New Orleans. On January 8, 1815, their commander, Sir Edward Pakenham, Wellington's brother-in-law, flung them into a frontal attack upon Andrew Jackson's line behind the Rodriguez Canal. Sheltered by ramparts, protected on one flank by the Mississippi and the other by a swamp, and aided by British ineptitude (a colonel was later cashiered because his regiment forgot the scaling ladders), the Americans chopped their opponents to bits. A secondary assault on the other side of the river gained only ephemeral success. The redcoats suffered 2,600 casualties, among them 700 dead including Pakenham, and the Americans only 13 before the General's successor called off the attack.

The news, soon followed by reports that the British had slunk away to their ships, reached Washington on February 5. Having anxiously awaited news for weeks, the nation greeted Jackson's victory with special enthusiasm. Many Americans, including the

[28] Crawford to Monroe, private, Aug. 17, 1814, Department of State Archives, National Archives, Despatches, France, Vol. XIV; Gallatin to Monroe, Aug. 20, 1814, Gallatin MSS; Bathurst to Castlereagh, Oct. 21, 1814, and encl., Papers of Robert Stewart, Viscount Castlereagh, Second Marquis of Londonderry, Mount Stewart, Newtownards, County Down. Bathurst did toy with the idea of bringing about the return of Louisiana to Spain, but even this he considered an extremely unlikely possibility dependent upon a popular rising in Louisiana.

General himself, ascribed the victory to divine interposition, but at least one Irish-American discounted it on the false hypothesis that regiments of cowardly Orangemen made up most of the British force.[29] Most citizens considered it, with Plattsburg, a vindication of American honor, a demonstration of national virility and strength to be shared only grudgingly with God, and a heartwarming triumph over Napoleon's conquerors. That New Orleans, like Plattsburg, was a defensive success fought within American boundaries made it no less glorious, perhaps the contrary, but did mean that it neither militarily nor psychologically encouraged a war of conquest. New Orleans became a glorious coda to an otherwise largely undistinguished symphony of war. For this the coincidence, or near coincidence, of the news of victory and the news of peace was largely responsible.

Deflected from Chesapeake Bay by bad weather, H.M.S. *Favourite* entered New York harbor after nightfall on February 11. As soon as the ship docked the pilot, a valuable *New-York Post* informant, hastened to the newspaper office, only to discover the journal put to bed and the last staffers about to leave. By word of mouth the news spread through lower Manhattan, and within twenty minutes candles of thanksgiving began to appear in house windows.[30]

At New York as elsewhere, celebration began with the bare news of peace, for the terms remained unknown until ratification in Washington. "In firing salutes for *'Madison's peace,'*" a sardonic Republican commented a month later, "—more guns have been fired, and more men wounded, in Massachusetts, . . . than during the whole of the war." Bitter Federalists considered the blind celebration clear proof that the nation detested Mr. Madison's war, and an occasional Republican journal warned against premature exultation. *Niles' Register* on the one hand and Feder-

[29] Marquis James, *The Life of Andrew Jackson* (Indianapolis, 1938), p. 252; John Goulding to Carey, Feb. 24, 1815, Lawrence F. Flick, ed., "Selections from the Correspondence of the Deceased Matthew Carey," American Catholic Historical Society, *Records*, XI (1900), 342.

[30] Baker #1 to Castlereagh, Feb. 19, 1815, FO 5/106; *New-York Evening Post*, Feb. 13, 1815; Robert G. Albion, *The Rise of New York Port* (New York, 1939), p. 9.

alist James Lloyd on the other excused the reaction by saying that all Americans knew the commissioners at Ghent incapable of accepting a disgraceful treaty.[31] Perhaps so, but the celebrations—violent in Boston and the convention's Hartford, astonished but thankful in Philadelphia, but above all general throughout the country—did reflect war weariness, a fear that continued war might lead to internal conflict, and eagerness to abandon demands put forward since 1812. Jackson's victory on the one hand, the Hartford convention on the other, made the nation willing to accept a standoff peace. Victory could be claimed later.

On the fourteenth the treaty reached Washington. Secretary Monroe hastened to the Octagon House, the former French legation occupied by Madison after destruction of the White House, and the President welcomed the terms. On Capitol Hill "hurly burly, congratulation and joy" disrupted debate, and exhilaration seems to have confused government offices as well, for an envelope intended to contain official news of the treaty proved, when opened at New Orleans, to cover only an old order respecting militia. Fortunately messengers from the British fleet had already given General Jackson the news.[32]

In the Senate, Rufus King carried a motion calling for Ghent correspondence more recent than that published in November, thus delaying action for a day. The papers, which showed the retreat from many demands in the American *projet* of November 10 as well as the wandering course toward silence on the fishery and Mississippi questions, gave King and his Federalist friends a tactical opening. The New Yorker reportedly poured forty minutes of

[31] *Niles' Register*, March 18, Feb. 25, 1815; *Evening Post*, Feb. 13, 1815: *Kentucky Gazette* (Lexington), Feb. 27, 1815; Lloyd to John Adams, March 8, 1815, James Lloyd Papers, Houghton Library, Harvard University; *Columbian Centinel* (Boston), Feb. 15, 1815; *Connecticut Courant* (Hartford), Feb. 21, 1815; *Aurora* (Philadelphia), Feb. 14, 1815. The *Courant* found gratification in the fact that after the celebration "our fellow-citizens, with their characteristic love of order, observing sobriety even in the midst of pleasure, quietly returned to their homes." Boston celebrations were more riotous.

[32] Brant, *op. cit.*, p. 367; Bigelow to Hannah G. Bigelow, Feb. 14, 1815, Clarence S. Brigham, ed., "Letters of Abijah Bigelow, Member of Congress, to His Wife, 1810–1815," American Antiquarian Society, *Proceedings*, n.s., XL (1931), 405; John S. Bassett, ed., *Correspondence of Andrew Jackson* (7 vols.; Washington, 1926–1933), II, 170–171n.

sarcastic oratory on the war and its backers. Clearly, however, no Federalist could vote against termination of a detested war. No war hawk insisted upon fighting for conquest. On February 16 the Senate unanimously approved the treaty. Its deliberations had been secret, and at the initiative of the administration floor leader the legislators voted to keep the new correspondence from the public.[33] Rather surprisingly, the Federalists observed this injunction.

There remained only the exchange of ratifications. Anthony Baker drifted rather than hastened to Washington with the official British documents, coming in for some American criticism as a result. He arrived on the evening of January 17, was summoned to the Department of State by Monroe, and exchanged ratifications that night at eleven o'clock. So hasty were the Americans that their instrument of ratification, marred by ink spots and bad spelling, had to be replaced with a fair copy two days later.[34] In this clumsy fashion a war of thirty-one months came to a close.

From editorial desks, pulpits, government offices, and the floors of Congress (forced by General Ross's torch to meet in the Patent Office) a flood of commentary spread over the nation. Madison's opponents, never having expected or even desired major British concessions, welcomed the treaty and above all, of course, the return of peace. At the same time, like the Opposition in England, they reminded the country that the administration deserved credit neither for the treaty nor for the conduct of the war. "Yes, the Olive Branch is . . . restored to our bleeding, suffering country," the *Virginia Patriot* admitted, but it emphasized that peace had come only "after . . . a long and gloomy night, in which scarce a ray of hope was seen or felt, by those devoted to the happiness and prosperity of America." [35] In short, Madison had placed the nation in jeopardy.

[33] *Journal of the Executive Proceedings of the Senate of the United States of America*, II (Washington, 1828), 618–621; Charles R. King, *The Life and Correspondence of Rufus King* (6 vols.; New York, 1894–1900), V, 470n.

[34] Baker #1 to Castlereagh, Feb. 19, 1815, FO 5/106; Baker to Hamilton, Feb. 19, 1815, *ibid.*

[35] *Virginia Patriot* (Richmond), Feb. 18, 1815.

Who deserved credit for the escape? Many Federalists gave thanks to "a most unexpected and wonderful interposition of Divine Providence." Others complimented the commissioners at Ghent. Few praised British moderation, for the published dispatches discouraged that tack. None gave credit to Madison, and indeed the *Connecticut Courant* argued that the negotiations succeeded only because the three thousand miles between Washington and Ghent prevented presidential meddling.[36]

Above all, Federalists argued, the terms of the treaty proved the futility of the war they had all along opposed. In 1806, by the Monroe-Pinkney settlement, or in 1812, through talks with Admiral Warren, America could have secured terms at least as good. The war, Federalists repeated over and over again, failed to gain a single objective—not Canada, not an end to impressment, not a code of neutral rights. In the words of a Federalist senator, the treaty was "disgraceful to the government who made the war and the peace." Thus, Senator Christopher Gore continued, the treaty would be judged once the outburst of joyous relief had subsided. Wiser Federalists anticipated efforts to fabricate a legend of victory, victory for which the Republicans might claim credit. "Indeed," commented the always saturnine, often accurate Samuel Taggart a few days after the *Favourite* docked, "I can see this game begun already, and it will probably be attended with some success." [37]

The Republican "game" sometimes involved misleading sleight of hand. The *Intelligencer,* forgetting its own more ambitious desires in 1812, argued that the United States had gone to war to defend her honor, to retaliate in kind for British seizures, to secure repeal of the Orders in Council and—here the newspaper disingenuously downgraded the administration position for two years

[36] Taylor to Monroe, May 26, 1815, James Monroe Papers, Library of Congress; Otis Thompson, *A Sermon Preached on the National Thanksgiving for the Restoration of Peace* (Providence, 1815), p. 17; *Courant*, March 7, 1815.

[37] *Alexandria Gazette*, Feb. 25, 1815; *Virginia Patriot*, Feb. 25, 1815; Gore to Strong, Feb. 18, 1815, Henry Cabot Lodge, *Life and Letters of George Cabot* (Boston, 1877), p. 563; Taggart to Cutler, Feb. 19, 1815, William P. Cutler and Julia P. Cutler, *Life, Journals and Correspondence of Rev. Manasseh Cutler, LL.D.* (2 vols.; Cincinnati, 1888), II, 332–334.

prior to June, 1814—to "oppose" impressment until it ceased. Having thus lowered the crossbar, the *Intelligencer* credited America with a triumphant leap. About two years later, ignoring the still-unpublished American *projet* with its list of rejected demands, to say nothing of available printed evidence, Hezekiah Niles maintained that "we did virtually dictate the treaty of Ghent." [38]

Less ingenious Republicans merely defended silence on the major issues. In any future war, Thomas McKean philosophized, Britain would ignore even the most solemn restrictions on impressment and blockade; thus their omission now was unimportant. Reed Paige, a New Hampshire clergyman whose published sermons supported Republicanism, pointed to the double-edged character of silence; British demands, too, had been ignored.[39] A good debating point in the recent context, Paige's view tested less well against the standards of 1812.

Responding to a presidential cue, many Republicans more effectively argued that only Don Quixotes would have continued the war after American maritime grievances ended. "With the general pacification of Europe," Hezekiah Niles told his readers even before news of peace arrived, "the chief causes for which we went to war . . . have . . . ceased . . . ; it is not for us to quarrel for *forms*—Britain may *pretend* to any 'right' she pleases; provided," Niles added with a show of bravado, "she does not *exercise* it, to our injury." Reverend Paige expressed the same theme more pacifically. Chastened war hawks accepted this reasoning. They could see little point in continuing the war for what Henry Clay dismissed as "mere abstract principle." [40]

As quickly as possible Republicans turned from the treaty to

[38] *National Intelligencer* (Washington), Feb. 23, 1815; *Niles' Register*, Sept. 14, 1816.

[39] McKean to John Adams, July 1, 1815, Thomas McKean Papers, Historical Society of Pennsylvania; Reed Paige, *Two Sermons, Delivered at Hancock, New Hampshire, April 13, 1815* (Concord, 1815), p. 20.

[40] James D. Richardson, ed., *A Compilation of the Messages and Papers of the Presidents* (10 vols.; Washington, 1907), I, 552; *Niles' Register*, Dec. 10, 1814; Reed Paige, *A Sermon, Delivered at Lyndeborough, New-Hampshire, April 20, 1815* (Concord, 1815), p. 15; *Annals of Congress*, 14th Cong., 1st sess., p. 782.

wildly distorted rhapsodies on the war itself. Here they had the enthusiastic coöperation of the American people, who have on the whole found it easier to remember Trenton than Long Island, Omaha Beach than Kasserine. John Quincy Adams, a patriot and also a hard-eyed realist, observed, "my country men . . . look too intently to their Triumphs, & turn their eyes too lightly away from their disasters." Americans forgot or minimized Hull's surrender, the feeble invasions of Canada, the tight blockade and the capture of Washington. They remembered and cherished their frigates' victories and the success of Perry, Macdonough, and Jackson.

The selective memory and the overweening pride of Americans irritated Englishmen. In 1816 a visitor to South Carolina complained, in the bantering tone so common in his Canningite circle, of having to endure frequent hints that "Wellington is inferior in the Military Art to Genl. Jackson, & that Nelson, Rodney, & S^t. Vincent were mere bunglers & drivellers in Naval Tactics, when compared with Ro[d]gers, Decatur, & *handsome* Porter." [41] British visitors chafed under similar suggestions for years after the war.

Sometimes Americans who would have been only too glad to escape from the war in the spring of 1814 retrospectively gave thanks to British stubbornness which continued the contest through the summer and autumn. Since the fall of Napoleon and the opening of direct negotiations America had depended upon her own resources; she owed no thanks, Clay noted with satisfaction, to any European monarch. "No Frenchmen now the conflict wage," a patriotic magazine rhapsodized, "The Briton finds another foe; / And learns amidst the battle's rage, / Columbia's hearts and hands to know." By standing alone after Napoleon's abdication, by gaining victories on the eve of peace, the United States proved its strength. "Peace has come in a most welcome time to delight and astonish us," Joseph Story wrote; ". . . we have stood the contest, single-handed, against the conqueror of Europe; and we are

---

[41] Adams to John Adams, May 29, 1816, Adams Family MSS, Vol. CXLIII; [? E. J.] Stapleton to Bagot, April 11, 1816, Sir Charles Bagot Papers, Levens Hall, Westmorland.

at peace, with all our blushing victories thick crowding on us." [42]

For Republicans and nationalists the war proved that Americans "fresh from the plow" could, like their fathers, defeat hired myrmidons of European tyranny. After all, trained regiments garlanded by victory over Napoleon fled the field at Plattsburg and New Orleans. On the water as well, "in single fight or in squadron," American seamen proved the superior courage of a free people. Our naval heroes, a Republican orator declaimed, "have discovered the grand secret, that the trident of Neptune is not hereditary in a British line." [43] Nationalistic myopia and the fortuitous coincidence of victory and peace converted the war, in American eyes, from a mixed canvas of honor and disgrace to an unrelieved study in success.

Still, it was not necessary, "A Citizen of Philadelphia" pointed out, to "keep the debts and credits of this war, with a mercantile accuracy," to prove its worth. The declaration of war, that "desperate ultimatum of a wronged and forbearing people," and the ability to endure the contest for some thirty months in themselves increased America's self-confidence and raised her reputation abroad. [44] These results became the central argument of those who defended the war against Federalist sneers.

By 1812 the United States government had attracted, in the brutal words of Henry Clay, who as a former war hawk bore no responsibility for the fact, "the scorn of foreign Powers, and the contempt of our own citizens." Since its founding the nation had

---

[42] Speech of Oct. 7, 1815, Hopkins, *op. cit.*, II, 68–69; *Niles' Register*, March 4, 1815; *Port Folio* (Philadelphia), XXVI (1816), 529; Story to Nathaniel Williams, Feb. 22, 1815, William W. Story, *Life and Letters of Joseph Story*, I (Boston, 1851), 254.

[43] *Niles' Register*, March 4, 1815; *Enquirer* (Richmond), Feb. 18, 1815; John Bailey, *An Address, on the Ratification of the Treaty of Peace* (Boston, 1815), pp. 4–5. Forgetting defeats and recapturing the spirit of 1812, Jefferson wrote, "in fighting we have done well. we have good officers at length coming forward, . . . who would soon have planted our standard on the walls of Quebec & Halifax. our men were always good; and after the affair of N. Orleans, theirs would never have faced ours again, and it is long since they have ceased to trust their frigates to sail alone." Jefferson to Gallatin, March 19, 1815, Gallatin MSS.

[44] A Citizen of Philadelphia, *The Second Crisis of America, or a Cursory View of the Peace* (New York, 1815), pp. 4–5.

suffered little but insult and made few effective protests. This line of argument ignored Pinckney's treaty with Spain and the acquisition of Louisiana, both important successes, and virtually invited criticism of Jefferson and Madison, but Republicans passed over the gains and ascribed their heroes' failures to seditious Federalists and cowards of all parties. John Jay's alleged surrender, the disgraceful retreat from the Embargo, the farce of the Cadore letter, and the eddying of Congress in 1810 and 1811 all invited Europe to treat America with contumely and made her own citizens fear for the nation's future.[45]

Then came the war. The declaration ended fears that a republican government could never act vigorously. The contest showed, Madisonian journals argued, that Washington could direct a war and finance it despite the opposition of a wealthy section of the country. The war stimulated industry and manufacturing, which many Republicans now cherished, and taught the nation to develop her always treasured agricultural resources. (William Duane of the *Aurora* even maintained that the new trade in merino wool would pay the cost of war ten times over.) At the very least, as admitted Matthew Lyon, a congressman who lost his seat to a war hawk in 1810 and still thought the war a mistake, the war gave cautious or cowardly men "a portion of National Confidence."[46] These benefits more than repaid the cost of war, in the Republican view.

This being so, the even more important gain of reputation abroad emerged as clear profit. "From a state of humiliation in the eyes of the world," the *Aurora* declared, "we stand on an elevation which now commands the respect of all the world." "Our character has been retrieved from ignominy, and instead of an insulted and pusillanimous people, we rank exalted in the opinion of the surrounding world," a pamphleteer echoed.[47] Such claims

[45] *Annals*, 14th Cong., 1st sess., p. 777; *Aurora*, Feb. 20, 1815; James T. Austin, *An Oration, Pronounced at Lexington, Mass.,* . . . *4th July, 1815* (Boston, 1815), pp. 7–10.

[46] *Aurora*, Feb. 14, 20, 1815; speech of Oct. 7, 1815, Hopkins, *op. cit.*, II, 70; *Enquirer*, Feb. 18, 1815; Lyon to Gallatin, Oct. 27, 1815, Gallatin MSS.

[47] *Aurora*, Feb. 20, 1815; *The Second Crisis*, p. 5.

overstated the case, for many a year would pass before the world admitted America to the company of major states, yet they also contained more than a germ of truth. After 1815 America's diplomatic opponents looked upon her in a different light.

Thus, whatever the terms of the Ghent treaty, the war conferred immense benefits upon the United States, most Americans believed. "Mr. Madison's Administration has proved great points, long disputed in Europe and America," commented ex-President Adams, whose own experience as a wartime president had been particularly unhappy.

1. He has proved that an Administration, under our present Constitution can declare War.

2. That it can make Peace.

3. That Money or no Money; Government or no Government, G. Britain can never conquer this country or any considerable part of it.

4. That our Officers and Men by land are equal to any [British troops] from Spain and Portugal

5. that our transalliganian States, in Patriotism, Bravery Enterprise and Perseverance are at least equal to any in the Union

6. That our Navy, is equal . . . to any that ever floated on the Ocean.[48]

On the floor of Congress in 1816 Henry Clay pressed much the same arguments. "Have we gained nothing by the war?" he asked. "What is our present situation? Respectability and character abroad—security and confidence at home. If we have not obtained in the opinion of some the full measure of retribution, our character and Constitution are placed on a solid basis, never to be shaken." In addition, the Kentucky gamecock reminded his colleagues, there had been a full harvest of glory.[49]

Those who celebrated the war ignored unpleasant facts today's historian must remember. The President and his party thrust an unprepared country into combat. The United States failed to conquer Canada when the task was easy and, after Napoleon's abdication freed British forces for transatlantic service, found itself in a

[48] John Adams to McKean, July 6, 1815, McKean MSS.
[49] *Annals*, 14th Cong., 1st sess., p. 783.

grim struggle for survival. A war begun to secure "indemnity for the past, and security for the future" ended in a treaty that provided neither. By later standards the price of war—2,260 battle deaths, $105 million in direct costs—was tiny; for a young nation it was impressive. From the experience, John Quincy Adams hoped the United States would learn "caution against commencing War without a fair prospect of attaining its objects as well as a good cause." [50]

The "blushing victories thick crowding on us" now seem less impressive than Republicans claimed. Had Jackson abandoned his rampart before New Orleans he would have deserved a firing squad, yet his defensive triumph was adjudged the greatest of the war. Victories won in the open field—the Thames, Chippewa, the more evenly balanced Lundy's Lane—involved tiny forces, had little permanent effect, and were followed by American withdrawals. The best honest claim was that, after starting slowly, American forces had fought British land forces to a standstill. Creditable enough, this achievement was far less than that claimed by patriots.

Unsullied by the cowardice and the mismanagement so frequently visible in land operations, the naval record was somewhat better. Oliver Hazard Perry at Put-in-Bay and Thomas Macdonough off Plattsburg fought with great gallantry and gained the two most important victories, by land or sea, of the war. Privateers and a few national vessels brought the war home to Britain, raiding even in the Irish Sea and the English Channel. Victories gained by American frigates evoked such enthusiasm that even Rufus King, a realist who should have known better, talked of seizing command of the ocean. Actually, as a Virginia congressman had the boldness to declare a few years later, the "victories . . . acquired renown for the American Navy; in that respect only were they valuable. In defending the nation, or obtaining peace, they were without effect." [51] Certainly they did not enable the United States to break the silent vise of blockade, the most important factor in

---

[50] Adams to Everett, March 16, 1816, Adams Family MSS, Vol. CXLIII.
[51] *Annals*, 15th Cong., 2d sess., p. 700.

the balance of naval accounts and one that threatened, after its extension to New England, to crush the nation into separate parts.

In their soberer moments Americans had to remember that until the spring of 1814 Britain fought, not merely with one hand tied behind her back, but really with only a finger or two free to claw the Americans. The surplus of ships made blockade possible, but neither troops nor able commanders nor adequate supplies for building on the lakes crossed the Atlantic. After gaining victory in Europe, Great Britain sent reinforcements to America. Interallied friction, demands for demobilization, a desire for economy, and logistic barriers to speedy deployment meant that only fifteen or twenty regiments from Europe saw action against the Americans.

Fortunately for the United States the British government decided to disembarrass itself of the conflict rather than risk new campaigns in 1815. Albeit less consistently than the public, the ministry sometimes dreamed of vengeance on the Americans. Deprived of this hope, at least for 1814, Downing Street abandoned its indecisive diplomatic offensive at Ghent and sought relief from what Castlereagh called "the millstone of an American war." [52] Without this burden the country could face the new challenges of European politics with stronger confidence. Thus in 1814, as in the two preceding years, European problems prevented England from bringing more than a fraction of its military or diplomatic power to bear upon the United States.

Military victory eluded the Madisonians, and Ghent was more an escape from potential disaster than a triumph. Yet the silent treaty served America well, for, as John Quincy Adams' historian grandson observed, the negotiators "gained their greatest triumph in referring all their disputes to be settled by time, the final negotiator, whose decision they could safely trust." [53] Thus, to look ahead, the Americans gained much of what they wished with respect to the fishery, whereas with the omission of articles reaffirm-

[52] Castlereagh to Liverpool, Jan. 2, 1815, Wellington, *op. cit.*, IX, 523.
[53] Henry Adams, *History of the United States during the Administrations of Jefferson and Madison* (9 vols.; New York, 1889–1891), IX, 53.

ing the right of British subjects to use the Mississippi River and to trade with Indians in American territory these matters disappeared. With them ended British interference in affairs between the tribes and the government at Washington.

Other gains, largely psychological rather than material, repaid the costs of the war. "In 1815," to quote Henry Adams once again, "for the first time Americans ceased to doubt the path they were to follow." [54] Before that year they had reason for their doubts. The bitter battles of Federalists against Republicans; the constant separatist plots, usually Federalist but sometimes Burrite; the apparent inability to develop positive policies after the retirement of Hamilton; the steady diet of diplomatic failure; the factionalism and the optimistic yet passive political philosophy of the ruling party—all made dubious the future of the nation-state. Could the Constitution survive? Was the United States really a nation?

The war answered these questions, not forever, for a sterner challenge later arose over slavery, but for more than a generation. Under the pressure of war, moderate Federalists turned their backs on the irreconcilables, and the moderates themselves learned from the fiasco of Hartford the political foolhardiness of attempting to use national troubles for factional advantage. On their part the Republicans shucked off some of the half-idealistic, half-doctrinaire tenets of twenty years' standing. The politics of the so-called "Era of Good Feeling" were filled with battles, but in none was the future of the nation called into question. The declaration of war showed that a republican government could act with vigor. The limited successes of the war, inflated by Americans into magnificent triumphs, showed that the government could mobilize an important fraction of national power even in the face of strong internal opposition. The failures taught the necessity for national union and sacrifice, held out the hope of greater accomplishments in the future.

Perhaps because his foreign birth and education gave him a perspective denied most Americans, Albert Gallatin was one of

[54] *Ibid.*, p. 220.

the most dispassionate political analysts of his day. In May, 1815, responding to Matthew Lyon's negative comments on the war, Gallatin wrote:

The War has been productive of evil & good: but I think the good preponderates. . . . Under our former system we were become too selfish, too much attached exclusively to the acquisition of wealth, above all too much confined in our political opinions to local & state objects. The war has renewed & reinstated the National feelings & character, which the Revolution had given, & which were daily lessened. The people have now more general objects of attachment with which their pride & political opinions are connected. They are more Americans: they feel & act more as a Nation, and I hope that the permanency of the Union is thereby better secured.[55]

"They are more Americans": this was the great political legacy of the war.

In the diplomatic sphere, too, the United States made impressive gains. From 1803 to 1812 Jefferson and Madison, though they did not always spurn compromise, sought goals their more realistic predecessors recognized could be obtained only at great cost. Humiliation and failure resulted, creating their own momentum. In Britain the feeling grew that the Americans would absorb any insult. "Our government," Reed Paige maintained with much justice, "was compelled to enter into war with her, or let the rights of our fellow-citizens be her sport, and our independence and our sovereignty be a mere name, and sink forever in the dust." [56]

The declaration of war and the ability to endure the contest for more than two years surprised Britain and made all Europe reëxamine its assumptions. In this sense, as Hezekiah Niles claimed, the war "REDEEMED THE INDEPENDENCE OF THE UNITED STATES." Never again would a European power look upon the Americans, as had Napoleon and Perceval, as a semicolonial, dependent people. Never again, not even during civil war at home, would the managers of American diplomacy face Europe with so weak an armory of weapons. "Hereafter," a

[55] Gallatin to Lyon, May 7, 1815, Gallatin MSS.
[56] Paige, *Two Sermons*, p. 18.

New York Federalist wrote, "we can look confidently in the Face of any Nation which may feel a Disposition to trample on our Rights." [57]

"All things considered," John Quincy Adams complained to his father, "my country men appear to me inclined to be rather more proud than they have reason [to be] of the War." Adams, himself not immune to the heady food of national pride, ought to have recognized that nationalism, having suffered privation for a decade, drew more than ordinary sustenance from the diet offered between 1812 and 1815. "The war of 1812," one orator assured fellow citizens who scarcely required the assurance, "has drawn into notice the republican virtue of the American people, and established the foundations of your national character." Projecting the same theme into the future, the Richmond *Enquirer* declared: "The sun never shone upon a people whose destinies promised to be grander." [58] The rebirth of national confidence was the overriding legacy of the war.

[57] *Niles' Register*, March 4, 1815; Decius Wadsworth to Wolcott, March 30, 1815, Wolcott Family Papers, Connecticut Historical Society, Vol. XXIII.
[58] Adams to John Adams, May 29, 1816, Adams Family MSS, Vol. CXLIII; Austin, *op. cit.*, p. 6; *Enquirer*, Feb. 18, 1815.

THE UNEASY ARMISTICE

Throughout 1815 fear, suspicion, and recrimination hung over relations between Britain and the United States. Despite their noisy claims few Americans truly believed the "triumph" over England assured permanent peace and, conditioned to insult, they watched Britain warily. Distracted by European events, Lord Castlereagh barely hinted at a policy that later gave him a place among the major architects of the permanent peace.

A spate of histories of the war in effect warned Americans to keep up their guard. The administration's attitude emerged, a few short weeks after peace, in the appearance, first serially in the *Aurora* and then in pamphlet editions, of *An Exposition of the Causes and Character of the Late War*. Written as war propaganda by Secretary of the Treasury Dallas from an outline by Madison and only modified by the insertion of "Late" in the title when the surprising news of peace arrived, the *Exposition* roundly denounced England. The administration tried to conceal its connection with the pamphlet, and indeed it is not certain that Madison authorized public release, although he did not disapprove and had himself circulated it privately. When word leaked out that

the Secretary of the Treasury had written the pamphlet, an up-
roar arose in America and then in England.[1] John Russell, Jr.,
hastily compiled a documentary *History of the War, Between the
United States and Great-Britain,* applying principles of selection
fanning the spirit to which Dallas' pamphlet appealed. In 1816
Robert B. McAfee, a Kentuckian wounded at the battle of the
Thames, published his *History of the Late War in the Western
Country.* In the preface McAfee confessed to "a natural attachment to his country and hostility to her enemies according to their
deserts." His *History* amply demonstrated these qualities.[2]

A book of a slightly different sort, Matthew Carey's *The Olive
Branch: or, Faults on Both Sides, Federal and Democratic,* gained
the widest circulation, passing through six editions before the end
of 1815. In the autumn of 1814, fearful for the fate of his country, "prostrate at the feet of a ruthless foe," this veteran publicist
hastily composed an appeal for national unity. To show his impartiality Carey criticized Republican weaknesses as well as Federalist obstructionism. He heavily garlanded his work with essays
and documents supporting his thesis that Americans ought to use
their energies to fight England, not one another. The *Olive
Branch,* first appearing in November, 1814, became immensely
popular after a slow start. Constantly revised and expanded by
Carey, the pamphlet came to exceed 400 pages in length. In the
preface to the first edition after the news of peace, Carey denied
that he wished to "perpetuate the hatred between the two countries." But, he continued, "I am much deceived, if a plain and
candid exposure of the vexatious, harassing, insulting, and out-
rageous policy pursued by . . . England . . . will not be the

[1] Alexander J. Dallas, *An Exposition of the Causes and Character of the Late War*
(Boston, 1815); Irving Brant, *James Madison: Commander in Chief* (Indianapolis,
1961), pp. 382–383; Joy to Madison, March 30, 1816, William C. Rives Collection,
Library of Congress. Jefferson, who advised release of the pamphlet, later inaccurately
stated that the government had tried but failed to suppress it. Jefferson to Madison,
March 23, 1815, Andrew A. Lipscomb and Albert E. Bergh, eds., *The Writings of
Thomas Jefferson* (Memorial ed., 20 vols.; Washington, 1903–1904), XIV, 290–291;
Jefferson to Mme. de Staël, July 3, 1815, *ibid.,* p. 332.

[2] John Russell, Jr., ed., *The History of the War, Between the United States and
Great-Britain* (Hartford, 1815); Robert B. McAfee, *History of the Late War in the
Western Country* (Lexington, 1816).

best means of preventing a recurrence of such impolitic and unjust conduct. They have deeply injured us." [3]

Stimulated by Dallas, Carey, and the others, most Americans found it easy to remember the past and to think of the future in similar terms. Jefferson, like John Quincy Adams, pronounced the treaty an armistice to last only until the first impressment or until any other old-style violation of the rights of the United States. He invoked Cato's motto, *Carthago delenda est,* and only half facetiously suggested that some "Scipio Americanus" might have to obliterate London. In 1816 Henry Clay declared: "That man must be blind to the indications of the future, who cannot see that we are destined to have war after war with Great Britain, until, if one of the two nations be not crushed, all grounds of collision shall have ceased between us."

Clay of course had once led the war hawks, while Jefferson often used language that belies his reputation as a pacifist. Yet Federalists spoke the same way, partly because the war they detested raised their confidence in American strength and partly because the obliteration of their bête noire, revolutionary France, destroyed some of the reason for their friendship for England. James Emott, in 1812 a vigorous, partisan opponent of war and in 1815 speaker of the New York assembly, predicted that "at no very distant time we shall have another English war, when," he added hopefully, "with a more vigorous administration, and an army and a navy . . . to commence with, the British must be driven from the continent if not from this quarter of the globe." Rufus King, a major figure in the Anglo-American rapprochement of the 1790's, forecast "repeated struggles . . . upon the Ocean before the undisputed Trident reposes in our Possession." [4]

In the spring of 1815 the President warned against overhasty

---

[3] Matthew Carey, *The Olive Branch: or, Faults on Both Sides, Federal and Democratic* (6th ed.; Philadelphia, 1815), pp. 6, 27–28, and *passim.*

[4] Jefferson to Crawford, Feb. 11, 1815, postscript, Lipscomb and Bergh, *op. cit.,* XIV, 244; Jefferson to Francis C. Gray, March 4, 1815, *ibid.,* p. 271; *Annals of Congress,* 14th Cong., 1st sess., p. 787; Emott to King, Feb. 19, 1815, Rufus King Papers, New-York Historical Society, Vol. XIV; King to Wolcott, Feb. 26, 1815, Wolcott Family Papers, Connecticut Historical Society, Vol. XXIII.

demobilization. "Neither the pacific dispositions of the American people nor the pacific character of their political institutions," he told Congress, "can altogether exempt them from that strife which appears . . . the ordinary lot of nations." He and Monroe, whose experiences as secretary of war and emergency scout during the British descent on Washington taught him the need for trained forces, saw their proposals suffer the usual fate of postwar military recommendations. Congress preferred a more Republican, economical course. The legislature pared standing forces to the bone. Algerian corsairs unwittingly saved the oceangoing navy, but on the Great Lakes construction ceased. Congress ordered the army reduced to half the size Madison desired.

Actual reductions followed slowly, primarily for administrative reasons, for the apparatus of government was no better prepared for rapid demobilization than for the demands of war. Perhaps, too, the administration dragged its feet. Certainly the government feared renewed conflict with those Indian tribes that still refused to make peace and, like the country, worried when British forces did not immediately evacuate their *points d'appui* on American territory. In 1815 the army demobilized only 5,000 men, less than one-seventh of its strength, and two years after the peace the armed forces were still one-third larger than they had been in 1812.[5]

John Quincy Adams, who during 1815 observed the British government at close range, shared his countrymen's suspicions. All the "combustible materials" in both countries, he sighed, made a long peace highly unlikely. His venerable father agreed, writing to Jefferson in 1816, "Britain will never be our Friend, till We are her Master."[6] For the Adamses, like most Americans, the

---

[5] James D. Richardson, ed., *A Compilation of the Messages and Papers of the Presidents* (10 vols.; Washington, 1907), I, 553; Monroe to Madison, Feb. 22, 1815, Rives Collection; *Niles' Weekly Register* (Baltimore), March 4, 1815; Brant, *op. cit.*, pp. 381–382; *Historical Statistics of the United States, Colonial Times to 1957*, Bureau of the Census (Washington, 1960), p. 737.

[6] Adams to Plumer, Oct. 5, 1815, Worthington C. Ford, ed., *The Writings of John Quincy Adams* (7 vols.; New York, 1913–1917), V, 401; John Adams to Jefferson, Dec. 16, 1816, Lester J. Cappon, ed., *The Adams-Jefferson Letters* (2 vols.; Chapel Hill, 1959), II, 502.

settlement of 1814 was an intermission in the Anglo-American quarrel, not adjournment sine die.

For a few months Napoleon's return from Elba seemed likely to reopen the debate. Henry Clay, then in London, wearily anticipated, or at least feared, renewal of the quarrels that preceded the War of 1812. The President shared Clay's fears. "It is . . . probable," he wrote, ". . . that a spirit of revenge, . . . a pride in shewing to the world that neither the war nor the peace with this country, has impaired her maritime claims, or her determination to exert them, will all unite, with the object of distressing France, . . . in stimulating her [Britain] into her former violences on the Ocean." As the British chargé reported, all Americans hoped to avoid involvement in European troubles. Yet, like their president, they feared a renewal of "former violences" and were determined not to tolerate them. At a Fourth of July celebration James Monroe toasted "American Neutrality; should Europe again be embroiled, let our neutrality be founded in justice, and," he added, "maintained with firmness." [7] The nation agreed.

Some Republican editors hailed the imperial eagle's progress from Elba to the Bay of Jouan to Grenoble to Paris. They ignored the bleak warning of the semiofficial *Intelligencer:* "This nation has nothing to hope, nothing to ask, from the favor of any foreign power." *Niles' Register,* the Richmond *Enquirer,* and the *Independent Chronicle* of Boston all maintained that the coup, an admittedly crude expression of the will of the French people, marked an important advance in the endless struggle against despotism and legitimacy. For the first time, Jefferson commented, Napoleon had the right on his side. The ex-President apparently forgot that he and his party had once justified 18 Brumaire in similar terms.

Since Brumaire, most Republicans had learned to distrust Napoleon. They cannot have given much credit to the myth, propagated in France by the despot himself, that he represented a sort of

[7] Clay to Crawford, March 23, 1815, James F. Hopkins, ed., *The Papers of Henry Clay* (Lexington, 1959———), II, 11; Madison to Monroe, n.d. [May, 1815], James Madison Papers, Library of Congress, Vol. LVIII, fol. 101; Brant, *op. cit.,* p. 389.

cryptorepublicanism. When Niles argued that a strong French state would check the "overgrown influence" of England he exposed the mainspring of his feeling, a deep fear and jealousy of Great Britain. This argument disgusted Albert Gallatin, always a voice of reason in the Republican party. Gallatin excoriated the stupidity of editors who, "carried away by natural aversion to our only dangerous enemy, . . . take up the cause of that despot & conqueror, and . . . represent him, as the champion of liberty, who has been her most mortal enemy." [8] Apparently the nation agreed, for the newspaper campaign ignited no flame of opinion in favor of Napoleon.

Marshal Ney's charge broke upon Wellington's squares of infantry before Anglo-American relations were put to severe trial. During the Hundred Days, British cruisers did reappear off New York, threatening once again to cut off American trade. There were a few instances of impressment, almost all in British ports, where His Majesty's right to recover the services of his own subjects, even those in American crews, had never been challenged. The American government never felt called upon to make formal representations to England.

Although a long European war would probably have driven Britain to harsher measures, the actual record suggests that the British government learned more from the War of 1812 than did the Americans. In June, Foreign Secretary Castlereagh assured the American minister that "the Admiralty was now occupied in prescribing regulations for the naval Officers which he hoped would prevent all cause of complaint." London neither promulgated orders in council along the old lines nor issued press warrants to officers at sea. The press-gangs at home almost always acted with great care. When a captain who overstepped the line called at a Dutch port the British minister ordered him home to explain his

---

[8] *National Intelligencer* (Washington), May 4, 1815; *Niles' Register*, May 20, 1815; *Enquirer* (Richmond), May 10, 1815; *Independent Chronicle* (Boston), May 1, 1815; Jefferson to John Adams, Aug. 10, 1815, Lipscomb and Bergh, *op. cit.*, XIV, 345–346; Gallatin to Jefferson, Nov. 27, 1815, Albert Gallatin Papers, New-York Historical Society. Gallatin's letter, nominally only a discussion of the newspapers, may also have been a veiled criticism of Jefferson himself.

conduct and forced him to release the seaman involved, quite possibly a British subject.[9]

The first accounts of Napoleon's return caused a flurry at Washington. Without waiting to consult the President, who was vacationing at "Montpelier," the secretaries ordered Commodore Stephen Decatur to postpone his departure for a campaign against Algiers. In the Mediterranean Decatur's squadron would be a hostage to the Royal Navy or might even, Monroe feared, be seized by the English. The President approved the cabinet decision, good evidence of distrust of Britain, and also agreed to slow army discharges. Secretary Dallas urged him to issue, upon the first official word of war in Europe, a strong statement of his determination to maintain American rights. Monroe agreed that only convincing evidence of that determination could prevent renewal of the old, sad story of neutrality.

This alarm quickly evaporated, partly because British troops finally began to evacuate Maine, thus indicating that Downing Street shunned a quarrel. The *National Intelligencer* stressed the importance of avoiding entanglement in European travails and minimized the chances of a new war for neutral rights. Although the *Intelligencer* demanded respect for American rights, it used language far milder than that of Dallas and Monroe only a few days before, and President Madison never issued an official proclamation of neutrality. The government soon decided to permit Decatur to sail after all, resumed army discharges, and rejected the Secretary of State's proposal for a special mission to England.[10]

So swiftly did events move that only one regiment engaged in the American war, the 4th Foot, reached Europe in time to serve at Waterloo. Early in August reports of this bloody struggle

[9] Adams #1 to Monroe, June 23, 1815, Department of State Archives, National Archives, Despatches, Great Britain, Vol. XIX; Eustis to Madison, private, Aug. 18, 1815, Madison MSS; Brant, *op. cit.*, p. 392.

[10] Crowninshield to Madison, May 1, 1815, Madison MSS; Monroe to Madison, April 30, 1815, Rives Collection; Madison to Monroe, May 2, 1815, James Monroe Papers, Library of Congress; Dallas to Madison, May 2, 1815, Madison MSS; Monroe to Madison, May 4, 1815, Rives Collection; *Intelligencer*, May 4, 1815; Dallas to Madison, May 12, 1815, Rives Collection; Dallas to Madison, May 23, 1815, Madison MSS.

reached the United States. The *Independent Chronicle*, as if to confirm its standing as one of the most prejudiced and inaccurate papers in the country, at first argued that the British casualty list showed that Wellington's army had been effectively destroyed.[11] Soon this hope collapsed. Napoleon sailed for St. Helena, there to compose memoirs which among other things reaffirmed his contempt for Jefferson and Madison. With him departed for a century the danger of serious quarrels over British interference with American neutral trade.[12]

Not only the imperial comet cast a harsh light upon Anglo-American relations in 1815. Flames of discord arose all along the Canadian-American frontier.[13] British evacuation of American territory proceeded far too slowly to satisfy the United States, which suspected, without justification except in one instance, that the delays masked unfriendly policy. The evacuation of Maine, which helped to lessen the concern aroused by Napoleon's return, took place late in April. British troops in the Niagara area did not withdraw to Canada until the latter part of May, although they had only a short distance to go. A party under Colonel Robert McDouall remained at Michilimackinac even longer, partly because no alternative station had been prepared and partly because Canadian authorities listened to merchants who urged them not to abandon the key to Indian trade. In riposte the Americans declined to quit their positions on Canadian soil across from Detroit. At last, in July, six months after the treaty, the Americans left Amherstburg and McDouall's men evacuated Michilimackinac.[14]

Amidst the delay and suspicion a different sort of episode passed almost unnoticed. When the British evacuated Castine, Maine, their plan to carry off several American ships long since condemned

---

[11] *Independent Chronicle*, Aug. 3, 1815.

[12] During the Civil War the roles were reversed, Britain complaining against American interference with English shipping.

[13] Alfred L. Burt, *The United States, Great Britain, and British North America from the Revolution to the Establishment of Peace after the War of 1812* (New Haven, 1940), pp. 373–387, provides much of the information on border friction used in the following paragraphs. See also the correspondence of Anthony Baker, Foreign Office Archives, Public Record Office, FO 5/106, 5/107, 5/112.

[14] Astoria, in Oregon, remained in British hands for some time. See pp. 246–247.

by prize courts met with forcible resistance. Major-General Gerard Gosselin declined to answer force with force, referring the matter to Baker for settlement. Washington agreed that the rioters had been in the wrong.[15]

The Americans found it hard to arrange peace with the Indians who had not capitulated before the Treaty of Ghent. Scattered evidence caused them to dust off old complaints against British intrigue. Newspapers printed angry editorials, and the Secretary of State emphasized his concern by protesting directly to Baker and through Adams to Castlereagh. At Baker's request Canadian authorities investigated, eventually satisfying Monroe that McDouall withdrew support from the Indian war as soon as news of the treaty, delayed by a faithless courier, reached Michilimackinac. Between July and October, 1815, the Americans concluded fourteen Indian treaties, and in the autumn an agent of the government reported the Indians more pacifically inclined than at any time for years past.

Both in 1815 and thereafter, British officials carefully avoided encouraging Indian resistance to the United States. In the fall of 1815 Bathurst formally advised a recalcitrant southern chieftain to make his peace with the United States. The governor of Canada warned tribes irritated by American plans to establish forts in their territory that they would get no assistance from His Majesty's government. In 1819 the *Courier*, once an earnest advocate of the barrier-state project, declared: "We might as well suppose that a race of barbarians could be permitted to exist in Cornwall or Yorkshire, with independent rights and privileges, as that the Indian tribes should oppose a barrier to the westward march of American civilization." [16] The Indian issue, so important from 1783 to 1815, ceased to trouble Anglo-American relations.

Throughout 1815 the British complained that Americans encouraged desertions from the forces in Canada. Once, they alleged,

---

[15] Baker #12 to Castlereagh, May 2, 1815, FO 5/106; Dallas to Madison, May 2, 1815, Madison MSS.

[16] Graham to Monroe, Sept. 28, 1815, Monroe MSS; Bathurst to chief of Muscogee tribe, Sept. 21, 1815, FO 5/108; Bagot #26 to Castlereagh, Aug. 12, 1816, FO 5/114; *Courier* (London), Feb. 2, 1819.

the Americans even provided horses to ease the flight of fifty men, and the United States Army enlisted many fugitives from British service. The Americans arrested royal officers dispatched, with cavalier disregard for international boundaries, to recover deserters, and one lieutenant on this service near Detroit was fined the precise sum of $631.48 for inciting a riot. Governor Lewis Cass of Michigan and military officers on both sides showed by their actions that peace did not yet cut very deep. London considered these events unfortunate and ultimately ordered restraint upon its subordinates.

As a gesture of friendship the Liverpool administration permitted Decatur's squadron to refit and replenish at Gibraltar during operations against Algiers, a decision contrary to the feelings of British officers who hoped the Algerians would defeat Decatur. The American navy used the base at Gibraltar spasmodically for several years. Aside from one incident in 1819, relations between the commands were cordial. The Admiralty, however, partly out of suspicion of the Americans, decided not to reduce the size of its Mediterranean squadron below that of Decatur and his successors.[17]

The positive gains of this gesture were as nothing compared with the fruits of Castlereagh's efforts to seal off a threatening episode. Six thousand prisoners at Dartmoor became surly when, because the treaty of peace caught the American agent for prisoners without transport to ship them home, they were not immediately released. On April 6, 1815, jittery guards opened fire, killing five Americans and wounding thirty-four, two mortally. The Foreign Secretary quickly arranged an investigation by one Briton and one American, the son of Rufus King. Their report, critical of the

[17] Adams #21 to Monroe, Nov. 21, 1815, Despatches, Great Britain, Vol. XXIX; Milne to George Hume, May 24, 1815, Edgar E. Hume, ed., "Letters Written during the War of 1812 by the British Naval Commander in American Waters (Admiral Sir David Milne)," *William and Mary Quarterly*, 2d series, X (1930), 296; Castlereagh #1 to G. Crawfurd Antrobus, Aug. 14, 1819, FO 5/143; Melville to Bathurst, Sept. 2, 1815, Francis Bickley, ed., *Report on the Manuscripts of Earl Bathurst* (London, 1923), pp. 380–381. In the letter cited above Melville laid down the principle that no British squadron anywhere should be smaller than its American counterpart. Two years later, although primarily for reasons of prestige, he sent a ship of the line to the Mediterranean when the Americans ordered one there. Melville to Bathurst, Aug. 11, 1817, *ibid*.

troops' lack of discipline, in general excused the affray as an unfortunate accident. Castlereagh extended the Prince Regent's regrets and offered compensation to families of the dead. This news reached the United States only a short time after news of the affair itself. A flurry of editorials on the "shocking massacre," as Niles called it, ended when the administration declared itself satisfied that no malice had been involved.[18]

Other issues that arose in 1815—and proved longer-lived—involved the meaning of the Treaty of Ghent. Article I prohibited the "carrying away . . . of . . . any Slaves or other private property" when British (or American) forces withdrew from enemy territory. Immediately after ratification, a dispute arose over the large number of slaves—the Americans later officially claimed more than 3,600—carried away by the Royal Navy. The British denied that Article I covered slaves on their ships, even ships in American territorial waters, when peace came. The Americans insisted that it did, and the evidence they presented showed that their commissioners at Ghent had drafted Article I with this question in mind.

After several years the two countries submitted their dispute to the Czar. Then secretary of state, John Quincy Adams found "something whimsical in the idea that the United States and Great Britain . . . should go to the Slavonian Czar of Muscovy to find out their own meaning, in a sentence written by themselves, in the language common to them both." The idea proved satisfactory as well as whimsical when Russia decided in favor of the Americans. After further disagreement over the amount of compensation, in 1826 the British agreed to pay $1,200,000 to quiet American claims.[19]

No one at Ghent expected silence to end the problem of the

---

[18] Report of F. Seymour Larpent and Charles King, April 26, 1815, FO 5/111; Castlereagh to Clay and Gallatin, May 22, 1815, *ibid.*; *Niles' Register*, June 24, 1815; Baker #25 to Castlereagh, July 20, 1815, FO 5/107.

[19] George Jackson #16 to Canning, Dec. 15, 1824, FO 5/188; June 26, 1820, Charles F. Adams, ed., *Memoirs of John Quincy Adams* (12 vols.; Philadelphia, 1874–1877), V, 160; Samuel F. Bemis, *John Quincy Adams and the Foundations of American Foreign Policy* (New York, 1949), pp. 231–233, 293.

fishery, and they were right. In May, 1815, Washington learned that British ships had turned away fishermen off Newfoundland. When the American government complained vehemently, the cabinet revoked Admiral Griffith's unauthorized orders and directed that, for 1815 only, he permit American fishermen to carry on their business. Downing Street did not abandon its claim that the right had ceased and, moreover, refused to permit curing on British shores even though it tolerated fishing in British waters.[20] Thus a threatening cloud hung over the fishery.

Although the American commissioners at Ghent had full powers in matters of commerce, from the very outset their British companions had declined to discuss trade questions. When the conference disbanded, Russell returned to his post at Stockholm and Bayard headed for the United States, landing only a week before death overtook him on August 6. The others decided to go to London in pursuit of a treaty of commerce. First, Albert Gallatin visited his childhood home at Geneva, while Adams and Clay went to Paris. Gallatin and Clay crossed the Channel in April. Adams waited in the French capital for the arrival of his wife and eight-year-old son after a long overland trip from Russia, and then for news of his appointment as minister to Great Britain. Only then, having indulged his insatiable appetite for the theater and observed Napoleon's return to the Tuileries, did he set off for London.

Although the Americans expected encouragement from Monroe, when at last his instructions did reach Europe they simply suggested reciprocal legislation to eliminate discriminatory duties. Castlereagh also showed no eagerness to tackle the thorny problem of commerce. The buzzing of Clay and Gallatin distracted him from the larger challenges of the Hundred Days, but he saw that, faced by a new European war, he must not annoy an important neutral. Thus when Clay and Gallatin, angered at British

[20] Baker #14, #24 to Castlereagh, May 6, July 19, 1815, FO 5/106; Monroe to Adams, July 21, 1815, Department of State Archives, National Archives, Diplomatic Instructions, All Countries, Vol. VII; Bathurst #10 to Baker, Sept. 7, 1815, FO 5/105; Bemis, *op. cit.*, pp. 234–235.

delays, hinted they would return home in a huff, Castlereagh appointed Goulburn, William Adams, and Frederick J. Robinson, vice-president of the Board of Trade, to negotiate.[21]

Gallatin and Clay opened the negotiations with an audacious statement of American requirements on commerce, neutral rights, and impressment. At informal conferences on May 11 and 16 Robinson and his colleagues brought the Americans down to earth. In reply to the American request that the British West Indies be opened to American ships they declared that their government could not change a policy followed without deviation for centuries. (This statement was not quite fair, for in practice shipping shortages had forced Britain to open the West Indies during the Napoleonic Wars.) The Englishmen warned that they expected no good to come of a discussion of neutral rights. "The Maritime Security of Great Britain was at stake on One side," they argued, "and a mere convenience of Navigation on the other." [22] Lacking weapons to force British reconsideration, Clay and Gallatin abandoned these issues.

Formal negotiations began with the presentation of an American *projet* on June 7, and continued four weeks. Robinson and Gallatin dominated proceedings, partly because John Quincy Adams, with unusual self-restraint, declined a major role in negotiations begun before his arrival. Both sides readily agreed to prohibit discriminatory charges, designed to encourage their respective merchant marines, on commerce between the United States and the home islands of Great Britain. As Congress had already passed legislation along these lines and England had long recognized she could not monopolize the carriage of transatlantic trade, this revivification of Article XIV of Jay's Treaty cannot be considered a major accomplishment.

---

[21] Monroe to Adams, March 13, 1815, Instructions, Vol. VII; Gallatin to Monroe, Nov. 27, 1815, Gallatin MSS; Clay and Gallatin to Monroe, May 18, 1815, Department of State Archives, National Archives, Records of Negotiations Connected with the Treaty of Ghent, Vol. I.

[22] Clay and Gallatin to Monroe, May 18, 1815, Ghent Negotiations, Vol. I; Heads of an unofficial conference . . ., May 11, 1815, FO 5/109.

The chief arguments arose over two other branches of trade formerly permitted by Jay's Treaty, trade across the Canadian-American border and with British possessions in India. The British wanted to resume the fur trade on the old basis, a suggestion that provoked apoplectic complaint from Clay and found no sympathy in his colleagues. The Americans' reaction, Robinson warned them, threatened to prevent agreement on trade with the British East Indies. Clay, Gallatin, and Adams declined to couple the two issues. Then, as if to ensure that all anger should not be on their side, they requested free use of the St. Lawrence from the interior to the sea. Without this, they maintained, no agreement to free Canadian-American trade from duties would be truly reciprocal. Deadlock ensued, and after two weeks Robinson was ready to drop the whole wearisome business.

Ultimately, by agreeing to limit the agreement to four years, the Americans got their way on India. They paid no other price for the concession. As neither side would give way on Canada, this subject was dropped. The convention—Gallatin objected to the grander title of "treaty"—dealt solely with trade across the Atlantic and with India.[23] In both instances it merely restored the *status quo ante bellum*, thus conforming to the pattern of Ghent.

At the last moment, when fair copies of the agreement were in preparation, John Quincy Adams stepped forward. Taking up a congenial task directed by Monroe's recent instructions, he insisted upon the principle of *alternat*, that the words "Great Britain" and "United States" should alternately take precedence throughout the document and that the plenipotentiaries should sign, each on their own copies, in the place of honor on the left-hand side. Omission of the *alternat* in the Treaty of Ghent, and indeed in most other American treaties, Adams felt, tacitly admitted the subordi-

[23] Robinson, Goulburn, and William Adams #1 to Castlereagh, June 7, 1815, FO 5/109; Adams, Clay, and Gallatin to Monroe, July 3, 1815, and enclosures, Ghent Negotiations, Vol. I; Robinson to Castlereagh, private, June 21, 1815, FO 5/109; Bemis, *op. cit.*, p. 224n; Gallatin to Monroe, Nov. 25, 1815, Gallatin MSS. William Adams received £500, one-quarter the sum given him for services at Ghent, for his role in these negotiations. Endorsement on William Adams to Hamilton, Feb. 4, 1816, FO 5/118.

nate status of the United States. He and Monroe had precedent on their side, for in Europe major powers never failed to insist upon the *alternat*. Clay and Gallatin scoffed at their colleague's interest in a mere matter of form. Adams found it more difficult to gain their support, which he did only after angrily threatening to withhold his signature, than to gain British acceptance. On July 3 both delegations signed the commercial convention of 1815, *alternat* and all.[24]

Aside from this symbolic, precedent-making triumph for American nationalism—and there is no evidence that the Englishmen felt the issue important enough to refer to Castlereagh—the convention of 1815 hardly represented a victory for either side or an important step in their commercial relations. The Americans, who gained reëntry into Indian markets, surrendered, at least for the term of the convention, the weapon of discriminatory charges on transatlantic commerce as a means of forcing open the British West Indies. The British protected their peacetime monopoly of trade with English islands in the Caribbean, but failed to gain permission for Canadians to resume a trade believed, but erroneously believed, to be a major factor in Canada's economic health.

Both nations greeted the convention with almost thunderous silence. A few Opposition papers, hypocritically bewailing the surrender of Canadian rights, attempted to make political capital. In identical articles the *Sun* and the *Times* more realistically dismissed the convention as comparatively unimportant, and in the end the government's enemies in Parliament did not challenge it.

When Clay and Gallatin, bearing the American copy, reached home in September, the President declined to call the Senate into special session. Some merchants grumbled at the failure to open the West Indies. At its regular session in December the Senate nearly unanimously approved the convention, "not because it will do much good," Rufus King commented, "but because it can do little harm: in truth it is scarcely worth the wax of its seals." Even Gallatin agreed. He considered the convention, although perhaps

---

[24] Bemis, *op. cit.*, pp. 225–227.

evidence that England sought no war of duties and discriminations with America, a very modest step forward.[25]

Ratification came at the end of an uncertain year in which England and the United States reaped the benefits of peace and wondered if the new day would last. Beginning with the *Milo* of Boston, Captain Glover, which arrived at Liverpool on the last day of March, a steady stream of American merchantmen entered British ports, taking advantage of the unexpected, unusual, and possibly short-lived reopening of Anglo-American trade. In 1815 America shipped more goods to the British Empire than in any year since 1807.[26] English merchants exported unprecedented amounts of manufactured goods to the United States,[27] often at prices so low that complaints against British "dumping" helped secure passage of a protective tariff by Congress in 1816.

Surging waves of commerce failed to wash away the obstacles to understanding. The commercial convention, omitting American trade with the West Indies or Canadian traffic with the Indians, demonstrated the strength of old prejudices. Friction and suspicion on the frontier, disagreement over the meaning of the Treaty of Ghent, Admiral Griffith's action against American fishermen, and the Foreign Secretary's obvious reluctance to open commercial negotiations all suggested that serious controversy had only been postponed.

Napoleon's return, which threatened to involve America and England in a second war over neutral and belligerent rights, ex-

[25] Adams to Russell, Dec. 14, 1815, Ford, *op. cit.*, V, 442; *Sun* (London), Jan. 18, 1816; *Times* (London), Jan. 18, 1816; Madison to Monroe, Sept. 12, 1815, Monroe MSS; King to Edward King, Dec. 23, 1815, Charles R. King, *The Life and Correspondence of Rufus King* (6 vols.; New York, 1894–1900), V, 495–496; Gallatin to Madison, Sept. 4, 1815, Gallatin MSS; Gallatin to Monroe, Nov. 25, 1815, *ibid.*

[26] *Liverpool Mercury*, March 31, 1815; Adam Seybert, *Statistical Annals . . . of the United States of America* (Philadelphia, 1818), pp. 134–140. Seybert's figures, which cover the year beginning October 1, 1814, show exports for that year, including three months of war, to have been worth $21,600,000, approximately $200,000 less than in 1810. Peacetime exports during the last three months of the calendar year 1815 undoubtedly allowed it to outstrip 1810.

[27] George R. Porter, *The Progress of the Nation*, ed. F. W. Hirst (rev. ed.; London, 1912), p. 479.

posed the underlying sympathies of American Republicans. At the same time it propelled Downing Street toward a limited commercial arrangement and made Americans remember the profits of neutrality. In these ways, and perhaps by causing England to recall troops to Europe with all possible speed, the Corsican tyrant served a cause he feared, reconciliation between the English-speaking peoples.

Such an outcome was by no means clear in 1815. On Independence Day a passionate Republican orator, James T. Austin, the son-in-law of Elbridge Gerry, declared:

If that iron colossus, who once bestrode the continent of Europe, was an object of alarm, how much more dangerous is that . . . tremendous tyranny, which claims empire over ocean, and would subjugate not a continent, but the world. That monstrous and gigantic power, which knows no law but its own pleasure, and freed from all moral obligation, carries on the most cruel desolation, with the accumulated terrors of pride, licentiousness, and plunder. . . . [Britain's] true character [is] vain-glorious, haughty, mean, profligate, unjust; uniting the barbarities of savage life to the more refined cruelties of civilized man.[28]

Passions in both countries, more virulent in America but more nearly unanimous in England, threatened the peace so laboriously constructed at Ghent. First of an endless series of peaceful years, at the time 1815 seemed an angry and uncomfortable harbinger of future trouble.

[28] James T. Austin, *An Oration, Pronounced at Lexington, Mass.,* . . . *4th July, 1815* (Boston, 1815), pp. 16–17.

WARFARE OF THE MIND

As part of their education, students at Westminster School wrote Latin plays performed before admiring parents. Just after the War of 1812 the young British thespians presented the tale of a misguided young man who planned to emigrate to America. "What!" the hero expostulated, "to that country which is beyond the ocean: a country barbarous in itself, and inhabited by barbarians? . . . Does a senatorial orator dextrously aim to convince his antagonist: he spits plentifully in his face. . . . The highest praise of a merchant, is his skill in lying; the great anxiety of a general, to manage his diarrhoea." The young actor, clutching his incongruous toga, pled with Geta to remain in England. "Let the ruined man, the impious wretch, the outlaw, praise America; if you are in your senses, Geta, stay at home."

This piece of billingsgate fell into the hands of the *Port Folio*, a Philadelphia review devoted, it claimed, to the arts. In a reaction entirely characteristic of the postwar period, the *Port Folio* published the Latin original and a translation, plus other British slanders and a rebuttal in kind, for the edification of American patriots.[1]

Deprived of old diplomatic quarrels and only occasionally provided with new ones, the nations seemingly sought to fill the void with what John Quincy Adams called the "warfare of the mind." American nationalism was cruder, brasher, and more narrowly focused against one enemy. In England it was nearly as pervasive and in addition maddeningly condescending. Americans resented, sometimes even denied, their subordination to the standards of a nation that did not respect them. Yet this dependence continued. Sir Walter Scott, for example, was almost as widely read in the United States as in England from the moment *Waverly* appeared in 1814, and many American writers, though seeking to avoid the feudalistic overtones of Scott's romances, aped his plots, forms, and language.[2] At the same time America rang with calls for the establishment of purely national modes in literature and other forms of expression, while even more numerous voices met British pretensions with often extravagant counterattacks.

Only a few Americans admitted, as did Josiah Meigs, a bureaucrat at Washington, that their hatred of England was passionate and instinctive. Most insisted that they acted in self-defense. Hezekiah Niles asked, "Can we love those who are ever . . . abusing and threatening us[?]" His appeal to national prejudices helped make *Niles' Register,* almost overnight, the most widely read American paper. Visitors to England bristled at their hosts' superciliousness, ignorance, and coldness. Young Edward Everett, cut from the Federalist pattern of the conservative and comfortable, returned home a convinced Anglophobe and joined the war against British misrepresentations and ignorance. John Adams and Thomas McKean, retired politicians with time for reflection, agreed after mulling over the record that Britain had never given a single sign of friendship for the United States.[3] Most Americans

---

[1] *Port Folio* (Philadelphia), XXVI (1816), 397–410.

[2] Adams to Robert Walsh, Jr., July 10, 1821, Adams Family Papers, Massachusetts Historical Society, Vol. CXLVII; Benjamin T. Spencer, *The Quest for Nationality* (Syracuse, 1957), pp. 38, 93–95.

[3] Josiah Meigs to Webster, Oct. 5, 1818, Emily E. F. Ford, *Notes on the Life of*

—Niles, Everett, Adams, McKean, and thousands of others—enjoyed the luxury of self-righteousness as they crusaded against England.

The realities behind the pose are not difficult to discern. War left a legacy of hatred—remember the prisoners massacred at the river Raisin! remember the arson at Washington!—as well as inflated self-confidence. Napoleon's downfall removed both a competing magnet for dislike and an excuse for English misdeeds, and thrusting, aspiring America naturally sought to round out the independence gained during the Revolution and confirmed by the Treaty of Ghent. The forms of society and politics, if not yet of culture, drifted slowly apart. Developments in the legal profession provide a good example. Fewer potential leaders sought education at Oxford or the Inns of Court. In American courts, citations of English precedent declined, partly because a native corpus was developing and partly because the country rejected less demo cratic principles. In 1816, to the dismay of some judges, the Supreme Court affirmed in *United States v. Coolidge* that common law had no standing before federal courts.[4] The law developed along national lines suggested by John Marshall and younger men similarly unbound by British-oriented training.

The new spirit particularly infected the young. "All the Young Men are AntiAnglican, and none of them can assign a decent reason for it," complained John Lowell, an unrepentant Anglophile. Like many Jeremiahs, Lowell oversimplified, but not by much. The youthful war hawks of 1812, in fact far less numerous than legend suggests, merely heralded a phalanx of combative postwar nationalists.[5]

Noah Webster (2 vols.; New York, 1912), II, 152; *Niles' Weekly Register* (Baltimore), Aug. 31, 1816; *North American Review* (Boston), XIII (1821), 34–36; Adams to McKean, Aug. 31, 1813, Thomas McKean Papers, Historical Society of Pennsylvania; McKean to Adams, Aug. 28, 1813, *ibid.*

[4] Charles Warren, *The Supreme Court in United States History* (2 vols.; Boston, 1922), I, 439–441.

[5] Lowell to Pickering, Sept. 24, 1820, Timothy Pickering Papers, Massachusetts Historical Society. In 1818 only fourteen or fifteen congressmen and one senator had as much as ten years of seniority. *Niles' Register*, March 21, 1818.

The downfall of Federalism—cautious, conservative, Anglo-phile—helped loose the flood of nationalism. In 1816 the Federalists lost a third of their congressional seats, in 1818 a third of the remnant, and in 1820 they did not even contest Monroe's re-election. On the state level the party remained active in old strong-holds, but it lost all real sense of purpose and much of its strength. In 1817 a coalition led by Oliver Wolcott, a Federalist apostate, captured Connecticut, purest of the party pure. In their weakness the Federalists could no longer afford, even if so inclined, the Anglophile declarations so harmful to them in the past.

Above all the party failed to produce a spokesman on foreign policy. The only important young Federalist, Daniel Webster, who opened his congressional career by charging the President with bias against England, turned to domestic issues after the war. Some older leaders, including Rufus King, followed young Webster's example. Others left the party—Wolcott, for one, and later Josiah Quincy—or relapsed, like Timothy Pickering, into grumbling silence. New England editors and pamphleteers no longer rallied in defense of England. Indeed, the collapse of Anglophilia in once Federalist Yankeeland was the most striking symptom of the new nationalism, and for young patriots like Edward Everett a very gratifying one.[6]

Simultaneously anti-Americanism flourished in England. Even the *Times,* a party in the quarrel, admitted, "In this country, unhappily, we look upon the Americans as the lees of society, and vainly think that the abuse of Jonathan will secure a pre-eminence to John Bull."[7] This spirit, although never so free from challenge as Americans maintained, became stronger after 1814 than it ever had been before the War of 1812. British animosity, John Quincy Adams declared, was "inspired by the two deepest and most malignant passions of the human heart—Revenge and Envy."[8] Only Adams' language was immoderate. The outburst of fury which accompanied the opening of negotiations at Ghent and the sullen

[6] *North American Review,* XIII (1821), 34.
[7] *Times* (London), April 20, 1817, quoted in *Niles' Register,* June 7, 1817.
[8] Adams to Walsh, July 10, 1821, Adams Family MSS, Vol. CXLVII.

reception of the compromise treaty reflected outraged pride. While no one seriously proposed a third war with the Americans, many hoped to put them in their place. Similarly, although economists and indeed the government insisted that American prosperity helped England, most Britons accepted the idea with visible distaste.

Stressing two factors, Adams neglected other roots of British passion, particularly the effect of Napoleon's fall. Even those Britons who criticized selfish aspects of their own country's wartime policy and defended the Jeffersonians against charges of being Napoleon's puppets believed that in resisting the Corsican England had served the world. Englishmen of all persuasions resented the Americans' unwillingness to recognize Britain's contribution to their own safety. "The mastery over France being obtained," commented the American minister at London, "we are destined permanently to take the place of that nation in the English odium." [9]

Moreover, most Britons simply refused to believe that a democratic, competitive society had merit or staying power equal to their own ordered one. Even those who saw some merit in republicanism and economic vitality wondered if the United States had not gone too far. Conservatives did not wonder; they knew. Robert Southey expected the Brazilians, then ruled by a Braganza exile from Portugal, to gain leadership of the transatlantic world. The citizens of the United States, he explained, totally lacked the necessary sense of honor and tended to "level down everything to the dead flat of vulgar influence." A leading London paper even pronounced America the most depraved nation in the civilized world.[10] In effect Southey and the *Star* objected to the Americanness of American society, its relative lack of deference, its comparative fluidity and liveliness.

The *Quarterly Review*, chief spokesman of London conserva-

---

[9] Rush #220 to Adams, Nov. 17, 1821, Department of State Archives, National Archives, Despatches, Great Britain, Vol. XXVI.

[10] Southey to Walter S. Landor, May 7, 1819, John W. Warter, ed., *Selections from the Letters of Robert Southey* (4 vols.; London, 1856), III, 134; *Star* (London), March 27, 1819.

tives, returned again and again to this theme. As late as 1823, a third of a century after the framing of the American Constitution, the *Quarterly* declared: "The experiment . . . which our brethren in America are trying, is to see, with how little government, with how few institutions, and at how cheap a rate men may be kept together in society. Is this a safe experiment? Can it possibly be a successful one?"[11] In the view of British conservatives America must, and therefore would, demonstrate by her failures the wisdom of British institutions and habits.

English nationalism drew strength from its transatlantic counterpart. Writers found it wonderfully satisfying to prick bubbles and scoff at pretensions while proclaiming their devotion to abstract truth. If the Americans complained they had only themselves to blame. "A people . . . eternally upon stilts," one newspaper explained, "must be expected to fret when they see the rest of the world laughing at their awkward self-elevation."[12] Thus Britishers, too, justified their own excesses by those of the enemy.

The Opposition failed to challenge prevailing sentiment. Unlike many prewar Federalists, the followers of Fox and Grenville did not consider the distant system better than their own, and after the American declaration of war they freely criticized the United States. Mostly noblemen and aristocrats, they mistrusted republicans as much as did the residents of Downing Street. The American minister, Richard Rush, correctly considered these grandees both ineffectual and basically anti-American—"Their trade is opposition, and republicanism one of their antipathies"—and he even had little faith in the democratic *fronde* challenging both government and Opposition.[13]

Yet the quarrel might have been even more frenzied. Some, particularly in England, took no part in the conflict. No important figure in either government, with one exception noted later, con-

---

[11] *Quarterly Review* (London), XXX (1823), 36.

[12] *Morning Post* (London), June 28, 1819.

[13] Rush to Monroe, private, April 22, 1818, James Monroe Papers, Library of Congress; Rush #50 to Adams, Dec. 31, 1818, Despatches, Great Britain, Vol. XXIII; Rush #108 to Adams, Jan. 28, 1819, *ibid.*, Vol. XXIV; Rush to Monroe, private, Dec. 7, 1819, Monroe MSS.

tributed to the public campaign, and in private the leaders often bewailed what Adams called "the voracious maw and the bloated visage of national vanity." English radicals and some reformers in effect considered themselves part of a republican community spanning the Atlantic; most businessmen went quietly ahead with their tasks; and religious groups in both countries often coöperated in a nobler war against sin and ignorance. Admiral Gambier even contributed money, perhaps earned at Ghent, to Kenyon College and other Episcopal institutions.[14]

A few British commentators did warn against activities that threatened to disturb peace. When expressed by the *Caledonian Mercury* or the *Liverpool Mercury* such views were not surprising, as spokesmen for manufacturers and exporters had pounded this theme even before the War of 1812. More interesting was the shift of the *Times* and the *Annual Register*, of Tom Moore and Samuel Taylor Coleridge, all formerly offensive critics of the United States. The *Register* carried its praise even into the political realm, congratulating the Americans on their "unbroken tranquility and prosperity" which proved "there is nothing incompatible in the coexistence of the most perfect good order with the most unlimited political freedom." Writing to Washington Allston, the American painter, Coleridge promised to devote an ode on General Ross's death to "lamentation on the [im]moral war between the child and the parent country" and above all to avoid "the feeding or palliating the vindictive antipathy of the one party, or the senseless, groundless, wicked contempt and insolence of the other." [15]

Finally, it must be noted that American travelers in England, official and nonofficial, admitted that ministers and indeed the ruling class as a whole received them with at worst a certain re-

[14] Dec. 31, 1817, Charles F. Adams, ed., *Memoirs of John Quincy Adams* (12 vols.; Philadelphia, 1874–1877), IV, 33; Frank Thistlethwaite, *The Anglo-American Connection in the Early Nineteenth Century* (Philadelphia, 1959), p. 81 and *passim*.

[15] *Annual Register, 1821* (London, 1822), p. 359; Irving to Henry Brevoort, Jr., March 10, 1821, Pierre M. Irving, *The Life and Letters of Washington Irving* (4 vols.; New York, 1862–1864), II, 37; Coleridge to Allston, Oct. 25, 1815, Jared B. Flagg, *The Life and Letters of Washington Allston* (New York, 1892), pp. 115–116.

served courtesy, at best with real kindness. Visitors protested the general mood of the country, not that of her rulers. A few Americans even gained spectacular social successes in England, most notably the three granddaughters of Charles Carroll of Carrollton. The girls visited Europe with their brother in 1816 and 1817. The Duke of Wellington and the Prince Regent, both notably susceptible to a full figure, an attractive ankle, and a vivacious mind, succumbed to their charms. Lord Glenbervie, a Pecksniff, complained that the eldest sister was "very transatlantic indeed," and he could not stand her brother, but the girls did well. One after another they married the Duke of Leeds, Marquis Wellesley, and Lord Stafford.[16] As so often in Anglo-American relations, the two aristocracies mingled more happily than the generality of the people.

These countercurrents failed to slow the tide of nationalistic fervor. Mutual hatred showed itself perhaps most clearly in the controversies evoked by the writings of Englishmen who visited America and by essays appearing in reviews on both sides of the Atlantic. Many British visitors, although seldom the discreet and aristocratic travelers for pleasure, felt compelled to commit to print their observations on America. The Americans made an issue of writings better left unnoticed. Even more than in the past they permitted published reports by British visitors to stir a fearful outcry. "It has been the particular lot of our country to be visited by the worst kind of English travellers," Washington Irving complained. Even more annoying, "it has been left to the broken-down tradesman, the scheming adventurer, the wandering mechanic, the Manchester and Birmingham agent, to be her oracles respecting America." Edward Everett avowed that his countrymen took up the cudgels only because all England accepted and endorsed the vicious untruths of unfriendly visitors to the United States.[17]

[16] Wellington to Mary Bagot, April 9, 1817, Josceline Bagot, ed., *George Canning and His Friends* (2 vols.; London, 1909), II, 42–43; Hughes to Bagot, Dec. 23, 1816, Sir Charles Bagot Papers, Levens Hall, Westmorland; Richard Rush, *A Residence at the Court of London* (3d ed.; London, 1872), p. 85 and n.; May 9, 1817, Francis Bickley, ed., *The Diaries of Sylvester Douglas (Lord Glenbervie)* (2 vols.; London, 1928), II, 227.
[17] Washington Irving (*pseud.* Geoffrey Crayon), *The Sketch Book* (rev. ed.; New York, 1849), p. 66; *North American Review*, XIII (1821), 36.

The writings of English visitors, some of them actually immigrants, did not remotely justify the violent American reaction, which must be explained in terms of the strong nationalism of the day. Only a few writers displayed real spleen, notably William Faux, and even the *Quarterly Review* found Faux's *Memorable Days in America* unconvincing. Many more authors generally favorable to the United States, for example Lieutenant Francis Hall, tempered praise with lesser amounts of criticism.[18] American readers, accepting praise as their due, objected to the reservations.

The most enthusiastic description of America was written by Frances Wright, the daughter of a Scottish liberal and later herself a leader of radical movements in the United States. "An awful responsibility has devolved on the American nation," she proclaimed; "the liberties of mankind are entrusted to their guardianship." Such sentiments affronted many English readers. The *Quarterly* described Fanny Wright's book as "a most ridiculous and extravagant panegyric on . . . the United States, accompanied by the grossest and most detestable calumnies against this country, that folly and malignity ever invented." [19] As the *Quarterly*'s rage suggests, no other traveler, not even Faux writing on the other side of the question, equaled Miss Wright's shrill tone.

Of the three most widely read reporters, only Henry B. Fearon really justified American complaints. The United States disappointed Fearon, who visited the country to spy out the land for immigration promoters, and his *Sketches of America* in effect sought to justify his shift from friendship to dislike. Fearon, who

---

[18] William Faux, *Memorable Days in America* (London, 1823); *Quarterly Review*, XXIX (1823), 340; Francis Hall, *Travels in Canada, and the United States, in 1816 and 1817* (2d ed.; 2 vols.; London, 1819); John M. Duncan, *Travels through Part of the United States and Canada in 1818 and 1819* (2 vols.; Glasgow, 1823); John Lambert, *Travels through Canada, and the United States of North America, in the Years 1806, 1807, & 1808* (3d ed.; 2 vols.; London, 1816); John Bradbury, *Travels in the Interior of America* (Liverpool, 1817); Adam Hodgson, *Letters from North America, Written during a Tour in the United States and Canada* (2 vols.; London, 1824).

[19] Frances Wright (*pseud.* An Englishwoman), *Views of Society and Manners in America* (London, 1821), p. 522 and *passim; Quarterly Review*, XXVII (1822), 73.

provoked bitter American outcries, gained many readers but little acclaim in England. The *Edinburgh Review* ridiculed his wild exaggerations, and the *Quarterly* objected that, in turning his back upon the United States, Fearon did not reëmbrace his homeland. Nevertheless the *Quarterly* devoted forty-two pages to Fearon's book, in excerpts and comments.[20]

Morris Birkbeck, a Quaker, political liberal, and successful Surrey farmer who emigrated to Illinois in 1817, sent his friend George Flower back to England largely to arrange publication of his *Notes on a Journey in America*. Because Birkbeck gloried in America and wanted others to follow him to Illinois, where he sought the role of country squire, his *Notes* fervently praised the United States. His book enraged English conservatives and aroused the curiosity of others, going through eleven editions in two years. Even the *Quarterly*, which threw darts at Birkbeck for years, admitted that his book was interesting and reasonably accurate. Birkbeck lived happily if not prosperously in America until 1824, when he drowned while crossing the Wabash River. His writings led several hundred emigrants to follow him to what he called the English Prairie.[21]

John Bristed, whose book appeared in 1818 along with Fearon's and Birkbeck's, was a remarkable man who emigrated to America in 1806 and during a long life worked successively as a doctor, lawyer, and clergyman. (Marriage to John Jacob Astor's daughter eased the monetary pain of shifting to the pulpit.) His book, *The Resources of the United States of America*, was more analytical, though clumsily so, and less purely descriptive than books by short-term visitors. Bristed candidly admitted American faults, including slavery and an underdeveloped intellectual life. He considered England a great nation, savior of the world during the Napoleonic Wars, but he was even more proud of America and sure the future lay in her hands. "These two countries will never cease to be commercial rivals, and political enemies," he said, "until one or the other falls." Bristed had no doubt which nation would fall, al-

[20] Henry B. Fearon, *Sketches of America* (London, 1818); *Edinburgh Review*, XXXI (1818), 133; *Quarterly Review*, XXI (1819), 145–146.
[21] Morris Birkbeck, *Notes on a Journey in America* (London, 1818); *Quarterly Review*, XIX (1818), 78; Thistlethwaite, *op. cit.*, pp. 48–51.

though he warned his new countrymen against forcing the pace of conflict.[22]

America's minister to England coupled Bristed's work with Fearon's—a preposterous idea revealing his own touchiness—and regretted its wide circulation. The *North American Review* harshly criticized it, nominally for stylistic or organizational weaknesses usually illustrated by wrenching critical passages out of context. Actually the *Resources of the United States* was particularly effective partly because of its balance. George Canning, who would have spurned a mere panegyric, praised the book but was not surprised Americans did not. The Earl of Liverpool read Bristed and commended him to cabinet members.[23] Certainly the success of Birkbeck, Bristed, and other friends of the United States far outweighed that of Faux and Fearon. Americans protested too much when, citing these volumes and their British reception, they accused the English of provoking a quarrel.

With more justification Americans found English reviews offensive. The two leading reviews, the *Quarterly* and the *Edinburgh,* circulated widely in the United States, probably more widely than such youthful emulators as the *North American Review* and the *Port Folio.* Both British journals angered the Americans with "their disgusting pretensions, their patriotic egotism, their silly sneers, their impudent sarcasms, and their unblushing contradictions," as the *Port Folio* so inclusively phrased the charge.[24]

The *Quarterly Review,* which spoke for the most conservative forces in English life and included Southey, Scott, and Canning among its contributors, steadily grew more hostile, or at best more condescending, toward America. In its first year, 1809, the review devoted a major article to a theme—the paucity of culture in the United States—which it stressed for years. The *Quarterly* concluded sanctimoniously: "This is an unfavourable picture, yet surely not an unfair one, nor has it been drawn by an unfriendly

[22] John Bristed, *The Resources of the United States of America* (New York, 1818), p. 246 and *passim.*

[23] Rush #50 to Adams, Dec. 31, 1818, Despatches, Great Britain, Vol. XXIII; *North American Review,* VII (1818), 401–427; Canning to Bagot, Aug. 24, 1818, Bagot, *op. cit.,* II, 83; Rush to Crawford, private, Aug. 4, 1818, William H. Crawford Papers, Library of Congress.

[24] *Port Folio,* XXXIII (1819), 505.

hand." Time and British tutelage would improve the United States.[25]

In 1814 editor William Gifford alloted forty-five pages to what was nominally a review of Charles Jared Ingersoll's anti-British pamphlet, *Inchiquin, the Jesuit's Letters*. This article, fairly described by a resentful American as "the most laboured, revolting libel," stimulated the cultural war. The *Quarterly* cast a wide net, attacking America's political system, courts, morals, vulgarity, use of the English language, and many other things. Commodore Rodgers was dismissed as a coward, and as for Franklin, he was half plagiarist and nearly half imbecile. The War of 1812, the *Quarterly* noted with approval, had killed sentimental talk of Anglo-American friendship. The magazine no longer saw any hope that time would redeem the Americans.[26]

This splenetic article, warmly received in England, kindled a different sort of heat in the United States. James K. Paulding, already angry at British criticism of his poetry, wrote a reply twice the length of the original. The *Port Folio*, answering strictures on American criminality, asserted that in one whole year all the courts in the nation would not "exhibit as black a catalogue of enormous crimes as . . . one session at Old Bailey." In the *North American Review* William Tudor, Jr., inserted thirty pages along a *tu quoque* theme. Even Timothy Dwight, a conservative, high Federalist type, published a pamphlet replying to the *Quarterly*'s article, erroneously ascribed by him and others to George Canning. When these strictures reached England, William Wilberforce hastened to John Quincy Adams to exculpate Canning, to explain that the British government disapproved efforts like the original article, and less accurately to assure Adams that the *Quarterly*'s sentiments were not representative of British opinion.[27]

Unrepentant, the *Quarterly Review* continued upon its way.

[25] *Quarterly Review*, II (1809), 337.

[26] *Ibid.*, X (1814), 524 and 496–539 *passim*; *North American Review*, I (1815), 65.

[27] James K. Paulding, *The United States and England* (New York, 1815); *Port Folio*, XXVI (1816), 52; *North American Review*, I (1815), 61–91; Timothy Dwight (*pseud*. An Inhabitant of New-England), *Remarks on the Review of Inchiquin's Letters, Published in the Quarterly Review* (Boston, 1815); July 10, 1815, Adams, *op. cit.*, III, 249–250.

Travelers' accounts and American books provided the excuse for long review articles ranging far afield. A naval hero was "a civilized barbarian . . . proficient in swinish sensuality." The country was peopled by "swarms of emigrants, renegadoes, and refugees," the West in particular by "the scum and wreck of society." America was, in short, "a land of misrule and impiety." Not until a decade after the war did the *Quarterly Review* again express a cautious hope, not yet a prediction, that the Americans would become "more worthy of their parentage." [28]

The *Edinburgh Review,* which angered Americans as much as the *Quarterly,* deserved less criticism. Before the war the *Edinburgh* ceaselessly criticized the Orders in Council and watched the American political experiment with sympathetic understanding. The editor, Francis Jeffrey, journeyed to the United States during the war and even called at the White House.[29] His visit, which resulted in marriage to an American, did not change Jeffrey's views. Although often criticizing slavery, the *Review* almost always spoke favorably of America when political matters were the subject of discussion. All administrations from Washington to Monroe, it maintained, had shown "forbearance, circumspection, constancy and vigour." [30] As journalistic spokesman for the Opposition, which often used similar tactics in Parliament, the magazine employed American developments to point up shortcomings in Lord Liverpool's England. A review article of 1824 perfectly captured the tone:

America seems, on the whole, to be a country possessing vast advantages, and little inconveniences; they have a cheap government, and bad roads; they pay no tithes, and have stage coaches without springs. . . . They have no collections in the fine arts; but they have no Lord Chancellor, and they can go to law without absolute ruin. . . . In all this the balance is prodigiously in their favor.[31]

Despite its views on American politics the *Edinburgh Review*

[28] *Quarterly Review,* XIII (1815), 383; XV (1816), 555; XXX (1823), 27; XXI (1819), 167; XXX (1823), 40.
[29] Jeffrey to Rush, Jan. 21, 1814, Rush Family Papers, Princeton University Library.
[30] *Edinburgh Review,* XXXI (1818), 202.
[31] *Ibid.,* XL (1824), 442.

attracted steady, often understandable criticism from across the Atlantic. Jeffrey once assured his readers he recognized their anti-American bias and did not himself intend to recommend the Yankees as "objects of our love." He and the magazine fully executed this promise when dealing with nonpolitical subjects. Like Englishmen of all persuasions, the *Edinburgh*'s writers considered Britain the cultural focus of the world. The United States lagged far behind. This was only natural, the magazine noted in 1818, since "a six weeks voyage brings them, in their own tongue, . . . science, and genius, in bales and hogsheads." [32] Americans squirmed at such condescension, but worse was yet to come.

In January, 1820, the magazine carried a famous attack upon American pretensions written by the Reverend Sydney Smith, an attack which unfairly caused Americans to consider Smith and the *Edinburgh* their most violent enemies. Actually the Yorkshire clergyman, a supporter of religious and political liberalism, considered himself a "Philoyankeeist." He criticized Fearon's book and wrote the article describing America as "a country possessing vast advantages, and little inconveniences." [33] Clearly he was not of a stripe with writers for the *Quarterly Review*.

In the autumn of 1819 Smith offered to review Adam Seybert's *Statistical Annals . . . of the United States*, itself a manifestation of nationalism. Editor Jeffrey approved, and Smith prepared what he considered an unexciting article. Most of it was a mere summary, and statistics are not the most romantic of subjects. "Thus far we are the friends and admirers of Jonathan," wrote Smith as he began a closing passage of quite different tenor. He warned the Americans to ignore claims they were "the greatest, the most enlightened, and the most moral people upon earth." After all, said Smith scathingly,

During the thirty or forty years of their independence, they have done absolutely nothing for the Sciences, for the Arts, for Literature, or even for the

[32] *Ibid.*, XXIV (1814), 263; XXXI (1818), 144.
[33] Smith to Jeffrey, Nov. 23, 1818, Nowell C. Smith, ed., *The Letters of Sydney Smith*, I (Oxford, 1953), 305; Smith to Lady Grey, Jan. 12, 1819, *ibid.*, p. 311; Robert E. Spiller, "The Verdict of Sydney Smith," *American Literature*, I (1929–1930), 3–13.

statesman-like studies of Politics and Political Economy. . . . In the four quarters of the globe, who reads an American book? or goes to an American play? or looks at an American picture or statue? . . . Under which of the old tyrannical governments of Europe is every sixth man a Slave . . . ?

Americans might begin to boast, Smith concluded, when they could expect favorable answers to these questions.[34]

This attack—fierce, exaggerated, gratuitous, petty, unwise, and provocative—was well received by proud Englishmen. Smith basked in London's approval but apparently failed to anticipate the bitter American reaction. How could this be? Why did the "Philoyankeeist" write such an article? Why did not Jeffrey ask him to modify it? We can only suggest answers to these questions.

Neither the magazine nor the Yorkshire cleric ever praised America's intellectual life. They considered her cultural subordination to England axiomatic, a price paid for political and commercial success. Thus, language aside, Sydney Smith's article repeated an old line. Carried away by anger or cleverness, or perhaps considering West and Allston now his own countrymen, Smith slandered American painting. But, after all, how many American books were read in Europe? how many American plays were performed? and in 1820 how many deserved to be? Not until later in the year did Washington Irving gain the first great critical success for an American author.

The *Edinburgh Review* and its contributor did not consider themselves anti-American. In the very next issue, reviewing another American book, Smith pointed out that Englishmen often criticized the *Edinburgh* for bias in favor of the young republic. The magazine, he rightly maintained, printed far more favorable than unfavorable comment. Smith did not point out, though he might have, that the *Edinburgh Review* consistently praised friendly travelers like Lieutenant Hall and Morris Birkbeck. Of course the *Review* did not go to extremes. A few years later Smith himself wrote a slashing review of Fanny Wright's book, but then,

---

[34] Smith to Jeffrey, Sept. 23, 1819, Smith, *op. cit.*, I, 338; Smith to Edward Davenport, n.d. [1820], *ibid.*, p. 347; *Edinburgh Review*, XXXIII (1820), 69–80, esp. 78–80.

fearing the Americans would be hurt, withdrew it.[35] Apparently he had learned a lesson. In his second article Smith expressed regret if "rash or petulant expressions" had slipped into the *Review*. The chief reason, at least for his own bitter blast, may well have been the recent flow of arrogant nationalism across the Atlantic. As men of peace Jeffrey and Smith condemned all American efforts to rouse animosity against England, and they considered denials of evident British cultural leadership part of such a campaign.[36]

The transatlantic audience sought out, devoured, and spat back criticism. English viciousness convinced the *Port Folio* that "although Great Britain is our mother country, she is now, as she has been from the beginning, a jealous and a cruel step-mother." By what right did she censure immorality and crudity, attack the slave system, bemoan the number of unpunished criminals, and even haughtily correct the language of American writers and orators? Was it not true, as Niles stated, that "the British reviewers have business enough at home, and are without any necessity of reaching across the Atlantic . . . in order to employ themselves"? [37] Americans convinced themselves that a bitter hatred of republicanism lay beneath the criticism, even that which was far afield from politics. In the interest of human happiness and freedom the United States must take up the gauntlet.

The turn-about-face of the *Port Folio* shows the broad appeal of republican nationalism. Before the war this magazine flew conservative colors under the editorship of Joseph Dennie, once secretary to the arch-Federalist, Timothy Pickering. Dennie's magazine praised Tom Moore's vehement anti-American poetry (though not specifically the verse in which Moore placed Jefferson in the arms of a slave mistress) and attacked "The Clamours of the Bellowers for Liberty." After Dennie's death and especially after the *Quarterly Review*'s "filthy invective" against Ingersoll's *Inchiquin,* the *Port Folio* brought its guns to bear upon England.

---

[35] *Edinburgh Review,* XXXIII (1820), 402, 409–410; XXX (1818), 120–140; XXXI (1818), 133; Spiller, *op. cit.,* p. 9.
[36] *Edinburgh Review,* XXXIII (1820), 406–407, 395–396.
[37] *Port Folio,* XXXIII (1819), 495; *Niles' Register,* May 24, 1817.

"It is at length high time to lay aside forbearance," the magazine declared long after it had in fact done so, "to show that the doctrines of passive obedience and nonresistance, are exploded among us; and that we neither want the power nor the will to repel aggressions of any kind." [38]

The *Port Folio*, the *Portico*, *Niles' Register*, and other journals bewailed cultural dependence upon England. So did the *North American Review*, founded by Boston Federalists in 1815 to "foster American genius, and . . . instruct and guide the public taste." An awareness of British leading strings caused these journals and other Americans to react with special sensitivity to Sydney Smith's lash. Why did not the nation develop a purely American art and literature? Why did republicans permit those who reviled them to be arbiters of their taste? Why, Niles asked, did Americans let the *Portico* of Baltimore, his home town, die from lack of patronage while they continued to buy English reviews of no better quality?[39]

Dr. Walter Channing, an able physician and a literary dabbler, reflected on these questions in two early issues of the *North American Review*. The title of his second installment, "Reflections on the Literary Delinquency of America," shows Channing's pessimism. A common language made it too easy to depend upon English forms and English books, he said. "Would not that we have already accomplished in literature be thought well for a young people," he asked, "if we wrote in our own tongue?"[40] Such modest questions did not appeal to his colleagues, and the *North American* carried no further speculations by Channing.

The doctor's pale patriotism ran counter to prevailing sentiment. Particularly when assailed by English critics, Americans maintained that they did indeed have a national culture, that they had produced important literature, and sometimes even that they had seized the lead from Great Britain. Anthologies of American writings, epic poems, pretentious essays, and soon-forgotten fic-

---

[38] *Port Folio*, VII (1806), 56–57, 204; XXVI (1816), 402; XXXIII (1819), 495.
[39] *Niles' Register*, May 24, 1817.
[40] *North American Review*, I (1815), 308 and 307–314; II (1816), 32–43 *passim*.

tion—*Rosalvo Delmonmort, a Tale; Demetrius, a Russian Romance; The Corsair, a Mello Drama*—issued from the presses along with an even larger number of biographies, collections of correspondence, sermons, medical reports, and other useful volumes. Most of them—for example, William Dunlap's life of the novelist, Charles Brockden Brown, which appeared in 1815, and the statistical collections published by Timothy Pitkin and Adam Seybert in 1816 and 1818, respectively—had at least collaterally a patriotic purpose.

The Americans even spawned travelers' accounts on the English model. Mordecai Noah, a sort of American Fearon, explained his country's superiority by saying that the people enjoyed "a greater familiarity with public affairs, and . . . a greater portion of rational liberty; for, though the English boast of being the only free people on earth, the greatest portion of this liberty, is enjoyed in imagination." [41] Such claims produced further British criticism and, in turn, American replies.

A few cool patriots argued for restraint. William Cullen Bryant, whose poetry soon provided a solid basis for American pride, warned that excessive praise of American writings—Joel Barlow's *Columbiad*, for example—invited European contempt and encouraged younger writers to copy bad examples. Bryant took comfort in the fact that the republic had done so well in the short years of its life and urged America to make haste gradually. [42]

Perhaps the most glaring repudiation of Bryant's advice, a volume entitled *An Appeal from the Judgments of Great Britain Respecting the United States of America*, burst upon the scene in the autumn of 1819. The author, Robert Walsh, Jr., formerly an Anglophile contributor to the *Port Folio* but now reformed, devoted more than two hundred pages to his task. He exposed the distortions of British commentators. He denounced in language seldom equaled in England or America the iniquities of the British

[41] Mordecai M. Noah, *Travels in England, France, Spain, and the Barbary States* (New York, 1819), p. 51.
[42] *North American Review*, VII (1818), 198–211.

government and the Opposition, the prejudice of reviewers and travelers. Very little escaped Walsh's acid pen.[43] The *Port Folio* praised its alumnus' volume. No doubt the British would find it irritating, but there seemed no other way to defend the United States.

When Walsh's *Appeal* reached England the *Quarterly Review* unaccountably ignored it. Others did not. George Canning and Sir Walter Scott, a dyed-in-the-wool reactionary, mentioned the *Appeal* to the American minister with scarcely concealed distaste.[44] The *Edinburgh*'s strange response, by Smith, denounced Walsh for stirring up discord, denied malice in the passages of which Walsh complained, and called upon the United States to join England in defense of liberty and constitutionalism. This reply, Adams told his friend Walsh, was in "every way exceptionable; it shuffles between candid avowal and ingenuous recantation, without either the spirit to defend or the generosity to atone for its offence." [45] Another leading journal, the *New London Magazine*, did not "shuffle." It delivered a counterbarrage.

Naturally enough the matter did not end there. Edward Everett replied in a bitter article for the *North American Review*, and Secretary of State Adams delivered a passionately patriotic address in the chamber of the House of Representatives on July 4, 1821. Adams, who particularly denounced Sydney Smith's plea for Anglo-American coöperation, did not limit himself to a reaffirmation of American isolation. He went on to reply to the "unrelenting war of slander and invective, waged by almost all the literature of Great Britain against the good name of his country." Some Americans, including Walsh himself, criticized Adams' style and others considered parts of his speech in bad taste, notably a passing allusion to George III's insanity. Generally the speech enjoyed

[43] Robert Walsh, Jr., *An Appeal from the Judgments of Great Britain Respecting the United States of America* (2d ed.; Philadelphia, 1819), p. vi and *passim*.

[44] *Port Folio*, XXXIII (1819), 493–515; Richard Rush, *A Residence at the Court of London, Second Series* (2 vols.; London, 1845), I, 311.

[45] *Edinburgh Review*, XXXIII (1820), 395–431; Adams to Walsh, July 10, 1821, Adams Family MSS, Vol. CXLVII.

an enthusiastic reception. The British minister rightly described it as an "extraordinary effusion." [46]

None of the disputants mentioned the fame gained in London by a small number of Americans whose success vindicated England from charges of complete intolerance and America from suggestions that she produced no men of talent. John Howard Payne, author and dramatist, gained renown, particularly in the latter role. "Brutus, or the Fall of Tarquin" received praise beyond its deserts and enjoyed a very long run during the season of 1818–19, but Smith felt free to ignore it in 1820. In painting, following the path of Benjamin West and John Trumbull (who returned in 1815 to finish his life in America), Washington Allston achieved great success. He might well have succeeded West as president of the Royal Academy had he not made the decision, so fatal to his talent, to return to the United States in 1818. America, as the *North American Review* admitted with embarrassment and regret, did not yet provide the stimulus or the support required by men of the arts.[47]

Washington Irving gained more fame in England than any other American. Shortly after the Treaty of Ghent, Irving crossed the Atlantic. Encouraged by Sir Walter Scott, who enjoyed his *Knickerbocker's History of New York*, Irving abandoned business to devote himself entirely to literature. Early in 1819 he began to send home essays, descriptive articles, and tales—even-

---

[46] *North American Review*, XIII (1821), 20–47; John Quincy Adams, *An Address Delivered ... on the Fourth of July, 1821* (Washington, 1821); Adams to Ingersoll, July 23, 1821, Worthington C. Ford, ed., *The Writings of John Quincy Adams* (7 vols.; New York, 1913–1917), VII, 119–123; Adams to Walsh, July 27, 1821, *ibid.*, pp. 127–137; Stratford Canning to Londonderry, separate, July 30, 1821, Foreign Office Archives, Public Record Office, FO 5/158; Samuel F. Bemis, *John Quincy Adams and the Foundations of American Foreign Policy* (New York, 1949), pp. 355–359. Arthur P. Whitaker, *The United States and the Independence of Latin America, 1800–1830* (Baltimore, 1941), chap. 12, points out other implications of Adams' speech.

[47] E. Allison Grant and Stanley T. Williams, "John Howard Payne," in Dumas Malone, ed., *Dictionary of American Biography*, XIV (New York, 1934), 327–329; Raymond Weaver, "Washington Allston," in *ibid.*, I (New York, 1928), 224–225; *North American Review*, I (1815), 440.

tually thirty-two in all—later collected in *The Sketch Book,* published in America and England in 1820. An instantaneous success in both countries, it caused *Knickerbocker's History* to be republished in England. Until it became known that the pseudonym "Geoffrey Crayon" belonged to Washington Irving, some Britons suspected that it masked Sir Walter Scott. No American could ask higher praise.

The Sketch Book contained one essay, "English Writers on America," which should have shown from the beginning that Scott could not have written the volume. In spirit this piece differed very little from diatribes by Walsh, Everett, and others. Irving repeated the usual denunciation of British travelers and reviews, and warned England she might come to regret a campaign that was destroying American affection for the mother country. At the same time he told his countrymen not to take the slanders too seriously: "We have but to live on, and every day we live a whole volume of refutation." [48]

The rest of *The Sketch Book* and *Bracebridge Hall,* published two years later, perfectly conformed to English tastes. Irving consciously followed English models, his descriptive pieces romanticized the Britain he loved, and his conservative views—had he not satirized Jefferson in *Knickerbocker's History?*—mirrored those of most British readers. Irving became the friend of Scott, Moore, and even Gifford, editor of the *Quarterly Review.* He luxuriated in the praise of George Canning and other famous men; he gulped down reviewers' congratulations. After a delay suggesting that Gifford found it uncomfortable to praise an American, even if he was a friend, in his magazine, the *Quarterly* climbed on the bandwagon. Noting Irving's verbosity and suggesting, not unprophetically, that major novels were beyond his talent, the review welcomed Irving "to the full freedom and privileges of

---

[48] Washington Irving, *op. cit.,* pp. 69 and 65–75 *passim.* For general information on Irving these paragraphs follow Stanley T. Williams, "Washington Irving," in Robert E. Spiller *et al.,* eds., *Literary History of the United States* (3 vols.; New York, 1948), I, 242–252.

the English guild of authorship." [49] America had not created a literature of her own, but through Washington Irving she penetrated the highest British circles.

Washington Allston and Washington Irving—their very names remind us of the brief span of time since the contest between redcoats and Continentals. Neither nation considered independence complete, neither fairly valued the other. Thus the battle raged, inflaming spirits on both sides of the Atlantic Ocean. In the summer of 1821 the British army ordered Major John André's body moved from New York to Westminster Abbey, where a monument honored this gallant, tragic figure. Consul James Buchanan planned a full-dress ceremony, a scheme the British minister at Washington feared would lead to riot and possibly end with André's bones at the bottom of the Hudson River. The Americans did complain—Adams considered it "impossible to do him honor without insulting all that was great and glorious in our cause"— and in the end, having toned down the plans, Consul Buchanan half smuggled the coffin out of the country.[50] The incident bespoke American bitterness in the years after the War of 1812.

The inflammatory spirit in both countries immensely complicated the diplomats' task. Only a few of them, nationalists rather than statesmen, welcomed it; for example, the British consul at Boston urged William Gifford to keep up the good work. More, notably Richard Rush, American envoy at the Court of St. James, both regretted the strife and silently shared their country's resentment. Still others, including Charles Bagot and Stratford Canning, Rush's opposite numbers, worked to restore peace. When in 1821 the *National Intelligencer* unfairly reproached the Foreign Secretary for allegedly anti-American remarks, Canning seized his pen to reply. The *Intelligencer* published his temperate explanation and withdrew its charges.[51]

[49] *Quarterly Review*, XXXI (1824), 487 and 473–487 *passim*.
[50] Stratford Canning to Londonderry, separate, Aug. 31, 1821, FO 5/159; Adams to Walsh, Aug. 4, 1821, Worthington C. Ford, *op. cit.*, VII, 137n; Stratford Canning to Londonderry, confidential, Sept. 4, 1821, FO 5/159.
[51] George Manners to Gifford, Feb. 4, 1823, FO 5/182; Stratford Canning to Londonderry, confidential, Sept. 4, 1821, FO 5/159.

This episode, like the one involving Major André's remains, is instructive. Although Adams, who self-righteously believed he acted only under extreme provocation, had contributed to the furor, neither he nor other members of the administration welcomed it. They permitted Canning to use the columns of the semi-official *Intelligencer* to whittle away at misunderstanding, and they even allowed him to write under a pseudonym so that his explanation could not be discounted as official British persiflage. American leaders, notably Adams, suspected and distrusted England; similarly, Liverpool and his colleagues often questioned American motives and purposes. Both groups nevertheless cherished peace and regretted the bitter, useless warfare of the mind. Their success is all the more remarkable for the existence of this warfare.

CHAPTER

VISCOUNT CASTLEREAGH
AND MR. ADAMS

A tardy coachman made John Quincy Adams, America's first post-war minister, an hour late for his opening appointment at Downing Street. When Adams at last arrived, he found Castlereagh closeted with a French visitor. Adams waited thirty minutes in an anteroom, then was ushered into an office he had not seen for nearly thirty years. He and the Foreign Secretary took each other's measure as they discussed problems which, at least in Adams' view, required attention. That night Adams wrote in his diary: "His deportment is sufficiently graceful, and his person is handsome. His manner was, cold, but not absolutely repulsive." [1] For the next seven years, at first directly and after Adams' promotion to the cabinet through intermediaries, the relationship between these two men became the very essence of Anglo-American relations.

Adams never learned, nor did most Americans or even the For-

[1] May 29, 1815, Charles F. Adams, ed., *Memoirs of John Quincy Adams* (12 vols.; Philadelphia, 1874–1877), III, 202–205.

eign Secretary's own countrymen, to appreciate Castlereagh fully while he lived. It remained for historians to place him in the front rank of British statesmen, although when Castlereagh committed suicide in 1822 his European policy lay in ruins. Far more lasting was the improvement in relations with America. Castlereagh, Sir Charles Webster comments, "was the first British statesman to recognize that the friendship of the United States was a major asset . . . , and to use in his relations with her a language that was neither superior nor intimidating." [2] Although Sir Charles ignores Lord Grenville, Pitt's foreign secretary in the 1790's, he does not otherwise misstate the case.

Of course, the Foreign Secretary did not impose his policy on unwilling colleagues. "The avowed & true Policy of Great Britain is, in the existing state of the World to appease controversy, & to secure if possible for all states a long interval of Repose," Castlereagh wrote in 1817. [3] Britain had had enough of war; she needed time to bind her wounds and expand new avenues of trade. Above all she needed peace for reasons of domestic politics. The years after Waterloo saw a deep social crisis, rising discontent, and a repressive reaction by the government. In 1819 cavalry charged a mass meeting at Manchester, killing eleven and wounding several hundred in an action derisively called "Peterloo" in imitation of Wellington's battlefield, and the next year police uncovered a plot to assassinate the cabinet.

Britain emerged from the wars in Europe the greatest single power in the world. "Here . . . , doubtless, dwells the ascendant will," commented the American minister at the Court of St. James in 1818, "and here are largely determined the political movements of Europe." [4] As the conference at Aix-la-Chapelle that fall showed, this statement had already become dated. Despite Castlereagh's labors to preserve the European alliance and particu-

[2] Charles K. Webster, ed., *Britain and the Independence of Latin America* (2 vols.; London, 1938), I, 42.
[3] Castlereagh #24 to Bagot, most secret and confidential, Nov. 10, 1817, Foreign Office Archives, Public Record Office, FO 5/120.
[4] Rush #11 to Adams, March 21, 1818, Department of State Archives, National Archives, Despatches, Great Britain, Vol. XXII.

larly Britain's leadership within it, the island kingdom drifted into conflict with European advocates of legitimacy and reaction. This quarrel broke into the open at the congresses of Troppau and Laibach in 1820 and 1821. Even the most powerful state in the world could not afford another foe, and Britain craved the understanding of a nation sharing her view of continental developments.

Economically, too, Britain needed the United States. Americans provided English manufacturers with their largest overseas market and paid for British goods with agricultural products, especially cotton, essential to the British economy. Postwar reconversion proved difficult, and a serious depression gave plausibility to the standard American charge that the British economy had become dependent upon war. Three hundred thousand veterans added to the unemployed, the end of government orders crippled many businesses, and the swollen national debt of some £850 million burdened the country. The riots and strikes that plagued the British government had an economic as well as a political origin. Peterloo, which counseled peace in general terms, specifically advised ministers not to risk the large, always growing trade with America.

Finally, there was Canada. Until 1812 British governments minimized the chances of an American invasion and even considered Canada a valuable base for attacks upon the United States. The War of 1812 forced a reconsideration. After conferences at Whitehall an officer assigned to American duty wrote, "we cannot keep Canada if the Americans declare war against us. I believe Ministry now view it in this light." In 1819 the Duke of Wellington, considered an infallible military expert, advised that Canada had no use as an offensive base and could be defended only with the greatest difficulty.[5] Thus in the years after 1814 British statesmen recognized that Canada had become a hostage to Anglo-American peace.

The new policy began immediately after the war and gained

[5] Milne to Hume, Jan. 29, 1817, Edgar E. Hume, ed., "Letters Written during the War of 1812 by the British Naval Commander in American Waters (Admiral Sir David Milne)," *William and Mary Quarterly*, 2d series, X (1930), 297; Wellington memorandum, March 1, 1819, Papers of Stratford Canning, Viscount Stratford de Redcliffe, Public Record Office, FO 352/9.

momentum as years passed. As Albert Gallatin observed to a doubting President, England's acceptance of commercial negotiations she did not desire in 1815 was "an evidence of friendly disposition." When John Quincy Adams arrived in London to join Gallatin and Clay in these negotiations and to take up his post as regular minister to England, the Prince Regent received him courteously, passing over the unpleasant past in silence. The next year a royal duke, Victoria's father, toasted James Monroe in language so expansive it caught newspaper attention.[6] These trivial incidents foreshadowed a policy that successfully challenged the supposed teachings of history and the efforts of contemporary editors.

Memories of controversy and then war made Americans doubt British *bona fides*. They reacted suspiciously to the new temper and searched for the truth behind it. English opponents of conciliation, less obtuse than most Americans, protested against the new departure. "I wish, sir," complained a Britisher of traditional views, "some person would show what quality it is in the disposition of the United States toward Great Britain that gives them a title to become the most favored government on this globe." [7] Liverpool's ministry deserves great credit for persevering in the face of nationalistic complaints at home and suspicion abroad.

Viscount Castlereagh, principal architect of this policy, challenges the historian to understand him. Castlereagh composed many impressive state papers, always on European affairs. His colleagues respected his judgment almost as much as the Duke of Wellington's. Yet, partly by design and partly through shyness, Castlereagh concealed his inner self, bearing his own burdens and thinking his own thoughts. Neither official nor private papers gave him away, and his speeches tended to be opaque rather than clear or philosophical.

[6] Gallatin to Madison, Sept. 4, 1815, Albert Gallatin Papers, New-York Historical Society; Madison to Gallatin, Sept. 11, 1815, *ibid.*; Adams to Abigail Adams, Aug. 30, 1816, Adams Family Papers, Massachusetts Historical Society, Vol. CXLIII.
[7] William Sabatier, *A Letter to the Right Honorable Frederick J. Robinson . . . on the Relative Situation of the British North American Possessions, with the United States of America and Great Britain* (London, 1821), pp. 14–15.

Castlereagh and his wife, a devoted but lighthearted and frivolous companion rather than a confidante, entertained widely at their town house on St. James Street or at North Cray, an estate —they called it a farm—on the capital's southern outskirts. These affairs tended, like the host, to be formal and reserved, not gay and relaxed. That deep passion lay behind the Secretary's hauteur and diffidence did not become apparent until shortly before that summer evening in 1822 when, only just fifty-three, he drew a pen knife across his throat.

As foreign secretary, Castlereagh devoted most of his time to the challenging problems of Europe. As leader in the House of Commons, where he remained even after becoming Marquis of Londonderry in 1821 because his was an Irish and not an English peerage, Castlereagh bore the additional duty of explaining his colleagues' domestic policies. This responsibility, leaving him comparatively little time for other matters, perhaps explains George Dangerfield's charge that the "Americans entered into his calculations only as an afterthought; his policy towards them had been a drowsy compound of appeasement and indifference." [8] This criticism is not quite just. Although Castlereagh only occasionally gave priority to American questions, he left an indelible mark on every important episode. Far more than anyone at Washington, he can claim credit for the postwar amelioration of spirit.

Castlereagh did not act as he did out of liking for the Americans. As a realist he announced repeal of the Orders in Council in 1812 and, insofar as he intervened in negotiations managed by Bathurst and Liverpool, supported a mild line at Ghent. During his journey to Vienna in 1814 he educated himself on American affairs and, his reading finished, commented: "I trust we shall never again commit the egregious folly of spoiling Americans by acts signally unjust to our own subjects and to all foreign powers." [9] This attitude lasted until his death.

[8] George Dangerfield, *The Era of Good Feelings* (New York, 1952), p. 267. The excellent study by Charles K. Webster, *The Foreign Policy of Castlereagh, 1815–1822* (London, 1925), contains much helpful material but only a short section specifically on American relations.

[9] Castlereagh to Bathurst, private, Oct. 4, 1814, Francis Bickley, ed., *Report on the Manuscripts of Earl Bathurst* (London, 1923), p. 296.

Yet, again as a realist, Castlereagh worked for concord. When he declined American requests he did so as inoffensively as possible. Unlike many predecessors he did not simply repeat arrogant British doctrine and defy the Americans to challenge it. He worked hard to eliminate some areas of friction, partly because he appreciated the growth of American power. The Rush-Bagot agreement on lakes disarmament, the convention of 1818 settling the fishery question and closing a long-disputed gap in the Canadian-American boundary, and his steady refusal to involve Britain in the Florida question all testify to his desire for reconciliation on realistic terms.

The Foreign Secretary particularly sought to avoid unnecessary controversy, for again unlike his predecessors he did not consider it Britain's task to teach international manners to the United States. When the two navies quarreled at Gibraltar, Castlereagh followed a characteristic line; instead of complaining of the Americans' abuse of British hospitality, he directed his representative at Washington not to discuss the subject unless Secretary Adams raised it. As Minister Rush observed after Castlereagh's death, "If anything unpleasant ever arose . . . , he threw around it every mitigation which blandness of manner could impart; whilst to announce or promote what was agreeable, seemed always to give him pleasure." [10]

In 1820, in a rare moment of expansiveness, Castlereagh composed instructions for a minister about to depart for Washington. He advised his subordinate to cultivate American friendship, "always holding in mind that there are no two States whose friendly relations are of more practical value to each other, or whose hostility so inevitably and so immediately entails upon both the most serious mischiefs." He forbade the envoy to seek help from any political faction, adding, in criticism of prewar connections with the Federalists, "we have never derived any advantage, but the reverse, from building any portion of our hopes upon such a foundation." Above all, he counseled his agent to avoid written disputes

[10] Castlereagh #1 to G. Crawfurd Antrobus, Aug. 14, 1819, FO 5/143; Richard Rush, *A Residence at the Court of London, Second Series* (2 vols.; London, 1845), II, 3.

with the Americans. "Their Official Notes are generally seasoned to the temper of their people," he justly observed, and historic feelings made Washington address Britain "in a tone of greater harshness than toward any other government whatever. . . . Time has done a good deal to soften these dispositions," and Britain would benefit "the more we can permit them to subside by avoiding angry discussions." [11] On these principles—the importance of friendly relations, the inadvisability of intrigue in American politics, the advantage of polite discussion over disputatious notes—the Foreign Secretary built his policy.

A few months after preparing these instructions Lord Castlereagh met Richard Rush at a dinner given by the French ambassador. Their exchange, a bantering reflection of the success of British policy, began when Castlereagh said, "Why, I have not seen you for these hundred years!" "My misfortune, my Lord," Rush politely replied, bowing. "It is a proof," Castlereagh continued, "how smooth the waters are between our two countries." Archly Rush responded, "But we must contrive to ruffle them a little, if their smoothness is to be followed by our separation." The Foreign Secretary threw up his hands in mock horror; "No, no," he said, "that won't do." [12]

Castlereagh made an almost inspired choice in selecting Charles Bagot as minister to implement the new policy. On social grounds alone, Bagot would have appealed to the Americans, for he was the son of a peer and had married the Duke of Wellington's niece, and his appointment as privy councillor just before leaving for America was a further bouquet to American pride. When he proved to combine good sense with an impeccable background the Americans were delighted.

Bagot, undersecretary in the Foreign Office during Canning's tenure from 1807 to 1809, was in 1815 secretary to the Duke of Wellington at Paris. When Napoleon's return from Elba deprived him of this pleasant employment Bagot asked Castlereagh for another job. The American position resulted. After a long delay

[11] Castlereagh #2 to Stratford Canning, confidential, Aug. 7, 1820, FO 5/150.
[12] Rush, *op. cit.*, I, 357.

—Mrs. Bagot awaited a child—the new envoy sailed for the United States. He arrived at Washington to replace Anthony Baker, who became consul general, in March, 1816, showed his pacific temper by eluding a quarrel with Monroe over etiquette, and put all his effort into improving relations between the two countries.

Bagot did not at first welcome the proffered American appointment. He considered Washington an uncouth, distant exile and professionally a blind alley; no British minister since Robert Liston in 1800 had returned with an enhanced reputation. Castlereagh personally undertook Bagot's conversion, stressing the importance the government attached to the appointment and thus the opportunity to use it as a route to the top of the diplomatic service.[13] After talking to Castlereagh, Bagot announced to friends that he intended to use oil rather than the traditional vinegar in dealing with the Americans. His former superior, George Canning, replied:

Your plan of treatment may or may not succeed with the Yankees—but it is obviously, for your own sake, the proper one. I am afraid indeed that the question is not so much how you will treat them, as how they will treat you, & that the hardest lesson which a British Minister has to learn in America is not what to do, but what to bear. But even this may come round. And Waterloo is a great help to you: perhaps a pretty necessary help after the (to say the least) balanced successes & misfortunes of the American War.[14]

Apparently Bagot received orally from Castlereagh the same counsel the Foreign Secretary penned for Bagot's successor five years later.

No one ever accused Bagot of genius. John Quincy Adams, who liked him, confessed that the Englishman's success undermined his own conviction that a nation ought to devote its best talents to diplomacy. What Bagot lacked in intellect he made up in tact and understanding and a willingness to work hard. Although he found travel difficult and boring—"when one has seen the principal

[13] Bagot to Wellington, private, June 6, 1815, Sir Charles Bagot Papers, Levens Hall, Westmorland.
[14] Canning to Bagot, private, July 14, 1815, *ibid.*

cities—one great river—and one great forest, an accurate idea can be formed of all the rest"—he did his "devoirs" by visiting all parts of the country during summer tours. Although the cost of entertainment frightened him—"I am as stingy as a weasel, and determined not be ruined"—he loyally performed his social duties from the opening of each Congress until "the wild and hairy deputies of which it is composed are gone back into their woods and wigwams." Although privately preferring Federalists to Republicans, he carefully avoided any impression of partisanship. Although he endorsed most of the *Quarterly Review*'s strictures on the Inchiquin letters, he concealed his contempt for American culture from the Americans themselves. Above all Bagot avoided the sarcasms that the touchy republicans, he said, had come to expect from foreign visitors, particularly Englishmen.[15]

In dealing with the secretaries of state, Monroe and then Adams, the minister showed equal tact. His desire to avoid controversy, apparent from the moment of his arrival, positively amazed Monroe. When Bagot left, Secretary Adams composed a fulsome letter of praise, which he sent to Richard Rush for transmission to Castlereagh and the Wellington connections. "Mr. Bagot's conduct and deportment have been not merely and invariably unexceptionable, but have been truly those of a minister of peace," commented Adams in a summary sentence.[16] That Bagot never had a serious quarrel with Adams made him literally unique in the diplomatic corps of the day.

London recognized Bagot's worth almost from the beginning, partly because the minister happily, indefatigably reported his own success. In 1817, after a cabinet meeting at which ministers vied with one another in praising Bagot, Castlereagh formally commended him. When Bagot returned in 1819 the government rewarded him with the Grand Cross of the Order of the Bath and

[15] Bagot to Lord Binning, private, Oct. 24, 1816, *ibid.;* Bagot to Edward Cooke, private, Sept. 1, 1816, *ibid.;* Bagot to Binning, Feb. 26, 1818, *ibid.;* Bagot to Binning, private, May 6, 1816, *ibid.;* Bagot to John Sneyd, June 12, 1816, *ibid.*

[16] Monroe to Madison, July 7, 1816, William C. Rives Collection, Library of Congress; Adams to Rush, May 2, 1819, Worthington C. Ford, ed., *The Writings of John Quincy Adams* (7 vols.; New York, 1913–1917), VI, 546–547.

promotion to St. Petersburg. The *Times* grumbled that anyone who simply acted as a conveyor of concessions would have been as popular at Bagot, but the cabinet knew better.[17]

Less than two years after his arrival Bagot began to seek relief from his post. Wellington urged Mary Bagot to convince her husband to stay at Washington, "as we were certainly never on such good terms (I believe never before on any terms at all) with the Gov[t]. of the United States, as we have been since he was appointed the Minister." Another relative warned Bagot he would jeopardize his career if he returned home too soon. Bagot agreed to stay a little longer.

Throughout his stay the envoy sent a steady stream of complaint, wry rather than hostile, across the Atlantic. "A Pint of American summer would thaw all Europe in ten minutes. Sir, it is dreadful—it is deleterious—it leads to madness," he wrote, adding thanks to God that Madison offered use of the presidential ice-house before fleeing Washington for the summer. Nine months later it was the cold: "Oh Sirs! I have had a prodigious winter—the busiest, the coldest, the ballest, the teaest, the dinnerest I ever passed. But it is over. The Congress and the Frost are both broke up." Luckily for Bagot, none of these letters ever leaked into public view. A similar effort by Mary Bagot, circulated with appreciative laughter through the Prince Regent's circle, did embarrass the envoy by getting back to the Americans.[18]

In July, 1818, Bagot received permission to leave Washington at a time of his own choosing. The mere assurance that he could leave "this worse than N. Indian climate" improved his morale, and Bagot stayed until the adjournment of Congress and the signing of the Spanish-American treaty on Florida in 1819. Late in the spring he, Mary, the three children, a secretary, and four servants shook the dust of the United States from their feet. Before their departure Washington society honored Charles and Mary Bagot

[17] Castlereagh to Bagot, private, March 22, 1817, FO 5/120; William Wellesley Pole to Bagot, March 27, 1817, Bagot MSS; *Times* (London), June 1, 1819.
[18] Wellington to Mary Bagot, Dec. 14, 1817, Bagot MSS; Wellesley Pole to Bagot, March 6, 1818, *ibid.*; Bagot to Sneyd, June 12, 1816, March 24, 1817, *ibid.*; Bagot to Binning, private, Oct. 24, 1816, *ibid.*

at a ball attended by the cabinet, Chief Justice Marshall and his brethren, military officers (including Stephen Decatur, a sponsor of the affair), and congressmen. United, miniature flags of the two countries decorated the dinner tables. "Upon drinking our health," Bagot reported,

the Band, to my infinite surprise, & somewhat to my apprehension for the effect, played God save the King, which the company heard standing. As this was a pierre de touche, I hinted to one of the managers to tell the Band to play Yankee Doodle the moment God save the King was finished, in order that it might be understood as a union of the two national airs, which I believe it was, for not a murmur was heard.

Responding to the toast, Bagot thanked the Americans for their kindness during his stay.[19]

For seventeen months, until September, 1820, Bagot's secretary of legation, G. Crawfurd Antrobus, served as chargé d'affaires. The long delay shows how difficult it was to find a leading diplomat willing to take on the Washington station. Meanwhile Antrobus suffered through what he called "the time of my banishment." [20] When his sentence expired he passed into historical limbo.

Bagot's ultimate successor, Stratford Canning, also considered the American position a stepping-stone to better things, and in time he gained a series of important embassies to Constantinople, a peerage, and finally the Order of the Garter. In 1820 Canning was still poor, his father having been disinherited for a bad marriage, and he grieved over the death of his own wife only a year after their union. (In America, rumor linked Canning with the widow of Stephen Decatur, who died in 1820, but the envoy escaped entanglement and remarried in England in 1825.) His cousin, George Canning, took Stratford into the Foreign Office in 1807, and Castlereagh boosted him up the ladder. He came to America after serving as minister to Switzerland.

An earnest man, Stratford Canning prepared carefully for his

[19] Bagot to Joseph Planta, Jr., private, July 29, 1818, FO 5/132; Bagot to Planta, private, March 5, 1819, FO 5/142.
[20] Antrobus to Bagot, private, June 30, 1819, Bagot MSS.

mission. He cultivated the American minister at London and secured Rush's blessing. He searchingly questioned Bagot, and he read and reread Castlereagh's instructions and other material. Before leaving he engaged eleven servants and amassed seventy tons of baggage which occupied naval stevedores for four days; one wonders how Canning paid for all these things. Like Bagot he became a privy councillor before he sailed, and the Foreign Secretary told Rush this practice would thenceforth be followed. The heavily laden H.M.S. *Spartan* sailed from England in August, 1820, and deposited Canning's party at Annapolis six weeks later.[21]

Stratford Canning never established rapport with Secretary of State Adams, not because he did not wish to do so but because the two men excited their mutual argumentativeness. For the first few months Canning observed Castlercagh's injunctions, and Adams even found him too reserved. In January, 1821, Canning's patience gave out, and he and the Secretary engaged in a slanging match over Oregon. Castlereagh shot back instructions to drop the subject. Canning obeyed, but he still maintained that it "was impossible to *slide out* of the debate, there was nothing for it but to set my back against the wall." [22] During the rest of his mission Canning and Adams dealt in a gingerly fashion with each other.

When Canning left the United States the Secretary of State confided an estimate to his diary:

He is a proud, high-tempered Englishman, of good but not extraordinary parts; stubborn and punctilious, with a disposition to be overbearing, which I have often been compelled to check in its own way. He is, of all the foreign Ministers with whom I have had occasion to treat, the man who has most severely tried my temper. . . . He has, however, a great respect for his word, and there is nothing false about him. . . . Mr. Canning is a man of

---

[21] Rush to Monroe, private, July 27, 1820, James Monroe Papers, Library of Congress; Stanley Lane-Poole, *The Life of the Right Honourable Stratford Canning, Viscount Stratford de Redcliffe*, I (London, 1888), 296; Rush #92 to Adams, Sept. 20, 1819, Despatches, Great Britain, Vol. XXIV; Stratford Canning #1 to Castlereagh, Sept. 30, 1820, FO 5/150.

[22] Jan. 17, 26, 27, 1821, Adams, *op. cit.*, V, 237, 243–259; Stratford Canning #3 to Castlereagh, Jan. 28, 1821, FO 5/157; Stratford Canning to Planta, private, Feb. 6, 1821, *ibid.*; Castlereagh #7 to Stratford Canning, April 10, 1821, FO 5/156; Stratford Canning to Planta, June 15, 1821, Lane-Poole, *op. cit.*, I, 308.

forms, studious of courtesy, and tenacious of private morals. As a diplomatic man, his great want is suppleness, and his great virtue is sincerity.

For his part Canning considered Adams flawed by gnawing political ambition and choler. Their unofficial relations were "not wanting in kindness," but business was different. Canning disliked Adams' habit of leaving the office door open so secretaries could hear, and presumably pass on, his nationalistic diatribes. He found Adams sometimes slow with business, his notes complicated and difficult to understand. At the end the British envoy lost faith in Adams' word.[23]

Canning, who modeled his public behavior after Bagot, found it just as difficult to keep the mask in place. During the summer he was bored to death and sought diversion in Scott's romances. In winter things changed. During a session of Congress, he wrote, the "diplomatic body . . . ought really to be reckoned among the laboring classes," for a minister must constantly entertain hypersensitive legislators and, "like a candidate at a popular election, . . . have his hand out for everyone, and a never-ebbing smile on his face." Canning fought an arduous battle to conceal his prejudices. This nervous strain, the alternating heat and cold, and frequent bouts with the flu combined to impair his health. In the last months of his mission he became so ill that, horror of horrors, he had to give up wine. Nevertheless he seems to have been a social success, albeit on a more modest scale than the Bagots, and Niles reported general regret when he left Washington.[24]

What troubled Stratford Canning, as it had Bagot, was "the vanity, the suspicion, and the irritability" of the Americans. He welcomed the depression of 1819 because he thought it would "sober down some of those brilliant fancies with which the good people, one and all, have been possessed since the pleasant days of

---

[23] June 24, 1823, Adams, *op. cit.*, VI, 156–157; Lane-Poole, *op. cit.*, I, 308–309, quoting Canning's memoirs; Stratford Canning to Planta, private, April 9, June 6, 1823, Stratford Canning MSS, FO 352/8.

[24] Elizabeth F. Malcolm-Smith, *The Life of Stratford Canning (Lord Stratford de Redcliffe)* (London, 1933), p. 68; Stratford Canning to Planta, June 15, 1821, Lane-Poole, *op. cit.*, I, 303; Stratford Canning to Planta, private, Jan. 4, 1823, Stratford Canning MSS, FO 352/8; *Niles' Weekly Register* (Baltimore), July 5, 1823.

neutral trade and the glories of Perry and Jackson." A pious and philosophical man, he reconciled himself to his situation, writing his mother, "I consider my residence in America as a second and rougher period of education; one's passage through it is not unattended with the privations and annoyances of school, but I do not quite despair of being able . . . to look back upon it as I now do with thankfulness on the restraints and disciplines of Eton." [25] Public school lasted a term of years, and from the beginning Stratford Canning determined to endure his new education for three sessions of Congress and no more. He left America without regret in June, 1823.

Once again a chargé succeeded the minister. Henry Unwin Addington, nephew of Lord Sidmouth, who was a cabinet member and former premier, served under Stratford Canning in Europe and owed his American appointment to him. Addington reached Washington six months before the minister left, was broken in by him, and took over the mission when Canning departed. For two years, until Charles Vaughan arrived in 1825, he served modestly and on the whole capably in Washington. [26]

Neither the chargés nor Stratford Canning could reasonably hope to equal Bagot's success. The first envoy had the good fortune to join in the liquidation of wartime difficulties. His successors dealt largely with problems—the slave trade, Oregon, West Indian commerce, Latin American independence—which grew toward a climax rather than away from one. Fortunately Adams, who perhaps recognized in Canning some of his own failings, never considered their differences signs of a major change in British policy, and Canning honestly sought to serve Castlereagh's policy of conciliation. On balance he compares well with most of his predecessors.

Of the postwar American leaders, James Monroe responded

[25] Stratford Canning to Planta, June 15, 1821, Lane-Poole, *op. cit.*, I, 303; Stratford Canning to Canning, private, Sept. 29, 1821, *ibid.*, pp. 305–306; Stratford Canning to Mehitabel Canning, Nov. 4, 1821, *ibid.*, p. 326.
[26] Addington to Canning, Sept. 17, 1822, and encl., George Canning Papers, Harewood House, Leeds, Bundle 125; Bradford Perkins, ed., *Youthful America* (Berkeley and Los Angeles, 1960), pp. 3–7.

most warmly to the new British approach. James Madison's more negative reaction hardly mattered because, exhausted by wartime labors, he virtually abandoned the management of diplomacy long before departing from Washington by steamboat, unnoticed and uncelebrated, in the spring of 1817.[27] During the closing months of Madison's administration, Secretary of State Monroe ritualistically warmed up old complaints against England. Almost as soon as Monroe moved to the White House he showed a new temper, and both Bagot and Canning liked and respected the new president.

Monroe quickly became a national president in a way unknown since Washington's time, riding to popularity on the wave of postwar patriotism. Aside from Chief Justice Marshall, he was the last combat veteran of the Revolution to hold important federal office, and during the second war with England Monroe gained kudos rightly withheld from most of the administration. Shortly after his inauguration he undertook a grand tour of the Northern states, a journey his Republican predecessors never risked. Alerted by Bagot, British officers on the Niagara frontier courteously greeted the President, who was grateful for their attention.[28] On the American side of the border, the tour stimulated outpourings of obeisance and loyalty Monroe accepted in the manner of a European monarch, albeit a modest and informal one, on a progress through his domains.

Monroe's early career had been most notable for instability, particularly in his attitude toward Great Britain. As president he showed balance and moderation, moving in an almost Olympian way through the hurly-burly of political strife. One historian describes him as "a lonely and sometimes bewildered figure, irreso-

---

[27] W. Penn Cresson, *James Monroe* (Chapel Hill, 1946), pp. 284–285. Retiring, Madison received few letters of praise for his long service to the United States. Albert Gallatin wrote: "Never was a country left in a more flourishing situation than the United States at the end of your administration; and they are more united at home and respected abroad than at any period since the war of the independence." Gallatin to Madison, July 17, 1817, Rives Collection.

[28] Bagot #50 to Castlereagh, Aug. 8, 1817, FO 5/122.

lute between two worlds." Another asserts that Monroe dominated even John Quincy Adams.[29] The truth seems to lie somewhere in between. Monroe, who disliked factional brawling, could not stop it, and toward the close of his administration permitted the government to become an engine for Adams' election. In foreign policy he usually left tactical control to Adams. On the other hand he determined the general outlines of American policy and often restrained overzealous subordinates, including Adams. Except on his tours, Monroe by no means played the role of constitutional monarch.

Adams brought to the cabinet the fruits of his long experience abroad, most recently as minister to England. He reached London in May, 1815; on the road he passed a regiment marching to serve under Wellington on the Continent. In June the Regent formally received Adams, expressing fond memories of his friend Pinkney (or was it Pinckney? and what was his first name?) and asking Adams if he had enjoyed Brussels (Ghent, said Adams).[30] The new minister gathered together possessions scattered over Europe—thirty-four trunks from St. Petersburg, twenty-six cases of wine from France, his own baggage—and settled into a mission that he rightly anticipated would provide few opportunities for glory.

Led by the cabinet ministers and their wives, English society threw open its doors to Adams, enticing him into a round of engagements he often considered wasteful in time and money. He made the acquaintance of Fox's political heir, the pro-American Lord Holland, and enjoyed conversations with intellectual leaders including Jeremy Bentham and Sir James Mackintosh. Sir William Scott's "great urbanity . . . and playful wit" so impressed Adams that he almost forgave the admiralty judge for his prewar condemnations of American ships. If Lord Walpole, an old rival

[29] Charles M. Wiltse, *John C. Calhoun, Nationalist* (Indianapolis, 1944), p. 146; Arthur P. Whitaker, *The United States and the Independence of Latin America, 1800–1830* (Baltimore, 1941), pp. 379–382.
[30] June 8, 1815, Adams, *op. cit.*, III, 214–215.

from St. Petersburg, tactlessly commented on Adams' growing girth, others were more careful. George Canning, introduced to Adams by Liverpool, tried to envelop him in charm. The suspicious Yankee commented, "I suppose [he] considers it as a rule of personal courtesy to make up by an excess of civility for the rancor which he has so constantly manifested against us." [31]

Neither Canning nor anyone else induced Adams to drop his guard. He dismissed the friendship shown to him as mere politesse. English hauteur and the animosity of the press affronted him as much as any other visitor. He considered the country "far more inveterate against us than it ever was before" [32] and feared trouble in the future, for he disagreed with some Republicans who believed that England's social upheaval forecast her downfall. Fortunately, like Bagot in Yankeeland, Adams kept these thoughts to himself.

Castlereagh sometimes irritated Adams. He forgot details—for example, the terms of the 1815 convention—and often kept Adams waiting, once being still in bed when the American arrived for a scheduled appointment shortly before noon. On the whole their relations were satisfactory. The Englishman smoothly accepted or suavely turned aside Adams' oral complaints and official notes—one on the fishery ran to twenty pages—and Adams did not take affront at refusals and evasions. When the American returned home, Castlereagh had great hopes that the new secretary would improve the tone of the Department of State. [33]

Only once did they quarrel. Questioned accusingly about rumored British designs on Florida, Castlereagh took offense at the implication he was playing America false. "If it is supposed that we have any little trickish policy of thrusting ourselves in there, between you, and Spain, we are very much misunderstood indeed," he complained. Before Castlereagh regained his poise he let slip a minatory declaration that an American threat to the Floridas

---

[31] Adams to Abigail Adams, June 6, 1816, Adams Family MSS, Vol. CXLIII; May 2, 1817, May 3, Aug. 25, 1816, Adams, *op. cit.*, III, 515–516, 351–352, 437.

[32] Adams to John Adams, Aug. 1, 1816, Adams Family MSS, Vol. CXLIII.

[33] June 18, April 9, 1816, Adams, *op. cit.*, III, 391, 329; Castlereagh to Bagot, private and confidential, Nov. 10, 1817, FO 5/120.

VISCOUNT CASTLEREAGH

Portrait by Thomas Lawrence

GEORGE CANNING

Portrait by Thomas Lawrence

might force a preventive English occupation,[34] something he never considered when the issue later became real.

Long before Monroe took office rumor appointed Adams to the Department of State. In terms of experience and diplomatic talent he had no rival, but Monroe later implied that he selected Adams very largely to lay at rest complaints against a Virginia dynasty.[35] Only after the Senate had confirmed Adams' appointment did the President ask him to accept the post.

This news reached London on an April morning. Adams accepted with conventional disclaimers about his unworthiness, and sailed from Cowes in June. After a fairly slow voyage and a month with parents he had not seen for eight years, he traveled to Washington in September, changing six times from stagecoach to steamboat and back again. Thanks to General Ross the White House smelled so badly of fresh plaster and paint that Monroe fled to Virginia after one brief evening meeting with his new lieutenant. For a week the secretary ad interim initiated Adams into the department's arcane mysteries. After that he was on his own.

The transmogrification from envoy to secretary did not change Adams' character, although in Washington he did permit his temper to show more often. Particularly near the end of his tenure, with the White House tantalizingly in view, Adams became extremely combative. At various times he quarreled with Stratford Canning, Luis de Onís of Spain, and France's Hyde de Neuville.[36] At that he never matched the fury of Hyde and Canning, who exchanged angry words at the White House and nearly fought a duel. As always, Adams showed cool nerve, an almost unimaginable capacity for work, a clear but pessimistic grasp of world politics, and deep faith in America's future.

[34] Adams #30 to Monroe, Feb. 8, 1816, Despatches, Great Britain, Vol. XX. In preparation for this conference the methodical Adams memorized a list of ten issues to raise with Castlereagh. He lettered them *A* through *J*, each letter the beginning of a key word which reminded him of the issue. Jan. 25, 1816, Adams, *op. cit.*, III, 280.
[35] Monroe to Jefferson, Feb. 23, 1817, Stanislaus M. Hamilton, ed., *The Writings of James Monroe* (7 vols.; New York, 1898–1903), VI, 3–4.
[36] Of all the ministers with whom he dealt, including Bagot, Adams preferred Hyde de Neuville despite the Frenchman's quick temper. June 2, 1820, Adams, *op. cit.*, V, 136–138.

Adams, who never trusted or loved England, responded half-consciously to Castlereagh's policy and became, as Sir Charles Webster observes, "almost against his will an instrument in the creation of better relations with Britain." [37] He obtained the Floridas and a boundary stretching to the Pacific Ocean, wisely managed the timing of American recognition of independent Latin-American states, and contributed mightily to the Monroe Doctrine, all without risking America's security or exposing her to the insults so often invited by his predecessors.

Adams' efforts exhausted him, particularly because he tested his own conduct by standards even more rigid than those he applied to others. About two-thirds of the way through his term of service, learning of Castlereagh's suicide, the Secretary wrote chillingly, even cruelly, to his wife: ". . . you think I am panting to be President when I am much more inclined to envy Castlereagh the relief he has found from a situation too much like mine, though I implore the mercy of God that I may be never so deserted of Him as to seek relief in the same manner." Later in the same letter Adams balanced this frightening passage by adding proudly, "Of the public History of Mr Monroes administration, all that will be worth telling to posterity hitherto has been transacted through the Department of State." [38] Nothing caused him to alter this view.

No more than Viscount Castlereagh was John Quincy Adams a political philosopher. The American inherited from his father a devotion to republicanism as opposed to monarchy on the one hand and egalitarian democracy on the other. Once, when Stratford Canning, "in that joking manner which he thinks witty," commented, "What a troublesome body this Congress is!" Adams quickly replied, "Not quite so manageable as your Parliament; and you find even that sometimes troublesome." He considered European upheavals grounded in the contest between the people and their parliaments and kings, not in international rivalries. [39] It

[37] Webster, *Castlereagh, 1815–1822*, p. 441.
[38] Adams to Louisa Adams, Oct. 7, 1822, Adams Family MSS, Vol. CXLVII.
[39] Dec. 29, 1821, Adams, *op. cit.*, V, 466; Adams #1 to Henry Middleton, July 5, 1820, Department of State Archives, National Archives, Diplomatic Instructions, All Countries, Vol. IX.

followed that Europe's ruling class hated America for the unsettling example she provided. Before the war, Adams wrote in 1817, many Englishmen despised America, "& contempt is a feeling far less active in spurring to acts of hostility than hatred and fear, which have taken its place." Now Englishmen of all parties considered the United States a dangerous enemy and rival. Since British influence extended far and wide, the United States had enemies almost everywhere and few or no friends.[40] Fear and antirepublicanism ensured foreign hostility.

Wisdom, it seemed to Adams as to most Americans from Washington's time to McKinley's, counseled America to "stand in firm and cautious independence of all entanglement in the European system." This self-abnegating policy had a positive corollary, that America should lead in the Western Hemisphere. "Europe and America, I understand him to say," Stratford Canning reported in describing Adams' rebuff of suggestions for Anglo-American concert, "had each a sphere of its own." [41] These sentiments clearly foreshadowed Monroe's famous declaration three years later.

Adams did not permit rigorous, even narrow, conceptual views to straitjacket his English policy. The Secretary, who detested British colonialism and watched like a hawk for signs of its expansion in the Western Hemisphere, counted on time, not force, to break up existing outposts of empire. He recognized that Liverpool's ministry was less hostile than the British press, the English people, and most Continental statesmen. As Castlereagh and then Canning rallied their country against reactionary European dynasts, Adams came to feel that Britain, perhaps against her will, was serving American interests.

Richard Rush, the representative at London during Adams' secretaryship, shared most of his views. His various memoirs, written years later, sometimes with the clear purpose of reducing tension, have given Rush an undeserved reputation for Anglo-

---

[40] Adams to Plumer, Jan. 17, 1817, Adams Family MSS, Vol. CXLIII.
[41] Adams #1 to Middleton, July 5, 1820, Instructions, Vol. IX; Stratford Canning #2 to Castlereagh, Oct. 3, 1820, FO 5/150.

philia. A tactful and successful minister, he concealed his dislike and distrust of England.

The son of Benjamin Rush, physician and Republican politician in Pennsylvania, young Richard became a protégé of James Madison. He gained national prominence with a Fourth of July speech in 1812 defending the declaration of war. Rush served as secretary of state ad interim under Monroe until Adams returned from London. Aside from giving his name (with Bagot's) to an already nearly completed agreement limiting naval strength on the Great Lakes, Rush accomplished little at the department, and politicians grumbled at his London appointment. Even friends questioned his judgment and determination, and Rufus King considered him a "soft and empty pedant." Adams apparently shared these doubts,[42] and when important business arose in 1818 he ordered Albert Gallatin from Paris to London to share in the negotiations.

At the end of 1817 Rush sailed up the Channel in U.S.S. *Franklin*, a seventy-four-gun monster. Catharine Rush, four children, masses of luggage, a box of sea-otter skins carried as a favor to Mrs. Bagot, and a milch cow, brought along over the captain's protests, accompanied the envoy. A spat with customs officials, who refused to pass Rush's trunks without inspection until so ordered by the Foreign Office, delayed him briefly at Portsmouth. On December 21 Rush reached London where he was greeted by the chargé and secretary of legation, John Adams Smith, the Secretary's nephew. Two days later he paid a courtesy call on Castlereagh, and shortly after the turn of the year returned to Downing Street for their first business session.

Four and a half years later, after Castlereagh's suicide, Rush wrote, "I must bear tribute to the uniform obligingness and conciliation of his personal temper and manners, in all the intercourse I have ever had with him." They worked smoothly together, with nary an important argument, and occasionally they agreed to bury silently an issue that might have become an unpleasant little con-

[42] Crawford to Gallatin, May 1, 1818, Gallatin MSS; Clay to Caesar A. Rodney, Oct. 5, 1817, Rodney Family Papers, Library of Congress; King to Gore, April 12, 1818, Charles R. King, *The Life and Correspondence of Rufus King* (6 vols.; New York, 1894–1900), VI, 140; May 25, 1820, Adams, *op. cit.*, V, 132.

troversy. The two men never became close friends, nor did they often discuss larger aspects of world politics. For Castlereagh reserve was instinctive, and pride prevented Rush from forcing the pace. Undersecretary Joseph Planta, who liked Rush, inaccurately set him down as a shy man.[43]

Only a few months in England convinced Rush that the Liverpool ministry sincerely wanted peace. He was positive no alternative government would be so conciliatory. Rush explained the ministry's favorable policy in terms of its desire for economic recovery. "Friendship, it is not natural that it should feel towards us; nor is it necessary," he asserted, for peace also served American interests and permitted the United States to close the power gap between the two countries. Frequently he commented on "the settled hostility of this throne and those who surround it," [44] and he praised the ministry only by comparison with the rest of the political world.

A conflict of political systems and an already developing economic rivalry explained, Rush believed, the inveterate hostility he descried in the British capital. Extravagantly, he described England as no more republican than Turkey and her ruling class as fully as hostile to republican ideas. He chafed at compulsory visits to the residences of royal dukes and carefully refrained from placing an illuminated "G IV" in his window on coronation day, although all other envoys did so and Rush himself spent thirteen hours in Westminster Abbey to see the erstwhile Prince Regent become George IV. He feared Britain so much, particularly her sea power, that he considered Bourbon France "our best and true connection abroad." Between England and the United States, he believed, there existed "an immense and growing rivalry, . . . at all points, in all quarters." [45] One can only marvel at Rush's

[43] Rush #261 to Adams, Aug. 13, 1822, Despatches, Great Britain, Vol. XXVII; Planta to Bagot, Jan. 10, 1818, Bagot MSS.

[44] Rush to Monroe, Nov. 25, 1820, Monroe MSS; Rush to Crawford, July 10, 1818, William H. Crawford Papers, Library of Congress; Rush to Monroe, confidential, May 10, 1818, Monroe MSS.

[45] Rush #101 to Adams, Dec. 3, 1819, Despatches, Great Britain, Vol. XXIV; Rush to Monroe, private, Feb. 19, 1818, Monroe MSS; Rush #203 to Adams, July 21, 1821, Despatches, Great Britain, Vol. XXVI; Rush to Ingersoll, private, Feb. 14, 1824, Rush Family Papers, Princeton University Library.

success in concealing his hatred of England from those with whom he came into contact.

The self-righteous American steadily resisted English blandishments. He faithfully reported honors done his official character when he visited the Chatham Navy Yard, the polite applause when the Chancellor of the Exchequer praised American efforts at a meeting of the English Bible Society. He accepted the freedom of three gentlemen's clubs in London. He disliked these pretenses of friendship, although he promised that on his side "no just efforts shall ever be pretermitted . . . , to convert them into the realities which they counterfeit." He hated the British habit of "carousing all night and sleeping all day, because people who work do the contrary," and in his own residence observed "the hours of a certain country 3000 miles off where good sense is so much more predominant." With one single exception, the ultra-republican Jeremy Bentham, Richard Rush made no personal friends in England. He quitted the island as he entered it, an enemy of English pretensions, manners, and politics.[46]

Fortunately for the postwar rapprochement, Rush never lost his poise. He and Catharine Rush performed their roles to perfection. The envoy wrote a marvelously insincere note of condolence to Castlereagh on the death of George III, and shortly after his return to the United States composed a similar letter, much less demanded by the proprieties, to George Canning:

I look back with great interest upon the seven years that I spent in England. Beautiful country, wonderful people! That it fell my lot to be all that while in harmony with you all, I account a singular happiness, the result at once of the good dispositions which I always found at the foreign office, and of the corresponding ones which it was my duty and my pride to cherish. Refer-

[46] Rush #211 to Adams, Sept. 19, 1821, Despatches, Great Britain, Vol. XXVI; Richard Rush, *A Residence at the Court of London* (3d ed.; London, 1872), pp. 213–214 and *passim;* Rush #50 to Adams, Dec. 31, 1818, Despatches, Great Britain, Vol. XXIII; Rush to Monroe, private, Jan. 20, 1818, James Monroe Papers, New York Public Library; Bentham to Catharine Rush, March 26, 1822, Rush Family MSS. Bentham wrote: "In revenge for the late outrage to his Monarchical feelings, by Mrs Rush's present of Republican Oranges, Mr Bentham insists on her acceptance of one of the few sample Bottles of Ultra-Monarchical . . . Wine, lately received, from an Estate of his Brother's at Montpellier." Other notes affected a similar tone.

ring to the large measure of personal gratification which I derived in the course of my residence, I shall ever recall, as standing in the first rank, many of the days that I spent at Gloucester Lodge.

When he left England at his own request, Rush allowed Canning to assume that he had reluctantly acceded to the President's request that he take over the Treasury.[47]

As early as 1820, after two years' service at London, Rush had sought transfer to St. Petersburg. In addition to his dislike of Britain and the psychological mask this forced upon him, the young envoy found it impossible to live on his $9,000 salary. Secretary of State Adams, always attentive to the misuse of public funds, objected when Rush charged more than two newspaper subscriptions to the government, and the cost of housing in the British capital proved so high that Rush took refuge in the suburbs for several years, maintaining only an office in London. At the end of 1823 the envoy officially requested recall the next autumn.[48] Ignoring earlier doubts, President-elect Adams asked Rush to join his cabinet, and the Pennsylvanian left England in the spring of 1825 after seven and a half years of successful service.

If, as is beyond challenge, Anglo-American relations improved after 1815, Lord Castlereagh deserves most of, but not all, the credit. All the diplomats, watched suspiciously by a memory-ridden public, faced postwar challenges in a spirit unknown before the war. The leaders, even Castlereagh, shared the prejudices of their constituents. They also knew that their larger roles prevented them from indulging these feelings. This changed outlook was an essential difference, although not the only one, between England under Perceval and under Liverpool, between Jefferson's regime and Monroe's America.

[47] Rush to Castlereagh, Jan. 30, 1820, FO 5/154; Rush to Canning, private, Nov. 2, 1825, Canning MSS, Bundle 125; Rush to Canning, April 20, 1825, FO 5/207.
[48] Rush to Monroe, private and personal, March 20, 1820, Monroe MSS, Library of Congress; Adams to Rush, private, May 25, 1818, Rush Family MSS; Rush, *Residence*, pp. 56–57. Even the office suffered harassment, for, to enforce a judgment against the landlord, law officers invaded the three sacrosanct rooms, an event that distressed Secretary Canning almost as much as it angered Minister Rush. Rush to Canning, Aug. 9, 1823, FO 5/181; Canning to George Herries, Aug. 18, 1823, FO 5/182.

CHAPTER

XII

COTTON AND TOBACCO, CALICOES AND CUTLERY

In the time of Jefferson and Perceval one theme—neutral commerce—and one man—Napoleon—dominated Anglo-American diplomacy. Postwar leaders faced less stark, more complex challenges. Some issues arose and were settled quickly. Others—for example, the American desire to trade with the British West Indies—lasted for years. Often two or more problems vied for priority. General instructions to the American minister in England in May, 1816, listed five major topics and several lesser ones. Negotiations two years later, leading to the most important agreement of the period, covered a range of problems: boundaries, the fishery, the omnipresent West Indian question, even the ancient differences over impressment.[1] To be understood, these tangled threads must be separated into three skeins. One involved questions left over

---

[1] Monroe to Adams, May 21, 1816, Department of State Archives, National Archives, Diplomatic Instructions, All Countries, Vol. VIII; Adams #5 to Rush, May 21, 1818, *ibid.*

from prewar and wartime days. A second included the sometimes opposed, sometimes shared interests of the English-speaking powers in the downfall of the Spanish Empire. The third, which largely inspired and certainly supported Castlereagh's policy of conciliation, concerned Anglo-American commerce.

Adam Smith died in 1790, a prophet not without honor but certainly not yet with broad appeal. Although necessity forced modifications in the mercantilist system, notably the opening of direct trade between the United States and England to American ships, defenders of the Navigation Acts usually refused to budge. In Lord Sheffield and the first Earl of Liverpool, father of Castlereagh's superior, they found indefatigable spokesmen, and William Pitt, who demurred, never forcefully challenged the conventional wisdom of the day.

The French war forced certain *ad hoc* relaxations of the hallowed system, particularly the admission of American ships to colonial ports, but these ended with the return of peace. Far more important, with enemy coöperation the war became a contest in restriction and monopoly, a war of deep mercantilist hue. Jealousy of foreign prosperity, rigid devotion to a favorable trade balance, a conviction that British strength rose and fell with shipping and colonial interests—these prejudices carried over into the postwar years. As late as 1821 the *Quarterly Review* pronounced the Navigation Acts the "happiest thoughts of legislation operating upon and regulating human actions. . . . The effects are, at once, moral and political."[2]

Before 1812, and to a lesser degree after 1815, Opposition leaders insisted that American well-being benefited England, that the United States provided an essential market for manufactures and an even more essential source of raw materials. Commercial interests agreed. In 1814, congratulating the country on peace with the Americans, the *Caledonian Mercury* commented: "Agriculture will be their main pursuit [for centuries]; and for the produce of . . . industry, they must chiefly depend on . . . other na-

[2] *Quarterly Review* (London), XXIV (1821), 298.

tions." Britain stood to profit from this situation far more than any other country.[3]

After Ghent some of the cabinet stole Opposition clothes (and the somnolent Opposition made little effort to steal them back again). When a break in American purchases deepened England's depression the younger Liverpool, otherwise a dutiful son, frankly stated his position:

. . . there is no country more interested than England is, that the distress of America should cease, and that she should be enabled to continue that rapid progress which has been for a time interrupted; for, of all the powers on the face of the earth, America is the one whose increasing population and immense territory, furnish the best prospect for British produce and manufactures.

This prophecy meant, the Earl affirmed, that everyone "who wishes prosperity to England, must wish prosperity to America." This theme, frequent in ministerial speeches, annoyed conservative Englishmen and, at the other extreme, Richard Rush, who unfairly interpreted it to mean that Liverpool blamed the United States for England's hard times.[4]

Liverpool, Castlereagh, and energetic lieutenants, notably Chancellor of the Exchequer Nicholas Vansittart and Frederick Robinson, vice-president and then president of the Board of Trade, grounded their economic views in part upon Adam Smith and David Ricardo, whose great work, *Principles of Political Economy and Taxation,* appeared in 1817. They also appealed to the shade of the younger Pitt and the more distant, almost forgotten Earl of Shelburne, an advocate of close commercial ties with the former colonies at the end of the American Revolution. Like Smith and Ricardo, Pitt and Shelburne, the members of the cabinet clique were liberal in a very limited sense. They believed, as Liverpool put it, that trade prospered despite and not because of regulation,

---

[3] *Caledonian Mercury* (Edinburgh), Dec. 29, 1814.
[4] *Hansard,* n.s., I, 574–575; Rush #102 to Adams, Dec. 20, 1819, Department of State Archives, National Archives, Despatches, Great Britain, Vol. XXIV.

and they therefore sought to free commerce from constricting controls.[5]

The ministers, practicing politicians rather than dogmatists or theoreticians, proceeded cautiously in the face of opposition from less imaginative colleagues and their own back-benchers. They never dreamed, for example, of dropping import controls. For several years they virtually excluded American grain,[6] supporting domestic producers including great political magnates at a time when the poor called for bread. Still, the ministers frankly rejected tradition, particularly the deep-seated hostility toward American shipping. They made no effort to replace decrepit barriers with effective ones, and they agreed to demolish some walls. They furthered Anglo-American commerce at a time when depression encouraged them to look inward.

Generally speaking, Americans also welcomed the drift toward freer trade, particularly the end of restrictions on shipping. Lower construction costs, more efficient design, and smaller crews (which compensated for higher wages) gave Americans an immense advantage in unfettered competition. "The deduction is irresistible," Rush commented, "that the ocean is to change ownership and pass to us."[7] Thus the Americans happily arranged to eliminate shipping preferences on the Atlantic run. They only regretted that Downing Street would not act so decisively with respect to West Indian trade.

Congress passed a reciprocity act early in 1815, providing a legislative base for the commercial convention a few months later. Some Americans complained that the convention, by promising not to discriminate against British ships engaged in direct trade, abandoned a powerful weapon to force open the West Indies. Within a few years these murmurs died as the Americans gained a near monopoly of transatlantic carriage. In 1816, according to English

---

[5] On this theme, see particularly George Dangerfield, *The Era of Good Feelings* (New York, 1952), pp. 251–262.

[6] Rush #208 to Adams, Aug. 28, 1821, Despatches, Great Britain, Vol. XXVI.

[7] Rush to Crawford, July 10, 1818, William H. Crawford Papers, Library of Congress.

figures—and all statistics in this area are open to question—British ships enjoyed three-eighths of the carriage. In the first eight months of 1818, 358 ships reached Liverpool from America, Richard Rush reported, and only 30 were British. The convention "pressed us most for the first year or two," the minister stated, "but I am under the belief that in the race of competition under its provisions, we are now fast outstripping her." [8]

To risk these gains in pursuit of rights in the West Indies would have been sheer quixotism, and in the important negotiations of 1818 the Americans did not do so. The loss of West Indian carriage, Secretary Adams observed, "has not been very essential" compared with gains on the Atlantic run. Even before formal negotiations began, Adams' agents readily accepted an English proposal to extend the convention of 1815. Almost without discussion, the old agreement became one of the most important provisions of the broader convention ultimately arranged. Within a few years the Americans carried about 90 per cent of the trade in their ships. [9]

The American position on a protective tariff was less clear-cut. For many Republicans Hamilton's ancient advocacy of protection determined them to oppose it. Farmers and planters considered protection a tax for the benefit of a small class of manufacturers. Many Federalists, owing allegiance to commerce rather than to industry, opposed restrictions on international trade. On the other side, in addition to a small group directly interested in manufacturing, less cohesive groups stood for economic self-sufficiency. During the war treasury requirements and a desire to encourage manufacturing led Congress to raise tariffs. Later, when traditional Republican views reasserted themselves, they came into conflict with the war-born desire to shake off British shackles.

In a tariff debate early in 1816 the legislators rejected John Randolph's complaint that all protection was "a scheme of public

[8] *Parliamentary Papers, 1817*, XIV, 224–225; encl. in Rush to Gallatin, Sept. 13, 1818, Albert Gallatin Papers, New-York Historical Society; Rush to Crawford, July 10, 1818, Crawford MSS.
[9] Adams #6 to Gallatin, May 22, 1818, Instructions, Vol. VIII; Rush memorandum, Nov. 10, 1818, James Monroe Papers, Library of Congress; George R. Taylor, *The Transportation Revolution* (New York, 1951), p. 440.

robbery" carried out at the expense of agriculturists. They insisted that protection would defend America against British "dumping" and create a balanced economy better able to prosecute a future war against England. A New York Federalist described with horror (and exaggeration) the deluge of British goods at low prices and asked, "Is it possible to see such a course of trade in any other light than as most ruinous to the country?"

John C. Calhoun most forcefully expressed the protectionist point of view. Piously beginning with the statement that as representative of an agricultural district he could not be accused of self-interest, he argued that the recent war proved the United States could not mobilize its full strength without developing industry. When "we have the misfortune to be involved in a war with a nation dominant on the ocean, and it is almost only with such we can at present be," the Carolinian stated, both commerce and agricultural exports ceased, thanks to the Royal Navy. The answer appeared clear to Calhoun: stimulate domestic manufactures which would absorb agricultural produce, strengthen the nation's wartime economy, and support the national government in time of war.[10]

The tariff of 1816, which passed the House of Representatives by 88 to 54 and the Senate by a larger proportion, fell far short of real protection. The new law did not restore the schedules of 1812 but, on the other hand, reduced wartime levies, and the new charges proved insufficient to give much impetus to American manufacturers. Nevertheless, if only in a limited and ineffective fashion, Republicans turned their backs upon party tradition to strike a blow against England.

The bill chartering a new national bank, passed only a few weeks before the tariff of 1816, also reflected economic nationalism. Republicans allowed the Hamiltonian bank to die in 1811, and wartime efforts to establish a bank foundered, the last of them failing primarily because news of the peace of Ghent made a bank seem less urgently needed. In 1816 Congress reversed itself. President

[10] *Annals of Congress*, 14th Cong., 1st sess., pp. 1328, 1323, 1330–1336, and *passim*.

Madison, an enemy of the first bank on constitutional grounds, signed the bill in April.[11] The charter excluded foreigners from the Board of Directors and from voting by proxy. Until Jackson's presidency the charge of foreign, or British, ownership did not plague this bank as it had the earlier one. The bank symbolized American nationalism and provided a foundation for war finance, if needed.

The bank and tariff bills of 1816 did not trouble Downing Street because neither law stifled the flow of capital or goods to the United States. An effort to raise the tariff failed in the Senate by one vote in 1820. In 1824, at the very end of the postwar period, a new tariff raised duties; in the opinion of the British chargé the law was aimed at England, which provided four-fifths of American imports.[12] For nearly a decade, however, the tariff of 1816 continued in effect. Despite its nominally protective and clearly anti-British purpose, Liverpool's government could afford to disregard it.

America's export trade failed to regain pre-Embargo heights after the War of 1812, although in 1818 it fell short by only a few million dollars. A major explanation lies in the decline of the reëxport trade, very largely an artificial, war-born device. From 1805 to 1807 reëxports averaged more than $55 million; in the postwar decade they only twice topped $20 million. The largest ingredient in the surviving reëxport trade was British cotton cloth, imported into the United States and then consigned to other markets.[13]

By contrast, exports of American produce, so long trammeled by belligerent edicts, Jeffersonian policy, and then by war, topped prewar levels. On the average, domestic exports from 1816 to

[11] Irving Brant, *James Madison: Commander in Chief* (Indianapolis, 1961), pp. 402–403.

[12] Addington #12, #19 to Canning, March 13, April 5, 1824, Foreign Office Archives, Public Record Office, FO 5/185.

[13] *Historical Statistics of the United States, Colonial Times to 1957*, Bureau of the Census (Washington, 1960), pp. 529–553, and Taylor, *op. cit.*, pp. 176–202, 440–452, provide the information for this and succeeding paragraphs, except as noted in footnotes below. American statistics are incomplete and somewhat unreliable, especially before 1821. Taylor, *op. cit.*, pp. 198–200.

1825 exceeded pre-Embargo figures by about one-third. As always, whether peace or war ruled in Europe, the bulk of these shipments went to Britain and increasingly to the banks of the Mersey, for Liverpool steadily tightened her grip on the American trade. In the postwar years the United Kingdom consistently purchased more than two-fifths of all American exports, about $25 million worth annually, four times the French share.

In dollar terms 1818 was the peak year, not exceeded until 1834. After 1818 the value of domestic exports to all countries zigzagged downward from $74 million, touching a postwar low of $44 million in 1821. (Even that figure had been exceeded only three times before 1812.) Falling prices almost alone explain the drop in dollar sales; American producers suffered as a result of the worldwide depression that followed the Napoleonic Wars. Shipping tonnage entering and leaving American ports declined hardly at all, and the volume, as opposed to the worth, of exports continued to rise. Even at lower prices, sales to England played a major part in American economic life and ultimately supported recovery from the depression of 1819.

Raw cotton dominated American exports. Two leading prewar challengers, wheat and tobacco, declined, particularly after the British restricted grain imports. In dollar value cotton comprised nearly two-fifths of all domestic exports from 1816 to 1820, and slightly less than half in the next five years. The volume of cotton exports grew rapidly but erratically, and a price drop of more than 60 per cent between 1816 and 1823 held the cash return at about an even level. Farmers running on this treadmill sometimes supported a protective tariff they hoped would create a strong domestic market, but in fact they remained dependent upon British purchases for half a century.

Before Jefferson closed trade in 1807 the United States had captured most of the British cotton market. From that year until 1814 rivals, particularly Brazil, made great strides. With the return of peace Americans quickly reëstablished their position. During the ten years after Ghent they steadily provided slightly more than half the cotton purchased by England, and in later years they did even better. Since British consumption skyrocketed, in absolute terms the American share became ever larger. American cotton landed at Liverpool more than tripled between 1815 and 1818, and in the first eight months of 1818 one ship arrived daily in the Mersey from the Southern states. The United States exported 203,000 bales of cotton to Britain in 1815, 423,000 bales in 1825.[14] American agriculture, British manufacturing, and even American shipping could not have lived without this great flood of cotton across the Atlantic.

Return shipments, less bulky and even more valuable, most often entered the United States through the port of New York, which handled more imports than Boston and Philadelphia, its two closest rivals, put together. New York and Liverpool developed close ties as a result of their mutual interest in Anglo-American trade. It is no coincidence that the Black Ball Line, the first regularly scheduled transatlantic packet service, established in 1818, shuttled the *James Monroe,* the *Courier,* and its two other ships between the Mersey and the Hudson. The packets provided regular information, passenger service, and some freightage. No rival service began until 1822, so for four years Liverpool and New York had an additional advantage over their competitors.[15]

Cargo after cargo of British goods came to New York and other ports in 1815. The flood continued on into 1816, for as quickly as American ships could unload in England they took on board the great store of manufactures accumulated during the War of 1812. Total American imports in these two years probably exceeded $250 million in value at the port of entry. Britain provided a far larger share than any other country. English figures, more reliable than American, show that about $110 million worth of exports went to the United States in 1815 and 1816, and this sum does not allow for the cost of shipment across the Atlantic.

The trade was huge; whether it was profitable or not is another question. Many Americans accused the British of "dumping" goods

[14] Encl. in Rush to Gallatin, Sept. 13, 1818, Gallatin MSS; Thomas Ellison, *The Cotton Trade of Great Britain* (London, 1886), Table I.

[15] Taylor, *op. cit.,* p. 106; Frank Thistlethwaite, *The Anglo-American Connection in the Early Nineteenth Century* (Philadelphia, 1959), p. 13; Robert G. Albion, *The Rise of New York Port* (New York, 1939), *passim.*

below cost to destroy infant American industry, and Henry Brougham, an English observer, doubted that his country gained any immediate profit from the great flow.[16] Not until 1835 did America import as much as she did in 1816.

In succeeding years shipments to the United States rose and fell according to fluctuations in both economies, averaging about $30 million plus freight charges down to 1825, slightly more as the depression eased. Americans received roughly two-fifths of their imports from England, far more than from any other country and approximately the same percentage as the British share of their own exports. They never commanded so large a share of the British export market, usually around one-sixth,[17] but they constituted the largest single purchaser of English goods.

All sorts of materials were shipped to the United States, even coal from Newcastle, for the Americans had not yet developed their own coal deposits. Cotton and woolen textiles predominated, providing in 1821 some 29 per cent of American imports,[18] though a small part came from countries other than England. Unfortunately, precise figures are lacking on the British end, and one may state only that the Americans absorbed far more textiles than any other market. As Liverpool and Castlereagh saw, English prosperity depended in large part upon the rate of exports to America.

Before 1812 economic ties drew the British and the Americans together. At the same time the Americans' quite natural desire to penetrate a European market closed by the Royal Navy drove them asunder. After the peace of Christmas Eve, 1814, both countries had an interest in the expansion of trade, particularly the direct trade across the Atlantic. The depression that struck America in 1819 and England slightly earlier might, like the depression of 1929, have encouraged experiments in autarky. It did not, although there were stirrings in the United States. The Americans sometimes chafed under their dependence upon England, particu-

---

[16] George R. Porter, *The Progress of the Nation*, ed. F. W. Hirst (rev. ed.; London, 1912), p. 479; William Smart, *Economic Annals of the Nineteenth Century*, I (London, 1910), 530. For conversion purposes the pound has been valued at $4.80 rather than the official $4.44. Taylor, *op. cit.*, p. 447n.

[17] Porter, *op. cit.*, pp. 477, 479.

[18] Taylor, *op. cit.*, p. 449.

larly for manufactured goods and for capital which kept trade moving, and in small ways they sought to destroy English primacy. In a larger sense Americans recognized that the transatlantic trade, the most important in the world, was a hostage to peace with Great Britain.

The flow of increasing quantities of goods across the Atlantic did not entirely satisfy the Americans. For years they sought to negotiate their way through imperial regulations closing West Indian ports to their ships, and in quick action just after the war they cut off Canadian trade with Indians in the territory of the United States.

Before the War of 1812 Canadian fur traders had crossed the international boundary to carry on their business with the red men. Americans, possessing the same rights except in the territory of the Hudson's Bay Company, scarcely exercised them at all. The people and the government of the United States increasingly objected that the fur trade masked political intrigue, and they considered it an infringement on their independence. At Ghent the American commissioners declined to renew the privilege, and the British government did not press them. Adams feared England might claim that the treaty, by restoring the Indians to their prewar state, implicitly confirmed their right to trade with agents from Canada, but the British never made such an assertion.[19]

During the commercial negotiations of 1815 Robinson, Goulburn, and Dr. Adams tried halfheartedly to renew the old arrangement in return for British concessions on trade with India. Clay and Gallatin refused even to consider the subject, and the Englishmen did not press it. The next year an American law prohibited foreigners from trading with the Indians, and the Washington government established military posts athwart the old routes.[20]

[19] Alfred L. Burt, *The United States, Great Britain, and British North America from the Revolution to the Establishment of Peace after the War of 1812* (New Haven, 1940), pp. 366, 376.
[20] Robinson, Goulburn, and Adams #1 to Castlereagh, June 7, 1815, FO 5/109; Clay and Gallatin to Monroe, May 18, 1815, Department of State Archives, National Archives, Record of Negotiations Connected with the Treaty of Ghent, Vol. I; Burt, *op. cit.*, pp. 376–377.

Thus ended a trade that often exacerbated Anglo-American relations.

On political grounds Americans opposed colonialism, particularly the imperial system against which they rebelled in 1775. For economic reasons they sought to penetrate markets open to them before the Revolution and, in practice if not always in law, during the Anglo-French contest. The convention of 1815 confirmed their privilege of trading with India. Commerce with British North America remained small and, aside from one small spat in 1823 [21] and nearly ritualistic requests for free use of the St. Lawrence, played no part in diplomacy except as an adjunct to the West Indian issue. Americans concentrated their fire upon the exclusion of their ships from the British West Indies.

The campaign, important in itself, was even more important as part of a general campaign against trade restrictions. Commenting on a proposal to close American ports to English ships from the West Indies, Rufus King wrote that "by adhering to its Principle, we shall accelerate the period of that Dominion on the Ocean, that we are hereafter to attain." The Americans believed that if the British system collapsed, less sturdy empires would abandon monopolistic practices. Negotiations with France, for example, paralleled those over the British West Indies, and after an arduous campaign Secretary Adams gained victory in 1822. As the issue dragged on it necessarily involved national prestige, and in 1822 Stratford Canning reported: "Few questions are capable of exciting a more lively interest in the United States." [22] The campaign became part of the larger crusade to complete the work of independence and the development of national power.

Americans exaggerated the economic stake involved, for the British West Indies took only a tiny share of American exports,

[21] *Annals*, 17th Cong., 2d sess., pp. 670–674, 1159.
[22] King to Gore, April 5, 1818, Charles R. King, *The Life and Correspondence of Rufus King* (6 vols.; New York, 1894–1900), VI, 136–138; King to Charles King, April 5, 1818, *ibid.*, pp. 138–139; Stratford Canning #30 to Londonderry, May 8, 1822, FO 5/168. F. Lee Benns, *The American Struggle for the British West India Carrying-Trade, 1815–1830*, Indiana University Studies, no. 56 (Bloomington, 1923), the standard work on this subject, is freely used in the following paragraphs.

less, for example, than Cuba. At first the monopoly aided British ships on the important North Atlantic run, for they could engage in a triangular trade—England to the United States to the Caribbean and home again—closed to their rivals, charging uneconomic rates where they competed with Yankees. After 1818, when an American law destroyed the triangle's western face, this advantage ceased. British tonnage entering American ports dropped by five-sixths from 1817 to 1819. Unsatisfied, Washington continued the economic war for less substantial goals.

From first to last shipowners alone stood to benefit from American policy. Restrictions on trade hurt the farmer; he would gain little if American ships forced their way into Caribbean ports and not much more through the removal of imperial preference, for his only possible rivals, the Canadians, could not begin to meet West Indian requirements. By 1822 there was extensive grumbling in the United States, but the policy continued.[23]

Many Englishmen in and out of government favored relaxation of the old system. Caught in a trade recession so sharp that the price of West Indian rum fell to a shilling per gallon, plantation owners pleaded for the opening of ports to American shipping. The *Edinburgh Review* described exclusion as "a measure . . . obviously founded on the worst principles of a grasping and avaricious policy," and Lord Grenville urged the government to open the West Indies (and the St. Lawrence) to American ships and to abandon all preferential tariffs on imperial goods. The cabinet's inner circle agreed. As early as 1816 Nicholas Vansittart wrote: "I more than doubt the wisdom of the principle of reciprocal monopoly in our colonial system."[24]

Powerful forces, perhaps more powerful ones, opposed major tinkering with the *status quo*. Driven from North Atlantic routes

[23] Benns, *op. cit.*, p. 36; Stratford Canning #5 to Londonderry, Feb. 7, 1822, FO 5/166.
[24] Petitions of Dominica and St. Vincent merchants, Feb. 28, 1823, Papers of the First and Second Earls of Liverpool, British Museum (Add. MSS 38190–38489, 38564–38581), Add. MSS 38292; *Edinburgh Review*, XXXIII (1820), 338–339; Grenville to Charles Wyman, March 8, 1824, Papers of Stratford Canning, Viscount Stratford de Redcliffe, Public Record Office, FO 352/9; Vansittart memorandum, Oct. —, 1816, FO 5/119.

by American competitors, shipowners had no desire for a rematch in the Caribbean. Canadians maintained that their lumber trade would collapse if American ships gained entry into the West Indies. Above all, conservatives opposed any retreat from a policy that had worked so well in the past. The Prince Regent thought this way, as did, within the cabinet, such important figures as the Duke of Wellington, Lord Eldon, and Earl Bathurst.[25] At least until American restrictions struck home, these men could count on a large part of the House of Commons.

Additionally, Liverpool and Castlereagh underestimated American determination. They simply did not understand that the Americans attached so much symbolic importance to their crusade. Thus London sought to buy off the Americans with minor concessions. They permitted the United States, like other foreign states, to trade with Bermuda, where goods could be transshipped to Caribbean colonies, and by the Free Port Act of 1818 they permitted cargoes destined for the West Indies to be imported into Nova Scotia and New Brunswick for transfer to British vessels. By such expedients they endeavored to encourage the flow of trade while preserving a large portion of the carriage to British vessels.[26]

Until 1822, whenever the Americans raised the question with Lord Castlereagh they received the same bland but discouraging answer: England could not consider major changes in her system but would not object to any retaliatory measures the Americans might devise. British negotiators so informed Clay and Gallatin in 1815. The next year Adams reopened the subject. Cabinet discussion followed, but in the end, "with the utmost courtesy and politeness of form," the Foreign Secretary told Adams that Britain preferred to leave things as they were.[27]

[25] George Lyall to Liverpool, July 9, 1823, Liverpool MSS, Add. MSS 38295; Board of Trade memorandum encl. in Thomas Lack to Hamilton, Jan. 10, 1817, FO 5/127; Bathurst memorandum, Oct. 6, 1816, FO 5/119; Dangerfield, *op. cit.*, p. 252.

[26] Memorandum encl. in Lack to Hamilton, Jan. 17, 1817, FO 5/127; Benns, *op. cit.*, pp. 66–67.

[27] Liverpool to Castlereagh, private and confidential, Sept. 26, 1816, and encl., FO 5/119; Vansittart memorandum, Oct. —, 1816, *ibid.*; Bathurst memorandum, Oct. 6, 1816, *ibid.*; Adams to Madison, private, Sept. 28, 1816, John Quincy Adams Papers, Library of Congress.

This mild rebuff led the Americans to pass a bill forbidding the entry of goods borne from the West Indies by English ships. Henceforth, the law provided, only West Indian or American ships could bring imports from the Caribbean colonies. Because agriculturists did not wish to jeopardize a $3 million trade, the act of 1817 did not prohibit British ships from carrying American exports to the islands; only imports were controlled. This tepid restriction did not disturb London. Shortly before Adams departed to take over the Department of State, Castlereagh told him that the British government considered the act fair and unexceptionable.[28]

A year later the United States stepped up the pressure. The act of 1818, passed by overwhelming majorities, prohibited exports to as well as imports from colonial possessions closed to American ships. Monroe hesitated before signing the act, fearing to harm Anglo-American relations. He need not have worried. Although the London *Sun* described the new law as "pregnant with war" and "an act of hostile policy," other newspapers discounted it as unimportant or excused it as fair, exact retaliation. Bagot, who feigned concern in talks with Adams, really expected the law to backfire, leading "the gentlemen of the landed interest . . . to change their note" when hit by the loss of a market. Lord Castlereagh repeated the usual assurances to Rush.[29]

During the large negotiations of 1818 the West Indian question generated no heat. Washington expected to have a stronger hand after the new act made itself felt. Gallatin and Rush, who presented a request for open ports, did not press the British negotiators. When Robinson and Goulburn discovered that the Americans would neither compromise nor pay any price for the opening of the West Indies, something Rush and Gallatin demanded as a matter of right and parity, they too lost interest.

In frequent conversations on the subject both sides merely

[28] Dangerfield, *op. cit.*, p. 255; Bagot #7 to Castlereagh, Feb. 5, 1817, FO 5/121; March 18, 1817, Charles F. Adams, ed., *Memoirs of John Quincy Adams* (12 vols.; Philadelphia, 1874–1877), III, 489–490.

[29] Benns, *op. cit.*, pp. 51 ff.; *Sun* (London), May 14, 1818; *Times* (London), May 14, 15, 1818; *Caledonian Mercury*, May 16, 1818; April 11, 1818, Adams, *op. cit.*, IV, 78; Bagot to Planta, private, July 29, 1818, FO 5/132.

sought to explain their position. Robinson in particular emphasized that His Majesty's government disliked the colonial system in the abstract, but for political reasons could not suddenly abandon it. "In the course of the discussions," Rush recounted, "it was said by Mr Robinson . . . , though with the greatest urbanity, (for he exhibits at all times in this respect the best qualities of a negociator,) that the very worst way in the world to drive G. Britain from her colonial system was to attempt to coerce her." At the end of the negotiations Robinson and Goulburn presented an article *ad referendum* to Washington. After only slight hesitation Secretary of State Adams rejected this compromise proposal.[30]

Disdaining Robinson's advice, the Americans further strengthened their system by cutting off the roundabout flow of goods through Bermuda and British North America. With Rufus King in the van, Congress overwhelmingly passed a new law in the spring of 1820 which closed American ports to ships from all British colonies, not merely those that refused to admit foreign ships, and admitted goods only if they came directly from the place of origin.[31]

Once more Castlereagh professed to be untroubled. There was, as Robinson had warned, a danger that American pressure would produce a nationalistic reaction. On the other hand the British government probably half welcomed the legislation, for it provided an excuse for moving in a direction ministers desired to go. West Indian interests shrieked for relief. The *Times*, once blandly confident that Britain could outlast the Americans in a contest of self-denial, urged concession, and even the *Quarterly Review* finally swung around. At the same time the Americans felt the pinch. Had London held out a few more months the American system might well have collapsed.[32]

---

[30] Adams #6 to Rush, May 30, 1818, Instructions, Vol. VIII; Rush memorandum, Nov. 10, 1818, Monroe MSS; Robinson and Goulburn #9 to Castlereagh, Oct. 20, 1818, FO 5/138; Feb. 20, March 29, 31, 1819, Adams, *op. cit.*, IV, 272-273, 316, 320-321.

[31] Benns, *op. cit.*, pp. 69 ff.

[32] Rush #134 to Adams, July 14, 1820, Despatches, Great Britain, Vol. XXV; *Times*, May 12, 1820, May 31, 1822; *Quarterly Review*, XXVI (1822), 522-540; Stratford Canning #5 to Londonderry, Feb. 7, 1822, FO 5/166; Stratford Canning to Londonderry, separate and confidential, Feb. 7, 1822, *ibid*.

Despite Stratford Canning's reports to this effect, ministers decided to go to Parliament with a bill upon which Frederick J. Robinson had been working for some months. In June, 1822, Robinson introduced the West India and American Trade Bill. He and William Huskisson, who supported him, spoke cautiously, even defensively, pointing out that the imperial system had already been breached (for example, in trade with India) and promising to protect Canada against American competition. The bill, which soon became law, permitted Americans to bring an enumerated list of articles to specified ports—the most important but not all—in the West Indies. The government reserved the right to impose discriminatory duties on imports, and indeed it soon levied charges of about 10 per cent to aid British North America. Finally, of course, the law required the United States to drop restrictions on British ships and goods.[33]

"Surely victory was never more complete," Rush exulted. The limitations stressed by Robinson, perhaps to soothe domestic critics, did not reduce the value of the concession in any significant way. Almost all important American exports appeared on the permitted list. (Adams even shrugged off as unimportant the omission of fish, perhaps the only desertion of the cod in his family's history.)[34] Discriminatory duties did not seriously penalize the Americans, for obviously British North America could provide only a small fraction of West Indian needs for years to come. In ships, as opposed to goods, the Americans gained complete parity with the British on the run to and from the colonies, and this was what they professed to seek. In the next few years they captured almost all the carriage between the United States and the British West Indies.

Most important of all, America had gone to the mat with England and had won the contest. That the inner cabinet always wished to give way scarcely lessened the feeling of victory. The Amer-

[33] Goulburn to [Bathurst], Oct. 1, 1821, Francis Bickley, ed., *Report on the Manuscripts of Earl Bathurst* (London, 1923), pp. 517–518; Robinson to Bathurst, Dec. 16, 1821, *ibid.*, pp. 524–525; *Hansard*, n.s., VI, 1414–1430.

[34] Rush to Monroe, June 13, 1822, Monroe MSS; Stratford Canning #56 to Canning, June 6, 1823, FO 5/176.

icans, Stratford Canning dourly observed, considered the British surrender a "national triumph" and clear proof of "the irresistible truth of the principles proclaimed by the American government." [35] The fight for West Indian carriage was almost as important, in terms of national morale, as Adams' lengthy effort to obtain the Floridas. The United States advanced another step toward equality and respectability.

Unfortunately the Americans cast away the victory. When, by proclamation, President Monroe reopened trade with the English colonies, he left untouched the discriminatory tonnage and tariff charges imposed on British shipping from those areas. Stratford Canning protested to Adams and to Rufus King, the congressional leader most deeply wedded to the campaign. They rejected his protests, arguing for nothing less than the complete abolition of imperial preferences. Discrimination would continue until American goods gained the same footing as Canadian or Irish or English goods.[36] Their insistence tested the commercial liberalism of Liverpool and his lieutenants too much. The diplomats quarreled for several years—Castlereagh's death and the succession of George Canning did not make things easier—and in 1826 Britain again closed colonial ports. A final settlement in 1830 virtually granted victory to England, removing American discrimination while permitting continued imperial preference.

This last act reminds one very much of pre-1812 diplomacy. Just as Jefferson in 1807 refused to accept an apology for the *Chesapeake* affair unless Britain gave up impressment, thus securing neither, so in the years after 1822 the Americans threw away positive advantages in a chimerical search for total victory. Monroe and Adams did so with far less reason than Jefferson, for the carrying trade they sought was a tiny fraction, much less than 5 per cent, of America's commerce with the British Empire.

The antediluvian climax of the West Indian negotiations should not conceal the broader picture. The noisy brawling should not

[35] Stratford Canning #56 to Canning, June 6, 1823, FO 5/176.
[36] Private memorandum of Conversations with Mr Rufus King & Mr Adams, Feb. 10–11, 1823, Stratford Canning MSS, FO 352/8.

make one forget the silent keels furrowing the North Atlantic. Christopher Hughes, a young American diplomat called upon to respond to a toast at a public dinner in Liverpool in 1822, summed up the true state of affairs. He congratulated his hosts for showing him

a scene made up of thick and almost impervious forests of English and American masts, topped, (if I may so express it), with the fair foliage of friendly flags. Long may the gallant tars of my country inflict upon Liverpool the hardships of *such* bold invasions; and all hands be beat to quarters, to pour into you, gentlemen, whole broadsides of cotton and tobacco, and manfully to receive a constant fire of calicoes and cutlery.

Hughes's audience greeted these sentiments with wild applause, and when he sat down the Foreign Secretary, who was present, reached over to grasp his hand.[37]

Until Castlereagh's death in 1822 an interest in trade led the English government to follow a very conciliatory policy. Those who made decisions on commercial legislation accepted with equanimity, perhaps even welcomed, American restrictions. Their major concern was the continuing, even expanding flow of goods directly across the Atlantic. Although the tariff of 1816 and other actions showed a mild American drift toward economic nationalism, this spirit did not become really important until almost a decade after the war. Until 1824 the American government, like the British, encouraged Anglo-American commerce at least by declining to interfere with it. As a result economic ties between the two countries, temporarily sundered during the War of 1812, mended. Even in their squabbles over the West Indies neither government hazarded these ties, so vital to the economies of the two peoples.

[37] *Niles' Weekly Register* (Baltimore), Oct. 25, 1823.

CHAPTER

XIII

DIPLOMACY OF THE PAST

Generals, it is said, prepare for the last war rather than the next one. Diplomats too sometimes labor over obsolete problems. After 1815, we can now see, this was true of impressment, which both sides permitted to become the symbol of Anglo-American conflict on the seas. "Impressment and peace, it must now be evident, are irreconcilable," Madison commented.[1] Because others shared his view the two countries sought to draw the fangs of impressment before it caused trouble. They seldom guessed that the truth of Madison's aphorism would never be tested.

Other old disputes continued to pose practical problems. American fishing privileges needed redefinition after the Ghent stalemate. Parts of the Canadian boundary, some ineptly drawn as far back as 1782 and others in doubt since the Louisiana Purchase, demanded settlement. The war itself taught the cost in lives and resources of a naval race on the Great Lakes. In postwar negotiations, notably those leading to the Rush-Bagot agreement of 1817

[1] Madison to Monroe, Nov. 28, 1818, Gaillard Hunt, ed., *The Writings of James Madison* (9 vols.; New York, 1900–1910), VIII, 418.

and the convention of 1818, the diplomats made progress with the continuing, real issues. Settlement of the obsolete eluded them.

To the congeries of antiquated problems the Foreign Secretary brought his usual attitudes. For several years he evaded negotiations on impressment simply because he saw little purpose in possibly irritating discussion when opinion in both countries forbade compromise. When success seemed possible, as it did on impressment by 1818, Castlereagh welcomed, even sought, discussion. All his proposals showed that the Foreign Secretary valued harmony far higher than, for example, exclusive fishing rights or naval superiority on the Great Lakes.

Whether at London or at the State Department, John Quincy Adams held less irenic views. Confident that time would bring American victory, he opposed compromise on maritime rights, on the fishery, and on other things. The more flexible inclinations of Monroe, secretary of state and in 1817 Madison's successor as president, came to naught until Rush and Gallatin settled the fishery question in 1818. Monroe and Adams, a loyal subordinate, were never at daggers drawn, and their differences were primarily tactical. They shared republican prejudices against English institutions and, even more than Castlereagh, never lost sight of their constituents' xenophobia.

Negotiations leading to the Rush-Bagot agreement of 1817, limiting armaments on the Great Lakes, clearly showed the American attitude. At war's end both sides were engaged in feverish building, particularly on Lake Ontario. The British had a 110-gun ship nearly ready for service, and the Americans had countered with two 74's. Shortly after the treaty of peace, for reasons of economy, Congress ordered most of the ships on the Great Lakes dismantled. Driblets of information, mostly false, suggested to Washington that Britain intended to keep building until she dominated the inland waters.

In November, 1815, therefore, the United States government directed Adams at London "to propose . . . such an arrangement respecting the naval forces to be kept on the Lakes by both governments, as will demonstrate their pacific policy and secure their peace." The President, these instructions stated, desired to limit armed ships to a fixed number, "and the smaller the number, the more agreeable to him; or to abstain altogether from an armed force beyond that used for the revenue."[2] Undoubtedly Madison and Monroe recognized, as did Castlereagh when the proposal reached him, that a power vacuum on the Great Lakes would benefit the United States. If war broke out the Americans could build much more rapidly than Britain, and until new squadrons were built they could more easily apply their manpower superiority over Canada.

Before approaching Castlereagh, Adams discussed the subject with Alexander Baring. The banker predicted that the ministry would agree to mutual disarmament. (For himself, Baring told Adams, he would go further and abandon Canada, as it was "fit for nothing but to breed quarrels.") Two weeks later the minister called at the Foreign Office to present the proposal; Castlereagh, generally receptive, agreed that "keeping a number of armed vessels parading about the Lakes in time of peace . . . would be absurd." Dredging from his memory an argument used at Ghent to support the demand for unilateral American disarmament on the lakes, Castlereagh pointed out that Britain, the weaker power in North America, had more need of naval protection. The suspicious American minister put too much significance on this ritualistic comment. He reported home that, lacking Castlereagh's support, the proposal would almost certainly die in cabinet. He failed to report Baring's contrary prediction.[3]

Six weeks later, in a note opening with a crotchety discussion of border friction near Detroit, Adams repeated the American offer. He argued that "mutual reliance upon good faith" would be more likely to preserve peace, and thus protect Canada, than "the jealous and exasperating defiance of complete Armour." Without making any difficulty at all Castlereagh replied that Britain would accept any reasonable American proposal. He knew that Britain could

[2] Monroe to Adams, Nov. 16, 1815, Department of State Archives, National Archives, Diplomatic Instructions, All Countries, Vol. VIII.

[3] Jan. 12, 25, 1816, Charles F. Adams, ed., *Memoirs of John Quincy Adams* (12 vols.; Philadelphia, 1874–1877), III, 277–279, 287–288; Adams #29, #30 to Monroe, Jan. 31, Feb. 8, 1816, Department of State Archives, National Archives, Despatches, Great Britain, Vol. XX.

not hope to gain superiority on the lakes except at ruinous expense. At this point Adams, who had pressed the issue, drew back, announcing that he lacked powers to make a specific agreement. The two men agreed to transfer negotiations to Washington. Meanwhile, they assured each other, building on the lakes would halt.[4] The assurances, although pleasant, merely confirmed existing policy.

Castlereagh's instructions to Bagot did not reach Washington for ten weeks. Meanwhile the Americans began to fret. Monroe talked with Bagot, who, lacking guidance from home, seemed as cold as Adams had considered Castlereagh, so the Secretary renewed his instructions to Adams. President Madison added threateningly that unless Britain gave up her (nonexistent) building program Congress would almost certainly order new American construction.[5]

Suspicion continued long after Bagot's orders arrived early in July. Castlereagh preferred an informal agreement to continue "abstaining from exertion," as he put it, on the lakes. This proposal did not satisfy Monroe, who wanted Britain formally bound. Bagot exercised the option Castlereagh had given him and assented. At first the talks went well. Then, when Bagot revealed that he could only make an agreement *ad referendum*, American doubts revived. "The views of the B. gov^t. I am willing to believe are candid," the President wrote with doubtful candor himself, "but the course it has taken . . . would tempt a different conclusion." Monroe was tempted to throw the whole affair back into John Quincy Adams' lap.[6]

Early in August the two negotiators finally reached a settlement embodied in three letters. In the first Bagot announced British

[4] Adams to Castlereagh, March 21, 1816, Foreign Office Archives, Public Record Office, FO 5/117; Castlereagh #7 to Bagot, April 23, 1816, FO 5/113; April 9, 1816, Adams, *op. cit.*, III, 329–330.

[5] Bagot #8 to Castlereagh, May 3, 1816, FO 5/114; Monroe to Adams, May 21, 1816, Instructions, Vol. VIII; Madison to Adams, May 10, 1816, James Madison Papers, Library of Congress.

[6] Castlereagh #7 to Bagot, April 23, 1816, FO 5/113; Bagot #24 to Castlereagh, Aug. 12, 1816, FO 5/115; Monroe to Madison, July 21, 1816, William C. Rives Collection, Library of Congress; Madison to Graham, n.d. [incorrectly dated as *circa* June 1, 1816], Hunt, *op. cit.*, VIII, 345; Monroe to Madison, July 31, Aug. 12, 1816, Rives Collection.

approval of the general principle put forward in London by Adams. In the second, probably rewritten after Bagot objected to the first draft, Monroe stated the American position in detail. The naval forces of each side should be limited to one ship on Lake Champlain, one on Lake Ontario, and two more on the upper lakes; construction should cease; and the vessels were to be used only to enforce revenue laws. In the final note Bagot promised to refer Monroe's proposals to London and offered—redundantly, because Castlereagh and Adams had already so agreed—to suspend building until his government's response reached Washington.[7]

Even this exchange did not still Monroe's doubts, and when London did not immediately return its approval the Secretary of State commented that the transfer of negotiations from London (actually suggested by Adams) and the failure to give Bagot definitive powers "had much the appearance, that the object, was, to amuse us, rather than to adopt any effectual measure." [8]

London's long silence did not reflect guile, as Monroe feared. In September Castlereagh wrote Bagot that summer vacations would delay approval. One of the envoy's relatives wrote: "Your management of the negotiation about the Lakes is highly approved. . . . It is some comfort to know that your banishment will probably lead to Fame & Promotion." Not until the end of January, 1817, did Castlereagh, with embarrassed apologies, forward his government's official assent. Three months later Bagot and Richard Rush, acting head of the State Department, exchanged formal approval of what is called the Rush-Bagot convention, although Rush played no part in arranging it.[9] After still further delay the

---

[7] Bagot to Monroe, July 26, 1816, Monroe to Bagot, Aug. 2, 1816, Bagot to Monroe, Aug. 6, 1816, all encl. in Bagot #24 to Castlereagh, Aug. 12, 1816, FO 5/115. A later exchange, designed to protect Monroe from possible criticism by Anglophobes, did not affect the essential character of the agreement. Monroe to Bagot, Aug. 12, 1816, Bagot to Monroe, Aug. 13, 1816, encl. in Bagot #24 to Castlereagh, Aug. 12, 1816, *ibid.*

[8] Monroe to Adams, Nov. 14, 1816, Instructions, Vol. VIII.

[9] Castlereagh #16 to Bagot, Sept. 30, 1816, FO 5/113; Wellesley Pole to Bagot, Sept. 20, 1816, Sir Charles Bagot Papers, Levens Hall, Westmorland; Castlereagh #2 to Bagot, Jan. 31, 1817, FO 5/120; Bagot #32 to Castlereagh, May 5, 1817, FO 5/122.

President, on Bagot's prodding, sought Senate approval, which came in April, 1818.

The agreement, certainly the best known accomplishment of the postwar years, scarcely deserves its reputation as a landmark in Anglo-American friendship. Although both parties agreed to virtually complete disarmament on the lakes, they continued to fortify the land frontier and considered it a likely scene of future conflict.[10] Moreover, as we have seen, the Americans negotiated all along in a spirit of intense suspicion. They knew lakes disarmament most directly benefited the United States and refused to believe Castlereagh sincerely desired it. An essential ingredient in postwar harmony, the Rush-Bagot agreement did not seem earthshaking at the time. Few saw it as a further step toward full recognition of American power.

A second problem inherited from the past had a much longer history. Thanks largely to inaccuracies in John Mitchell's *Map of the British and French Dominions in North America,* the sole reliance of negotiators at Paris in 1782, much of the Canadian-American boundary remained in doubt for years. America's purchase of Louisiana in 1803 added new problems since the United States acquired ill-defined French claims stretching far to the west, perhaps to the Pacific. A commission set up under Jay's Treaty of 1794 settled a small part of the disputed Maine boundary. In 1803 Rufus King and the Foreign Secretary (who later became the Earl of Liverpool, Castlereagh's chief) negotiated a further settlement which failed of ratification, and in 1807 Monroe and Pinkney carried on abortive discussions at London. Thus in 1815 the issues remained unsettled.

The Ghent treaty established three binational commissions to deal with eastern sections of the boundary; failing agreement the disputes were to be arbitrated by a third power. One commission completed its work in 1817, fixing the boundary through Passamaquoddy Bay in a fashion generally favorable to the British. The other two commissions dawdled, partly to await the reports of

[10] Charles P. Stacey, "The Myth of the Unguarded Frontier, 1815–1871," *American Historical Review,* LVI (1950–1951), 1–18.

surveyors mapping the areas in dispute, a task further complicated when one party lost its instruments and papers to thieves. Ultimately the Anglo-American agents settled the precise location of the waterline from the St. Lawrence to Sault Ste. Marie in 1821, but the same commission could not agree on the boundary westward to Lake of the Woods.

Surveyors for the commission to fix the line from the St. Lawrence eastward discovered in 1818 that American fortifications at the outlet of Lake Champlain stood upon territory undeniably Canadian because north of the forty-fifth parallel! The old boundary had been inaccurately drawn! The discovery alarmed Bagot, who hastened to Adams' office. The Secretary of State reassured him, saying that the day before "the President and Calhoun laughed at the idea of the apprehended rebellion against the astronomers in Vermont." Still, the problem was an awkward one, and in addition the commissioners faced sharply conflicting claims about the northern boundary of Maine. When they finally met in 1822 they agreed only to disagree.[11] Deadlocks, slowness, alleged costliness, and the unfavorable award of 1817 caused grumbling in America and discouraged further recourse to arbitration.

Eastern problems paled by comparison with territorial questions west of Lake of the Woods. For more than a thousand miles there simply was no boundary, accurately drawn or not, between Canada and the United States. Particularly at the western end, in Oregon, trouble loomed. Britain inclined to deny the existence of any American rights in that country and was determined, in any event, to push the Americans south of the Columbia River. Secretary Adams, sometimes held in check by the more pacific Monroe, wanted to throw back the advance of empire.

[11] Oct. 28, 1818, Adams, *op. cit.*, IV, 145; Alfred L. Burt, *The United States, Great Britain, and British North America from the Revolution to the Establishment of Peace after the War of 1812* (New Haven, 1940), pp. 422–426. The British member of the third commission suggested that the Americans be asked to provide a special guard to protect the Champlain fortifications from pilferage before they were transferred to Britain. Barclay to Bagot, private and confidential, Oct. 26, 1818, Bagot MSS. See also Duke of Richmond to Bagot, private, Dec. 29, 1818, *ibid.* At last, in 1842, Lord Ashburton agreed to let the Americans have the disputed territory at the northern end of Lake Champlain.

For more than two years after the Treaty of Ghent the Oregon country caused no real trouble. In 1815 Monroe, then secretary of state, told Anthony Baker the United States intended to re-occupy Astoria, a trading post on the Columbia taken over by the British during the war, under the provision of the treaty calling for the restoration of conquered territory. Baker responded frostily that Britain had never recognized American claims in the Oregon country. Other Britishers, consulted by the chargé, pointed out that the North West Company had acquired Astoria by purchase before H.M.S. *Raccoon* arrived in December, 1813, to carry out the change of flags; thus, they argued, the post did not fall within the treaty's purview because it was not really a conquest. The dis-agreement remained moot because the Americans did not in fact dispatch the expedition announced by Monroe.[12]

At last, in the autumn of 1817, the American government sent the warship *Ontario* around Cape Horn toward Astoria. Bagot took alarm, particularly because Washington did not inform him in advance, leaving him to learn of the *Ontario*'s departure from a North West Company agent who picked up the rumor in New York.[13] Bagot naturally assumed that the administration, remem-bering Baker's attitude, had decided to seize Astoria by a *coup de main*. The dispatch of the *Ontario* threatened to touch off a nasty incident on the Pacific coast. It also showed that despite the new president's professed appreciation of British candor and friendship, the administration did not trust London. John Quincy Adams' later excuses, that the Americans believed no one at Astoria had authority to transfer control and, probably truthfully, that the failure to inform Bagot was an administrative oversight, only slightly mollified the envoy and his superiors.[14]

Shortly after receiving the news Bagot had his first extensive

---

[12] See Burt, *op. cit.*, pp. 411–416; Samuel F. Bemis, *John Quincy Adams and the Foundations of American Foreign Policy* (New York, 1949), pp. 280–286; and especially Frederick Merk, "The Genesis of the Oregon Question," *Mississippi Valley Historical Review*, XXXVI (1949–1950), 583–612, for this entire episode. For Monroe's statement in 1815 see Baker #24 to Castlereagh, July 19, 1815, FO 5/107.

[13] Bagot #74 to Castlereagh, Dec. 2, 1817, FO 5/123.

[14] Bagot #48 to Castlereagh, June 2, 1818, FO 5/132; Adams #4 to Rush, May 20, 1818, Instructions, Vol. VIII.

talk with Adams, who arrived at Washington to take over the Department of State after the *Ontario* sailed. Adams dominated the conversation, raising American grievances against Britain. At the end Bagot asked if the *Ontario* had really set off for Oregon. Adams paused in embarrassment, then admitted the fact. Recovering his savoir faire he disputed Bagot's assertion that the entire Oregon area belonged to Britain, and added that "it would hardly be worth the while of Great Britain to have any difference with the United States on account of the occupation of any part of so remote a Territory." This line of logic scarcely impressed Bagot, who reported the threat to comity and to British interests without delay. At more leisure he prepared a note of complaint to Adams, who did not reply, perhaps because he could think of no good answer.[15]

Despite America's insulting, even ominous behavior, the Foreign Secretary declined to quarrel, though he did complain to Richard Rush, nonplussing that uninstructed, uninformed minister, and had Bagot make the same complaint to Adams. He contemptuously dismissed the suggestion that Britain might, on highly legalistic grounds, maintain that the Treaty of Ghent did not require the restoration of Astoria. He ordered the post handed over to the Americans, leaving the matter of rightful title to later settlement. Accordingly, H.M.S. *Blossom* conveyed an American agent to the Columbia in the fall of 1818. On October 6 the Stars and Stripes replaced the Union Jack over the settlement. The *Ontario* arrived some time later, having been delayed in South America.

Castlereagh did not stop there. In characteristic spirit and—alas!—equally characteristic, and thus tortured, prose he wrote Bagot that

the difficulty of drawing the [boundary] line is likely to encrease from year to year, and . . . until we can localize with precision our respective Sovereignties, the harmony of the Two Governments is not only always exposed

[15] Nov. 24, 1817, Adams, *op. cit.*, IV, 24–25; Bagot #72, #74 to Castlereagh, Nov. 24, Dec. 2, 1817, FO 5/123; Adams #4 to Rush, May 20, 1818, Instructions, Vol. VIII.

to be compromised by the irregular habits of our advanced and intermixed Population, but an additional obstacle thrown in the way of any regulated intercourse of mutual accommodation.

To settle the entire northern boundary he suggested a binational commission like those already at work. The commission should begin with the Columbia Basin, the most pressing problem, and proceed eastward if it succeeded there.[16]

The Americans transformed Castlereagh's proposal into something much larger and quite different. At first Adams seemed impressed by the commission approach. Soon he called for direct negotiations, quite properly pointing out that the problem was political rather than legal or cartographic. Only responsible statesmen could engage in the necessary give-and-take.[17] Instructions to Rush made it clear that the American government intended to demand extensive territories in the Far West. Adams pointed out that Britain already had a great empire on four continents. "We may very fairly expect," he went on, "that she will not think it consistent either with a wise or a friendly policy, to watch with eyes of jealousy and alarm, every possibility of extension of our national domains in North America," particularly since in the long run America must succeed. As Adams asserted, Britain did possess large territories and needed Oregon far less than the United States. Still, this unusual diplomatic argument was irrelevant in a dispute over rightful title.

Adams did not want to limit the negotiations to boundary questions brought to the fore by the rude dispatch of the *Ontario*. At the President's suggestion he proposed conversations on the fishery, colonial trade, and the expiring convention of 1815 as well. "It is not our desire," he added soothingly, "to embarrass the . . .

---

[16] Rush #7 to Adams, Feb. 14, 1818, Despatches, Great Britain, Vol. XXII; Castlereagh #7 to Bagot, Feb. 4, 1818, FO 5/129; Castlereagh to Bathurst, Jan. 26, 1818, FO 5/139; Castlereagh to Bagot, secret and confidential, Feb. 4, 1818, FO 5/129; Castlereagh to Bagot, private, Feb. 4, 1818, Bagot MSS. The quotation is from the last cited letter.

[17] Adams later added that commissioners would certainly disagree, that Russia would probably become the mediator, and that the United States feared the Czar's agents might be interested in the Northwestern question or be influenced by Great Britain. Adams to Gallatin and Rush, July 28, 1818, Instructions, Vol. VIII.

Negotiations with any of the questions of maritime regulations adapted to a state of warfare, . . . even Impressment," unless Britain so desired.[18] Out of these suggestions, framed in instructions to Rush and to Gallatin, ordered from Paris to join the resident minister in England, came the convention of 1818.

The offer to negotiate on the fishery made Adams' suggestion welcome in England. With each fishing season there came a risk of serious collision, something Castlereagh avoided prior to 1818 by temporary, unsatisfactory expedients. On the American side Monroe too favored a settlement. Until 1818 domestic political factors and Adams' intransigence prevented serious negotiations. The best hope for success seemed to lie in melding the fishery with other issues, drawing its poison by making it part of a general settlement.

The conflict of legal views seemed unbridgeable, and in the end both sides agreed to pass by the question. "The right . . . required no new stipulation to support it," Secretary of State Monroe declared in 1815. "It was sufficiently secured by the treaty of 1783." At London and later at Washington Adams expanded on this view, arguing that the post-revolutionary division of empire was by nature permanent and unaltered by war.[19] In practice the United States recognized certain weaknesses, particularly because the Treaty of Paris spoke of a fishing "liberty" rather than a "right." Adams garnished his arguments with appeals that the fishery supported many deserving citizens and financed the purchase of British manufactures, and both he and Monroe offered to consider limits on the curing privilege.[20]

In theory Britain took the simple position that "the War abro-

[18] Bagot #48 to Castlereagh, June 2, 1818, FO 5/132; Adams #6 to Gallatin, May 22, 1818, Instructions, Vol. VIII; Adams #4, #6 to Rush, May 20, 30, 1818, *ibid.;* May 19, 1818, Adams, *op. cit.,* IV, 97.

[19] Sometimes Adams, loyal son of the framer of the old provision, gratuitously assumed the role of advocate. Once he responded to a British note, "It is for the Government of the United States alone to decide . . . ," and then spent twenty pages attacking the proposal he said he had to refer home. Adams to Castlereagh, Jan. 23, 1816, FO 5/117.

[20] Monroe to Adams, July 21, 1815, Instructions, Vol. VII; Adams to Bathurst, Sept. 25, 1815, FO 5/110; March 18, 1818, Adams, *op. cit.,* IV, 61; Monroe to Adams, Feb. 27, 1816, Instructions, Vol. VIII.

gated the Treaty [and] it determined the Privileges." Although this proposition required some modification—did England mean, then, that American independence ceased with the war? Adams asked—and the tortuous discussion at Ghent somewhat undermined the British position, on the whole Britain had a strong case. The British did not fail to emphasize, as they had failed to do at Ghent, the importance of the word "liberty." To those who considered only international law the matter seemed clear. "They are in fact as I told Monroe," Baker stated, "poaching upon our Manor." [21]

The cabinet saw that legal right did not settle the question. Americans had fished and cured around Nova Scotia and Newfoundland since colonial days. To end this traditional practice would alienate the most friendly section of the United States. To exclude American ships would require a sizable squadron and quite possibly lead to bloodshed. Castlereagh and his colleagues, determined to build good relations with the United States, flinched from such a course. They sought a negotiated settlement cutting down old privileges, enabling the Americans to share in but not to monopolize the fishery, and making it more difficult for smugglers masquerading as fishermen to carry on their trade. At the outset, in 1815, the British government offered to compromise along these lines.[22] The problem lay in getting Washington to enter discussions in the same spirit.

Castlereagh consistently refused to use the one weapon, closure of the fishery, which would have driven the Americans to negotiate because such a course might well have involved the two countries in the very difficulties he wanted to avoid. In 1815 the local commander, Admiral Griffith, sought to break up the onshore fishery and even to clear international waters on the Grand Banks. London quickly countermanded Griffith's orders. The next year, with negotiations at Washington in the offing, Castlereagh once more required the Royal Navy to stay its hand. When Secretary Monroe evaded a settlement, the Foreign Secretary ordered the

[21] Bathurst to Adams, Oct. 30, 1815, FO 5/110; Adams to Bathurst, Sept. 25, 1815, *ibid.*; Baker to Bagot, private and confidential, July 9, 1816, Bagot MSS.
[22] Bathurst to Adams, Oct. 30, 1815, FO 5/110.

fishery closed in the spring of 1817. Minister Adams quickly protested, and Castlereagh reversed himself, declaring that as a mark of favor to the incoming American administration and in anticipation of a negotiated settlement the fishermen would be tolerated for one more year. In 1818 similar orders went to North America.[23]

These piecemeal concessions, successful in preventing a major clash, failed to bring the basic issue closer to settlement. Hoping to stimulate negotiations, London dispatched the annual permissions as late as possible. As a result irritating seizures took place at the opening of each fishing season, and release came only after delays and court proceedings expensive to both sides. The American government apparently considered this a fair price for continued exercise of a claim Britain denied in theory. Washington came to count on, indeed to demand in rather cheeky fashion, the yearly relaxations.[24]

Naturally American leaders found this state of things relatively satisfactory. They were willing to accept restraints on fishermen designed to reduce smuggling and protect private property. Beyond that they preferred not to go, since in practice fishermen enjoyed almost all their prewar privileges. "It will be better to do nothing," Madison opined in 1816, "than to surrender the point of right, or to accept what may be of small value, with an actual privation of the residue formerly enjoyed." [25] American tradition and American interests alike discouraged compromise.

So did American politics. The fishery involved New England alone, particularly Massachusetts. As Republicans dared not risk charges that they had betrayed the Yankees, in effect they conferred upon New Englanders a right of veto. When, shortly after his inauguration, the President set out upon a Northern tour, Bagot observed that his trip would delay negotiations. "One of

[23] Bathurst #10 to Baker, Sept. 7, 1815, FO 5/105; Castlereagh #8 to Bagot, April 16, 1817, FO 5/113; Castlereagh #5 to Bagot, March 22, 1817, FO 5/120; Castlereagh to Adams, May 7, 1817, FO 5/126; Bathurst to Lords Commissioners of the Admiralty, May 10, 1817, encl. in Goulburn to Hamilton, May 12, 1817, FO 5/127; Barrow to Planta, June 10, 1818, FO 5/139.
[24] Monroe to Adams, Feb. 5, 1817, Instructions, Vol. VIII; Adams to Castlereagh, April 21, 1817, FO 5/126.
[25] Madison to Monroe, July 11, 1816, James Monroe Papers, Library of Congress.

the President's principal objects in this excursion," he reported, "is to ingratiate himself with the Eastern States of the Union, whose attachment and support he probably could not court in any surer way, than by appearing to consult their wishes . . . upon a subject so intimately connected with one of their chief interests." Later, Adams, who knew more about the fishery than most, carefully consulted New England congressmen.[26]

Such factors necessarily made negotiations stillborn. In 1816, on orders from London, Bagot sought a settlement. Monroe reacted favorably. Secretary of the Navy Benjamin Crowninshield, a knowledgeable Yankee, approved the first British offer because he considered the basic American claim untenable. Madison jerked his subordinates back into line. On his orders Monroe rejected Bagot's three successive proposals to open specific sections of coast to American fishermen and reserve the rest for British use. Fearing to undermine Britain's claim that her generosity, not American rights, inspired these offers, Bagot declined to receive counterproposals, and negotiations dragged to an end after six wearisome months.[27]

The Foreign Secretary, who praised Bagot's caution, nevertheless urged him to get the Americans to send an offer to London. None was forthcoming. According to Bagot, John Quincy Adams' arrival at the State Department in the fall of 1817 scotched a compromise proposal President Monroe and Richard Rush had in mind. In general instructions handed to Rush on his departure for England, Adams rehearsed the old legal arguments in rigid terms, and a few months later he told Bagot the fish migrated too frequently to make any territorial arrangement satisfactory. Bagot at last began to suspect the Americans did not want a settlement.[28]

[26] Madison to Monroe, Aug. 4, 1816, Madison MSS; Monroe to Adams, Aug. 13, 1816, Instructions, Vol. VIII; Bagot #2 to Castlereagh, Jan. 7, 1817, FO 5/121; Bagot #20 to Castlereagh, June 3, 1817, FO 5/122; Jan. 5, 1818, Adams, *op. cit.*, IV, 34.

[27] Monroe to Madison, July 7, 1816, Rives Collection; Benjamin Crowninshield to Monroe, July 25, 1816, *ibid.*; Madison to Monroe, July 11, 1816, Monroe MSS; Madison to Monroe, Aug. 4, 1816, Madison MSS; Bagot #2 to Castlereagh, Jan. 7, 1817, and encl., FO 5/121.

[28] Castlereagh to Bagot, private, March 22, 1817, FO 5/120; Bagot to Castlereagh,

Despite frequent, ultimately anguished appeals from the Foreign Office, the promised American offer did not arrive until the negotiations of 1818 began. In the spring of that year, when concern over Oregon and the western boundary paved the way to full-dress talks, the American cabinet at last turned its attention to the fishery. Adams wanted simply to instruct Rush and Gallatin to hold out for the full American claim. Monroe overruled him, so in May the Secretary told Bagot the two envoys would offer a compromise.[29] At last, after three years of remarkable British tolerance, serious negotiations approached.

Like the fishery, impressment, another major issue in 1818, involved deeply felt historical differences. Nothing symbolized British primacy more sharply than the memory of boarding officers who, backed by gun-studded black hulls a few cable lengths away, tore American seamen from their ships. To Englishmen, nothing seemed more essential to British naval power than the right to pursue fugitives from royal service even to the decks of foreign ships. The Ghent treaty passed over impressment, like the fishery, in silence. Although no matter of concern while Europe remained at peace, the momentum of the issue inevitably propelled it into postwar diplomacy. During their London visit after the treaty of peace, Clay and Gallatin perfunctorily sought agreement on impressment and neutral rights. They readily admitted that agreement was not a *sine qua non* to a commercial convention, and discussion died.

At about the same time, to encourage British concession, President Madison asked Congress to limit service in American merchantmen to native-born citizens and those already naturalized. Armed with this proposal, Adams argued that Britain need no longer impress seamen from American ships. Castlereagh replied that, if the President's proposal became law, negotiations could be forgotten; American vessels would no longer serve as refuges

---

private, June 2, 1818, Papers of Robert Stewart, Viscount Castlereagh, Second Marquis of Londonderry, Mount Stewart, Newtownards, County Down; Adams to Rush, Nov. 6, 1817, Instructions, Vol. VIII; Bagot #29 to Castlereagh, April 7, 1818, FO 5/131.
[29] May 15, 1818, Adams, *op. cit.*, IV, 95–97.

for English tars. Before Adams and Castlereagh could pursue their differences Congress dropped Madison's bill.[30] For a few months the subject lay dormant.

In May, 1816, Secretary Monroe instructed Adams to present proposals on several issues of which disarmament on the lakes, trade with British colonies, and impressment were the most important. After some delay, possibly reflecting his own misgivings, Adams presented Monroe's suggestions. Castlereagh, on the verge of departure for Ireland himself, replied that the cabinet could not discuss American affairs until summer absentees returned.[31] The proposals died without formal answer, a treatment of unpleasant issues entirely characteristic of the Foreign Secretary, and Adams left for home the next spring.

Unbeknownst to the outgoing minister his proposals touched off a flurry of correspondence within the ministry. All those consulted welcomed Monroe's offer to limit merchant crews to native-born citizens and those already naturalized, thus admitting by treaty what Congress refused to legislate, a ban on the employment of seamen naturalized in the future. Liverpool, who welcomed the proposal as a palliative and feared "we never shall be engaged in a Maritime war with any Power without its leading to a war with the United States," nevertheless refused to consider the plan a substitute for impressment. He insisted that in wartime British boarding parties must continue to search for fugitives, even detain them.[32]

[30] Clay and Gallatin to Monroe, May 18, 1815, Department of State Archives, National Archives, Records of Negotiations Connected with the Treaty of Ghent, Vol. I; Heads of an unofficial conference, May 11, 1815, FO 5/109; James D. Richardson, ed., *A Compilation of the Messages and Papers of the Presidents* (10 vols.; Washington, 1907), I, 555; James F. Zimmerman, *Impressment of American Seamen*, Columbia University Studies in History, Economics and Public Law, Vol. CXVIII, no. 1 (New York, 1925), pp. 222–225.

[31] Monroe to Adams, May 21, 1816, Instructions, Vol. VIII; Adams to Castlereagh, Sept. 17, 1816, FO 5/117; Castlereagh to Adams, Sept. 28, 1816, *ibid.*

[32] Memorandum encl. in Liverpool to Castlereagh, private and confidential, Sept. 26, 1816, FO 5/119. Neither later scholars nor the Americans at the time seem to have been aware of this discussion within the cabinet. Yet it alone makes understandable the discussions carried on in 1818 first by Rush alone and then by Rush and Gallatin.

Earl Bathurst thrust his pen into Liverpool's logic. He agreed that after "what has passed the U: States cannot submit to the exercise of this right," but drew conclusions diametrically opposed to those of his chief. He proposed, without allowing the legality of impressment to come into question, to suspend it for a fixed term of years in return for an American promise not to employ British seamen. "A limited evasion of the Regulations in time of war," the Secretary argued, "would be far less prejudicial to us, than the hostility of the United States." Besides, in boarding neutral ships for other purposes the Royal Navy could easily spot flagrant violations of the agreement, thus justifying renunciation or at least pinpointing protest to Washington.[33]

For the moment Bathurst's suggestion foundered. Vansittart and later Robinson sided with the premier.[34] Castlereagh did not challenge them, probably because Adams' uncompromising attitude discouraged him. Instructions from Monroe said nothing of any British renunciation of impressment. Apparently Madison and Monroe believed that, with British seamen expelled from American crews, England would see no point in impressment. Yet Adams took it upon himself to say that his country expected formal, permanent assurances.[35] This demand exceeded even Bathurst's view of an acceptable compromise. The Foreign Secretary abandoned the subject rather than quarrel with Adams and his own colleagues at the same time. Apparently he accepted Robinson's view that "all discussions in detail on this subject will only widen the difference between the two Governments."[36] Since Adams disapproved of the American offer he did not present it again before leaving England.

In the spring of 1818 the newly arrived Richard Rush broached

[33] Bathurst memorandum, Oct. 6, 1816, ibid.; Robinson to Castlereagh, Jan. 17, 1817, FO 83/2205.
[34] Vansittart memorandum, Oct. —, 1816, FO 5/119.
[35] Monroe to Adams, May 21, 1816, Instructions, Vol. VIII; Bagot #8 to Castlereagh, May 3, 1816, FO 5/114; Adams #56 to Monroe, Sept. 27, 1816, Worthington C. Ford, ed., The Writings of John Quincy Adams (7 vols.; New York, 1913–1917), VI, 95.
[36] Robinson to Castlereagh, Jan. 17, 1817, FO 83/2205.

the subject once more.[37] Following preliminary jousting he offered, in return for an agreement to suspend—not renounce—impressment, to stipulate that "all British subjects or seamen now in the United States, and not heretofore naturalized, will be excluded from their service, and that all who arrive there in future will also be excluded." After some delay Castlereagh declined this proposal in the cabinet's name.

Yet Bathurst's arguments had gnawed at him. He told Rush he was inclined to accept the plan even to the extent of suspending impressment by formal agreement. Would Rush approve two amendments? Britain wanted the agreement terminable on six months' notice, and she desired that officers boarding a neutral ship for other purposes have the right to examine crew lists and take formal note of any of their countrymen in the crew. Rush, who declined comment pending Gallatin's arrival, referred the amendments home.[38]

The Foreign Secretary told Rush that in asking for the two amendments he spoke for himself alone. This was almost certainly a diplomatic white lie. The Foreign Office archives contain a long memorandum written under the Secretary's direction if not by him. After sympathetically recounting Rush's propositions this paper virtually recommends their acceptance, provided the Americans agreed to the two amendments. If the scheme worked, the memorandum declared, "G[t]. Britain will have . . . gained her main object," stifling the flow of seamen to the American marine to avoid British service. She would also "escape the danger of an American War, [this] being the probable concomitant of every other War in which She may be engaged." If the scheme failed England could resume impressment.

The Foreign Office memorandum circulated through the cabinet

[37] Rush's instructions (Adams to Rush, Nov. 6, 1817, Instructions, Vol. VIII) do not specifically authorize the successive proposals he put forward. Bemis (*op. cit.*, p. 287n) surmises that Rush acted on oral instructions given him by the President before he left Washington. Probably Rush also drew upon the older instructions to Adams for guidance.
[38] Rush memoranda, April 18, June 20, 1818, FO 5/137; Rush #14, #15, #24, #34 to Adams, April 15, 20, June 26, Aug. 15, 1818, Despatches, Great Britain, Vol. XXII; Rush to Monroe, private, June 29, 1818, Monroe MSS.

and back to the Secretary. Only two brief, noncommittal comments are preserved. In August, however, the Foreign Secretary referred to the document as "a reasoned Mem[oran]dum . . . which has been approved by the P.R.'s Gov^t. as opening for discussion a general outline, which may be matured into some practical arrangement." [39] It seems clear that his colleagues authorized Castlereagh to feel out Rush without committing England in advance.

The fate of Monroe's offer reveals the extraordinary difficulty of the impressment issue. In 1816, hoping to prevent future quarrels and well aware that earlier offers to expel Britishers from American crews had not tempted England, Monroe offered to sacrifice the use of naturalized citizens as well. As a further concession he did not ask a formal British surrender, correctly calculating that the agreement would end impressment and that once ended it would never be resumed. Adams, who valued American pride over harmony with England, insisted upon a triumph rather than an accommodation. When Rush dusted off the plan sixteen months later he too asked Britain for a *quid pro quo,* though a lesser one, either on his own or because Adams had by this time converted Monroe, or possibly because the President feared public criticism if he conceded more than his subordinates considered wise. [40] Perhaps an informal understanding to end impressment would not have satisfied the American people. Monroe apparently thought so, but Adams and Castlereagh prevented the experiment.

At least until the spring of 1818 the British cabinet, like Adams, thought in terms of pride rather than reality. Only Bathurst drew the logical conclusion from the conviction that impressment would draw America into any future maritime war. When Castlereagh came around to Bathurst's way of thinking in 1818, he spoiled his conversion by injecting suspicion and detail. The privilege of

[39] Unsigned memorandum, n.d., with Ellenborough and Bathurst endorsements, FO 5/137, incorrectly filed at April 18–23, 1818; Castlereagh #1 to Robinson and Goulburn, Aug. 24, 1818, FO 5/138. The memorandum mentions Rush's second offer of June 20, 1818, but not the envoy's reaction to suggested amendments. It seems safe, therefore, to assign it to the period between June 20 and August 14, when Castlereagh suggested the amendments to Rush.

[40] These speculations are necessary because of the doubt concerning Rush's instructions and particularly Monroe's oral directives to him, if any. See n. 37 above.

annulling the agreement, perhaps necessary to convert the cabinet, reeked of distrust of American pledges. (Monroe and his lieutenants also suspected that Britain would enjoy the benefits of the agreement until she needed seamen, whereupon she would denounce it and resume impressment.) The elaborate procedure suggested to check on and report violations was a gratuitous insult. Since, as Bathurst observed, boarders on other errands would soon learn if the Americans recruited large numbers of British seamen, even at best Castlereagh's proposal was redundant. At worst— and the Americans so interpreted it—it suggested crews mobilized for British inspection, an intolerable infringement on sovereignty.[41] Castlereagh's proposals show how far apart the two countries stood. Bitter memories prevented a settlement.

John Quincy Adams, who opposed compromise on impressment, knew Britain was not ready to give in. Hence his instructions to Rush and Gallatin suggested silence unless Britain raised the issue. Yet past history and particularly Rush's revival of the old plan of 1816 made discussion inevitable. Impressment joined the fishery, the western boundary, and commercial relations as a central theme at London in the autumn of 1818. All these questions went back to prewar days, the fishery and the boundary as far as 1782. The American offer to discuss them, John Quincy Adams told Bagot, was "suggested by a spirit of the sincerest conciliation, and a desire to leave nothing unarranged between the two Countries which can again become matter of serious jealousy." [42] To achieve this end, or even part of it, the negotiators needed to cut their way through tangled thickets of misunderstanding and conflict.

[41] Oct. 29, 30, 1818, Adams, *op. cit.*, IV, 147–150.
[42] Bagot to Castlereagh, private, June 2, 1818, Castlereagh MSS.

CHAPTER

XIV

THE CONVENTION OF 1818

In July, 1818, Lord Castlereagh broke his Irish vacation to return to London. While there he received Richard Rush, who half-heartedly presented a request for general negotiations. The envoy considered most of the outstanding issues unnegotiable, and he thought Britain would refuse to waste time discussing them. She already had enough trouble on her hands in Europe, and Castlereagh had returned from Ireland very largely to prepare for a congress at Aix-la-Chapelle in the autumn.[1]

Castlereagh surprised Rush by accepting his request after consulting the cabinet. Having invited negotiations in the first place, England could not easily decline when the Americans broadened the frame of reference. The growing split with Europe encouraged rather than, as Rush believed, discouraged negotiations. More than ever it seemed good policy to settle disputes before they burst into flame.

[1] Rush to Gallatin, July 2, 13, 20, 1818, Albert Gallatin Papers, New-York Historical Society; Rush to Monroe, private and confidential, July 21, 1818, James Monroe Papers, Library of Congress.

The Foreign Secretary asked Rush to send for Gallatin right away. He wanted to get the talks started before leaving for Aix. After that Henry Goulburn and Frederick J. Robinson would take over.[2] Like all Americans, Rush remembered Goulburn's aggressiveness at Ghent. Robinson, on the other hand, had gained respect during the commercial negotiations of 1815. Even the Secretary of State, who did not waste compliments, considered Robinson fair, candid, and conciliatory.[3] One friend, one suspect, both experienced—the Foreign Secretary had not done too badly by the Americans.

Albert, Hannah, and three young Gallatins reached London from Paris in three weeks, settling in at a West End hotel. The newcomer quickly took charge from Rush; "to lead was his privilege," the resident minister later reported, "nor could I complain of his using it freely, while he used it so well." Without a Clay or an Adams to carry the war to the enemy, Gallatin felt called upon to adopt firmer tones. He did an able job, disproving the distant Bagot's prediction that "Ce rusé Genevois M. de Gallatin . . . will give trouble both by his trickiness and his settled hatred of England." [4]

On August 22 Gallatin and Rush drove the sixteen miles to North Cray, where the Foreign Secretary was in semiseclusion preparing for his European trip. They found that Robinson and Goulburn had preceded them by a few hours. After the usual preliminary banalities—the "two countries," Castlereagh said, ". . . should strive to make each other rich and happy"—the Foreign Secretary sketched in a tentative agenda: commercial relations, slaves carried off at the end of the war, the Canadian-American boundary and the Columbia Basin, and the fishery. The Americans naturally agreed to what was really Adams' list of topics. They

[2] Rush to Gallatin, July 24, 1818, Gallatin MSS.
[3] Adams #5 to Rush, May 21, 1818, Department of State Archives, National Archives, Diplomatic Instructions, All Countries, Vol. VIII.
[4] Rush to Monroe, private, Aug. 18, 1818, Monroe MSS; *Courier* (London), Aug. 19, 1818; Rush memorandum, Nov. 10, 1818, Monroe MSS; Bagot to Planta, private, Sept. 2, 1818, Foreign Office Archives, Public Record Office, FO 5/133. Rush's memorandum provides the best contemporary account of the negotiations from the American side, although a few dates are wrong.

had not received (and would not for another fortnight) the Secretary's final instructions, but they knew his views well enough to proceed except, as Gallatin told Castlereagh, on the fishery.

To Adams' agenda Castlereagh proposed to add impressment, a remarkable sign of his interest, as this problem would certainly make the entire negotiations more difficult and perhaps jeopardize other settlements. Again warning that he spoke without cabinet approval, the Foreign Secretary repeated the offer recently given to Rush. Gallatin objected. A ban on British seamen, he pointed out, would raise wage costs in peacetime; if Britain could denounce the agreement on short notice in time of war the Americans might well gain almost no return for their sacrifice. After some discussion the conferees set the subject aside for later treatment.[5]

When the informal conference ended the five men took a walk around the grounds examining Castlereagh's menagerie—lions, ostriches, kangaroos, and other beasts—and then joined the ladies for dinner. The Americans spent Saturday night at North Cray, watched Lord and Lady Castlereagh set off for church followed by a parade of pious servants, and then returned to London.

Robinson and Goulburn apparently stayed on to work out their instructions with Castlereagh, for these are dated the very next day and mention points raised at North Cray. After this the Foreign Secretary, aside from one short talk with Rush, left negotiation to his lieutenants, and no one in the cabinet seems to have stood in for him—as Bathurst did during the Ghent negotiations —after his departure for Europe. Robinson and Goulburn received only one other, quite minor directive from their superior.[6] Probably Liverpool kept a loose check on them, but on the whole they had no guidance beyond their original instructions.

Negotiations proceeded slowly. The two duos met half a dozen times at Robinson's office at the Board of Trade and also exchanged

[5] Rush memorandum, Nov. 10, 1818, Monroe MSS; Gallatin memorandum, Aug. 22–23, 1818, Gallatin MSS.

[6] Castlereagh #1 to Robinson and Goulburn, Aug. 24, 1818, FO 5/138; Rush memorandum, Sept. 1, 1818, Gallatin MSS; Castlereagh to Robinson, private and confidential, Oct. 8, 1818, FO 5/138. Castlereagh's letter to Robinson was written from Aix-la-Chapelle.

written proposals. "It is all full of interest, but would seem to be intrinsically incompatible with expedition," Rush commented after struggling with details. "Spare us . . . ; it is the first day of partridge shooting!" the Britons pleaded when Rush and Gallatin sought to advance an appointment. The Americans did not permit delays to upset them. With one exception, when Gallatin and Goulburn crossed swords, the negotiations proceeded, Rush said, with "perfect harmony on all sides." The Englishmen agreed.[7]

Equanimity was the more remarkable since the two sides deadlocked on several issues including a central one, impressment. As an ancillary to that question, introduced by Castlereagh, the Americans raised neutral rights, and from time to time sterile discussions of this issue intruded into the negotiations.[8] The four men spent more hours in vapid debate over trade with British colonies in the Western Hemisphere, and neither side came close to accepting the other's views. As a minor counterweight to these disagreements, the negotiators easily agreed to arbitrate American claims for compensation for slaves carried off at the end of the War of 1812.

Some Americans, including Rufus King, Congress' leading commercial expert, believed it doubtful wisdom to continue the commercial convention of 1815 unless Britain consented to open the colonial trade. The administration disagreed and sought renewal from the first. Castlereagh approved even before Gallatin reached London, and at their very first meeting the negotiators agreed to extend the commercial convention for ten years.[9] The Americans

[7] Rush to Monroe, private, Oct. 17, 1818, Monroe MSS; Richard Rush, *A Residence at the Court of London* (3d ed.; London, 1872), p. 323; Gallatin memorandum, Oct. 16, 1818, Gallatin MSS; Rush to Monroe, private, Nov. 21, 1818, Monroe MSS; Robinson and Goulburn #10 to Castlereagh, Oct. 20, 1818, FO 5/138.

[8] The Americans apparently believed that Adams desired them to couple impressment and neutral rights, keeping silent on both or discussing both if the British raised one of them.

[9] Nov. 25, 1818, Charles F. Adams, ed., *Memoirs of John Quincy Adams* (12 vols.; Philadelphia, 1874–1877), IV, 181; Madison to Monroe, Oct. 2, 1818, Gaillard Hunt, ed., *The Writings of James Madison* (9 vols.; New York, 1900–1910), VIII, 415; Adams #5 to Rush, May 21, 1818, Instructions, Vol. VIII; Rush to Gallatin, July 24, 1818, Gallatin MSS; Rush memorandum, Nov. 10, 1818, Monroe MSS.

welcomed this sanction of their domination of transatlantic carriage; the British sighed with relief because Gallatin and Rush had not tied Atlantic to West Indian trade; and both sides welcomed the continuation of untroubled commerce between the British home islands and the United States.

The fishery, far less important economically, evoked much more discussion. Reconciled to compromise, both sides sought to preserve national prestige. By offering to surrender the general liberty in return for a permanent right on specified coasts, the United States admitted into question its claim that the post-Revolutionary treaty had survived the War of 1812. By repeating her offer to open certain coasts, Britain likewise admitted a shadow over her legal argument. Neither side would openly confess to any doubt, and each tried to frame the compromise so that it seemed to justify earlier contentions.

The long-promised American offer, which finally arrived on September 3, proved only a rehash of the compromise Britain had suggested two years earlier. The Secretary of State sought fishing and curing privileges on precisely those coasts Bagot mentioned in his final, most generous offer (part of the southern shore of Newfoundland and some of the Labrador coast within the Gulf of St. Lawrence), plus the Atlantic shores of Labrador. Robinson and Goulburn readily agreed. They did more. They accepted an additional proposal, put forward by Rush and Gallatin on their own, to open other shores within the Gulf of St. Lawrence for fishing but not curing purposes.[10]

Obviously Britain considered even a generous arrangement better than unsettled conditions which really left the Americans free to fish almost anywhere. Gallatin and Rush took pride in having secured more than their chief asked. They abandoned some onshore fisheries, particularly in Nova Scotian waters, where actually almost no fishing took place, and they gave up some old curing grounds. In return they secured extensive fishing rights on the

[10] Adams to Gallatin and Rush, July 28, 1818, Instructions, Vol. VIII; Rush memorandum, Nov. 10, 1818, Monroe MSS.

best coasts and generous areas for curing, including Newfoundland beaches from which the treaty of 1782 excluded Americans.[11]

The permanence of the fishery article, rather than the geographical area open to Americans, led to sharp exchanges. Secretary Adams demanded an explicit statement establishing "a permanent right, not liable to be impaired by any war." The British demurred, rightly concluding that the Americans wanted to justify their old legal claim. After argument back and forth Gallatin and Rush accepted an article granting fishing rights "for ever" without specifically saying these rights would survive a war. Even this did not quite end the issue. Gallatin erupted when he thought he caught the Englishmen inserting the British legal argument into the protocol of one conference, and Robinson and Goulburn prepared a long note, virtually a lawyer's brief, which they had to withdraw when the Americans angrily declared that if it was presented they would not accept the article.[12]

The American commissioners half apologized to Adams for letting his instructions slide. In justification they pointed out that they had secured language almost as good for the future, if not a vindication of past claims. "To stave off all danger of immediate collision," Rush reported, he and Gallatin had accepted the modified language as the only route to agreement.[13] For similar reasons Robinson and Goulburn had willingly paid a large geographical price. A triumph for neither side, the fishery article benefited both because it settled the fishery question for a generation.

With boundaries the negotiators had less success. They fixed part of the northern boundary and dampened the Columbia controversy but could not agree on a boundary in Oregon. Adams'

[11] Gallatin and Rush to Adams, Oct. 20, 1818, Department of State Archives, National Archives, Despatches, Great Britain, Vol. XXIII; Alfred L. Burt, *The United States, Great Britain, and British North America from the Revolution to the Establishment of Peace after the War of 1812* (New Haven, 1940), pp. 418–420.

[12] Adams to Gallatin and Rush, July 28, 1818, Instructions, Vol. VIII; Rush memorandum, Nov. 10, 1818, Monroe MSS; Robinson and Goulburn #3 to Castlereagh, Sept. 5, 1818, FO 5/138; Robinson #6 to Castlereagh, Oct. 10, 1818, *ibid.;* Robinson and Goulburn #8 to Castlereagh, Oct. 19, 1818, *ibid.;* Gallatin memorandum, Oct. 16, 1818, Gallatin MSS.

[13] Gallatin and Rush to Adams, Oct. 20, 1818, Despatches, Great Britain, Vol. XXIII; Rush to Monroe, private, Oct. 22, 1818, Monroe MSS.

instructions breathed fire on the latter. In past conversations, particularly at London in 1806 and 1807, he observed, British and American diplomats virtually settled on the forty-ninth parallel as far as the Rockies. The negotiators at Ghent, he continued with dubious accuracy, planned to extend this line to the Pacific Ocean, until the question became mixed with the dispute over use of the Mississippi River. How then could Britain challenge America's claim to Oregon south of 49°? Two sinister explanations suggested themselves: "a design . . . to encroach . . . upon the forty-ninth parallel, South of which they can have no valid claim . . . , or . . . a jealousy of the United-States . . . of which it might have been supposed that experience would . . . have relieved them." This vigorous language discouraged Gallatin and Rush from breaking their instructions to insist upon 49°, as they were tempted to do.[14]

By comparison Castlereagh's written instructions to Goulburn and Robinson are vague and forceless, although it seems clear that he added oral warnings not to give up any of the Oregon country. In writing he merely urged his agents to arrange an easily marked boundary or, negotiation failing, to propose outside arbitration.[15] Apparently he had no doubt of the justice of Britain's claim to all territory north of the Columbia and believed arbitration would allow the United States to abandon a foolish demand without open humiliation.

The first American offer had at least the virtue of clarity. Rush and Gallatin prepared a draft article calling for a short leg north or south from Lake of the Woods to 49° and then along that parallel all the way to the Pacific Ocean. In a vain effort to tempt approval the Americans proposed to open the ocean shores and rivers crossing the boundary (meaning primarily the Columbia) to citizens of both countries. They had already made clear their unwillingness to agree to arbitration, in part because, the British commissioners skeptically reported, of "an alleged desire to keep

[14] Adams to Gallatin and Rush, July 28, 1818, Instructions, Vol. VIII. See, however, n. 20 below.
[15] Castlereagh #1 to Robinson and Goulburn, Aug. 24, 1818, FO 5/138.

their concerns altogether separate from the influence of European Connection." Robinson and Goulburn had to discuss the American proposal or admit total failure.

To feel out their opponents the Britishers asked, with a proper air of bewilderment, on what grounds the Americans claimed "an extent of Territory beyond what had ever been contemplated as belonging to them." The answers, they felt, showed Rush and Gallatin more interested in the mouth of the Columbia than any other part of the Oregon country. They also thought they detected "a disposition not to insist pertinaciously on the pretensions, which were advanced in their projet." Hoping to drive Gallatin and Rush southward from 49° they rebuffed suggestions to abandon the issue and concentrate on less difficult ones.[16]

Their counterproposal on October 6 combined obvious guile and a desire for compromise. The British demanded freedom to use the Mississippi, an antiquated idea they perhaps foolishly hoped to employ as a bargaining point. More seriously they proposed a northern border along the forty-ninth parallel to the Rocky Mountains; from there to the sea, they suggested, neither government should exercise authority between 45° and 49°, leaving the area open to citizens of both nations.[17]

In a so-called private note the next day Gallatin and Rush, after flicking off the Mississippi proposal, turned their attention to Oregon. They complained particularly that the English scheme would "throw into a common stock" only the territory most strongly claimed by the United States.[18] The proposal implied English sovereignty north of 49°, something the Americans could not admit if only for bargaining purposes, and seemingly forecast proposals to divide the area between 45° and 49° at the Columbia River or perhaps on a parallel of latitude. As Robinson and Goulburn doubtless understood these implications of their proposal,

[16] *Projet* encl. in Robinson and Goulburn #3 to Castlereagh, Sept. 5, 1818, FO 5/138; Robinson and Goulburn #1, #4 to Castlereagh, Aug. 29, Sept. 26, 1818, *ibid.;* Rush memorandum, Nov. 10, 1818, Monroe MSS.
[17] *Projet* encl. in Robinson and Goulburn to Castlereagh, Oct. 13, 1818, FO 5/138.
[18] Rush memorandum, Nov. 10, 1818, Monroe MSS; Gallatin and Rush to Robinson and Goulburn, Oct. 7, 1818, Gallatin MSS.

they probably intended primarily to probe the weakness they thought they had descried in the Americans.

When the British estimate proved wrong, Frederick J. Robinson, who in Goulburn's absence met the Americans alone on October 9, readily agreed to abandon the Mississippi bagatelle. He and his government wanted to reduce the chance of friction even if they could not fix the boundary all the way to the Pacific Ocean, but neither at this conference nor during a stormy interview between Gallatin and Goulburn a week later could a solution be found.[19]

Finally, on October 19, the day before negotiations ended, the two parties reached agreement. The British paid a substantial price to secure a truce in the Oregon country. The first of the two articles comprising this agreement drew the border from Lake of the Woods to 49° and then westward to the summit of the Rocky Mountains. The other article declared all territory claimed by Great Britain or the United States west of the mountains "free and open . . . to the citizens and subjects of the two powers." This arrangement threw the claims of both countries into a common stock, and for the first time Britain tacitly admitted that the Americans had claims worth discussing north of the Columbia and even north of 49°.

At Gallatin's insistence the second article had a limited life of ten years. The Americans did not want a permanent vacuum on the Pacific Coast. They consented to a decade's intermission during which, they somewhat optimistically calculated, settlers and traders would greatly strengthen the American position. Robinson and Goulburn accepted the time limit simply because they did not want to jeopardize other agreements—Gallatin talked of extending the convention of 1815 and dropping all others matters—and welcomed any muffling, even temporarily, of the controversy touched off by the *Ontario*.[20]

[19] Robinson #6 to Castlereagh, Oct. 10, 1818, FO 5/138; Gallatin memorandum, Oct. 16, 1818, Gallatin MSS.

[20] Gallatin and Rush to Adams, Oct. 20, 1818, Despatches, Great Britain, Vol. XXIII; Gallatin memorandum, Oct. 16, 1818, Gallatin MSS; Robinson and Goulburn #9 to Castlereagh, Oct. 20, 1818, FO 5/138. Frederick Merk, "The Ghost River Caledonia in the Oregon Negotiation of 1818," *American Historical Review*, LV

Impressment, the leitmotiv of the negotiations, arose at almost every formal and private meeting. The English, expecting Gallatin and Rush to pant for a settlement, thought it clever to withhold an offer until their fellow negotiators produced the long-awaited proposal on the fishery. Actually the British did not have the leverage they thought. Even Rush, the most tempted toward compromise, considered Castlereagh's proposed mechanisms unacceptable, and Adams' instructions virtually directed his agents to avoid an agreement if they could.[21] The Americans were no longer supplicants. Rather than compromise national rights they preferred silence.

Thus the initiative passed to Britain and particularly to the Foreign Secretary. At the North Cray meeting Castlereagh introduced impressment into the conversation. The subject, dismissed by Adams in a phrase, dominated the instructions to Robinson and Goulburn. Castlereagh surrounded the proposal to end foreign enlistments and impressment with qualifications similar to those previously suggested to Rush. He sought thereby, he explained, to make agreement palatable to the British people.[22] "By authoriz-

---

(1949–1950), 538, points out that the copy of Rush's memorandum of the negotiations now in the Gallatin MSS—but not the copy in the Monroe MSS—records the Americans as having offered to recede from 49° to a line dividing Oregon along the watershed between the Columbia River and the streams running into the Gulf of Georgia. Presumably because it was an informal offer made in violation of Adams' instructions, this suggestion is not recorded in the formal protocol.

Why, if they understood this offer, did not Goulburn and Robinson seize upon it, since they already thought they had discerned weakness in Rush and Gallatin? They need not have accepted it or even have reported it in a formal dispatch to Castlereagh, but one would expect them to pass the information on to the Foreign Secretary in a private dispatch, or at the very least not to state so strongly as they did in their official report (Robinson and Goulburn #9 to Castlereagh, Oct. 20, 1818, FO 5/138) that the Americans adamantly refused to budge. Very tentatively one may guess that the Americans made this suggestion as unobtrusively and noncommittally as possible and that, in the heat of argument over many other aspects of the Oregon question, the Englishmen failed to understand it. As the proposal formed no important part of the negotiations of 1818 and was never referred to thereafter, it is ignored in this account of the discussions at London.

[21] Bagot to Planta, private, Sept. 2, 1818, FO 5/133; Robinson and Goulburn #3 to Castlereagh, Sept. 5, 1818, FO 5/138; Rush to Monroe, private, Aug. 18, 1818, Monroe MSS; Adams to Gallatin and Rush, July 28, 1818, Instructions, Vol. VIII.

[22] The Foreign Secretary also sought to exempt from prohibition impressment "in

ing . . . a modification of this ancient practice, so important to the naval security of the Country and upon which the Public Sentiments are so much alive," Castlereagh declared proudly, the Prince Regent's ministers gave "unequivocal proof of His desire to cultivate . . . the most friendly understanding." At the Secretary's request Frederick J. Robinson immediately set to work on a *projet* for submission to the Americans.[23]

Because the Americans showed little interest at the first two meetings of the commissioners, Castlereagh called Rush to his home in St. James Square. Amidst the hurly-burly of departure for Aix-la-Chapelle—his carriage waited at the door—the Foreign Secretary sought to infect Rush with his own enthusiasm. He revealed for the first time that the cabinet endorsed the proposal. He hoped, he said, this approval would show the government's "wishes for a durable harmony." He no longer asked the Americans to let boarding officers call for crew lists and take formal note of Britons they thought they saw in ships' companies. He urged Rush to meet the concession in the same spirit. The "great principle"—no enlistment, no impressment—must not become bogged down in details that would prevent agreement. Richard Rush listened coolly, offered no opinions, and then asked about neutral rights. Weary and discouraged, Castlereagh replied: "I think this point had better not come into view; at least I do not see how we should be able to settle it." [24] He understood Rush's reaction as a rebuff.

When Robinson finished his *projet* he and his colleague handed it to the Americans, who returned an amended version on Septem-

---

British Ports, or within the maritime jurisdiction of Great Britain." The Americans never challenged England's right forcibly to enlist Britons on ships in her harbors, but they always denied the British claim that Channel waters lay within the "maritime jurisdiction of Great Britain."

[23] Rush memorandum, Nov. 10, 1818, Monroe MSS; Castlereagh #1 to Robinson and Goulburn, Aug. 24, 1818, FO 5/138; Robinson to Castlereagh, Aug. 27, 1818, FO 83/2205; Robinson to Liverpool, private, Sept. 13, 1818, Papers of the First and Second Earls of Liverpool, British Museum (Add. MSS 38190–38489, 38564–38581), Add. MSS 38272.

[24] Rush memorandum, Sept. 1, 1818, Gallatin MSS.

ber 25. In what they considered a substantial concession, Rush and Gallatin agreed to permit renunciation of the agreement at short notice. They deleted a phrase excepting the so-called Narrow Seas from the ban on impressment, and Goulburn and Robinson passed over this change without contest, although an effort to settle the impressment question in 1803 had foundered over just this question of British sovereignty over waters in the English Channel.[25]

The only other substantial change Rush and Gallatin suggested proved fatal to the entire project. The British plan required each power to deliver a list of naturalized citizens born in the other country—and thus eligible to serve in the marine—along with places of birth and dates of naturalization. Rush and Gallatin objected that, because naturalization records were incomplete, their country could not make an accurate list. They declined to risk complaint if a naturalized seaman inadvertently omitted from the list later served on an American merchantman.[26] This objection, although valid, reflected their general lack of interest in a settlement.

The lists clogged discussion for the remainder of the negotiation. The Americans wanted to delete or substantially to modify the British proposal. The Englishmen insisted that to do either would reopen the vexing question of citizenship in hundreds of individual cases.[27] It was just the sort of argument against which Castlereagh had warned. His instructions did not suggest any such device, and it had no real importance for either side except as it showed doubt of American good faith. Obviously no British tar would enroll under his proper name if he had violated the inter-

---

[25] Apparently to meet Gallatin's objection that Britain would benefit while her seamen were excluded from American ships in peacetime, and then might deprive the United States of reciprocal benefit by denouncing the agreement as soon as war came, Robinson and Goulburn inserted a provision by which either power might waive its right to the exclusive use of its seamen. Presumably Britain would have done so in peacetime.

[26] Robinson and Goulburn #3 to Castlereagh, Sept. 5, 1818, and encl., FO 5/138; Rush memorandum, Nov. 10, 1818, Monroe MSS; Robinson and Goulburn #4 to Castlereagh, Sept. 26, 1818, FO 5/138.

[27] Rush memorandum, Nov. 10, 1818, Monroe MSS; Robinson #6 to Castlereagh, Oct. 10, 1818, FO 5/138; Robinson and Goulburn #7, #8 to Castlereagh, Oct. 13, 19, 1818, ibid.

national agreement, and the Foreign Secretary had already agreed not to mobilize crews for inspection and interrogation. The lists would have been utterly useless.

Rush later maintained that if Viscount Castlereagh had not been called to Aix-la-Chapelle he would have arranged a settlement. In principle Castlereagh desired to do so, but at the critical moment an outside factor discouraged him. When Britain learned that General Andrew Jackson had executed two Englishmen for aiding his Indian enemies, nationalists screamed for revenge. The pressure rose as weeks passed without any apology or explanation from Washington. From Aix the Foreign Secretary wrote: ". . . we should not deem it prudent to risk the fate of so delicate a Question as that of Impressment, with such a Topick of Inflammation open against us." [28] Domestic political considerations deterred the cabinet from directing Robinson and Goulburn to drop a ridiculously rigid demand. Surprisingly, this possibility never occurred to the Americans.

Four days before negotiations ended Gallatin observed philosophically that failure to agree was not too unfortunate, for no compromise could satisfy opinion in either country. He doubted that Britain would ever again attempt impressment. Goulburn responded pessimistically that he expected it to cause trouble. On October 19, at their last business meeting, the two commissions "finally determined that we could come to no agreement." [29]

"Upon impressment we have again completely failed; nor do I see . . . a hope of the question ever being laid to rest by treaty," Richard Rush reported to ex-President Madison. "I fear, sir, that it will only be left for some future administration to follow with more means, (with more justice and glory it never can,) the precedent of a remedy which you were forced at last to set." [30]

---

[28] Richard Rush, *A Residence at the Court of London, Second Series* (2 vols.; London, 1845), II, 3–4; Castlereagh to Robinson, private and confidential, Oct. 8, 1818, FO 5/138.

[29] Gallatin memorandum, Oct. 16, 1818, Gallatin MSS; Rush memorandum, Nov. 10, 1818, Monroe MSS.

[30] Rush to Madison, Dec. 13, 1818, Richard Rush Papers, Historical Society of Pennsylvania.

Failure never had the bloody consequences anticipated by Rush, Goulburn, and Castlereagh. The future proved John Quincy Adams right in disapproving any compromise of American rights to secure renunciation of a practice outmoded by time. The negotiations themselves showed that Castlereagh earnestly sought to settle this long-standing issue. Until Andrew Jackson muddied the waters the British government pressed for agreement, while the Americans, previously eager, allowed the question to drift. Then both sides let an inconsequential side issue prevent compromise.

On October 20 Gallatin, Rush, and Goulburn met in Whitehall to sign the finished convention. Goulburn gave the Americans a little history lesson, pointing out that the unfortunate Duke of Monmouth had once used the room as a bedchamber and that Edward Gibbon wrote at the very desk upon which the convention lay. Robinson had left for the country—more partridges?—and copies had to be sent after him for signature. Without even waiting for the courier's return, Gallatin set off for his regular post at Paris. Rush forwarded the convention to Washington accompanied by a final report, primarily Gallatin's work.[31]

Two weeks later the Foreign Office sent British ratification to Bagot. As at the time of Ghent the ministers feared American trickery; they directed Bagot to insist upon unconditional ratification. London need not have worried. The American political world welcomed the convention, and, after a delay caused by deference to Rufus King, who was ill, the Senate approved it unanimously at the end of January, 1819.[32]

Englishmen were not so universally pleased. They objected in

[31] Rush memorandum, Nov. 10, 1818, Monroe MSS; Rush to Monroe, private, Oct. 22, 1818, *ibid.*; Gallatin and Rush to Adams, Oct. 20, 1818, Despatches, Great Britain, Vol. XXIII.

[32] Bathurst (acting for Castlereagh), #22, #23 to Bagot, Nov. 7, 9, 1818, FO 5/129; Bagot #8 to Castlereagh, Feb. 1, 1819, FO 5/141; *Journal of the Executive Proceedings of the Senate of the United States of America*, III (Washington, 1828), 169. In later years Secretary Adams' candidacy for the presidency caused his opponents to reëxamine the convention. Thomas Hart Benton strongly implied that, to secure fishery concessions beneficial to New England, Adams and his agents accepted ambiguous language calling into question America's title to Oregon. *Annals of Congress*, 17th Cong., 2d sess., pp. 250–251.

particular to the fishery compromise and also to the tacit admission of American claims to part of Oregon. The London *Sun* attacked "gratuitous concessions." The *Times* declared that Rush and Gallatin "could not have finished the business assigned to them in a more successful manner," from the American point of view. The United States, this paper maintained, had no right whatsoever to the fishery yet received concessions of "frightful magnitude." Robinson and Goulburn might as well have ceded Newfoundland to the United States, for the concession would ruin that colony.[33] The government ignored this criticism, and it quickly petered out.

In one sense the convention of 1818 accomplished little. As a leading historian has observed, the agreement postponed the Oregon question, settled the boundary east of the Rockies along lines really arranged as far back as 1807, merely confirmed earlier agreement to renew the convention of 1815, compromised the fishery question, and referred the dispute over slaves to outside arbitration. "It settles at best but a few of the many disputed points between the two nations," Rush commented. Because so much remained unsettled, the negotiators agreed to call their work a convention rather than give it the grander title of treaty.[34] Robinson and Gallatin left before quite finishing the business, and neither party considered it necessary to charter a special packet to carry the convention to the United States.

When Richard Rush penned his memoirs fifteen years later he took a more favorable view of his handiwork, even though he regretted the failure to settle impressment (and neutral rights) and West Indian trade. He welcomed extension of the commercial convention and the advance toward settlement of the slave question. "In settling the controversy about the fisheries," Rush asserted, "the calamity of a war was probably warded off." Moreover, by fixing the northern boundary "the seed of future disputes

---

[33] *Sun* (London), March 16, 20, 1819; *Times* (London), March 1, 4, 1819.
[34] Merk, *op. cit.*, p. 538; Rush to Caesar Rodney, n.d., John H. Powell, *Richard Rush, Republican Diplomat* (Philadelphia, 1942), pp. 119–120; Rush memorandum, Nov. 10, 1818, Monroe MSS.

was extinguished." As to Oregon, the convention left the final decision to "time . . . , the best negotiator." [35]

Rush's mature judgment was better than his hasty one. The deadlock on impressment had no substantive importance. The failure to settle, even seriously to discuss, the West Indian question was outweighed by other successes, even if renewal of the commercial convention, the arrangement to arbitrate the slave question, and establishment of the 49° line are dismissed as trivial. Perhaps Rush exaggerated when he said the fishery dispute would have led to war. Still, serious friction would certainly have followed a failure at London, for British patience was nearly exhausted. England would probably have ended the annual dispensations which allowed the Americans free use of the fishery. Similarly, lack of any understanding on Oregon would almost certainly have had unfortunate consequences. To postpone a clash gave immediate benefit to both countries although, as Rush observed and the British doubtless knew, time would probably serve the United States. The fishery and Oregon settlements, one a compromise and the other inconclusive, markedly eased Anglo-American relations.

On the fishery Castlereagh once said "he thought it of less moment which of the parties gained a little more or lost a little more . . . than that so difficult a point should be adjusted and the harmony of the two countries . . . be made secure." [36] The observation applied equally well to the convention as a whole. At the very least, failure would have brought back the suspicion-ridden, combative mood of 1815. Moreover, the agreement left John Quincy Adams free to concentrate on the acquisition of Florida and Lord Castlereagh unembarrassed by lesser issues as he faced the Continental powers.

Impressment, which gave most trouble at London, never again seriously vexed Anglo-American diplomacy. Castlereagh's pre-negotiation offer, not discussed by Monroe and his cabinet until autumn, touched off a sharp two-day debate. Adams and Secretary

---

[35] Richard Rush, *Memoranda of a Residence at the Court of London* (Philadelphia, 1833), pp. 414–415.

[36] Rush, *Residence, Second Series*, II, 58–59.

of War Calhoun vigorously opposed the Foreign Secretary's two amendments. President Monroe gave in to his subordinates. In instructions which Secretary Adams generously described as a compromise between the President and himself the American government rejected one suggestion and severely modified the other. These instructions reached London after the negotiators broke up, and Rush ignored them.

Two years later Adams told the British minister at Washington that, recognizing the depth of British feeling, the United States would not press the issue so long as peace continued. "In this sentiment we heartily concur," Castlereagh's successor added at a later date, when Adams showed signs of shifting.[37] As the subject of negotiation, impressment practically passed from the scene.

The obsolete controversy cast a discouraging shadow over efforts to break up the slave trade. The problem was not inconsiderable, for every year slavers brought thousands of Negroes to the United States.[38] First a reluctant and then an enthusiastic convert to the cause, Lord Castlereagh pressed for international agreements directed against a noxious traffic carried on in defiance of the law of most nations, including the United States. After strenuous efforts Britain secured permission for her officers to board suspected vessels flying the flags of the important maritime powers of Europe. Castlereagh and his successor, George Canning, sought similar permission from the United States, offering in return to allow American warships to inspect suspected slavers under British colors.

These efforts ran afoul of American loathing of search and impressment, a feeling so deep that even enemies of slavery and the slave trade resisted the British proposal. Rufus King, a declared

[37] Oct. 29, 30, 1818, Adams, *op. cit.*, IV, 147–150; Adams to Rush and Gallatin, Nov. 2, 1818, Instructions, Vol. VIII; Oct. 26, 1820, Adams, *op. cit.*, V, 192–193; Canning #3 to Huskisson and Stratford Canning, May 31, 1824, FO 5/191.

[38] *Quarterly Review* (London), XXVI (1821), 80, and Samuel F. Bemis, *John Quincy Adams and the Foundations of American Foreign Policy* (New York, 1949), p. 412, present estimates of 14,000 and 60,000 in single years. The standard treatment of the subject is Hugh G. Soulsby, *The Right of Search and the Slave Trade in Anglo-American Relations, 1814–1862*, Johns Hopkins University Studies in Historical and Political Science, Series LI, no. 2 (Baltimore, 1933). See also, Bemis, *op. cit.*, pp. 409–435.

foe of slavery willing to risk the union on the Missouri question, urged President Monroe to take care before "allowing to England a Right to search american vessels: inasmuch as under the belligerent Right of Search, they justified the practice of Impressment." John Quincy Adams, likewise no friend of slavery, steadily set his face against British suggestions, and in 1821 he gruffly told Stratford Canning the United States government did not want to hear any more on the subject. The English minister observed in 1822, "the personal opinion of M^r. Adams is particularly hostile to an admission of the right of search," surely a fair comment, and the next year he added that Adams' presidential ambitions made him doubly reluctant to permit British officers to search American ships.[39]

Very few Americans condoned the slave trade, and in 1820 a combination of British pressure and rising feeling in the United States drove the administration a small way along the path Castlereagh desired. The Secretary of State offered to send an American squadron to coöperate with British ships in African waters. Although the Admiralty rightly objected that this gesture offered little help, the Foreign Secretary felt it best to accept it.[40] There the matter rested for more than two years.

In March, 1823, by a vote of 131 to 9, the House of Representatives called upon the President to make diplomatic arrangements "for the effectual abolition of the African slave trade, and its ultimate denunciation, as piracy, under the law of nations." Several months later the administration proposed that England and the United States declare the slave trade an act of piracy for their citizens, thus placing traders in effect at war with all nations, like ordinary pirates. This done, America offered to agree to a recipro-

[39] King to Monroe, July 27, 1818, James Monroe Papers, New York Public Library; Stratford Canning to Castlereagh, private and confidential, March 8, 1821, FO 5/157; Stratford Canning #49 to Londonderry, June 29, 1822, FO 5/168; Stratford Canning #54 to Canning, June 6, 1823, FO 5/176. The American argument does not make too much sense, for it failed to distinguish between the right of search in peacetime and the same right in time of war. Great Britain never engaged in impressment except in time of war.

[40] Stratford Canning #1 to Castlereagh, Jan. 2, 1821, and encl., FO 5/157; Croker memorandum, March 15, 1821, FO 5/163; Croker to Planta, April 6, 1821, ibid.; Castlereagh #6 to Stratford Canning, March 25, 1821, FO 5/156.

cal right of search for the sole purpose of destroying the trade. In 1824 Richard Rush signed a convention along these lines. The Senate attached amendments designedly unacceptable to England, primarily by excepting waters off the American coast.[41]

London's *Quarterly Review* had once warned Britons "not to be duped by fine speeches and lofty pretensions . . . into the belief that we have a real co-adjutor, in our own honest exertions for putting an end to this detestable traffic, in the government of the United States." The convention of 1824 failed, not because the administration or other Americans secretly approved the slave trade, but because Adams' political enemies saw an opportunity to embarrass him. They appealed chiefly to feelings roused by impressment and search, turning against the Secretary of State and presidential candidate arguments he had used prior to 1823. The memory of brutal infringements on American sovereignty delayed concerted action against the slave trade until the year of the Emancipation Proclamation.[42]

Weaknesses in the fishery compromise did not become immediately apparent. As time passed American fishermen sought more extensive rights and sometimes took them without permission, whereas their rivals sought to cut privileges to the bone. By the Marcy-Elgin Treaty of 1854 the Yankees won the use of all coastal waters of British North America, but controversy continued on into the twentieth century. For the moment the convention brought peace to the fishing grounds. In 1820 the local British commander reported only a single altercation, with more than 600 American ships visiting imperial waters.[43]

In the years after 1818 the Oregon country caused slightly more difficulty. The North West Company and the Hudson's Bay Company, which absorbed the former in 1821, gained fairly effective control of the area. This raised the hackles of patriots interested in the fur trade or in a Pacific base for commerce with China.

---

[41] Bemis, *op. cit.*, pp. 427–435.

[42] *Quarterly Review*, XXVI (1821), 80; Stratford Canning #26 to Canning, secret and confidential, May 21, 1824, FO 5/185; Bradford Perkins, ed., *Youthful America* (Berkeley and Los Angeles, 1960), pp. 86–90; Bemis, *op. cit.*, pp. 433–435.

[43] Sir Charles Hamilton to Croker, Oct. 24, 1820, extract encl. in Goulburn to Planta, Dec. 29, 1820, FO 5/155.

In 1819 Congressman John Floyd got himself appointed chairman of an investigatory committee. In 1821 his committee reported that no European state had any valid claims on the Pacific Coast south of 60°, approximately the latitude of Anchorage, Alaska! This extreme assertion made Floyd's legislative proposal, for occupation of the Columbia Basin, sound positively mild.

Congress shied away from a direct confrontation with Great Britain, and Floyd's bill failed, as it did when he reintroduced it in January and again in December, 1822. Floyd and his friends made a great deal of noise, partly to embarrass the Secretary of State, but the Oregon men by no means commanded a majority in Congress. In the words of a Kentuckian, "separated by the Rocky Mountains, and at a distance of three thousand miles, the wholesome blood which flowed from the heart of this confederacy cannot reach the confines of Oregon." Such modesty, forgotten in the exhilarating days of Manifest Destiny later on, helped defeat Floyd. After a brief flurry in 1825 the subject of Oregon dropped away for fifteen years.[44]

In his heart Secretary Adams, who opposed Floyd's proposals for tactical reasons, was fully as good an imperialist. At a cabinet meeting in 1819 he said that

the world [should] . . . be familiarized with the idea of considering our proper dominion to be the continent of North America. From the time when we became an independent people it was as much a law of nature that this should become our pretension as that the Mississippi should flow to the sea. Spain had possessions upon our southern and Great Britain upon our northern border. It was impossible that centuries should elapse without finding them annexed to the United States; not that any spirit of encroachment or ambition on our part renders it necessary, but because it is a physical, moral, and political absurdity that such fragments of territory, with sovereigns at fifteen hundred miles beyond [the] sea, worthless and burdensome to their owners, should exist permanently contiguous to a great, powerful, enterprising, and rapidly-growing nation.[45]

[44] On the Oregon question in these years, see Bemis, *op. cit.*, pp. 482–509. The quotation is from *Annals*, 17th Cong., 2d sess., p. 693.

[45] Nov. 16, 1819, Adams, *op. cit.*, IV, 438–439.

This spirit led Adams to watch warily for danger on the Pacific Coast, to contest British (and Russian) claims there, and later to play the central part in drafting the noncolonization doctrine in Monroe's famous message. For the most part, except in his oratorical outburst on the Fourth of July, 1821, Adams kept these thoughts from view outside the cabinet.

An exception occurred in January, 1821. The day after Floyd's report Stratford Canning visited the Department of State, as usual without appointment. Canning asked if the United States intended to establish a new settlement in the Oregon country. Adams rather loosely and casually replied that "it was very probable that our settlement at the mouth of [the] Columbia River would at no remote period be increased." "Am I to understand this," the British envoy then asked, "as the determination of the American Government?" Irritated by the Englishman's frosty and peremptory manner, the Secretary replied in kind. "No sir," he said, "you are to understand nothing as the determination of the American Government that I say to you without consultation with and directions from the President. What I have now said to you is merely an opinion of my own."

The two men quarreled the rest of that afternoon and much of the next. They argued over Canning's alleged impropriety in making an issue of mere newspaper reports and speeches, and they brawled over Adams' declaration that he would receive further complaints only in writing. Above all they fought over the Columbia. Adams denied that the convention of 1818 recognized the existence of British claims, pointing out that England had restored Astoria and agreed to leave the northwest coast open for ten years. "We certainly did suppose," he angrily concluded, "that the British Government had come to the conclusion that there would be neither policy nor profit in cavilling with us about territory on this North American continent," present possessions excluded.[46]

The outbreak surprised both men, particularly Canning, who until then considered himself on excellent terms with Adams de-

[46] Jan. 26, 27, 1821, *ibid.*, V, 243–252; Stratford Canning #3 to Castlereagh, Jan. 28, 1821, FO 5/157.

spite the Secretary's "continual coarseness, & ravenous enmity to England." Only ten days before, Adams' memoirs reveal, the two men had conversed pleasantly for three hours on "a great variety of topics, political and literary," when Canning dropped in at the State Department. At the time Adams wondered if he did not allow his tongue too much freedom in the dialogues Canning obviously cultivated.[47]

Both men deserve blame for the unfortunate episode. By failing to define their terms—did "settlement" mean a private venture or a military and administrative post established by the government? —they invited the disagreement too readily converted into a foolish quarrel. At least twice on the first day Stratford Canning tried to bring the clash to a close, and he considered the rupture of his developing personal relations with Adams a serious blow to his mission. Still he was by no means blameless, and deserved the rebuke Castlereagh returned across the Atlantic.[48]

Adams never admitted any responsibility, and during Canning's next visit, wisely postponed by the British envoy for six weeks, said nothing of the quarrel, although he spoke sharply on another subject, the slave trade. In April Adams fulsomely expressed appreciation of minor courtesies extended to Rush by the Prince Regent, just the sort of ceremonial he usually discounted or disliked. Adams said, Canning reported, that "he should view with pleasure any thing which tended even to draw closer the amicable relations of the two countries." [49] Perhaps Adams meant indirectly to apologize for the past or at least to downgrade it.

Adams and Canning, good haters both, never forgot the episode. More important, they never again quarreled. On the two occasions when Floyd reintroduced his bill Canning avoided mentioning Oregon to Adams, and at the end of 1822 he informed his superiors that the proposal did not have government sanction. London too refused to get excited. The cabinet clung to what

[47] Canning to Planta, private, Feb. 6, 1824, FO 5/157; Jan. 17, 1821, Adams, op. cit., V, 237.
[48] Castlereagh #7 to Stratford Canning, April 10, 1821, FO 5/156.
[49] Stratford Canning to Castlereagh, private and confidential, March 8, 1821, FO 5/157; Stratford Canning #25 to Castlereagh, April 27, 1821, FO 5/158.

Bathurst called "the policy of waiting to see." After the Czar's ukase of 1821 closed a broad stretch of coastal waters above Vancouver Island to all foreigners, England and the United States had an outside enemy who drew off some of their suspicion of each other. As soon as Adams learned of the ukase he called in Canning to announce American disapproval and ask what Britain intended to do.[50]

The two-day argument of January, 1821, so lovingly recorded in Adams' diary and minutely recounted in Canning's dispatches, is often allowed to cast a false light on the Oregon question in postwar years. Actually it was an isolated episode. Aside from men like Floyd, the politicians of both countries accepted, though they did not embrace or consider permanent, the arrangement reached at London in 1818. In 1827, after only half-serious efforts to fix a permanent boundary, the two countries extended the provisions of 1818 indefinitely.

These various forward glances show that the convention of 1818 did not wipe away suspicion as one might wash dirt from a pane. Few international agreements do. This one succeeded so well that of all the old issues only trade with the British West Indies seriously troubled relations for years after 1818. Failure on the slave trade and a silly quarrel on Oregon proved only that Americans, particularly Adams, had long memories.

A few days before Lord Castlereagh accepted Rush's request for general negotiations the *Courier*, certainly not well known for love of the Yankees, declared that since Ghent relations had steadily improved. "As far . . . as human foresight can drive into futurity," the paper continued, "we have, from the friendly spirit now happily existing, on each side of the Atlantic, every ground for expecting a lasting peace."[51] Daniel Stuart, of the *Courier*, did not in this instance lie for his patrons. Since 1815 progress had been made in liquidating old issues, and in 1818 America and

---

[50] Stratford Canning to Bathurst, separate, Nov. 21, 1822, FO 5/169; Bathurst to Planta, March 8, 1822, FO 5/166; Stratford Canning #5 to Bathurst, Oct. 28, 1822, FO 5/169.

[51] *Courier*, Aug. 17, 1818.

Britain took a further step forward. No one could be sure that their new comity, always fragile and subject to popular attack, often undermined by effusions of publicists and editors, would survive the challenge presented by the downfall of the Spanish Empire in Latin America and the consequent struggle for spoils.

SPANISH SPOILS

In the age of Castlereagh and Adams, Spain clearly deserved the dubious title, actually not yet invented, of "sick man of Europe." Accumulated misfortunes and miscalculations threatened the entire Spanish fabric. Ferdinand VII, the cruel and reactionary coward who occupied the throne, brawled constantly with the Cortes, the legislative body which preëmpted power during the struggle against Napoleon. In Latin America insurgents challenged imperial authority, and despite frequent defeats time clearly was on their side.

Spanish royalists had long repented the "unpardonable error" of aiding the North Americans' struggle for independence. Driven backward by Pinckney's Treaty, mulcted of Louisiana by grace of Napoleon, robbed of West Florida, Madrid viewed the United States with loathing and fear. Too weak and distracted to act alone, Spain sought common action with Britain "with the view of checking the enterprizes of an ambitious Power and of extinguishing the contagious fire of rebellion and insurrection." [1] British sympa-

[1] Conde de Fernán-Nuñez to Castlereagh, Oct. 17, 1816, Charles K. Webster, ed., *Britain and the Independence of Latin America* (2 vols.; London, 1938), II, 347.

thies often lay with Spain, if not with Ferdinand personally, but Lord Castlereagh was far too wise to cast away his rapprochement with the United States.

Almost as soon as peace with Britain freed their hands the Americans resumed efforts to acquire that part of the Floridas still in Spain's possession, and shortly after John Quincy Adams took over the State Department he began marathon negotiations with Luis de Onís, the Spanish envoy. From the beginning Onís and his superiors saw they could not hold Florida, where Spanish authority had already begun to rot. In return for cession they sought the cancellation of American claims against Spain, a favorable boundary between their Mexican province and the United States, and assurances that the Americans would not aid insurgents in Latin America. These last Adams declined to give, nor would he accept Onís' boundary proposals, which began with a demand for the Mississippi line—in other words, surrender of the Louisiana Purchase by the United States—and receded more slowly than an Alpine glacier in summer. By the spring of 1818 the two men had reached a deadlock.[2]

Americans sometimes blamed England for the difficulty. "A strong suspicion is entertained here by many," Monroe wrote in 1816, "that the Spanish government relies on the support of the British, if it is not instigated by it." Above all Americans feared that Onís' evasions masked an intention to transfer Florida to Great Britain, either as a reward for English services in arranging an accommodation between Spain and her rebellious colonies or to establish a stronger buffer against American expansion southward. This plan, actually suggested by Onís in 1815, never received British encouragement. In 1816, presuming upon their acquaintance at Ghent and London, Goulburn chided Clay for countenancing the story. Rumors lasted until 1819, another example of the baleful legacy of the past.[3]

[2] Philip C. Brooks, *Diplomacy and the Borderlands: The Adams-Onís Treaty of 1819* (Berkeley, 1939), the standard monograph, is heavily used here and in following paragraphs. For general information see also Samuel F. Bemis, *John Quincy Adams and the Foundations of American Foreign Policy* (New York, 1949), pp. 300–340.

[3] Monroe to Adams, Feb. 2, 1816, Department of State Archives, National Archives, Diplomatic Instructions, All Countries, Vol. VIII; Monroe to Adams, Dec. 10, 1815,

The activities of unauthorized Englishmen in Florida encouraged suspicion. Shortly after Ghent a British officer who organized Creek and Seminole resistance to the Americans during the war, Colonel Edward Nicholls, signed a treaty of alliance with the Creeks. London quickly disavowed Nicholls—his action, Bathurst wrote, "may have been occasioned by an ill-judged zeal in the prosecution of . . . Military Duties . . . , but was in no way sanctioned by His Majesty's Government"—but received Creek chieftains and bestowed presents. Not until 1818 did the Foreign Secretary forbid visits by Indian leaders. As a result of this order a Creek chief was refused permission to land at Spithead and was sent back to America without setting foot on English soil.[4]

After Nicholls' departure two British officers not on active duty, George Woodbine and Robert Ambrister, a Waterloo veteran cashiered for dueling, appeared in Florida, stirring up the Indians. A Scottish trader among the tribes, Alexander Arbuthnot, bombarded Bagot and Governor Charles Cameron of Bermuda with pleas for British aid to the Indians. Bagot and Cameron, as well as superiors at the Foreign and Colonial offices, rejected Arbuthnot's appeals. Because these actions remained secret, American suspicions continued.[5]

At first the British government tried, as it had before the War of 1812, to discourage American designs on Spanish territory. Early in 1816, irritated by Adams' close questioning, Castlereagh angrily denied that Britain wanted Florida. Then he went on, in what Adams described as a "tone of struggling irritation and complacency," to warn, "Do you only observe the same moderation. If we should find you hereafter pursuing a system of encroachment upon your neighbors, what we might do *defensively* is another con-

---

ibid.; Charles R. Vaughan #34 to Castlereagh, Nov. 16, 1815, Webster, *op. cit.*, II, 344; Goulburn to Clay, March 8, 1816, James F. Hopkins, ed., *The Papers of Henry Clay* (Lexington, 1959——), II, 172–173; *Annals of Congress*, 15th Cong., 2d sess., pp. 612–613.

[4] Bathurst #11 to Baker, Sept. —, 1815, Foreign Office Archives, Public Record Office, FO 5/105; Hamilton to Croker, Sept. 14, 15, 1818, FO 5/140; Bemis, *op. cit.*, p. 303.

[5] Bagot #9 to Castlereagh, Feb. 5, 1817, FO 5/121; Goulburn to Hamilton, April 2, 1817, FO 5/127; Colonial office memorandum, June —, 1817, and encl., *ibid.*; Bagot #28 to Castlereagh, April 7, 1818, and encl., FO 5/131; Bagot to Planta, private, Nov. 4, 1818, FO 5/133.

sideration." [6] Although Adams never forgot this threat, the Foreign Secretary neither repeated it nor even thought of seizing Spanish territory when the United States gained Florida. Quite the contrary. Soon convinced that the drive was too strong for Spain to resist, Castlereagh urged Madrid to cede Florida in return for a favorable Mexican boundary.

Madrid repeatedly sought British assistance, and in 1817 Castlereagh felt he had to respond to the importunities. Just before Adams left for America, the Secretary offhandedly inquired if the United States would welcome an offer of British good offices. Adams, at first receptive, naturally recoiled when Castlereagh mentioned a settlement transferring Florida to the United States and fixing the western boundary along the Mississippi River.[7]

Pressed by Spain, Castlereagh went through the motions of repeating his offer a few months later. After cabinet discussion he sent three long directives to Bagot on November 10, 1817. At Spanish urging, he said, Great Britain wished to suggest the possibility of mediation. The Foreign Secretary hedged this proposal with qualifications designed, he told Bagot, to avoid the danger of damaging Anglo-American relations. Castlereagh did not even formally propose mediation; he merely asked if the United States would welcome an offer. He made it clear that while ideally speaking Britain would prefer Spain to retain East Florida, he now considered this solution impossible and would not even suggest it. He informed Bagot—and through him Adams—that England had refused Spanish urging "to press . . . Intervention somewhat in a tone of Menace," and promised to steer a middle course between the parties if mediation went forward; talk of the Mississippi boundary ceased. Finally, Castlereagh made it clear he expected America to decline mediation and would not be upset if she did.[8]

[6] Adams #30 to Monroe, Feb. 8, 1816, Department of State Archives, National Archives, Despatches, Great Britain, Vol. XX. For Castlereagh's milder but belated memory of this conversation, see Castlereagh to Bagot, private and secret, Nov. 11, 1817, Sir Charles Bagot Papers, Levens Hall, Westmorland.

[7] June 7, 1817, Charles F. Adams, ed., *Memoirs of John Quincy Adams* (12 vols.; Philadelphia, 1874–1877), III, 560.

[8] Castlereagh to Bathurst, Oct. 31, 1817, Francis Bickley, ed., *Report on the Manuscripts of Earl Bathurst* (London, 1923), p. 441; Castlereagh #23, #24 (most secret

All in all this was pretty mild beer for the Spaniards, far short of the support Madrid desired.

Late in January Bagot conveyed these thoughts to Adams, carefully pointing out that the initiative had come from Spain. The cabinet discussed this development at two sessions (surprisingly, Adams was less obdurately opposed than his colleagues) and decided to decline the British offer with thanks. The Secretary of State, with care and grace equal to Bagot's (again a surprise), explained that the American government was "entirely convinced of the good faith, the friendliness, and the impartiality" of London. The administration had a "decided preference" for England over any other potential mediator. Public opinion, however, would not tolerate outside interference, particularly British interference, and the government must decline Bagot's proposal. Adams added that, if mediation went forward, England would probably draw to herself some of the hostility presently reserved for Spain, "and a check [would] thus be given to the amicable feelings which were daily arising toward Great Britain." [9] He welcomed escape from this misfortune, he said.

Castlereagh showed no disquiet when Bagot's report reached his desk. In all England only the *Times* publicly regretted the decision at Washington, and even the *Times* admitted "the quarrel belongs not to us." [10] Thanks to careful management on both sides of the Atlantic and to an unusual lack of touchiness on the part of Adams, who reserved his spleen for Onís, the one tentative British effort to ease Spain's path failed to roil Anglo-American relations. Onís, who in January had told Bagot that only British assistance could save his country from humiliation, was angry with the English. He never expected the Americans to accept mediation

and confidential) to Bagot, Nov. 10, 1817, FO 5/120; Castlereagh to Bagot, private and confidential, Nov. 10, 1817, *ibid.* Quotations are from #24.

[9] Jan. 27, 28, 31, Feb. 3, 1818, Adams, *op. cit.*, IV, 48–52; Bagot #14 to Castlereagh, Feb. 8, 1818, FO 5/130. See also memorandum on British offer to mediate, Feb. 2, 1818, Worthington C. Ford, ed., *The Writings of John Quincy Adams* (7 vols.; New York, 1913–1917), VI, 294–298.

[10] Rush to Gallatin, April 22, 1818, Albert Gallatin Papers, New-York Historical Society; *Times* (London), April 22, 1818.

but hoped the offer, if firmly pressed, would lead to friction between the English-speaking powers from which Spain might benefit.[11]

A few days after the American rejection became known in London, an event at a backwoods fort in Florida 3,500 miles away threatened to bring about the clash Onís desired. In March, 1818, at the head of an Indian-fighting army of 1,700 men, General Andrew Jackson crossed the border between the United States and Florida. He seized Spanish posts at St. Marks and later at Pensacola, quite accurately alleging that local authorities had failed to prevent raids upon the United States by tribes living in Spanish territory. At St. Marks the General captured Alexander Arbuthnot, the Scottish trader, and in the interior Robert Ambrister, the veteran of Waterloo, fell into American hands. On April 29, 1818, the two Britons, convicted by a court-martial of aiding Indian enemies of the United States, were executed by order of Jackson.

President Monroe's administration faced a difficult choice. The General had entered Florida without official orders (although there is some evidence that the President knew what Jackson had in mind) and executed two British citizens without waiting for Washington to confirm their sentences. Should the government repudiate him? Jackson had apparently defied both military and international law, jeopardized a settlement with Spain, and threatened to embroil England and America. On the other hand the American people detested Spain, the Indians, and British intriguers with almost equal passion; the brusque action might (as it actually did) bring procrastinating Spaniards to their senses, and certainly had the effect of chastising tribes that took American lives.

Luis de Onís, supported by the French minister, Hyde de Neuville, strenuously protested to Adams. Without even waiting word from Orange County, where the President was vacationing, the Secretary replied that "we could not suffer our women and children on the frontiers to be butchered by savages, out of complaisance to the jurisdiction which the King of Spain's officers

[11] Bagot #7 to Castlereagh, Jan. 6, 1818, FO 5/130; April 14, 1818, Adams, *op. cit.*, IV, 79–80; Bagot #14 to Castlereagh, Feb. 8, 1818, FO 5/130.

avowed themselves unable to maintain against those same savages." [12]

After Monroe's return his cabinet met five times in a week. Adams fought for Jackson and at first even wanted to hold the Spanish posts. Secretary of War Calhoun, affronted at the insult to his authority, called for disavowal. The President as usual took a middle ground, and in the end the cabinet decided to restore Pensacola and St. Marks, at the same time defending Jackson's admittedly unauthorized actions on the ground Adams indicated. An official note so informed Onís on July 23, 1818. Four months later a perfect blunderbuss of a note, nominally instructions to the minister at Madrid but actually an appeal to British and American opinion, repeated the justifications at great length and with characteristic Adams vigor. The *Times* denounced this note as "unworthy sophistry" in defense of a murderer and pirate.[13]

During these exciting days Charles Bagot exercised remarkable and, for a British minister, almost unprecedented tact. He never protested what he personally considered "unjust and sanguinary proceedings" and "a crying outrage." He assured Adams that neither Arbuthnot nor Ambrister had government sanction for their activities, he discountenanced Onís' scheme for a joint protest by the diplomatic corps, and he even refrained from asking for Arbuthnot's belongings so as not to give a handle to Anglophobes. As far as possible he avoided discussion, except to press for a full record of the court-martial. Castlereagh praised his circumspection.[14]

Months later the Foreign Secretary claimed credit for avoiding war over the executions. "Such was the temper of Parliament, and

---

[12] July 8, 1818, Adams, *op. cit.*, IV, 105; Adams to Monroe, July 8, 1818, Ford, *op. cit.*, VI, 384.
[13] July 15, 16, 17, 18, 20, 1818, Adams, *op. cit.*, IV, 107–115; Adams to Onís, July 23, 1818, Ford, *op. cit.*, VI, 386–394; Adams to George W. Erving, Nov. 28, 1818, Instructions, Vol. VIII; *Times*, Jan. 28, 1819.
[14] Bagot #52, #56, #57 to Castlereagh, June 29, July 24 (2), 1818, FO 5/132; Bagot #87 to Castlereagh, Dec. 3, 1818, FO 5/133; Bagot to Planta, private, July 29, 1818, FO 5/132; Adams to Monroe, Aug. 20, 1818, James Monroe Papers, Library of Congress; Bagot #74 to Castlereagh, Sept. 19, 1818, FO 5/133; Planta to Bagot, private, Jan. 13, 1819, Bagot MSS.

such the feeling of the country," he told Rush, "that . . . WAR MIGHT HAVE BEEN PRODUCED BY HOLDING UP A FINGER; and . . . an address to the Crown might have been carried for one, BY NEARLY AN UNANIMOUS VOTE." Rush, who watched the British reaction with his usual combination of suspicion and hostility, apparently did not demur.[15] Yet examination of the British press suggests Castlereagh claimed too much. That Britain was angry is beyond question; that her citizens really wanted a confrontation with the United States is much less certain.

Time and distance helped reduce the threat to peace, for news of the two executions and of subsequent events reached London in driblets rather than all at once. First reports arrived in copies of *"The Milledgeville Journal,* an American Paper of an inferior class," at the end of June. Until better information came to hand a month later most papers suspended judgment. Then London seethed, and a fellow diplomat told Rush "we have had nothing of late so exciting—it smacks of war." During the summer the British press took up the issue, its vigor somewhat inhibited by initial feelings that Washington would punish Jackson, by appeals on the part of America's friends to await her official explanation, and by general satisfaction when the President offered to return the Spanish posts.[16] After an autumn hiatus Adams' argumentative exculpation of Jackson—and, no doubt, the approaching session of Parliament—brought forth a violent outburst. By this time, in January, 1819, Arbuthnot and Ambrister were eight months dead. Editors and politicians who blistered the Americans often added that war was unthinkable.

Moreover, some British journals excused the United States although none justified Jackson. American designs upon Florida, the

[15] Richard Rush, *A Residence at the Court of London, Second Series* (2 vols.; London, 1845), I, 140.
[16] *Morning Chronicle* (London), July 1, 1818; Richard Rush, *A Residence at the Court of London* (3d ed.; London, 1872), pp. 292–293; *Courier* (London), Aug. 10, 1818; *Chronicle*, Aug. 15, Sept. 5, 1818; *Times*, Sept. 14, 1818; *Courier*, Sept. 4, 1818.

Liverpool Mercury commented, were perfectly understandable, for such a "colonial province on the frontiers of a great republic is at once a political and moral nuisance." The *Morning Chronicle* considered bloodthirstiness a necessary ingredient of Indian warfare. The *Times* admitted that if Spain could not maintain order among the tribes she must surrender the territory. Several papers argued that, however reprehensible Jackson's conduct, "we should not embroil ourselves in any degree with a matter so foreign to our interests," and the London *Sun* warned against action that would disturb Anglo-American harmony.[17]

Despite Rush's blanket indictment of the London press the *Star* carried the burden almost alone during the summer campaign against the United States. That paper accused the Americans of provoking Indian war to manufacture an excuse for invading Florida, compared the campaign with the unprovoked attack on Canada in 1812, and denounced Jackson's "war of pillage and extermination." The *Times,* which at the very beginning explained that "Restless, foolish or mischievous adventurers" lost the protection of their government, later adopted a hostile if somewhat inconsistent tone.[18] Other papers, almost universally critical of Jackson, used milder language toward the United States.

Early in 1819 British newspapers published the record of "the Trial (*read* MURDER) of our countrymen" and "Mr. ADAMS's cold-blooded extenuation of this military murder" in the instructions to Madrid. Now the *Star* found plenty of companions. "Military butchery," "brutal ferocity of the sanguinary Jackson," "a sentence which would have reflected disgrace on Morocco"—such were some of the epithets. The *Times* raised the specter of Englishmen killed all over the world if Jackson remained unpunished, and even the *Chronicle,* relatively mild in the summer, now demanded a formal American apology. Only the *Times* hinted at

[17] *Liverpool Mercury*, Aug. 7, 1818; *Chronicle*, Aug. 7, 1818; *Times*, Sept. 5, 1818; *Caledonian Mercury* (Edinburgh), Aug. 1, Sept. 7, 1818; *Sun* (London), Jan. 12, 1819.

[18] Rush to Monroe, private, Aug. 13, 1818, Monroe MSS; *Star* (London), Aug. 1, 3, Sept. 1, 1818; *Times*, June 30, Aug. 10, 13, 15, 1818.

war, and the *Caledonian Mercury,* which vigorously castigated Jackson, added: "The notion of a war on account of this transaction is, we think, totally out of the question." [19]

Against this background the cabinet's achievement seems less striking than Castlereagh claimed. British opinion against Jackson ran high—Rush even reported placards in the streets—but more than a figurative finger would have been required to convert this feeling into war spirit. The cabinet deserves praise, not for preventing war, but for minimizing the irritating episode. Quicker than his countrymen, Castlereagh saw that Arbuthnot and Ambrister had forfeited British protection, and he refused to seek cheap political profit by racketing against Jackson for no real purpose.

An item in the *Courier* on July 1, 1818, commenting on the execution of the two Englishmen, bore the mark of cabinet inspiration: "If they were really guilty . . . , their fate was such as the law of nations warrants. But as to the idea of their being emissaries of the British Government, it is too ridiculous a supposition to be seriously refuted." This comment foreshadowed Castlereagh's reaction. Time and again the minister asked if Rush had information showing the men "really guilty," but he always spoke casually and without resentment. "It strikes me," a colleague commented, "that it will turn out that Arbuthnot and his companion deserv'd their fate." Clearly this was Castlereagh's view. The Foreign Secretary, like Bagot, worked hard to allay suspicions that the two Englishmen were government agents. Rush several times praised the cabinet's attitude, Castlereagh did not force things to a climax before leaving for Aix-la-Chapelle, and the ghosts of Arbuthnot and Ambrister cast no shadow over negotiation of the convention of 1818. [20]

[19] *Star,* Jan. 7, 1819; *Morning Post* (London), Jan. 29, 1819; *Star,* Jan. 28, 1819; *Courier,* Jan. 11, 1819; *Chronicle,* Jan. 9, 1819; *Times,* Jan. 13, 1819; *Chronicle,* March 25, 1819; *Caledonian Mercury,* Jan. 17, 1819.
[20] *Courier,* July 1, 1818; Pole to Bagot, Sept. 3, 1818, Bagot MSS; Castlereagh #16, #17 to Bagot, Aug. 18, 31, 1818, FO 5/129; Rush to Gallatin, Aug. 7, 1818, Gallatin MSS; Rush to Monroe, private, Aug. 13, 1818, Monroe MSS.

Early in 1819, having returned from his Continental trip and a Christmas vacation in Ireland, Castlereagh called Rush to his house, where gout confined him. From his bed he read instructions prepared for Bagot a few days earlier. These spoke of Jackson's apparently "harsh and unwarrantable" actions but, far more important, announced that the British government would make no formal protest. Ministers had decided that the activities of "the unfortunate Sufferers . . . deprived them of any claim on their own Gov^t. for interference on their behalf." Rush, who felt it necessary to justify American suspicions of the British government by recapitulating the whole sorry history of Anglo-Indian intrigue, nevertheless repeatedly assured Castlereagh that in the present instance Washington believed suspicion unjustified. Naturally Rush welcomed Castlereagh's decision and shared the Secretary's regret at the second wave of tumult then disturbing England.[21]

The government delayed parliamentary discussion until May, by which time Adams and Onís had signed a treaty ceding Florida to the United States. An Opposition peer, the Marquis of Lansdowne, criticized Jackson and asked why the ministry had not prevented the Florida cession, "the aggrandizement of another power, in such a way as to completely subvert our influence in the West Indies." Bathurst and Liverpool ignored the latter point. As for Jackson they replied that, Ambrister and Arbuthnot having forfeited British protection, "the fate of these unfortunate men formed a question to be settled between the government of the United States and its commander, and not between the two nations." Lansdowne's attack came to naught.[22] Britain had lost interest.

The long episode is instructive. Jackson's invasion of Florida and his execution of two Englishmen reflected impatient, self-con-

---

[21] Castlereagh #1 to Bagot, Jan. 2, 1819, FO 5/141; Rush #52 to Adams, Jan. 12, 1819, Despatches, Great Britain, Vol. XXIII; Rush to Castlereagh, Jan. 24, 1819, and encl., FO 5/146; Rush, *Residence*, pp. 339–351. Castlereagh directed Bagot to avoid the entire subject unless Adams raised it. Castlereagh to Bagot, private, Jan. 2, 1819, FO 5/141.
[22] *Hansard*, XL, 287–302.

fident American nationalism. Monroe's decision against punishment placed his government in the same camp, and after fiery, politically inspired debate Congress followed along by refusing to condemn the General. In Britain the government's reaction confirmed its devotion to conciliation based on economic need and growing recognition of American power. While the violence of popular feeling showed that dislike of the Americans had by no means died, the often unnoticed limits of and challenges to prevailing sentiment revealed a growing if reluctant acceptance of the truths that influenced ministers.

Jackson's incursion jarred Madrid and Onís into action. If Spain did not act promptly there might be no Florida province to trade for a firm boundary between Mexico and the United States. Pressed by Hyde de Neuville, the French minister, who feared America would formally recognize and perhaps assist Latin-American revolutionaries if Spain did not make a settlement,[23] Onís revived the negotiations. On Washington's birthday, 1819, he and Adams signed a treaty transferring Florida to the United States, quieting American monetary claims against Spain, and—Adams' particular pride—drawing a western boundary to the Pacific Ocean. Onís might have conceded more, and in later years Adams' opponents castigated him for surrendering Texas. At the time the treaty seemed an American triumph.

Late in March news of the treaty reached England. The *Star* permitted itself a spasm of hatred:

What with unpunished murders and territorial acquisition, the Americans are drunk with exultation. The acquisition of Florida is a matter of great triumph, and its fruits rich in anticipation, as giving her great facilities in annoying our West Indian possessions in the event of any future war; bringing her into contiguity with the mines of Peru; and extending her western boundary to the Pacific Ocean. . . . Add to all this the rights of fishery on the Coasts of Newfoundland, secured to them by their late treaty with this country, and it will be allowed that they are as much to be praised in point of

[23] Calhoun to Monroe, Sept. 6, 1818, Monroe MSS; Hyde to Onís, Jan. 24, 1819, and Duc de Richelieu to Hyde, Sept. 1, 1818, Guillaume-Jean Hyde de Neuville, *Mémoires et Souvenirs*, II (Paris, 1890), 390, 394–395; Adams to Rush, May 2, 1819, Ford, *op. cit.*, VI, 547–548.

diplomacy, as to be execrated in point of morality. Of civilized nations, the Americans are unquestionably the most depraved in principles, and the duties of social relation, of any upon the face of the earth.

The *Times* grumbled, and the *Sun* predicted that American ambition would now turn against English territory. Richard Rush masochistically devoured these items. He ignored the *Morning Post*'s resigned comment, more representative of prudent British opinion, that "This arrangement has long been upon the tapis; the event, under existing circumstances, was unavoidable, and of course can excite no surprise." [24]

"Let me deal candidly," Castlereagh said to Rush at a party at the French embassy, "it can little be supposed, were it an abstract question, that we would not prefer Spain's owning the Floridas, to their falling into your hands. Spain is weak. You are strong." Yet Britain recognized that continued Spanish control was impossible, welcomed a peaceful settlement between Spain and the United States, and hoped no hitch over ratification would jeopardize the treaty. The Foreign Secretary warned that "a spirit of encroachment" might cause Britain to "take exception" to American actions, "but . . . he did not consider the present case as open to such views." [25] In one sense the cabinet's moderation is even more remarkable precisely because Britain ideally preferred to see Spain in Florida, and feared that the Florida triumph would lead to further American projects.

For exactly two years Madrid's duplicity and resentment blocked ratification of the treaty. During the first months Castlereagh pursued a double-barreled policy. Through his ambassador at Madrid he urged Spain to stop her foolishness before the Americans, losing patience, took Florida by force. He also did his best to allay American suspicions, more annoying because exactly contrary to fact, that British intrigues delayed ratification. His assurances convinced Rush and then President Monroe, who praised England's attitude in messages to Congress in December, 1819,

[24] *Star*, March 27, 1819; *Times*, March 26, 1819; *Sun*, March 26, 1819; Rush, *Residence, Second Series,* I, 46; *Post*, March 26, 1819.
[25] Rush #87 to Adams, Aug. 26, 1819, Despatches, Great Britain, Vol. XXIV.

and March, 1820. The Foreign Secretary's efforts bore no immediate Spanish fruit, but by 1820 even Hezekiah Niles, whose *Register* almost never gave England the benefit of any doubt, withdrew charges of British machinations.[26]

In 1819 and early 1820 many Americans, having hailed a treaty that cost Spain one colony, feared that Britain would reply by taking Cuba, a far more valuable one. Indeed the *Times* urged such a course, partly to forestall further American conquests. The *Chronicle* printed articles by Freeman Rattenbury, later published as a pamphlet, which pressed the same argument. The *Courier* scarcely calmed the Americans by observing that "it would be strange if the Washington Cabinet should interpose . . . to prevent our acquisition of Cuba, when we taught it a lesson of so much moderation while the surrender of the Floridas was completed." [27]

Since most Americans expected Cuba, as Secretary Adams later phrased it, to fall into their laps like a ripe apple, the possibility that Britain might pluck the fruit troubled them. Niles even talked of fighting, if necessary, to drive off the apple picker. Although Rush discounted the rumors he felt it wise to quiz Castlereagh, who assured him "with the [same] carelessness that I had thrown into the question" that Britain had no such plans.[28] Cuba passed temporarily from the scene.

Cuba and Florida, though infirmly held by Spain, were among the few dominions that did not revolt. Aided by Augustín de Iturbide, the home country temporarily reduced Mexico to obedience. Elsewhere the war flamed or smoldered; the insurgents won with a San Martín, a Bolívar, an O'Higgins, or a Sucre, and lost with

[26] Rush #91 to Adams, Sept. 17, 1819, *ibid.*; Planta to Antrobus, private, Oct. 9, 1819, FO 5/143; James D. Richardson, ed., *A Compilation of the Messages and Papers of the Presidents* (10 vols.; Washington, 1907), II, 58, 59; Antrobus to Planta, private, Jan. 2, 1820, FO 5/148; *Niles' Weekly Register* (Baltimore), Jan. 8, 1820.

[27] *Times*, June 19, 25, 26, Oct. 6, 1819; *Chronicle*, June 28, 1819; *Courier*, June 24, 1819.

[28] Adams to Hugh Nelson, April 28, 1823, Ford, *op. cit.*, VII, 373; *Niles' Register*, Jan. 8, 22, 1820; Rush #86, #87 to Adams, Aug. 24, 26, 1819, Despatches, Great Britain, Vol. XXIV.

other commanders. Only Ferdinand VII and a few equally pur-
blind ministers unwaveringly believed that in the end the old empire could be reconstructed. America, England, and the Continental powers made their plans on the assumption that history could
not be turned back to 1808, the year the bonds began to loosen.
The interplay of British and American policy again demonstrated
the new character of their relations.

From the beginning of the revolt the Americans knew where
they stood—in favor of independence—and concerned themselves
merely with timing and tactics. The British government faced a
more complex problem involving domestic politics, initial sympathy with Ferdinand VII, American policy, a reluctance to break
with Europe, and above all commercial considerations. Down to
about 1820, Sir Charles Webster, the closest student of this problem, informs us, Britain sought to mediate the quarrel between
Ferdinand and his subjects; thenceforth she drifted toward recognition.[29]

When, after 1814, Ferdinand sought to regain control of his
fractious colonies, the British government at first sided with him.
The world's greatest imperial power naturally distrusted antico-
lonialism; as Samuel Eliot Morison has commented, speaking of
Chile and Ireland, "Recognition of O'Higgins might encourage
O'Connor!" Yet Britain, having enjoyed South American trade
since 1808, did not wish to see the old imperial monopoly restored.
She opted for a looser system which would preserve Spanish sovereignty, grant limited political powers to the Latin Americans,
and keep trade open to foreigners. Such a scheme satisfied neither
Ferdinand nor the rebels, and Britain never considered using force
to impose it.

Ultimately she lost patience with Spain. Although conservatives
and the King held back, key ministers began to consider permanent
separation inevitable. In 1822 Undersecretary Planta caught
Castlereagh's later policy in a sentence, writing, "If I were to de-

[29] Webster, *op. cit.*, I, 12. The following paragraphs rest heavily upon the introduc-
tion to Webster's volumes and William W. Kaufmann, *British Policy and the Independence of Latin America, 1804–1828* (New Haven, 1951).

scribe our Line, I should say it would be one of as little *overt act* as possible; but our securing to Our Subjects all the Commercial Advantages enjoyed by any other Nation with the South American Prov[ince]s." [30]

In 1818 and 1819, largely in response to queries from Rush, the Foreign Secretary explained his policy to the Americans. Britain hoped to effect a reconciliation between Spain and her colonies by moral suasion; she would not consent to the use of force. Above all she wanted open trade with the southern continent, and she sought no special privileges for herself. (Although Castlereagh did not say so, Britain was confident that in a commercial contest she could defeat America.) The Foreign Secretary sought, as he had before, to discourage recognition by the United States, partly by declining to tell Rush how England would react if Monroe recognized a former colony. Actually he had already rejected a Spanish request to warn the United States against receiving rebel ambassadors, and with Rush he used language that led the American minister to guess that recognition would not bring down upon Washington the wrath of London. [31]

Castlereagh's promise not to seek a commercial monopoly never quite convinced the Americans. Each nation was anxious to secure a predominant share of a market which, like Asia at the end of the

[30] Samuel E. Morison and Henry S. Commager, *The Growth of the American Republic* (5th ed.; 2 vols.; New York, 1962), I, 455; Planta to Stratford Canning, May 11, 1822, Papers of Stratford Canning, Viscount Stratford de Redcliffe, Public Record Office, FO 352/8.

[31] Rush to Gallatin, April 22, 1818, Gallatin MSS; Rush #30, #32, #40, #46, #57 to Adams, July 25, Aug. 3, Oct. 12, Nov. 20, 1818, Feb. 15, 1819, Despatches, Great Britain, Vol. XXIII; Castlereagh to Bagot, private and confidential, Aug. 8, 1818, FO 5/129; Oct. 19, 1818, Adams, *op. cit.*, IV, 136–139; Castlereagh #7 to Sir Henry Wellesley, March 27, 1818, Webster, *op. cit.*, II, 366–367; Kaufmann, *op. cit.*, pp. 106–107, 113, 118. John Quincy Adams described British policy at this time with cynicism and considerable accuracy: "The Revolution in South-America had opened a new World to her Commerce, which the restoration of the Spanish Colonial Dominion, would again close against her. Her Cabinet therefore devised a middle term, a compromise between Legitimacy and Traffic; a project by which the political Supremacy of Spain shall be restored, but under which the Spanish Colonies should enjoy Commercial Freedom, and intercourse with the rest of the World. She admits all the pretensions of Legitimacy until they come in contact with her own Interest; and then she becomes the patroness of liberal principles and colonial emancipation." Adams to George W. Campbell, June 28, 1818, Instructions, Vol. VIII.

century, seemed capable of bestowing prosperity upon those who controlled it. The hope of commercial advantage reinforced recognition demands in the United States; similarly, a desire for trade and particularly a wish to forestall special privileges for the United States led many Englishmen to agitate for the change in policy which actually began in 1820. Adams considered such rivalry unrealistic. "Do what we can," he said in cabinet, "the commerce of South America will be much more important and useful to Great Britain than to us, . . . for the simple reason that she has the power of supplying their wants by her manufactures." [32] Others failed to reach the same conclusion, and commercial jealousy helped keep England and the United States apart.

Britain's differences with European powers worked in the opposite direction. As early as 1817 Castlereagh warned France that although England hoped to help arrange an accommodation between Spain and Latin America, "H.R.H. cannot consent that his Mediation shall under any circumstances assume an armed character." This did not satisfy the Continental allies for, whatever the turnings and inconsistencies of their plans, they were almost always ready to use at least a threat of force to bring Latin America to heel. In the summer of 1818 and at Aix-la-Chapelle that fall the Russians and the French pressed Castlereagh to reconsider. He refused, and the proposed interference was perforce dropped. For the moment the European powers even professed to believe that Spain must change her unrealistic attitude before anything could be done to reconstruct her empire.[33]

The United States grudgingly began to admit that perhaps England was not cut from the same pattern as the legitimist powers. In August, 1818, Adams concluded that "the real policy of Great Britain is to promote the cause of the independents." That fall, at Castlereagh's orders, Bagot showed Adams the British warning of 1817 against the use of force, and the Secretary of State soon learned from Rush that Castlereagh even talked of inviting the

[32] June 20, 1822, Adams, op. cit., VI, 24–25.
[33] Foreign office memorandum, Aug. 20, 1817 [communicated to France], Webster, op. cit., II, 352–358; Charles K. Webster, The Foreign Policy of Castlereagh, 1815–1822 (London, 1925), pp. 413–421.

United States to take part in the proposed mediation. These signs pleased Adams.[34] Somewhat more slowly his less well informed countrymen moderated their suspicions, although a residue remained at least until England finally recognized three Latin states in 1824, more than two years after Castlereagh's suicide.

The Americans would have betrayed their ancestors had they not welcomed an anticolonial revolt.[35] The young nation, always prone to consider itself the fountainhead of republican virtue, often doubted that Latinos would meet the rigorous standards of the north. "The resemblance between their revolution and ours is barely superficial," John Quincy Adams instructed his son; ". . . there is not an instance, in which the Patriot Commanders have shewn the slightest respect for individual rights or personal liberty." Even Jefferson, the apostle of liberty, commented: "Ignorance and bigotry, like other insanities, are incapable of self-government." [36] Such doubts did not prevent Americans from siding with rebels against European tyranny. Nor did they prevent congressional orators, particularly Henry Clay and his followers, from hailing Latin progress and denouncing the administration's refusal to recognize South American states.

Adams detested colonialism as much as any man; he once told Stratford Canning, "The whole system of modern colonization was an abuse of government, and it was time that it should come to an end." For various reasons he and Monroe resisted the popular clamor for recognition. In Adams' view a former colony should not be recognized until "the chance of the opposite party to recover their dominion [is] entirely desperate." [37] Moreover, the administration feared that recognition of one or more of the former col-

---

[34] Adams to Thomas Sumter, Jr., Aug. 27, 1818, Ford, *op. cit.*, VI, 452; Oct. 19, 1818, Adams, *op. cit.*, IV, 136–138; Webster, *Castlereagh, 1815–1822*, p. 417.

[35] For a broad treatment of the question see Arthur P. Whitaker, *The United States and the Independence of Latin America, 1800–1830* (Baltimore, 1941).

[36] Adams to Thomas B. Adams, April 14, 1818, Adams Family Papers, Massachusetts Historical Society, Vol. CXLV; Jefferson to LaFayette, May 14, 1817, Andrew A. Lipscomb and Albert E. Bergh, eds., *The Writings of Thomas Jefferson* (Memorial ed.; 20 vols.; Washington, 1903–1904), XV, 116.

[37] Nov. 25, 1822, Adams, *op. cit.*, VI, 104; Adams to Monroe, Aug. 24, 1818, Monroe MSS.

onies would lead Spain to refuse the cession of Florida. Finally the government believed recognition or open aid might well unite Europe, including perhaps Great Britain, in support of the Spanish cause. Thus the administration held back, and neutrality acts of 1817 and 1818 limited the activities of friends of Latin-American independence.

For some months in 1818 and 1819 Monroe and his advisers considered recognizing Buenos Aires and perhaps other stable governments. Throughout they sought England's coöperation, partly to widen the breach between Britain and her erstwhile allies. At the same time the Americans did not have complete faith in England; Rush received orders to find out if Britain would take violent exception, perhaps go to war, if the United States unilaterally recognized any Latin-American state.[38] Adams never liked the joint-recognition scheme, particularly after Aix-la-Chapelle showed the depth of the split between Castlereagh and European ministers. He told the cabinet "we should not have the appearance of pinning ourselves too closely upon her sleeve; . . . we should carefully preserve the advantage of taking the lead in advancing the recognition of the South American Governments, and, while using persuasion with England to move in concert with us, take care to let her know that we shall ultimately act independently for ourselves." [39]

More cautious counsel prevailed. The American government, read instructions sent to Rush in May, 1818, wished "to proceed in relation to South-American affairs, in good understanding and harmony with Great-Britain. . . . The time is probably not remote, when the acknowledgement of the South-American Independence, will be an act of friendship toward Spain herself." This approach came to nothing, Castlereagh preferring to await the outcome at Aix-la-Chapelle before settling future policy. Adams prevented renewal of the overture later in the year. When the subject came up again early in 1819 the President toned down the

---

[38] Adams #9 to Rush, Aug. 15, 1818, Instructions, Vol. VIII. Similar inquiries went to the American ministers in France and Russia.

[39] Jan. 2, 1819, Adams, *op. cit.*, IV, 207.

strong language by which Adams proposed to tell England that the United States was on the verge of recognizing Buenos Aires. On the other hand the instructions, as sent, virtually demanded British acceptance of American principles. In February Castlereagh declined to proceed on this basis.[40]

For three years recognition projects were held in abeyance while the United States sought Spanish approval of the Florida treaty. At last, in March, 1822, President Monroe sent a special message to Congress asking for funds to establish missions in five Latin-American states. The legislators responded enthusiastically, and in June the President formally received the first South American envoy.[41] The United States had cast caution to the winds, acting "independently for ourselves" as Adams advised once Florida had changed hands and Spanish prospects in Latin America had begun to dim.

Most of London, Richard Rush reported, welcomed American recognition as proof that Latin America had triumphed. Although the *Sun* grumbled that the United States had ignored diplomatic proprieties, other papers accepted or welcomed the action and merely urged the ministry to protect English commercial interests in the former provinces.[42] In reply the government opened British ports to the flags of Latin-American states, a sort of demirecognition limited to the commercial sphere. Then the Foreign Secretary, known as the Marquis of Londonderry since his father's death in 1821, sidled in the direction of full recognition, preferably in coöperation with other European powers.

By an act of tragedy this problem, like Cuba, became part of the series faced by Londonderry's successor, George Canning. In the summer of 1822 the Foreign Secretary broke down. On August 10 both Wellington and the King concluded, after talking with Londonderry, that he needed a doctor's care. Despite precautions he managed to cut his throat with a small knife from a washstand

---

[40] Adams #4, #15 to Rush, May 20, 1818, Jan. 1, 1819, Instructions, Vol. VIII; Rush #57 to Adams, Feb. 15, 1819, Despatches, Great Britain, Vol. XXIII; Whitaker, *op. cit.*, pp. 260–266.

[41] Bemis, *op. cit.*, p. 359.

[42] Rush #242 to Adams, April 22, 1822, Despatches, Great Britain, Vol. XXVII; *Sun*, April 10, 1822; *Courier*, April 9, 1822; *Chronicle*, April 10, 1822.

only two days later. "It required great anatomical Skill to do what he did so effectually with the Instrument," a colleague commented with rather gruesome admiration.[43]

The same colleague, reporting that Canning might succeed his great rival, added: "My own opinion is that we want that link which we had in Lord Londonderry, & that matters will end ill." Particularly after the King and Lord Liverpool clashed, as they did in 1820, the Foreign Secretary had become an essential figure in domestic as well as diplomatic matters. The other ministers and George IV mourned his passing, though not all the country shared their feelings. A small group cheered the passage of his coffin into Westminster Abbey, unjustifiably blaming Londonderry, government spokesman in the House of Commons, for the ministry's repressive acts. The *Times,* taking a different tack, gloomily observed that "the manifest mediocrity of his genius" was typical of the times and of the Liverpool government.[44]

Some Americans found it impossible to grieve over the death of any English statesman, even the architect of reconciliation. "Cruel man that he was, may his sins be forgiven," Niles editorialized. On the other hand, if Stratford Canning reported correctly, most Americans seemed willing to forget their prejudices and recognize that England had lost, not only an able statesman, but also an advocate of Anglo-American understanding. Certainly John Quincy Adams and Richard Rush, the two Americans who knew Londonderry best through their service at the Court of St. James, regretted his passing and doubted that any successor would be so devoted to good relations.[45]

Adams and Rush rightly mourned the suicide; the dissenters

---

[43] Bathurst to Harrowby, private, Aug. 23, 1822, Papers of Dudley Ryder, First Earl of Harrowby, Sandon Hall, Staffordshire; Webster, *Castlereagh, 1815–1822,* pp. 482–489.

[44] Bathurst to Harrowby, private, Aug. 23, 1822, Harrowby MSS; George IV to Liverpool, private, Sept. 15, 1822, Papers of the First and Second Earls of Liverpool, British Museum (Add. MSS 38190–38489, 38564–38581), Add. MSS 38190; *Times,* Aug. 13, 1822.

[45] *Niles' Register,* Sept. 28, 1822; Stratford Canning to Planta, Oct. 1, 1822, Stanley Lane-Poole, *The Life of the Right Honourable Stratford Canning, Viscount Stratford de Redcliffe,* I (London, 1888), 334; Adams to Louisa Adams, Sept. 29, 1822, Ford, *op. cit.,* VII, 309–310; Rush #261 to Adams, Aug. 13, 1822, Despatches, Great Britain, Vol. XXVII.

simply vomited traditional Anglophobia. During his decade at the Foreign Office Viscount Castlereagh, to give him his more familiar title, turned the American policy of Great Britain in a new, unprecedented direction. Insofar as he played a role in the Ghent negotiations he spoke for moderation. After the war he labored without cease to smooth relations almost always tempestuous since the first volley echoed across Lexington green.

An instinctive conservative, certainly an antirepublican, Castlereagh adopted his policy as a matter of realism rather than sympathy. Sooner than most Europeans he grasped the importance of growing American power, the wisdom of treating the young republic without contempt. He anticipated and then symbolized a development enthusiastically reported by Richard Rush in 1819: "from a sentiment of total indifference towards us, or nearly so, . . . there has been a vibration quite to the other extreme. We have assumed, for the first time, a settled importance in their eyes. Our nation has been swelled out, morally and politically." [46] Complete independence lay only a short distance over the horizon.

[46] Rush #70 to Adams, May 24, 1819, Despatches, Great Britain, Vol. XXIII.

CHAPTER

XVI

CANNING SEEKS AN ALLY

For five weeks after Castlereagh's suicide, the cabinet resisted selection of a successor. The conservative mediocrities who made up a majority of Liverpool's colleagues disliked the inevitable choice, George Canning. The King hated Canning for opposing a royal divorce, and many M.P.'s distrusted his flippancy, egotism, and alleged lack of principle. Canning's talents, experience, and recently regained standing with the public (largely the result of his support of Queen Caroline) ultimately won out. The Duke of Wellington, no more friendly than other ministers, brought around the cabinet and then the King by arguments of sheer necessity. "This is the greatest sacrifice of my opinions and feeling that I have ever made in my life," George IV protested, but the very next day, August 9, 1822, an offer went forward. Abandoning his appointment to "gilded and imperial exile" as governor-general of Bengal, Canning took the place of his great rival.[1]

---

[1] Charles D. Yonge, *The Life and Administration of Robert Banks, Second Earl of Liverpool* (3 vols.; London, 1868), III, 199; Harold Temperley, *The Foreign Policy of Canning, 1822–1827* (London, 1925), p. 28. The following paragraphs rest heavily upon Temperley, esp. pp. 27–49.

His colleagues and his sovereign always caused Canning as much difficulty as foreigners. Only the premier wholeheartedly supported him. Within a few months the Duke of Wellington grumbled, "Canning can[not] be depended upon; . . . he often decides in haste & then writes in haste & . . . what he does write has better sounding phrases than good solid sense." [2] The Foreign Secretary never escaped his reputation for somewhat shifty brilliance, and often had to fight hard for the new departures he proposed.

Canning's flashing declamations, savage sarcasms, natural gregariousness, and boldness made him seem to differ startlingly from Castlereagh. The glaring contrasts—between character and genius, contemporaries liked to say—concealed important similarities. On domestic policy the two men differed little despite Canning's occasional attacks upon the aristocratic principle. Canning liked to consider himself "English," his predecessor "European," but actually the break with Europe began well before Castlereagh's suicide. The differences between the two men were differences of tone and temperament. Canning welcomed conflict and challenge; Castlereagh sought always to avoid them. Castlereagh spoke for a not dead but dying age of private or at most parliamentary statecraft. Canning spoke for a day yet aborning when the mobilization of public opinion through speeches and state papers became a major part of diplomacy.

Policy toward America changed not a whit when Canning took over the seals of office. Perhaps because he knew the Americans distrusted him, Canning exercised special tact. Once, in 1825, he endorsed a long state paper, "Twiddle twaddle but ack[nowled]ge with thanks," then thanked the American minister for presenting "a very interesting & able Paper." Canning gained remarkable success with Rush, who gave him affection he withheld from Castlereagh. Years later Rush paused while bundling together letters from Canning to write on the wrapper: "These off-hand

[2] Charles Arbuthnot to Liverpool, private and confidential, Dec. 23, 1822, Papers of the First and Second Earls of Liverpool, British Museum (Add. MSS 38190–38489, 38564–38581), Add. MSS 38291.

notes, . . . flowing from the good personal intercourse existing between us, show the point and playfulness of his mind." [3]

With those insulated from Canning's charm by 3,000 miles of salt water he succeeded less well. When, in a parliamentary speech, the Foreign Secretary praised Washington's neutrality in Latin America, *Niles' Register* sourly commented that it was "probably the first time that this famous 'joker of jokes' ever said any thing honorable to us," and discounted the passage as a justification of British neutrality, which in part it was.[4] Americans never forgot the sarcasm and the extravagant language Canning used during his tenure at the Foreign Office from 1807 to 1809.

At a diplomatic dinner Canning drank Monroe's health and, Rush reported to the President, spoke warmly of the time, fifteen years earlier, when he was foreign secretary and Monroe the American minister. Monroe, who doubtless remembered the *Chesapeake* period differently but was not a good hater, considered Canning an improvement on Castlereagh but did not trust him. "Canning has more talents, & a better heart than his predecessor," he wrote, "but yet, I fear that he . . . cannot . . . therefore be thoroughly relied on, for a persevering effort . . . in support of the right cause." [5] Like Wellington, Eldon, and British Neanderthals, but from quite a different angle of vision, Monroe and Adams distrusted Canning's stability.

Events crowded Canning hard during his first year at the For-

[3] Endorsement on King to Canning, confidential, Nov. 18, 1825, Foreign Office Archives, Public Record Office, FO 5/207; Canning to King, private, Nov. 21, 1825, *ibid.*; wrapper, n.d., Rush Family Papers, Princeton University Library.

[4] *Niles' Weekly Register* (Baltimore), June 7, 1823.

[5] Rush to Monroe, April 24, 1823, James Monroe Papers, Library of Congress; Monroe to Jefferson, April 14, 1823, Stanislaus M. Hamilton, ed., *The Writings of James Monroe* (7 vols.; New York, 1898–1903), VI, 307. When Adams succeeded Monroe, Canning ordered the British chargé at Washington to read the following passage to the new President: "It is no compliment to him to say, how much my personal wishes have been on his side, against all his Competitors: because it is but natural to feel that the Intercourse, which has passed between us constitutes a bond of good will, which would have been wanting, with any Stranger; and because one naturally values more any thing that, after being accustomed to it, one has been on the point of losing." Canning to Addington, private, March 16, 1825, George Canning Papers, Harewood House, Leeds. Addington reported that this letter gratified Adams and evoked similar sentiments from him. Addington to Canning, private, May 1, 1825, *ibid.*

eign Office. A French army invaded Spain to protect Ferdinand from the Cortes. Many observers feared that, once Spain was reduced to obedience, the Continental powers planned to subject Latin America to similar control. The Czar's claim to extensive territories and offshore waters on the Pacific Coast of North America challenged both Britain and America, and a flare-up of suspicions over Cuba threatened Anglo-American relations. All these issues contributed in one way or another to the climacteric that came with Canning's dramatic proposals to Rush in the summer of 1823.

Cuba reëntered the picture in the autumn of 1822. Underground leaders offered to rise against Spain if the United States would take the island into the union. Washington held back, fearful of English countermeasures and of reopening the slavery question only recently, tenuously closed by the Missouri Compromise. The annexation of Cuba might "shake our system," Monroe wrote.[6] Despite cabinet disapproval, loose talk about acquiring the island circulated through the United States.

Soon the rumors reached London, seriously troubling Canning, who asked his cousin Stratford to ferret out the facts. In November the Foreign Secretary wrote Wellington, then on a European mission: "I hope I may not have to tell you, before your return, that the Yankees have occupied Cuba; a blow which I do not know how we can prevent, but which as a government I hardly know how we should survive." [7] This uncharacteristic pessimism reflected Canning's awareness of the growth of American power since the feeble days of Jefferson and Madison. He had never spoken this way between 1807 and 1809.

Fortunately for the Secretary's peace of mind, his cousin turned up no evidence of aggressive American intentions. The envoy believed America dared not risk war with England by annexing Cuba. On the other hand, partly because Secretary Adams evaded efforts

[6] Monroe to Madison, Sept. 26, 1822, William C. Rives Collection, Library of Congress.

[7] Canning #7 (secret), #9 to Stratford Canning, Oct. 11, Dec. 7, 1822, FO 5/165; Canning to Wellington, Nov. —, 1822, Dexter Perkins, *The Monroe Doctrine, 1823–1826* (Cambridge, Mass., 1927), p. 62.

to pin him down, the British minister slightly qualified his analysis. Investigations, he said, "have brought me, not indeed to a conviction, but to a very strong impression that the American Government have no intention at present of attempting to extend their dominion over the Island of Cuba." [8] This report cheered George Canning without absolutely quieting his fears.

The Americans, too, had their apprehensions. Late in 1822 the British government ordered a squadron to Cuban waters to protect commerce from corsairs based on the island. There is not a shadow of evidence that rumored American plans influenced the cabinet. Canning carefully explained the squadron's limited objective, and after six weeks the Royal Navy recalled Commodore Edward Owen when Spain promised to curb the raiders and pay spoliation claims. Nevertheless for some time Americans suspected a British plot to take over the island, with or without Spanish concurrence.

Rumors picked up in London and Paris increased the administration's concern. The stories also "had the effect of reviving . . . feelings of jealousy in the public mind," Stratford Canning reported in March. Calhoun even talked of fighting if Britain made a move. The Secretary of State, in this instance amazingly like his opposite number in London, replied that such a war would inevitably fail. President Monroe, taking up a suggestion by Gallatin, proposed a mutual Anglo-American denial of Cuban ambitions. Adams, who expected America to acquire Cuba in the long run, was unwilling to tie his country's hands. For the moment the Americans contented themselves with an extremely harsh warning to Madrid, dispatched late in April, not to cede Cuba to England.[9]

At a dinner at his home Lord Liverpool earnestly assured Rush

[8] Stratford Canning #18 to Canning, secret, Feb. 7, 1823, FO 5/175.
[9] Rush #287 to Adams, Jan. 7, 1823, Department of State Archives, National Archives, Despatches, Great Britain, Vol. XXVIII; Gallatin #242 to Adams, Jan. 6, 1823, Department of State Archives, National Archives, Despatches, France, Vol. XXI; Stratford Canning #34 to Canning, March 19, 1823, FO 5/176; March 15, 17, 1823, Charles F. Adams, ed., *Memoirs of John Quincy Adams* (12 vols.; Philadelphia, 1874–1877), VI, 138; Adams to Hugh Nelson, April 28, 1823, Department of State Archives, National Archives, Diplomatic Instructions, All Countries, Vol. IX. William W. Kaufmann, *British Policy and the Independence of Latin America, 1804–1828* (New Haven, 1951), p. 144, interprets the British expedition as a step toward recognition.

that Britain did not covet Cuba. The premier added, perhaps as a veiled warning, that he felt it best for all if Cuba remained under Spanish control.[10] Liverpool's statement, which satisfied the American minister, did not entirely reassure Washington. Unjustified suspicions continued on both sides of the Atlantic, although by the summer of 1823 the feeling of immediate danger had passed.

Rivalry, this time over Oregon, also affected the two powers' reaction to a Russian thrust southward along the Pacific Coast of North America. In September, 1821, annoyed by American incursions into Alaskan waters, Czar Alexander issued a ukase claiming exclusive control down to 51°, a great extension of Russian claims. The ukase closed the coast to foreigners and, most pretentious of all, excluded them from waters within a hundred Italian miles of the shore. In London the *Quarterly Review* denounced the "wholesale usurpation of 2000 miles of sea-coast."[11] Americans and Englishmen had become accustomed to think that they alone would settle the title to Oregon.

In 1818 John Quincy Adams had written that the Oregon area "can never form a subject of serious difficulty, or jarring interest between that Emperor and the United States." He did not believe Russia could deploy real power in the Northwest. Consequently he protested only temperately when he learned of the ukase early in 1822. He did make clear that the United States challenged Russia's territorial claim and her effort to change maritime law by extending her jurisdiction scores of miles out to sea. In August the American minister at St. Petersburg reported that the Russian government, after American and British protests, had suspended execution of the ukase and invited negotiations.[12]

Might not the English-speaking powers act together in the

[10] Rush #298 to Adams, March 10, 1823, Despatches, Great Britain, Vol. XXVIII.
[11] *Quarterly Review* (London), XXVI (1822), 344. On the ukase and the reaction to it, see Perkins, *op. cit.*, pp. 4–8, and Samuel F. Bemis, *John Quincy Adams and the Foundations of American Foreign Policy* (New York, 1949), pp. 493–495, 514–519.
[12] Adams to Campbell, June 28, 1818, Instructions, Vol. VIII; Adams to Pierre de Poletica, Feb. 25, April 24, 1822, Worthington C. Ford, ed., *The Writings of John Quincy Adams* (7 vols.; New York, 1913–1917), VII, 212–213, 245–246; Adams #12 to Henry Middleton, May 13, 1822, Instructions, Vol. IX; Bemis, *op. cit.*, pp. 497–498 and 498n.

forthcoming discussion? The idea occurred almost simultaneously to Canning and Adams. In instructions to Rush in July, 1823, Adams suggested a tripartite convention opening unsettled coasts to fishermen and traders, an idea clearly acceptable to Britain. Adams also proposed that Russia make no new, permanent settlements south of 55°, Britain none except between 51° and 55°, and the United States none above 51°. Clearly the Foreign Secretary would balk. He was equally unlikely to endorse the ringing declaration, a forecast of part of Monroe's message four months later, with which Adams closed the instructions. The Secretary declared that, the Pacific question settled, "the American continents, henceforth, will be no longer subjects of colonization," and avowed that the "application of colonial principles of exclusion . . . cannot be admitted by the United States as lawful upon any part of the North West Coast of America." [13]

Adams must have known that Canning would challenge these principles. Indeed, Rush's recent reports showed the Foreign Secretary alert to the danger of strengthening American claims to northern Oregon.[14] Presumably the Secretary of State thought Russia might help him pen England between 51° and 55°; probably he refused even tacitly to accept colonialism and commercial monopoly. It is tempting to guess, too, that, as it became clear that Russia could not enforce her edict, joint action seemed less necessary. In any event Adams asked Britain to pay a substantial price for American coöperation. Otherwise he preferred to act alone.

Only a few weeks later Canning offered coöperation on a different problem, arising from events in Spain and prospects in Latin America. A rebellion in 1820 forced Ferdinand VII to approve a liberal constitution giving the Cortes extensive power. At the Congress of Verona late in 1822, over strong British protests and despite differences among themselves, the Continental monarchies denounced this constitution as a threat to the rights of kings.

---

[13] Rush #309 to Adams, May 24, 1823, Despatches, Great Britain, Vol. XXVIII; Stratford Canning #47, #54 to Canning, May 3, June 6, 1823, FO 5/176; Adams #70 to Rush, July 22, 1823, Instructions, Vol. X.
[14] Rush #309 to Adams, May 24, 1823 (endorsed received July 14, 1823), Despatches, Great Britain, Vol. XXVIII.

France, quickly appointing herself executive agent of the legitimists, prepared to invade Spain on Ferdinand's behalf. Canning, in trying to dissuade Paris, suffered a sharp diplomatic defeat. In April an army under the Duke d'Angoulême, Louis XVIII's nephew, crossed the frontier. Angoulême entered Madrid in May, then continued on to free Ferdinand and capture the constitutionalist bastion at Cadiz.[15]

Lacking weapons to stop France, Canning and Liverpool announced a policy of neutrality. The King and some conservative ministers sympathized with France on royalist grounds; Liverpool, Canning, and the country cheered the Spaniards. Ferdinand, Canning wrote Bagot, "is as bad a King and the Cortés as bad a Government as one can conceive. But between invaded and invader the choice is clear." Before Parliament the Foreign Secretary declared: "Indifference we can never feel towards the affairs of Spain, and I earnestly hope and trust that she may come triumphantly out of the struggle." His policy of benevolent neutrality won an overwhelming mandate from the Commons.[16]

Thus Britain moved into open opposition to royalist policemen with whom she had acted in uneasy concert since 1814. "Events," the Foreign Secretary commented to his sovereign, ". . . have gradually but unavoidably, relaxed . . . the bonds, by which the Great Despotick Powers of the Continent assumed Your Majesty to be inseparably tied to all their principles & projects."[17] The new foreign secretary faced the challenge foreshadowed during Castlereagh's last years.

The United States instinctively sided with the constitutionalists. Americans hated the European concert described by Niles as a " 'holy alliance' against liberty and justice" and "a conspiracy of villains against HEAVEN's own ordinances, granting free will and imposing consequent responsibility on the human race." The attempt to dictate Spain's form of government so angered Jeffer-

---

[15] Temperley, *op. cit.*, pp. 10–24, 53–99.
[16] Canning to Bagot, private, July 14, 1823, Josceline Bagot, ed., *George Canning and His Friends* (2 vols.; London, 1909), II, 181–182; Temperley, *op. cit.*, p. 87.
[17] Canning to George IV, July 11, 1823, Royal Archives, Windsor Castle.

son that he half recommended to Monroe a bold, public declaration in favor of the Cortes. A senator soon sent to Argentina as the first American minister had much the same idea. "Would it not be sound policy," Caesar Rodney asked, "to throw the moral weight of this country, into the scale of freedom?" [18]

Most Americans welcomed Canning's declarations in favor of Spain, although Jefferson, for one, remained suspicious of his sincerity. Rodney considered English sympathy for the cause of liberty more than adequate apology for many past sins. British policy, Stratford Canning informed his cousin early in May, "has had the effect of making the English almost popular in the United States. . . . On the whole I question whether for a long time there has been so favorable an opportunity—as far as general disposition & goodwill are concerned,—to bring the two Countries nearer together." [19]

In this private letter the envoy noted that "even Adams has caught a something of the soft infection." As early as March the Englishman noted a change. Discussing English efforts to dissuade France from intervention, Adams maintained that the Spanish issue "affected the great principle of National Independence" and probably marked the beginning of a conflict between autocracy and representative government. The Secretary of State welcomed Canning's efforts to stop the conflict before it started. [20] His friendly attitude became even more pronounced after Angoulême invaded Spain.

In June, 1823, having served nearly three years of penance in an uncongenial environment, Stratford Canning prepared to return home. Before leaving he had several long conferences with the Secretary of State. In these discussions the talk ranged wide, Adams in particular leading the conversation to world politics.

[18] *Niles' Register*, Oct. 19, Nov. 30, 1822; Jefferson to Monroe, June 11, 1823, Monroe MSS; Caesar A. Rodney to Monroe, April 6, 1823, *ibid.*

[19] Jefferson to Monroe, June 11, 1823, Monroe MSS; Rodney to Monroe, April 6, 1823, *ibid.*; Stratford Canning to Canning, private, May 6, 1823, Papers of Stratford Canning, Viscount Stratford de Redcliffe, Public Record Office, FO 352/8.

[20] Stratford Canning to Canning, private, May 6, 1823, Stratford Canning MSS, FO 352/8; Stratford Canning #35 to Canning, March 27, 1823, FO 5/176.

Much that the Secretary said confirmed Stratford Canning's view that Adams had caught the "soft infection."

The American pronounced the European alliance "virtually dissolved" and anticipated speedy British recognition of Latin-American independence. Adams recorded himself as saying, "Great Britain had separated herself from the counsels and measures of the alliance. She avowed the principles which were emphatically those of this country, and she disapproved the principles of the alliance, which this country abhorred." Adams thought this "coincidence of principle" a hopeful augury for negotiations then planned; Stratford Canning hoped the new spirit would do more than affect talks on the West Indies or the slave trade and inspire joint action against the ukase. He saw the glimmering prospect of a firmer connection,[21] and infected his cousin with the same hope.

When George Canning received Stratford's reports he had turned his sights from Spain to Latin America. Rumors spread over Europe that when France completed the occupation of Spain she, perhaps supported by other Continental powers, would forcibly discipline Ferdinand's overseas subjects. Actually European statesmen worked at cross-purposes, and even within the French government there was no agreement on policy. The premier, Count de Villèle, supported the most feasible but still highly unlikely scheme, a plan to establish cadets of the Spanish royal house upon Latin-American thrones with a minimum use of force and a maximum of persuasion. Even this Bourbon monarchy scheme, as it was called, depended upon Ferdinand's concurrence. As he stubbornly refused all compromise, neither the monarchy scheme nor shadowy Russian plans, likewise contingent upon Spanish moderation, had a ghost of a chance.[22]

Nevertheless the rumors frightened Canning and many others in England and America. For reasons of domestic politics as well as diplomacy the Foreign Secretary could not permit another defeat so close on the heels of France's scornful disregard of his ef-

[21] Stratford Canning #56 to Canning, June 6, 1823, FO 5/176; June 20, 1823, Adams, *op. cit.*, VI, 151–153.

[22] Perkins, *op. cit.*, pp. 104–143.

forts to prevent intervention in Spain. When French troops crossed the Iberian frontier, Canning delivered a state paper through his ambassador, Sir Charles Stuart, warning Paris not to press England too far. Permanent military occupation of Spain or interference in Portugal, he stated, would lead to a "collision" between France and Britain.

The heart of the paper, for Anglo-American relations, lay in the third warning:

With respect to the Provinces in America, which have thrown off their allegiance to the Crown of Spain, time and the course of events appear to have substantially decided their separation from the Mother Country; although the formal recognition of those Provinces, as Independent States, by His Majesty, may be hastened or retarded by various . . . circumstances. . . . Disclaiming in the most solemn manner any intention of appropriating to Himself the smallest portion of the late Spanish possessions in America, His Majesty is satisfied that no attempt will be made by France, to bring under her dominion any of those possessions, either by conquest, or by cession, from Spain.[23]

This paper, published only five days after delivery in Paris, created a great stir in England, Europe, and America. It speeded the "soft infection" and seemed to reduce the presumed threat to Latin America.

Immediate publication of Canning's letter to Stuart and his strong speech to Parliament, both so much in contrast with Castlereagh's methods, caused the world to overlook an important omission. True, the Foreign Secretary declared South American independence almost inevitable and warned against attempts to create French colonies. He did not threaten to prevent outside assistance to Spain, either to regain outright control or to establish Bourbon principalities, nor did he hint that Spain had no right to try to regain control of Latin America.

Quite probably, confronted by a real threat along any of these lines he would have acted against it. In the summer of 1823 he knew a majority of the cabinet still hoped to see Spain preserve

[23] Canning #29 to Sir Charles Stuart, March 31, 1823, Temperley, *op. cit.*, pp. 84–85.

315

some form of suzerainty. He himself was not ready to recognize any former colonies, partly because he dared not invite charges that he gave a *coup de grâce* to Spanish hopes in South America when she had troubles enough at home. Canning still wanted Spain—king or constitutionalists—to admit colonial independence, thus easing English and European recognition and assuring the uninterrupted flow of commerce.

These thoughts apparently dominated Canning's mind when, early in August, Richard Rush sought an appointment to discuss instructions just received from Adams. On August 16 the two men met. At the close of their conversation, devoted mostly to more prosaic subjects, Rush commented approvingly on the note to Stuart. "On my having referred to this note," the American reported, Canning "asked me what I thought my government would say to going hand in hand with this, in the same sentiment." [24] Thus began oral and written discussions Canning later described as a "flirtation." Shortly after the first interview the Englishman left on a visit to the Midlands, half political trip and half vacation. Notes then flowed in both directions. After a month Canning returned, and a pair of interviews followed before the Foreign Secretary dropped his efforts to cajole Rush into agreement.

In Canning's first note he stated a proposition never significantly changed:

Is not the moment come when our Governments might understand each other as to the Spanish American Colonies? And if we can arrive at such an understanding, would it not be expedient for ourselves, and beneficial for all the world, that the principles of it should be clearly settled and plainly avowed?

For ourselves we have no disguise.

1. We conceive the recovery of the Colonies by Spain to be hopeless.

[24] Rush #323 to Adams, Aug. 19, 1823, Despatches, Great Britain, Vol. XXIX. The entire "flirtation" may be followed in this dispatch and in Rush #324, #326, #330, #331, #334, #336 to Adams, Aug. 23, 28, Sept. 8, 19, Oct. 2, 10, 1823, *ibid.* Copies of the notes exchanged by Rush and Canning are enclosed in these dispatches. Most of them may also be found in the Rush Family Papers and in the George Canning MSS. The exchanges, followed chronologically, are conveniently summarized in Bemis, *op. cit.*, pp. 376–380. The footnotes below cite only specific references.

2. We conceive the question of the Recognition of them, as Independent States, to be one of time and circumstances.

3. We are, however, by no means disposed to throw any impediment in the way of an arrangement between them, and the mother country by amicable negotiation.

4. We aim not at the possession of any portion of them ourselves.

5. We could not see any portion of them transfered to any other Power, with indifference.

He invited Rush to join in a declaration that "would be at once the most effectual and the least offensive mode" of discouraging scheming by France or other European powers.[25]

Rush accepted the Foreign Secretary's first and last points, largely evaded the fourth, and virtually ignored the third. He concentrated on the second, at the outset suggesting that British recognition of one or more of the former colonies would encourage him to take the responsibility of acting without instructions and then peremptorily demanding recognition as the price of his acquiescence. At first enthusiastic or at least receptive, Rush came to feel that England "has no more sympathy with popular rights and freedom now, than it had on the plains of Lexington." [26]

The American's caution is understandable, for Canning asked him to assume an immense responsibility. A good isolationist, Rush disliked mixing the United States in the politics of Europe's "federative system," inviting trouble with France or linking his country with a traditional enemy.[27] Viewing Canning's letter to Stuart as a guarantee against French colonies, he could see no reason to accept involvement to get the pledge reaffirmed. If Canning agreed to go further Rush was prepared to act, for British recognition would advance the cause of Latin America to which his own country had pledged itself. Failing recognition he refused to move. Canning's third point perhaps hinted disapproval of earlier American recognition, and certainly left England free to support a set-

---

[25] Canning to Rush, private and confidential, Aug. 20, 1823, encl. in Rush #323 to Adams, Aug. 23, 1823, Despatches, Great Britain, Vol. XXIX.

[26] Rush #336 to Adams, Oct. 10, 1823, *ibid.*

[27] Rush #323, #326 to Adams, Aug. 23, 28, 1823, *ibid.*

tlement restoring limited ties between the mother country and the rebels.[28] In Rush's view America had no need of foreign assistance on these terms.

Canning's far more complicated motives invite speculation and defy certainty. Pointing to the Foreign Secretary's abrupt turn to a unilateral and in some ways anti-American policy after his conversations with Rush, an American historian writes: "His conduct in this affair was marked by a levity and shortsightedness that seriously mar his record as a statesman." On the other hand, emphasizing that the Royal Navy required no assistance to block France, an Englishman concluded that Canning "seems to have thought that he was conferring a favor rather than soliciting aid." [29] Both verdicts are oversimplified.

The Foreign Secretary clearly sought an American entente for its own sake and for the effect upon Europe. Stratford Canning's reports of the "soft infection" reached London shortly before the talks began, and the retiring envoy arrived in time to sit in on the closing interviews. George Canning hoped to improve the rapprochement by permitting America to join in a denunciation of colonialist principles both he and Rush knew could be frustrated, if attempted, only by British power. Canning also hoped "the simple fact of our being known to hold the same sentiment would, . . . by its moral effect, put down the intention on the part of France, admitting that she should ever entertain it." The unity of two great maritime powers on a question primarily of sea power and overseas deployment must, he felt, give pause to adventurers.[30]

[28] Rush to Monroe, private, Sept. 15, 1823, Monroe MSS; Rush #326 to Adams, Aug. 28, 1823, Despatches, Great Britain, Vol. XXIX.

[29] Arthur P. Whitaker, *The United States and the Independence of Latin America, 1800–1830* (Baltimore, 1941), p. 448; Charles K. Webster, ed., *Britain and the Independence of Latin America* (2 vols.; London, 1938), I, 47. For a particularly interesting assessment of Canning's motives see Kaufmann, *op. cit.*, pp. 150–155.

[30] Rush #323 to Adams, Aug. 19, 1823, Despatches, Great Britain, Vol. XXIX. Canning did not rule out the possibility that force might become necessary. Commenting on Rush's reaction to his first proposal, he wrote, "You will not fail to observe that Rush, . . . in declaring against the dishonesty and perniciousness of any appropriation of the provinces in revolt against Spain by France, . . . avoids intimating . . . that his Government would concur in measures to prevent it." Canning to Liverpool, private, Aug. 26, 1823, George Canning MSS.

While corresponding with Rush the Foreign Secretary visited Liverpool. At the same time Christopher Hughes arrived there en route to a diplomatic appointment in Scandinavia. To Hughes's enormous gratification the great Englishman lavished him with attention. Canning sought the American's company for an "acquatic excursion" on a new steamboat, spent a long time visiting the American ship in which Hughes had crossed the Atlantic, invited Hughes to sit in his box at the theater (the American's entry touched off a round of cheers), and delayed his departure four hours to discuss Latin-American affairs and the ukase. The most dramatic moment came at a banquet on August 25. "The Mayor gave every other Toast," Hughes later recalled, "but when it came to *my health* the Mayor, Mr. Molyneux, delegated the office to Mr. Canning, who rose & made a beautiful speech."

Canning's theme may be caught in one sentence: "The force of blood again prevails, and the daughter and the mother stand together against the world." Canning delivered this eulogium, he said later, "in response . . . to Adams's harangue" of the previous year. He hoped to show that the rivalry between America and the Old World, emphasized in Adams' Fourth of July oration, did not extend to relations between Britain and the United States. (Canning counted it a great success when Adams later "used the phrase 'the mother & the daughter' as quite familiar to their vocabulary.") The attention bestowed upon Hughes was part of the flirtation with America, not the inconsequential matter Rush rather jealously considered it.[31]

At this time almost four months had passed since the letter to Stuart. Perhaps because he had designed it primarily as a manifesto, Canning did not demand French acceptance of his principles. Paris offered voluntary promises against the permanent occupation of Spain and interference in Portugal. She did not comment on the

[31] Hughes to Mrs. ——— Moore, Dec. 17, 1823, Christopher Hughes Papers, William L. Clements Library, Ann Arbor; Sir Roger Thierry, ed., *The Speeches of the Right Honourable George Canning* (3d ed.; 6 vols.; London, 1836), VI, 414; Canning #1 to Bagot, private and confidential, Jan. 22, 1824, Sir Charles Bagot Papers, Levens Hall, Westmorland; Rush to Monroe, private, Oct. 22, 1823, Monroe MSS.

third point. Did this mask a secret purpose to invade Latin America? Canning so feared, although he did not accept at face value all the rumors circulating through Europe, and he impressed Rush with the sincerity of his fears.[32] A joint declaration with the United States seemed the best way to reinforce the earlier warning.

Canning feared a European congress on the Spanish colonies nearly as much as he feared a French invasion of Latin America. Reports from Europe suggested a plan to convene one as soon as France completed her Spanish campaign. Canning knew he would be under heavy pressure from English conservatives to send a representative. He and Liverpool, in close touch throughout the discussions with Rush, knew England would find herself in a minority of one at such a congress.

Canning also knew—and Rush explicitly so stated—that the United States denied the right of a European congress to meddle in what it considered entirely an American affair. If Rush agreed to a public statement, England could oppose a European conference, arguing that decisions on Latin America required the concurrence of the United States, one of the powers most deeply involved. If the Continental monarchy unexpectedly agreed to invite republican America and somehow inveigled her into attending, Britain could count on an ally. "Something may perhaps be made out of this," Canning commented on Rush's statement against a congress, ". . . on the occasion . . . of a proposition from the Continental Powers, to take Spanish America into consideration." Should Latin America "be proposed as the Subject of *Joint Deliberation*," Liverpool replied, "I think I see my Way to a Course to which no one could object." [33] The premier apparently meant that he planned to use a joint Anglo-American declaration to silence demands within the cabinet for participation in a conference on Latin America.

Canning attached considerable importance to his proposed fourth point: "We aim not at the possession of any portion of them [the

---

[32] Rush #324 to Adams, Aug. 23, 1823, Despatches, Great Britain, Vol. XXIX.

[33] Rush to Canning, Aug. 27, 1823, George Canning MSS; Canning to Liverpool, secret, Aug. 30, 1823, Liverpool MSS, Add. MSS 38193; Liverpool to Canning, private and confidential, Aug. 30, 1823, George Canning MSS.

former colonies] ourselves." He pointed out to Liverpool that "Rush, in accepting my disavowal of any design upon Cuba, evades any reciprocal dis-avowal, on the part of his government in return." [34] The Foreign Secretary hoped to settle the nagging Cuban problem by joint declaration, improving Anglo-American relations and at the same time making the broader agreement more attractive to his cabinet colleagues.

Central to any understanding of Canning's offer and his refusal to modify it is the vulnerability of the Foreign Secretary and the premier, who plotted behind the backs of colleagues and king. Canning, willing to flirt, dared not marry without their approval. He and Liverpool felt they must produce a dowry to justify the match, particularly American acceptance of the English line on Latin America and a promise not to take Cuba. If Rush had accepted Canning's proposal, the Foreign Secretary wrote him, "I would immediately have taken measures for assembling my Colleagues, in London, upon my return, in order to be enabled to submit to you, as the *act* of my Government, all that I have stated to you as my own *sentiments* &," Canning added with more hope than certainty, "theirs." [35] Failing agreement, Liverpool and Canning wished to conceal the illicit romance.

Rush's well-meant assurances that he would inform the President of all that transpired threw the British plotters into consternation. They feared a leak at Washington—with good reason, for the Rush-Canning exchanges became almost common knowledge in the American capital—and, after news returned to London, sharp questioning by colleagues and the King. Canning briefly considered convening the cabinet to approve his offer retrospectively. Liverpool, wiser in the ways of his colleagues, advised against it.

Late in November a bundle of dispatches arrived with accounts of John Quincy Adams' discussion of the overture with the British

[34] Canning to Rush, private and confidential, Aug. 20, 1823, encl. in Rush #323 to Adams, Aug. 23, 1823, Despatches, Great Britain, Vol. XXIX; Canning to Liverpool, private, Aug. 26, 1823, George Canning MSS. Canning was perhaps too suspicious, for Rush virtually accepted the Foreign Secretary's third point. Rush to Canning, Aug. 23, 1823, *ibid.*

[35] Canning to Rush, Aug. 31, 1823, Rush Family Papers.

chargé, nephew of a leading British reactionary. This revelation proves, Canning clucked, "how impossible it is to have any confidential communication with that Government." "N° 18 is certainly awkward in some respects, if it must be communicated to the King," Liverpool agreed. They asked the chargé to withdraw his dispatch and recast it as a private letter which Canning need not show to king or colleagues.[36]

Canning still held much of the view revealed by the silences in his letter to Sir Charles Stuart. Rush reported him, perhaps too baldly, as believing "the day had arrived when all America might be considered as lost to Europe, so far as the tie of political dependence was concerned." This definitely did not mean he had abandoned all hope of a negotiated settlement between Spain and her quondam colonies. Six months later Canning summarized the exchanges with Rush in a private letter to Charles Bagot, a crony then serving at St. Petersburg:

> I inquired of Mr Rush, in August, whether he had, or was likely to have, any Instructions . . . ? He said that he had none; but, that, *if we would place ourselves on the same line with the U. States,* by *acknowledging* the S.A. States, he would say, swear, sign, any thing, *sub spe rati,* & with perfect certainty of not being disavowed, to prevent any interference on the part of the Continental Powers *or Spain.* We were not prepared to acknowledge immediately; and of course we would not stipulate against *Spain.* Our flirtation therefor went off; but it left a tenderness behind it.

In an official dispatch Canning wrote that if the President intended to outlaw Spanish efforts at reconquest "there is . . . as important a difference between his view of the subject and ours as perhaps it is possible to conceive." [37] He scarcely exaggerated.

[36] Samuel Smith to Hughes, Dec. 4, 1824, encl. in Hughes to Canning, Jan. 20, 1824, George Canning MSS; Canning to Liverpool, private, Aug. 26, 1823, *ibid.;* Liverpool to Canning, private and confidential, Aug. 29, 1823, Liverpool MSS, Add. MSS 38568; Canning to Liverpool, private, Dec. 2, 1823, George Canning MSS; Liverpool to Canning, private, Dec. 2, 1823, *ibid.;* Lord Francis Conyngham to Addington, Dec. 8, 1823, FO 5/177; Addington to Canning, private and confidential, March 15, 1824, George Canning MSS. Desiring to keep matters in his own hands, and perhaps also because he did not trust the chargé who took over from Stratford Canning, the Foreign Secretary sent no instructions, on Latin America or any other subject, to America between July and November.
[37] Canning #1 to Bagot, private and confidential, Jan. 22, 1824, Bagot MSS; Canning to Bagot, Jan. 9, 1824, Bagot, *op. cit.,* II, 208.

Canning, then, sought to bring America to accept British policy. He offered an alliance he expected the United States to welcome because it would force European capitals to consider Washington's views and strengthen the protection of Latin America against non-Spanish incursions. In return the Foreign Secretary expected American concessions. He was, after all, an English statesman, not an altruist, certainly not a sentimental republican.

Rush never really assimilated this simple truth. When the exchanges ended he accused Canning of sinister motives. "It is France that must not be aggrandized, not South America that must be made free," he stated, adding, "The former doctrine may fitly enough return upon Britain as part of her permanent political creed; but not having been taught to regard it as also incorporated with the foreign policy of the United States, I have forborne to give it gratuitous succour." [38] Why the discovery that Britain acted in her own interests so shocked Rush is hard to see.

Liverpool and Canning never denied that above all they sought to assure a continued market in Latin America. They considered recognition in advance of Spain only one of several possible ways to this end, and therefore refused Rush's request, although Canning finally asked if a promise of future British recognition would change Rush's mind. (Rush said "No.") The premier, outlining for Canning a reply to Rush, wrote: "Would there be any harm . . . in telling Rush fairly that you w^d. have submitted to the Cabinet the expediency of concluding Engagements . . . upon the Principle—if he had been prepared to agree to them, but as he is not, that we cannot commit ourselves as to what it might be practical or convenient for us to do under . . . unforeseen Circumstances[?]" This position, communicated to Rush in a note of August 31, practically settled the fate of a joint declaration. In two interviews after Canning's return from the north neither man agreed to budge, and Rush referred the British offer to Washington for instructions.[39]

[38] Rush #336 to Adams, Oct. 10, 1823, Despatches, Great Britain, Vol. XXIX.
[39] Liverpool to Canning, private and confidential, Aug. 29, 1823, Liverpool MSS, Add. MSS 38568; Canning to Rush, private and confidential, Aug. 31, 1823, encl. in Rush #330 to Adams, Sept. 8, 1823, Despatches, Great Britain, Vol. XXIX; Rush #331, #334 to Adams, Sept. 19, Oct. 2, 1823, *ibid.*

Events moved rapidly in the summer of 1823. Masses of information, some true and some false, flowed into the Foreign Office. The constitutionalists' collapse, Ferdinand's continued obduracy, and reports of French ambitions all alarmed Canning, and Rush had made it clear that he would not lend himself to a scheme to frustrate a European congress.

Rather than waste further time on the American, Canning opened conversations with the French ambassador. By this time the possibility of French entry into Latin America had excited even conservative members of the cabinet. "The D. quite agrees that We cannot permit France to get a footing in Spanish America, on pretense of aiding Spain," Canning wrote.[40] When even Wellington endorsed a policy to frustrate France the Foreign Secretary could proceed with assurance. He advanced a step, putting his country on record as opposing intervention to aid Spain as well as the establishment of new, non-Spanish colonies.

After consulting Liverpool and then the cabinet Canning called the French ambassador to the Foreign Office. They met several times early in October, and Canning reduced their talks to a memorandum he required Polignac to submit to Paris for approval. As early as October 9 Canning reported to his superior, "Polignac has received his Courier. His assurances as to L.A. are satisfactory." For three weeks the Ambassador squirmed, trying in particular to adjust the memorandum so France would not appear to have given in to British menace. At the beginning of November he finally approved it. Still another three weeks later the Foreign Secretary reported the talks to Rush, and after a further delay he sent a copy of the memorandum to Rush for transmission to Washington.[41]

In the Polignac memorandum Canning insisted that no nation, other than Spain, should have special commercial privileges in Latin America. France agreed. The Foreign Secretary warned that European interference in the quarrel between Spain and her colonies would force England to recognize the rebels, and Polignac

[40] Canning to Liverpool, private, Sept. 27, 1823, George Canning MSS.
[41] Canning to Liverpool, private, Oct. 9, 1823, *ibid.*; Temperley, *op. cit.*, p. 114; Rush #346, #354 to Adams, Nov. 26, Dec. 23, 1823, Despatches, Great Britain, Vol. XXIX.

replied that France entertained no such plans. (At about the same time Villèle told Sir Charles Stuart he had abandoned "visionary schemes" for Bourbon monarchies, Spain proving too stubborn.) Finally, Canning said Britain disapproved of a congress on Latin-American affairs and virtually declared England would not take part unless the United States received an invitation. Polignac reserved France's position on these points but, for himself personally, accepted Canning's argument that American interests in the ex-colonies made it logical to invite her to a congress.[42] This suggestion later roused the anger of European monarchs and Polignac's superiors.

In the closing months of 1823 the threat of French interference in Latin America—for herself, for Bourbon princelings, for Spain —faded away. For this the Polignac memorandum was largely but not totally responsible, and France found it a good excuse when the European powers pressed her to send troops to South America in March, 1824. Transmitting the memorandum to Rush, Canning wrote: "You will see that we were not unmindful of your claim to be heard: but I flatter myself that neither you nor we shall now have to lift our voices against any of the designs which were apprehended a few months ago."[43] Canning did not then know that ten days before the President of the United States had indeed lifted his voice, speaking out forcefully but alone along much the same lines as the Polignac memorandum. Canning's flirtation encouraged the Americans to value themselves as highly as the Foreign Secretary said he did.

[42] Webster, *op. cit.*, II, 115–120; Stuart #562 to Canning, Nov. 3, 1823, *ibid.*, p. 122.
[43] Temperley, *op. cit.*, p. 119; Canning to Rush, private and confidential, Dec. 13, 1823, George Canning MSS.

XVII

THE MONROE DOCTRINE

Rush reported his exchanges with Canning in two sets of dispatches. The first, describing their correspondence but not the discouraging interviews following the Foreign Secretary's return to London, reached Washington on October 9, 1823, the very day Polignac approved in principle the memorandum Canning thrust upon him. Adams was still rattling across Pennsylvania on his return from Massachusetts, where he had visited his lonely father, a widower since 1818. President Monroe, who only awaited Adams' return before taking a short vacation of his own, interrupted preparations to scan the dispatches.

James Monroe and those he consulted agreed that Canning's offer posed "the most momentous [question] which has ever been offered . . . since that of Independence." [1] In the early years of

---

[1] Jefferson to Monroe, Oct. 24, 1823, Andrew A. Lipscomb and Albert E. Bergh, eds., *The Writings of Thomas Jefferson* (Memorial ed.; 20 vols.; Washington, 1903–1904), XV, 477.

This entire chapter owes a great deal to the information and particularly the insights provided by Dexter Perkins, *The Monroe Doctrine, 1823–1826* (Cambridge, Mass., 1927); Arthur P. Whitaker, *The United States and the Independence of Latin*

the republic European powers usually called the tune. The War of 1812 showed America's impatience with passive defense, while the Treaty of Ghent and Castlereagh's postwar policy revealed a growing, somewhat grudging British recognition of her power. Now Canning offered a limited alliance, an understanding nominally between equals, really an entente on British principles. Should the United States accept? The isolationist spirit, the almost universal conviction that America and Europe occupied distinct spheres, urged refusal. Yet during the Revolution, the undeclared war with France, and the Louisiana crisis, the Americans sought foreign assistance. Had Castlereagh's policy unintentionally taught them to value their own worth? Had they now the confidence to strike out on their own?

The President first turned to his old mentors, Jefferson and Madison. Forwarding the correspondence to them, Monroe stated his opinion that Britain at last found herself forced to choose between autocracy and constitutionalism, that if the Europeans succeeded in Latin America they would attack the United States, and that "we had better meet the proposition fully, & decisively," thus encouraging her to serve "in a cause which tho' important to her, as to balance of power, commerce &c, is vital to us, as to government." The President did not explicitly recommend acceptance of Canning's five points.[2]

Thomas Jefferson and James Madison advised Monroe to accept Canning's offer even though it meant, as Jefferson pointed out, postponing Cuban ambitions. "Great Britain is the nation which can do us the most harm of any one, or all on earth," Jefferson wrote; "and with her on our side we need not fear the whole world." The separation of Europe and America would be assured. More specifically the two Virginians, ignoring gaps in Canning's proposal, expected current threats to collapse in the face of Anglo-American union. "Whilst it must ensure success, in the event of an appeal to force," Madison predicted, "it doubles the chance

---

America, 1800–1830 (Baltimore, 1941); and Samuel F. Bemis, *John Quincy Adams and the Foundations of American Foreign Policy* (New York, 1949).

[2] Monroe to Madison, Oct. 17, 1823, William C. Rives Collection, Library of Congress.

of success without that appeal." [3] For the moment Monroe kept this advice secret, even from Adams.

The President, who returned to Washington on November 4, convened his cabinet on the afternoon of the seventh. Five men— Monroe, Adams, Secretary of War Calhoun, Secretary of the Navy Southard, and Attorney General Wirt—settled the reply to Britain, an important declaration to Russia, and Monroe's message at the opening of Congress on December 2.[4] William Wirt and Samuel Southard, old friends of the President's, contributed little to the first meeting or the half dozen that followed. On Latin America, the most debated question, Calhoun spoke the language of caution and his elder, Adams, the language of bold independence. The President heard all views, at times inclined toward Calhoun's, and ultimately backed Adams'.

Until November 21, when Monroe read a preliminary version of his message, none of the secretaries expected the President to make a general declaration of principles in his message to Congress. As was then customary, each secretary prepared a few paragraphs on his department for the President's guidance. Adams' suggestions, submitted on November 13, ignored the Latin-American question, the Secretary expecting to handle this in diplomatic correspondence. His draft concentrated on the Pacific Coast. The ukase, Adams observed, had led to discussions in which the American government asserted that "the American Continents by the free and independent condition which they have assumed and maintain, are henceforth not to be considered as subjects for future Colonization by any European Power." [5] The President accepted this passage almost verbatim.

As a maxim the noncolonization doctrine, a less acid expression of the views Adams inflicted on Stratford Canning in their worst

---

[3] Jefferson to Monroe, Oct. 24, 1823, Lipscomb and Bergh, *op. cit.*, XV, 477–480; Madison to Monroe, Oct. 30, 1823, Gaillard Hunt, ed., *The Writings of James Madison* (9 vols.; New York, 1900–1910), IX, 157–159. See also Madison to Jefferson, Nov. 1, 1823, and Madison to James Barbour, Dec. 5, 1823, *ibid.*, pp. 157, 173.

[4] Illness prevented Secretary of the Treasury William H. Crawford from attending.

[5] Adams memorandum, Nov. 13, 1823, James Monroe Papers, New York Public Library.

quarrel, challenged England more than any other power. Yet although the Secretary sometimes considered it applicable to British claims in the Oregon country, the doctrine never played a major part in that dispute, nor did it have relevance to current British ambitions. Noncolonization was laid down at this time solely because of the Russian ukase.

When Monroe read his draft Adams, happy to hear the paragraph on colonization, took exception to another presidential passage. The Chief Executive cast a benevolent eye upon the Greeks, then struggling to cast off their Turkish yoke, and spoke "in terms of the most pointed reprobation of the late invasion of Spain by France, and of the principles upon which it was undertaken by the open avowal of the King of France." Like many Republicans at the opening of the French Revolution and many contemporaries as well, the President allowed enthusiasm for self-government and dislike of tyranny to undermine his devotion to isolation. A strong antimonarchist, an even stronger isolationist, Adams protested that Monroe's proposed statement, by breaking down the idea of two spheres, weakened the noncolonization doctrine and objections to European projects in the Western Hemisphere. The statement might even involve the country in serious controversy over non-American issues.

The President apparently felt the force of Adams' arguments. Despite Calhoun's contrary opinions he altered his plans. After expressing sympathy for Spain the message delivered to Congress added, "In the wars of the European powers, in matters relating to themselves, we have never taken any part, nor does it comport with our policy, so to do." [6] Monroe thus made explicit the traditional isolationism of his people, a feeling as old as and more realistic than their prorepublicanism. This became the second tenet of the doctrine bearing his name. The third required much more discussion.

When the President returned to Washington Adams showed

[6] Nov. 21, 22, 24, 1823, Charles F. Adams, ed., *Memoirs of John Quincy Adams* (12 vols.; Philadelphia, 1874–1877), VI, 194–199; James D. Richardson, ed., *A Compilation of the Messages and Papers of the Presidents* (10 vols.; Washington, 1907), II, 217.

him a note delivered on October 16 by Baron Tuyll, the Russian minister. Tuyll announced and justified Russia's adamant refusal to recognize the rebellious colonies. He also praised the American decision to remain neutral even after recognition. This warning against American aid to Latin America, if indeed it was a warning, was temperate enough to permit Adams to reply, for the President, with a mild defense of recognition and a hope that Russia too would remain neutral. Otherwise the United States might reconsider its own neutrality.[7]

Tuyll returned to the charge. On the afternoon of the seventeenth, after Adams had already spent a long day drafting instructions to Rush, discussing them with Monroe, and interviewing the British chargé, the Russian appeared in his office. Tuyll presented extracts from circular instructions recently received. These reviewed in "a tone of passionate exultation," Adams observed, French success in Spain, put Russia on record as opposing revolution in principle, and announced the Czar's intention to act as world policeman. Did the imperial constable, Adams asked, still consider Latin America to be Spanish property? Yes, Tuyll replied. This declaration, Adams said a few days later, was "bearding us to our faces upon the monarchical principles of the Holy Alliance." In his view and that of his colleagues, "It was time to tender them an issue."[8]

Because Europe had no real plans the administration often dealt in rumor, and in the autumn of 1823 Tuyll and Canning tempted Monroe and his lieutenants to forget contrary, consoling information. Months earlier Rush had reported that, although Canning's letter to Stuart did not quite say so, Great Britain would prevent French counterrevolutionary efforts in Latin America. On the heels of this wise conjecture Adams received from Gallatin, just returned from Paris, a soothing report of his last conversation with Foreign Minister Chateaubriand. Pressed by Gallatin to disavow ambitions "either to take possession of some of her [Spain's]

[7] Nov. 7, 8, 1823, Adams, *op. cit.*, VI, 178–182; Bemis, *op. cit.*, pp. 384–386.
[8] Nov. 17, 25, 1823, Adams, *op. cit.*, VI, 189–190, 201.

colonies, or to assist her in reducing them under their former yoke," Chateaubriand gave categorical assurances that France had no such plans and would in no way interfere in American questions.[9] Of course Chateaubriand and Villèle, his chief, notoriously worked at cross-purposes. Still this was as explicit an assurance as one could ask.

Adams thought Canning feigned alarm to draw the Americans to his own position. He concealed this suspicion from the British chargé, of course, but he did tell Henry Addington he considered the danger negligible. Talking of the South Americans, he told Addington "nothing could [be] more absurd than the notion that they could ever be again brought to submit to the Spanish yoke." Moreover Adams felt sure that British and American disapproval, already clear to Europe, would suffice to prevent intervention. "Any mere declaration on the part of the European Sovereigns he considered as a dead letter, and as for active and substantial interposition the bare idea was too absurd to be entertained for a moment." [10]

Monroe and Calhoun considered the danger genuine, and so apparently did Wirt and Southard. Less than a week after receiving Rush's first reports the President asked Gallatin to return to Paris, urging the need of an experienced hand in a period of crisis. Adams tried to argue Monroe and Calhoun out of their alarm. "Calhoun," he complained, "is perfectly moon-struck by the surrender of Cadiz, and says the Holy Alliance . . . will restore all Mexico and all South America to the Spanish dominion." The Secretary of State maintained that allied forces could make no more than a temporary impression in Latin America. Did he doubt the rebels' ability to fend off attack, he said, he would advise against "embarking our lives and fortunes in a ship which . . .

[9] Rush #302 to Adams, April 17, 1823, Department of State Archives, National Archives, Despatches, Great Britain, Vol. XXVIII; Gallatin to Adams, June 24, 1823, Department of State Archives, National Archives, Despatches, France, Vol. XXI.
[10] Nov. 17, 1823, Adams, *op. cit.*, VI, 188; Addington to Canning, private and confidential, Nov. 3, 1823, Bradford Perkins, ed., "The Suppressed Dispatch of H. U. Addington," *Hispanic American Historical Review*, XXXVII (1957), 485.

the very rats have abandoned." [11] Monroe and Calhoun, who wanted to support Latin America, had no answer to this argument.

On November 16, the day after Adams found Calhoun "moonstruck," further dispatches arrived from Rush. Describing the conversations following Canning's return to London, they showed that the Foreign Secretary had markedly cooled. Monroe interpreted this to mean that Canning had somehow discovered that the danger to Latin America had become less immediate. He took comfort in this guess. During the second fortnight of November, when he framed his message and whipped it into shape, Monroe seemed less fearful than before. He never entirely abandoned his old concern, and certainly Calhoun did not, but the President's hopes rose.[12] At least he did not fear that French troops at Cadiz would immediately board ship for South America.

This declining sense of urgency did not destroy the appeal of Canning's proposal. For some days the cabinet, aware of the cost, wrestled over the attractive, unprecedented invitation to join the club of major powers. Perhaps unnecessary at the moment, a joint declaration would certainly discourage future European plans, and all the cabinet preferred an investment of words to a later investment of force. Even more important, in the view of Monroe and his advisers, union with Britain would cement her break with the Continent.

The idea, fatuous after Verona and the Stuart letter, that Britain teetered near the brink of an understanding with the allies troubled Monroe, Wirt, Calhoun, and Jefferson. Their concern showed the depth of their distrust of England as well as a simplistic republican inability to distinguish among types of monarchy. Even the more sophisticated Adams, denying the need to bind England, merely maintained that her past actions committed her against the allies, not that her system was different.[13]

Distrust cut both ways, arguing also against a connection with Albion. At the height of the cabinet discussions a letter from

[11] Monroe to Gallatin, Oct. 15, 1823, James Monroe Papers, Library of Congress; Nov. 13, 15, 1823, Adams, *op. cit.*, VI, 185–186.
[12] Nov. 17, 18, 21, 1823, Adams, *op. cit.*, pp. 188, 190, 195–196.
[13] Nov. 25, 26, 1823, *ibid.*, pp. 203–207.

George W. Erving, a former diplomat traveling privately in Europe, came into Monroe's hands. An alliance with England horrified Erving, who was "perfectly persuaded . . . that in such alliance either her system or ours would suffer, & equally persuaded that it would not be hers." Better abandon Latin America, counseled Erving, than join England "at the imminent risk of exposing our health by the poisonous contact." [14] Adams, who did not respect Erving, nevertheless shared his feelings, as to a lesser degree did the President. Castlereagh's years of endeavor, strikingly successful on the diplomatic level, barely touched the visceral Anglophobia of the American people.

Adams, the cabinet member most hostile to understanding with England, attached as much importance to recognition as did Rush. At an early interview with Addington, Adams permitted the chargé to hope for some way to bypass the issue. As time passed he tightened his position. English recognition of at least one of the new states, he told Addington after receiving Rush's report of the deadlock with Canning, was indispensable so that "whatever events may happen, the concord in the views and measures of the Governments may be preserved unbroken, and that confusion avoided, which a discrepancy of principle might engender." [15] The United States denied the right of any power including Spain to challenge states already living in freedom. If a twist of events led Britain to support reconstruction of the empire, albeit on a less rigid basis, a real crisis might develop. To eliminate this possibility Monroe and Adams, like Rush, required England to take a public stand by the act of recognition.

Pointing to the statement, proposed by Canning, that neither Britain nor America had territorial ambitions, Adams argued that the Englishman sought a pledge only "ostensibly against the forcible interference of the Holy Alliance between Spain and South America; but really or especially against the acquisition to the

[14] Erving to Crawford, Sept. 25, 1823, Stanislaus M. Hamilton, ed., *The Writings of James Monroe* (7 vols.; New York, 1898–1903), VI, 304n.
[15] Addington to Canning, private and confidential, Nov. 3, 1825, Bradford Perkins, *op. cit.*, p. 484; Addington #20 to Canning, secret and confidential, Nov. 20, 1823, Foreign Office Archives, Public Record Office, FO 5/177.

United States themselves of any part of the Spanish-American possessions." He was not willing, although Calhoun was, to foreclose the possibility of admitting Cuba or even Texas into the union at the request of local inhabitants, and he was willing to give up the advantage of a self-denying British pledge to preserve his own country's freedom of action.[16]

The Americans saw serious risk in acting at England's call. "Had we mov'd first in London," Monroe later observed, "we might have appeared . . . a secondary party, whereby G.B. would have had the principal credit with our neighbors" in Latin America. Adams was equally reluctant to allow her the lead. "As the independence of the South Americans would then be only protected by the guarantee of Great Britain," he said, "it would throw them completely into her arms." He urged independent action partly to strengthen political and commercial ties with the new states.[17]

In more general form the discussion reached the heart of America's position as an independent power. At the first cabinet meeting after Monroe's return, Adams pointed out that Tuyll's *démarche* provided an opportunity "to take our stand against the Holy Alliance, and at the same time to decline the overture of Great Britain. It would be more candid, as well as more dignified, to avow our principles explicitly to Russia and France, than to come in as a cock-boat in the wake of a British man-of-war." The cabinet agreed. The day after Tuyll's second note Adams told Addington, who visited him to discuss Latin America, that "Foreign Powers . . . should not be left in ignorance of the views and opinions of the United States. . . . These views would be openly and distinctly declared to them." [18] National self-respect urged such a course rather than action as England's junior partner.

Proceeding along these lines the President prepared a long, heated passage for his address to Congress. His diatribe against

[16] Nov. 7, 1823, Adams, *op. cit.*, VI, 177–178.
[17] Monroe to Madison, Dec. 20, 1823, Rives Collection; Nov. 26, 1823, Adams, *op. cit.*, VI, 207–208.
[18] Nov. 7, 1823, Adams, *op. cit.*, VI, 178–179; Addington #20 to Canning, secret and confidential, Nov. 20, 1823, FO 5/177.

antirepublican endeavors everywhere—in Greece, in Spain, in Italy, in Latin America—upset Adams, who successfully urged the President to tone down denunciations of purely European activities, to promise to abstain from European politics, and to concentrate his fire against outside intervention in the New World. Speaking past Congress to the allies James Monroe wrote:

We owe it . . . to candor, and to the amicable relations existing between the United States and those powers, to declare that we should consider any attempt on their part to extend their system to any portion of this hemisphere as dangerous to our peace and security. . . . With the Governments who have declared their independence and maintained it, . . . we could not view any interposition . . . by any European power, in any other light than as the manifestation of an unfriendly disposition toward the United States. . . .

It is impossible that the allied powers should extend their political system to any portion of either continent without endangering our peace and happiness; nor can anyone believe that our southern brethren, if left to themselves, would adopt it of their own accord. It is equally impossible, therefore, that we should behold such interposition, in any form, with indifference.[19]

Thus was phrased the third tenet of Monroe's famous message, the nonintervention doctrine.

Secretary Adams, who approved the final version of Monroe's message, altered his draft reply to Tuyll to correspond with it and considered the result a "firm, spirited, and yet conciliatory answer to all the communications lately received from the Russian Government, and at the same time an unequivocal answer to the proposals made by Mr. Canning to Mr. Rush." Calhoun considered the note far from conciliatory and wanted to eliminate it altogether, merely sending the presidential message to Tuyll. Monroe found Adams' draft not a little strong, but after the Secretary pled his case in a private interview Monroe allowed Adams to proceed much as he had planned. The Secretary of State read his note to Tuyll on November 27 and promised soon to send a written copy.[20]

[19] Nov. 21, 22, 24, 1823, Adams, *op. cit.*, VI, 194–199; Richardson, *op. cit.*, II, 217–219.
[20] Nov. 25, 26, 27, 1823, Adams, *op. cit.*, VI, 199–202, 204–216.

Statements to the world through Tuyll and Congress made it plain that the American government intended to act as an independent power rather than as a British satellite. They did not make a reply to Canning less necessary. Unwillingness to act as "a cock-boat in the wake of a British man-of-war," in other words, made it certain Canning's plan would not gain unconditional, immediate approval, but did not disbar negotiations on the basis of that plan.

Adams' diary pictures the President as uncertain of the proper reply to England, not as inclined to accept Canning's offer. Even Calhoun, the most alarmed member of the inner circle, proposed to give Rush only discretionary authority to accept the offer in an emergency. All apparently agreed to seek modifications if time permitted, particularly to request or require British recognition of Latin states. At one point the President endorsed Calhoun's suggestion. Adams rather easily talked him out of this idea, and in the end the President adopted Adams' sterner position.[21]

Instructions to Rush, revised several times as the President edged toward decision, bore date of November 29, a few days after Monroe had completed his forthcoming address. At Monroe's direction Adams struck out an explicit statement that until Britain granted recognition "we can see no foundation upon which the concurrent action of the two Governments can be harmonized." The instructions made the point in more diplomatic language. Only if Britain extended recognition was Rush authorized to move "in concert" with her. This last clause, whatever courses it approved, clearly did not mean joint action along the lines Canning originally proposed, even should the Foreign Secretary bring his colleagues around to recognition. Monroe and Adams promised to consider joint as opposed to parallel action only if, a new emergency arising, Rush referred home further proposals.[22]

---

[21] Nov. 7, 13, 15, 20, 26, 1823, *ibid.*, pp. 177–181, 185–186, 192, 210.

[22] Nov. 26, 1823, *ibid.*, p. 210; Dexter Perkins, *op. cit.*, p. 93; Adams to Rush, Nov. 29, 1823, William R. Manning, ed., *Correspondence of the United States Concerning Independence of the Latin-American Nations* (3 vols.; New York, 1925), I, 210–212.

Adams, who never claimed credit for rejecting the British offer (he took pride chiefly in the noncolonization doctrine), stood nearer his colleagues than is often said. No one desired unconditional approval. In his first comments on Canning's offer the President merely said that his inclination was to "meet" it, not that he favored the joint manifesto Canning urged. Obviously the President wished to widen the breach between Britain and the allies and to protect Latin America. He believed the reply to Tuyll and the message to Congress did so. "We certainly meet, in full extent, the proposition of M^r. Canning," he wrote Jefferson. "With G. Britain, we have, it is presumed, acted fairly & fully to all her objects, & have a right to expect, a corresponding conduct on her part," he wrote his immediate predecessor. Forwarding the President's message to Rush, Adams observed, "The concurrence of these sentiments with those of the British Government as exhibited in the proposals of Mr. Canning, will be obvious to you. It will now remain for Great Britain to make hers equally public. The moral effect upon the councils of the Allies, to deter them from any interposition of force between Spain and America, will be complete." [23] The form might differ from Canning's scheme. The effect did not, President and Secretary both believed.

On December 2, 1823, instructions having gone to Rush and a reply to Tuyll, Congress heard the President's message. Three of fifty-one paragraphs dealt with foreign affairs, an early one stating the noncolonization doctrine and two later ones mingling isolationist sentiments and warnings against intervention by Europe.

Not for thirty years did Americans name these three paragraphs the Monroe Doctrine. From the beginning, however, they valued the principles laid down by the last of the Virginia dynasty. Within a week Adams noted that the nation universally approved the message. The British chargé agreed. "The explicit and manly tone," he informed Canning a month later, "has evidently found in every

[23] Monroe to Jefferson, Dec. [8], 1823, Hamilton, *op. cit.*, VI, 344; Monroe to Madison, Dec. 20, 1823, Rives Collection; Adams to Rush, secret, Dec. 8, 1823, Bemis, *op. cit.*, p. 577.

bosom a chord which vibrates in strict unison with the sentiments so conveyed. They have been echoed from one end of the union to the other." [24] Monroe's decision to ignore the advice of his two neighbors and predecessors, to strike out boldly and independently with a declaration of principle despite possible risks, drew support throughout the nation.

Just after the message Washington received a rumor, in fact unfounded, that 12,000 French troops were about to sail for South America. This alarmed editors Niles and Gales as well as the President, who talked briefly of the need to "unite with the British Govt, in measures, to prevent the interference of the allied powers." Monroe soon cooled, perhaps under Adams' influence. New instructions to Rush, carried by a secret agent sent to Europe to ferret out allied plans, spoke only of a "concert of operations" and studiously avoided any mention of joint action.

In a few days a dispatch arrived from Daniel Sheldon, the chargé at Paris. Sheldon reported that, neither the Bourbon monarchy scheme nor any other having come to a focus, the United States need not fear an immediate descent on Latin America. A second dispatch two weeks later repeated this prediction. The scare passed. In the spring Henry Clay withdrew a resolution endorsing the nonintervention doctrine, saying, "Events and circumstances, subsequent to the communication of the Message, evinced, that if such a purpose were ever seriously entertained, it had been relinquished." [25]

Monroe's message, aimed partly at Latin America, had no clear effect there. The leader of the fight for liberty, Simón Bolívar, completely ignored it in his correspondence. Most South American

---

[24] Richardson, *op. cit.*, II, 209, 217–219; Dexter Perkins, *op. cit.*, pp. 144–149; Adams to Rush, secret, Dec. 8, 1823, Bemis, *op. cit.*, p. 578; Addington #1 to Canning, Jan. 5, 1824, FO 5/185.

[25] Dec. 4, 1823, Adams, *op. cit.*, VI, 226; *Niles' Weekly Register* (Baltimore), Dec. 6, 1823; Monroe to Adams, Dec. 3, 1823, Bemis, *op. cit.*, p. 398n; Adams to Rush, secret, Dec. 8, 1823, *ibid.*, pp. 578–579; Sheldon #13 to Adams, Oct. 18, 1823 (received Dec. 12), Despatches, France, Vol. XXII; Sheldon to Adams, private, Oct. 30, 1823 (received Jan. 3, 1824), *ibid.*; *Annals of Congress*, 18th Cong., 1st sess., pp. 1104, 2673–2764.

leaders continued to regard England as their chief defense against European intervention.[26]

Europeans, who also felt that the message scarcely altered the practical situation, nevertheless reacted strongly to the President's sentiments. Liberals contrasted Monroe's enlightened views with those of their own governments. The dominant groups denounced his presumption. The noncolonization doctrine challenged international law; the warning against intervention denied legitimist ambitions; the prorepublican theme threatened traditional European doctrines. The United States, Prince Metternich complained, "have suddenly left a sphere too narrow for their ambition, and have astonished Europe by a new act of revolt, more unprovoked, fully as audacious, and no less dangerous than the former. . . . If this flood of evil doctrines . . . should extend over the whole of America, what would become of . . . that conservative system which has saved Europe from complete dissolution?" [27]

In Britain praise outweighed criticism. The message reached Falmouth by government packet on December 24 and passed to all the kingdom. The *Caledonian Mercury*, usually friendly to the United States, scoffed at Monroe's "obscure innuendos." Other papers gave the message the attention it deserved, the *Chronicle* pronouncing it "worthy of the occasion and of the people, who seem destined to occupy so large a space in the future history of the world." [28] No editor denounced the republican cast which so upset Metternich. All withheld comment on the isolationist passages, apparently considering them mere truisms. The papers concentrated upon the noncolonization and nonintervention doctrines.

Several editors objected to the former, a "startling general principle," a "curious idea," a "grave and somewhat novel doctrine." The *Star*, most critical of the entire message, declared: "The plain *Yankee* of the matter is, that the United States wish to

[26] Dexter Perkins, *op. cit.*, pp. 149–161.
[27] *Ibid.*, pp. 161–178. Quotation on p. 167.
[28] Rush #354 to Adams, Dec. 27, 1823, Despatches, Great Britain, Vol. XXIX; *Caledonian Mercury* (Edinburgh), Dec. 29, 1823; *Morning Chronicle* (London), Dec. 27, 1823.

monopolize to themselves the privilege of colonising . . . every
. . . part of the American Continent." In the Oregon country and
elsewhere Britain must not accept this proposition.[29] Not one
British voice defended Monroe, but many papers passed over
noncolonization in silence.

Britons regarded the nonintervention doctrine as the heart of
the message, and on the whole they liked it. Even the *Star*, which
considered Monroe hypocritical "to place on the basis of a bounden
duty, what is, in plain truth, a matter of the sheerest self-interest,"
welcomed his reinforcement of British efforts. "The President has
made just such a declaration . . . as it is to the interest of this
country that he should have made," opined the *Herald*. "This is
plain speaking, and it is just speaking," pontificated the *Times*.
Both the *Times* and the *Chronicle* contrasted America's boldness
with the British government's alleged lack of courage. The latter
paper even maintained that an English declaration as forthright
as Monroe's would have prevented the French invasion of Spain
which began the whole crisis.[30]

The *Courier*, once bitterly anti-Yankee and long a mouthpiece
of British conservatism, capped British comment. "The question
of the Independence and recognition of the South American States,
may now be considered as at rest," the paper declared. Europe
would no longer dare to plan action against the former Spanish
colonies. "Protected by the two nations that possess the institutions,
and speak the language of freedom—by Great Britain on one side,
and by the United States on the other, their independence is placed
beyond the reach of danger." [31] On the great issue of the day England and the United States stood together as allies for freedom.

Canning reacted less favorably to the message and the decision,
unknown to the public but to him painful, to refuse the offer of
joint action. Six months earlier his cousin's overoptimistic reports
led to dreams of a virtual alliance, an agreement far transcending

[29] *Morning Post* (London), Dec. 27, 1823; *Morning Herald* (London), Dec. 29,
1823; *Times* (London), Dec. 27, 1823; *Star* (London), Dec. 27, 1823.
[30] *Star*, Dec. 27, 1823; *Herald*, Dec. 29, 1823; *Times*, Dec. 27, 1823; *Chronicle*,
Dec. 27, 1823. See also *Sun* (London), Dec. 27, 1823.
[31] *Courier* (London), Dec. 27, 1823.

a joint statement on Latin America. In October, after discussing general negotiations with Rush and Stratford Canning, he turned to his cousin, who remained in the office, and said "he should be inclined to take this opportunity to make a clearance of all American questions." [32] The collapse of hopes for an entente on Latin America destroyed Canning's interest in other negotiations. Rush's conversations with Stratford Canning and Huskisson dwindled slowly into nothing during the first half of 1824. Canning made little effort to stir the negotiations into life.

Nor did the Foreign Secretary show interest when Rush read Adams' instructions of November 29, laying down terms on which coöperation might develop.[33] With the Latin-American problem anesthetized by the Polignac memorandum, Canning saw no need for a joint statement, particularly one quite different from his original proposal, and felt free to take up new questions posed by Monroe's message.

Canning particularly objected to the noncolonization doctrine. He complained so strongly that Rush quickly dropped the matter. Canning drew up but wisely did not deliver an argumentative note in which he compared Alexander's ukase with "the new doctrine of the President," concluding that "we cannot yield obedience to either." Later, in instructions to Stratford Canning and Huskisson, he declared the British government "prepared to reject [Monroe's principle] in the most unequivocal manner, maintaining that whatever right of colonizing the unappropriated parts of America had been hitherto enjoyed . . . may still be exercised in perfect freedom, and without affording the slightest cause of umbrage to the United States." [34]

Although Canning saw advantages in acting hand in hand with the United States he shrank from appearing at St. Petersburg with a power avowing principles so different. He also did not like or

[32] Stratford Canning memorandum, Oct. 8, 1823, Papers of Stratford Canning, Viscount Stratford de Redcliffe, Public Record Office, FO 352/8.

[33] Rush #361 to Adams, Feb. 9, 1824, Despatches, Great Britain, Vol. XXX.

[34] Rush #356 to Adams, Jan. 6, 1824, *ibid.*; Canning to Rush [not sent], Jan. —, 1824, FO 5/194; Canning #3 to Huskisson and Stratford Canning, May 31, 1824, FO 5/191.

even profess to understand the American proposal to limit permanent British settlements to the area between 51° and 55°, and when the American minister presented this plan Canning replied, "Heyday! What is here? Do I read Mr Rush's meaning aright?" Consequently he ordered his ambassador in Russia to negotiate separately.[35] No harm resulted. Russia abandoned her claim to broad maritime jurisdiction and, by separate agreements with her two adversaries, abandoned the Oregon country.

George Canning considered the nonintervention doctrine in some ways useful to England. He even professed unconcern at the refusal to act jointly. After Polignac he did not fear an allied descent upon South America. He counted on Monroe's message to give pause to planners of a European congress on Latin-American affairs. "The Congress was broken in all its limits before, but the President's speech gives it the *coup de grace*," he felt, over-optimistically as events proved. "The effect of the ultra-Liberalism of our Yankee cooperators, on the ultra-despotism of our Aix la Chapelle allies, gives me just the balance that I wanted," he informed his friend Bagot.[36]

In more important ways the presidential announcement unsettled Canning. A proud and practical politician, he disliked having Monroe steal a march on him. "Are you not," Lord Grey asked Holland, "delighted with the American speech? What a contrast to the conduct . . . of our Government. . . . Canning will have the glory of following in the wake of the President of the United States." Canning did not like to have his enemies free to speak this way, particularly since he believed, and said Rush agreed, that "his Gov^t. would *not* have spoken out, but for what passed

---

[35] Canning memorandum, n.d. [Dec., 1823], FO 5/183; Stratford Canning to Canning, private, Dec. 24, 1823, *ibid.*; Canning to Rush, Dec. 17, 1823, Rush Family Papers, Princeton University Library; Canning #1 to Bagot, private and confidential, Jan. 22, 1824, Sir Charles Bagot Papers, Levens Hall, Westmorland.

[36] Canning to Lord Granville, Dec. 28, 1823, Harold Temperley, *The Foreign Policy of Canning, 1822–1827* (London, 1925), p. 129; Canning to Sir William à Court, private, Dec. 31, 1823, Augustus G. Stapleton, *George Canning and His Times* (London, 1859), p. 395; Canning #1 to Bagot, private and confidential, Jan. 22, 1824, Bagot MSS.

between us." [37] Canning felt Monroe had tricked and defeated him.

More than mere pique upset the Foreign Secretary. Canning did not want close economic and political ties between the United States and South America, partly because these might lead to discrimination against English commerce and partly because Britain, already at odds with Europe, would find herself isolated. The Foreign Secretary still hoped for negotiations between Spain and the Latin Americans, a course Monroe clearly disapproved. Because Canning, in the words of an admiring biographer, considered "constitutional monarchy . . . the true *via media* between democracy and despotism," he hoped to keep monarchist ideas alive in South America. Monroe's message was a paean on popular government. Canning felt he must regain the lead from one who blew "a blast on the republican trumpet, while sheltered behind the shield of England." [38]

The Polignac memorandum, circulated to European diplomats shortly after its signature and sent by Canning to Rush a few weeks later,[39] remained secret from the public until 1824. At the opening of Parliament in February, Canning, assailed for following a less decisive tack than Monroe, defended ministers with a paraphrase. On March 4 he presented the memorandum, still with deletions, to the House of Commons, and government spokesmen exploited it. Lord Liverpool asked if such a *démarche,* which the

[37] Grey to Holland, Jan. 2, 1824, George M. Trevelyan, *Lord Grey of the Reform Bill* (2d ed.; London, 1929), p. 374; Canning #1 to Bagot, private and confidential, Jan. 22, 1824, Bagot MSS.

[38] Temperley, *op. cit.,* pp. 139, 127.

[39] Rush professed to accept Canning's excuses for the tardy delivery of the memorandum, although he felt the document itself, which promised recognition only if Europe acted against the colonies, proved England "devoid of all justice, of all magnanimity, and even of all true foresight and policy." Canning later hinted that the delay in communicating the memorandum was not unintentional, although it is hard to see what purpose he hoped to serve by delay, particularly since, as he said, French diplomats disseminated the memorandum so widely it was bound to fall into American hands. In any event Monroe did not know of the Polignac memorandum before he delivered his message to Congress. Rush to Canning, Dec. 27, 1823, FO 5/181; Rush to Monroe, Dec. 1, 1823 [?], Monroe MSS, NYPL; Canning to Bagot, Jan. 9, 1824, Josceline Bagot, ed., *George Canning and His Friends* (2 vols.; London, 1909), II, 208–209.

French had been forced to accept, was not "worth a thousand official declarations." [40] The government also revealed its refusal to attend a congress on Latin America, a proposal reluctantly made by Ferdinand. These actions showed Europe and Latin America, neither of whom needed much convincing, that Britain still posed the most effective barrier to outside interference in the imperial war.

Fostering monarchical principles in Latin America proved more difficult, even impossible. After the downfall of Iturbide in Mexico they virtually disappeared. Moreover King Ferdinand, obdurate as ever, refused to countenance negotiations with his erstwhile subjects, and the continued presence of French troops in Spain angered Canning. Supported by Liverpool he decided to challenge the cabinet majority.

In August, 1824, Canning forced agreement to recognize Buenos Aires, although George IV objected that "the whole proceedings . . . are premature"—at a time when, except in Peru, Spain had no armies on the mainland. On the last day of the year, after a lengthy battle during which Canning threatened to resign, the Foreign Secretary won cabinet approval of a note to Spain announcing England's intention to recognize Buenos Aires, Mexico, and Colombia. The King again objected to his ministers' precipitancy —"I have already expressed my wishes . . . & wishes when coming from the King are always to be considered & understood as Commands"—but recognition proceeded as Canning and Liverpool planned.[41] A year and a half after Canning first approached Rush the British and American governments were aligned. They were also rivals for Latin-American favor and commerce.[42]

Canning's efforts to counteract the nonintervention doctrine,

[40] Hansard, n.s., X, 74, 708–712, 997.

[41] Temperley, op. cit., pp. 142–151; George IV to cabinet, n.d. [Aug., 1824], Arthur Aspinall, ed., The Letters of King George IV, 1812–1830, III (Cambridge, 1938), 97; memorandum of George IV, n.d., on Liverpool to George IV, Dec. 17, 1824, Royal Archives, Windsor Castle.

[42] In arguing for recognition Liverpool laid heavy stress on the danger of throwing "the Wealth, the Power & the Influence of these great Dominions into the hands of the People of the United States." Such a course, Liverpool warned, would lead to the rapid development of American maritime power and, eventually, to a war between

usually carried out with a tact belying his reputation, failed to pull the wool over Richard Rush's hypercritical eyes. Late in 1824 he wrote: "It would be an entire mistake to suppose, that because of the partial and guarded approach to us by Britain last year, on the south American question, she feels any increase of good will towards us." [43]

Most Americans disagreed, and in 1824 and 1825 Anglo-American friendship reached unprecedented levels. Early in 1824 an alliance on Latin-American questions gained wide support although, as Addington reported, it could be "attributed as much to the hope of acquiring additional security to their own institutions as from any inherent affection for Great Britain, or disinterested ardour in the cause of transatlantic Liberty." Alliance talk died with the collapse of threats to Latin America; friendship did not. The tariff debate of 1824 totally lacked the anti-British emphasis of that of 1816. At a White House reception the President, speaking in a tone to be overheard, praised British policy and welcomed the growth of Anglo-American concord. [44]

In the spring of 1825, learning of Charles Vaughan's appointment as minister to the United States, Addington requested a leave to escape the oppressive Washington heat. He looked back upon his tenure with satisfaction. "It is scarcely possible that a man should arrive under better auspices than Vaughan," he reported, "for 2/3^{ds} of the Americans are just now well-disposed towards us, and Clay [the former war hawk now secretary of state] says that he is quite in love with Mr Canning." An honest man well aware that outstanding issues or new ones could spoil the scene, Addington added: "How long this may last I do not pretend to conjecture." [45]

Britain and the United States in alliance with France. How seriously the premier took these arguments is open to question. Liverpool memorandum, Dec. 1, 1824, Royal Archives.

[43] Rush to Crawford, Sept. 18, 1824, William H. Crawford Papers, Library of Congress.

[44] Addington to Canning, private and confidential, Jan. 5, 1824, George Canning Papers, Harewood House, Leeds; Addington #12, #20 to Canning, March 13, April 30, 1824, FO 5/185.

[45] Addington to Planta, private, June 4, 1825, FO 5/198.

Addington's ease paid tribute to George Canning and perhaps even more to Lord Castlereagh, for Canning reaped where Castlereagh had sown. From the spring of 1814 onward, at first slowly and almost inadvertently, British policy moved toward conciliation. The Rush-Bagot agreement and the convention of 1818 were positive sides of this policy. Probably more important, Castlereagh and then Canning sought to stifle controversy before it became serious or, better, to avoid it altogether. "Let us hasten settlement, if we can; but let us postpone the day of difference, if it must come; which however I trust it need not," Canning wrote. This policy had the disadvantage of leaving issues like Oregon and West Indian trade for future dispute. In the immediate sense it paid impressive dividends.

Even Rush, hostile and suspicious, admitted, "Mine have been plain-sailing times," and in general the American political world praised England for muffling winds of controversy. An observant British traveler, no mere panegyrist of the United States, wrote in 1823 that "there are few, whose good opinion is worth having, who do not unite in good will towards the people of my native country." [46] This much had the climate changed since 1812.

In the Liverpool speech which charmed Christopher Hughes, George Canning "express[ed] the gratification which he felt, in common with the great mass of the intelligent and liberal men of both countries, to see the animosities necessarily attendant on a state of hostility so rapidly wearing away." He welcomed the growth of friendship between "two nations united by a common language, a common spirit of commercial enterprise, and a common regard for well-regulated liberty." [47] Appropriately, Canning did not mention contrary factors—the continuing British air of superiority, American touchiness and ambition, commercial rivalry, England's distrust of republicanism, and America's of monarchy. Still

[46] Canning to Rush [not sent], Jan. —, 1824, FO 5/194; Rush #220 to Adams, Nov. 17, 1821, Despatches, Great Britain, Vol. XXVI; John M. Duncan, *Travels through Part of the United States and Canada in 1818 and 1819* (2 vols.; Glasgow, 1823), II, 271.

[47] *Speeches of the Right Hon. George Canning Delivered on Public Occasions in Liverpool* (Liverpool, 1825), p. 386.

he fairly described a process taking place on both sides of the Atlantic.

Basically the new relationship reflected the growth of American power and stability and of Britain's sometimes half-reluctant recognition of this growth. America has "already taken her rank among the first powers of Christendom," the *Annual Register* observed in the volume for 1824. Few Englishmen yet placed the United States on a par with their own country. They did see that the American form of government "has survived the tender period of infancy, and outlived the prophecies of its downfall. . . . It has been found serviceable both in peace and war, and may well claim from the nation it has saved . . . the votive benediction of 'Esto perpetua.' " [48] Perpetual or not—Calhoun and Jefferson Davis would speak to that—the union had gained a position beyond foreign challenge. Capable and bold diplomacy followed a dangerous and ill fought war. The new American generation vindicated the aspirations of their fathers in 1776.

[48] *Annual Register, 1824* (London, 1825), p. 295; Francis Hall, *Travels in Canada, and the United States, in 1816 and 1817* (2d ed.; 2 vols.; London, 1819), I, 420–421.

NOTE ON THE SOURCES

The student of Anglo-American relations from 1812 to 1823, frequently aided by works of larger or smaller scope, searches in vain for a cohesive treatment of the entire theme. This work rests primarily upon an examination of manuscript materials and contemporary publications in England and the United States. A large proportion of these sources aided in the preparation of an earlier volume, *Prologue to War: England and the United States, 1805–1812* (Berkeley and Los Angeles, 1961). The Note on the Sources in that work (pp. 439–446) contains many comments it does not seem worthwhile to repeat here, and at appropriate points in this narrative the footnotes call attention to useful contributions by other scholars bearing upon particular episodes.

Of general accounts, the most helpful for this study is Samuel Flagg Bemis' magnificent *John Quincy Adams and the Foundations of American Foreign Policy* (New York, 1949), which deals with Anglo-American relations as part of Adams' broader concerns. Sympathetic yet shrewd, grounded in a careful reading of Adams' official and private correspondence, Bemis' work is necessarily less concerned with British than with American developments. Alfred L. Burt, *The United States, Great Britain, and British North America from the Revolution to the Establishment of Peace after the War of 1812* (New Haven, 1940), judicious, sober, and helpful, closes with the convention of 1818. George Dangerfield's lively and provocative *The Era of Good Feelings* (New York, 1952) touches upon the most important diplomatic developments and penetratingly assays the outlook of Liverpool, Castlereagh, and Canning. Both Dangerfield and Burt depend almost entirely upon printed sources.

Studies of British diplomacy during this period slight, if they do not ignore, Anglo-American relations to concentrate upon developments in Europe. Nevertheless the classic accounts, Charles K. Webster's two volumes, *The Foreign Policy of Castlereagh, 1812–1815* (London, 1931) and *The Foreign Policy of Castlereagh, 1815–1822* (London, 1925), and Harold Temperley, *The Foreign Policy of Canning, 1822–1827* (London, 1925), are essential to an understanding of British diplomacy. All three are based upon close reading of British and sometimes European official documents, printed and unprinted.

Official American policy is best followed in the manuscript records of the

349

Department of State, available on microfilm from the National Archives. For this study the following departmental files have been used: Diplomatic Instructions, All Countries, Vols. VII-X; Despatches, Great Britain, Vols. XVIII-XXX; Despatches, France, Vols. XIV-XXII; and two volumes entitled Records of Negotiations Connected with the Treaty of Ghent. William R. Manning, ed., *Correspondence of the United States Concerning Independence of the Latin-American Nations* (3 vols.; New York, 1925), provides information essential to an understanding of one aspect of Anglo-American relations. *Annals of Congress,* 12th Congress–18th Congress (Washington, 1853), is far less helpful than similar volumes for the years before 1812.

The Madison and Monroe collections at the Library of Congress contain many documents not available in printed selections. The William C. Rives Collection of Madison materials at the Library of Congress and Monroe manuscripts at the New York Public Library, particularly helpful on events in 1823, help to fill out the larger collections. John Quincy Adams' papers, part of the Adams Family Papers, Massachusetts Historical Society, now available on microfilm, are voluminous and helpful. They supplement rather than displace Worthington C. Ford, ed., *The Writings of John Quincy Adams,* Vols. IV-VII (New York, 1914–1917), which, however, stops at June, 1823, and Charles F. Adams, ed., *Memoirs of John Quincy Adams,* Vols. II-VI (Philadelphia, 1874–1877).

All the American negotiators at Ghent left records of one sort or another. Adams' papers have already been mentioned. The Albert Gallatin Papers, New-York Historical Society, and the Jonathan Russell Papers, Brown University Library, contain important observations from quite different points of view. Clay's position emerges, albeit not in much detail, in the first two volumes of James F. Hopkins, ed., *The Papers of Henry Clay* (Lexington, 1959——), and Bayard's in Elizabeth Donnan, ed., *Papers of James A. Bayard, 1796–1815,* American Historical Association, *Annual Report, 1913,* Vol. II (Washington, 1915). The papers of William H. Crawford, American minister at Paris, in the Library of Congress also provide helpful information on the peace negotiations.

Richard Rush, American minister at London during most of the postwar decade, wrote several volumes of memoirs including *A Residence at the Court of London* (3d ed.; London, 1872) and *A Residence at the Court of London, Second Series* (2 vols.; London, 1845). These retrospective and somewhat propagandistic efforts must be used with great caution. The Rush Family Papers, Princeton University Library, and the Richard Rush Papers,

Historical Society of Pennsylvania, are disappointing, although the former collection includes the notes exchanged by Canning and Rush in 1823. Rush's account of the negotiations of 1818 is in the Monroe Papers and, in slightly different form, in the Gallatin Papers. In the latter collection there is also important material on these negotiations from Gallatin's pen.

Only a few other manuscript collections in the United States need be singled out for comment. The Rufus King Papers, New-York Historical Society, contain useful information on Federalism and trade, particularly with the West Indies. On the former, see also the Timothy Pickering Papers, Massachusetts Historical Society, and Samuel E. Morison, *The Life and Letters of Harrison Gray Otis* (2 vols.; Boston, 1913). Christopher Hughes's papers, William L. Clements Library, Ann Arbor, include several interesting comments on Canning's "flirtation" in 1823 but nothing on Hughes's services at Ghent.

Official British records are at the Public Record Office. The Foreign Office file on American affairs, FO 5/85–194, covers these years. For selections primarily from other files, see Charles K. Webster, ed., *British Diplomacy, 1813–1815* (London, 1921), which sheds important light on England's position at the time of the Ghent negotiations, and, edited by the same scholar, *Britain and the Independence of Latin America* (2 vols.; London, 1938). The latter contains a masterful preface analyzing British policy.

The Law Officers Reports (FO 83/2205) throw some light on policy toward the United States, as do the wartime minutes of the Board of Trade (BT 5/21–22) and scattered material in Colonial Office records. The Ind series makes it possible to find relevant correspondence in the otherwise unmanageable files of the Admiralty. The correspondence between the Prince Regent, later George IV, and his ministers in the Royal Archives, Windsor Castle, helps to elucidate the break with Europe and development of the policy toward Latin America. Like the *Annals of Congress, Hansard* is far less useful than for earlier years.

The semiofficial or private correspondence of British leaders is now available either in manuscript or in print. The last collection to be opened, the papers of George Canning, Harewood House, Leeds, makes available fresh material on the Foreign Secretary's colloquies with Rush in 1823. The Liverpool Papers, British Museum, Add. MSS 38190–38489, 38564–38581, have important scattered material. Charles W. Vane, Marquess of Londonderry, ed., *Correspondence, Despatches, and Other Papers, of Viscount Castlereagh, Second Marquess of Londonderry*, Vols. X–XI (London, 1853), does not completely obviate the need to examine the Castlereagh MSS, Mount Stewart, Newtownards, County Down. Francis Bickley, ed., *Report on the Manuscripts of Earl Bathurst* (London, 1923), is helpful for the Ghent negotiations, as is Arthur R. Wellesley, Duke of Wellington, ed., *Supplementary Despatches, Correspondence, and Memoranda of Field Marshal Arthur Duke of Wellington, K.G.*, Vol. IX (London, 1862). The latter volume contains much intracabinet correspondence not addressed to Wellington.

Less concentrated but still useful material may be found in the papers of the Earl of Harrowby, Sandon Hall, Staffordshire, and of Viscount Sidmouth, County Record Office, The Castle, Exeter, Devon, and in other collections mentioned only in the footnotes. Unfortunately neither the papers of Earl Grey, The Prior's Kitchen, Durham University, nor those of Lord Grenville, Boconnoc, Lostwithiel, Cornwall, nor those of Lord Auckland, British Museum, Add. MSS 34412–34471, 45728–45730, reveal much more than the fact that, in sharp contrast with prewar years, the Opposition paid little attention to relations with the United States.

For negotiations during the first part of the War of 1812, the papers of Sir John Borlase Warren, Sudbury Hall, Derbyshire, are helpful, as are Warren's letters to the first lord of the Admiralty, Greenwich Naval Museum MSS 9629. Two volumes of Henry Goulburn Papers on the Ghent Negotiations, among the most important collections for the negotiations themselves but remarkably empty on the formulation of British policy, are in the William L. Clements Library, Ann Arbor. These documents were abstracted before the deposit of Goulburn's papers in County Hall, Kingston-on-Thames; as a result the latter collection has little of value for this study. See also Wilbur D. Jones, ed., "A British View of the War of 1812 and the Peace Negotiations," *Mississippi Valley Historical Review*, XLV (1958–1959), 481–487. The only available Gambier material is in Georgiana, Lady Chatterton, *Memorials, Personal and Historical of Admiral Lord Gambier, G.C.B.* (2d ed.; London, 1861). Fittingly enough, Dr. William Adams seems to have left no papers.

The two postwar British ministers to the United States saved large quantities of manuscripts. A tiny fraction of Charles Bagot's papers, Levens Hall, Westmorland, is printed in Josceline Bagot, ed., *George Canning and His Friends* (2 vols.; London, 1909). The Stratford Canning Papers are in the Public Record Office, FO 352/7–9. This collection is almost but not quite as helpful as the Bagot Papers. The Henry U. Addington Papers, collected with those of his uncle, Lord Sidmouth, consist entirely of copies of official correspondence (including one dispatch suppressed at George Canning's order) and a retrospective description of life in America.

Newspapers and pamphlets are best and most conveniently examined, in the United States, in the voluminous collection of the American Antiquarian Society, Worcester, Massachusetts, and, in England, in the Goldsmiths' Collection, University College, London, and the British Museum, including its newspaper branch at Colindale. The text makes clear the political position of individual papers, but see also *Prologue to War*, p. 445. The *Port Folio* (Baltimore) and the *North American Review* (Boston) represent the American drive for cultural independence, while the *Quarterly Review* (London) and the *Edinburgh Review* provide the British answers—or the British provocation.

In addition to the broad studies mentioned at the beginning of this note, particularly helpful books and articles deserve special mention. Fred L. Engelman, *The Peace of Christmas Eve* (New York, 1962), draws upon printed sources and the Goulburn MSS to paint a graceful picture of the negotiations of 1814. Frank Thistlethwaite, *The Anglo American Connection in the Early Nineteenth Century* (Philadelphia, 1959), Benjamin T. Spencer, *The Quest for Nationality* (Syracuse, 1957), and George R. Taylor, *The Transportation Revolution*, Vol. IV of *The Economic History of the United States* (New York, 1951), help to develop the nondiplomatic aspects of Anglo-American relations. F. Lee Benns, *The American Struggle for the British West India Carrying-Trade, 1815–1830*, Indiana University Studies, no. 56 (Bloomington, 1923), traces this highly complicated subject. Philip C. Brooks, *Diplomacy and the Borderlands: The Adams-Onís Treaty of 1819* (Berkeley, 1939), provides essential information. The complex of factors resulting in the Monroe Doctrine is examined in many works, notably William W. Kaufmann, *British Policy and the Independence of Latin America, 1804–1828*, in Lewis P. Curtis, ed., *Yale Historical Publications, Miscellany*, Vol. LII (New Haven, 1951); Arthur P. Whitaker, *The United States and the Independence of Latin America, 1800–1830* (Baltimore, 1941); and Dexter Perkins, *The Monroe Doctrine, 1823–1826*, Vol. XXIX of *Harvard Historical Studies* (Cambridge, 1927).

INDEX

Adams, John, 175–176; on John Q. Adams, 41; on gains of war, 150; fears renewal of war, 159

Adams, John Q., 20; and Britain, 2, 175, 176, 191–192, 194, 214–215, 258, 265, 313–314; arrives at Ghent, 39; character and views of, 40–42, 214–215, 219, 240; and colleagues at Ghent, 46–47, 49–50; travels of, 48; and impressment, 53, 72, 253–255, 268, 272, 274–275; and British commissioners, 60–61, 85, 106, 116; gloom and optimism of, 78, 89, 110, 119–120; and barrier state, 83; on Congress of Vienna, 100–101; on fishery, 116, 118, 124–125; and *status quo ante bellum*, 118–119; on War of 1812 and Treaty of Ghent, 126, 129, 130–131, 215; on patriotic exaggeration, 147, 155, 179; fears renewal of war, 159; and slaves removed by Britain, 166; and *alternat*, 169–170; as minister to England, 196, 211–213; and Bagot, 203, 204; and Stratford Canning, 207–208, 209, 279–281; and Monroe, 211, 240; and George Canning, 212; and Castlereagh, 212, 213, 214, 299–300, 303; as secretary of state, 213; and Rush, 216; and trade with West Indies, 224, 231, 233, 235–237; and disarmament on Great Lakes, 240–242; and Oregon country, 245–249, 264–265; anti-imperial views of, 248, 300; and postwar fishery, 249, 251, 252–253, 263–264; on Robinson, 260; and slave trade, 276–277, 280; and territorial ambitions, 278–279; and Russian ukase, 281, 310–311, 329–330; and Florida negotiations, 284–287, 293–294; on Jackson, 289–291; on independent action, 301–302, 334, 336; and Cuba, 309, 333–334; and noncolonization doctrine, 328–329; answers George Canning, 330, 336–337, 341; and threat to Latin America, 331–332. *See also*

Commercial convention of 1815; Ghent, Treaty of; Monroe Doctrine

Adams, Dr. William, 59, 60, 62, 77, 230. *See also* Commercial convention of 1815; Ghent, Treaty of

Addington, Henry U., 226; as chargé, 209; and John Q. Adams, 321–322, 331, 333, 334; on Monroe Doctrine, 337–338; on American sentiment, 345

Aix-la-Chapelle, conference at, 197, 259, 269, 271, 293, 299, 301

Alexander I, Czar of Russia. *See* Mediation offered by Russia; Ukase, Russian

Alexandria (Va.) *Gazette*, 113

Allston, Washington, 192, 194

Alternat, 169–170

Ambrister, Robert, 285, 288

André, John, 194

Anglophobia, American, 42, 156–160, 163, 172, 174–175, 188, 199, 244, 332–333

Angoulême, Duke d', 312

Annual Register (London), 179, 347

Antrobus, G. Crawfurd, 206

Arbuthnot, Alexander, 285, 288

Armstrong, John, 42–43

Astoria, 245–247, 279

Atcheson, Nathaniel: on barrier state, 83–84; on boundary revision, 91, 103; on fishery, 123

Aurora (Philadelphia), 149, 156

Austin, James T., 172

Bagot, Charles, 210; as minister at Washington, 202–203; and United States, 203–205; departure of, 205–206; on West Indian trade, 234; on Canadian boundary, 245; and Oregon country, 246–247; and fishery, 251–253; and Gallatin, 260; and ratification of convention of 1818, 272; and aid to Creeks, 285; and proposed British mediation, 286–288; and Jackson's invasion of Florida, 289, 293. *See also* Rush-Bagot agreement

Bagot, Mary, 202–203, 205–206

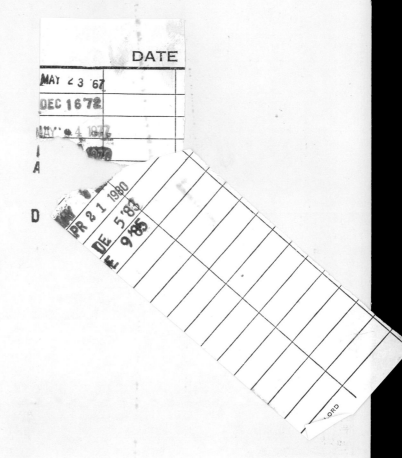